Beginning
Ajax with ASP.NET

Beginning
Ajax with ASP.NET

Wallace B. McClure, Scott Cate, Paul Glavich, Craig Shoemaker

Wiley Publishing, Inc.

Beginning Ajax with ASP.NET

Published by
Wiley Publishing, Inc.
10475 Crosspoint Boulevard
Indianapolis, IN 46256
www.wiley.com

Copyright © 2006 by Wiley Publishing, Inc., Indianapolis, Indiana

Published simultaneously in Canada

ISBN-13: 978-0-471-78544-6
ISBN-10: 0-471-78544-X

Manufactured in the United States of America

10 9 8 7 6 5 4 3 2 1

1B/QT/QY/QW/IN

Library of Congress Control Number: 2006016507

Credits

Executive Editor
Bob Elliott

Senior Development Editor
Kevin Kent

Technical Editor
Steven A. Smith

Production Editor
Pamela Hanley

Copy Editor
Foxxe Editorial Services

Editorial Manager
Mary Beth Wakefield

Production Manager
Tim Tate

Vice President and Executive Group Publisher
Richard Swadley

Vice President and Executive Publisher
Joseph B. Wikert

Graphics and Production Specialists
Carrie A. Foster
Lauren Goddard
Joyce Haughey
Barbara Moore
Heather Ryan
Alicia B. South

Quality Control Technicians
John Greenough
Brian Walls

Project Coordinator
Jennifer Theriot

Proofreading and Indexing
Techbooks

For my wife, Ronda, my two children, Kirsten and Bradley, and the rest of my family.

—Wallace B. McClure

My contribution to this project is dedicated to my newborn son, Cameron. I'd like to thank Michael Schwarz both for authoring the Ajax.NET Professional library and for his research assistance, as well as all of the myKB.com staff, who were very helpful and supportive of this project. Special thanks go to Lorin Thwaits, who helped me with research and provided several great ideas for my chapters.

—Scott Cate

To my wonderful wife Michele for her enduring love and patience; my three children, Kristy, Marc, and Elizabeth, for being so lovable and great people; my two grandchildren, Olivia and William, for just being themselves; my loving parents for all their support; and everyone else I have met on the way to getting where I am, good or bad, thank you for helping me get here.

—Paul Glavich

I dedicate this work first to God, then my Peachy, TyRy, Zachy-zoo, and baby Jacob—who started to make his appearance as I write this text.

—Craig Shoemaker

For Michelle, for putting up with me longer than anybody should have to do so.

—Steven A. Smith

About the Authors

Wallace B. "Wally" McClure graduated from the Georgia Institute of Technology in 1990 with a Bachelor of Science degree in electrical engineering. He continued his education there, receiving a master's degree in the same field in 1991. Since that time, he has done consulting and development for such organizations as The United States Department of Education, Coca-Cola, Bechtel National, Magnatron, and Lucent Technologies, among others. Products and services have included work with ASP, ADO, XML, and SQL Server, as well as numerous applications in the Microsoft .NET Framework. Wally has been working with the .NET Framework since the summer of 2000. Wally McClure specializes in building applications that have large numbers of users and large amounts of data. He is a Microsoft MVP and an ASPInsider, and a partner in Scalable Development, Inc. You can read Wally's blog at `http://weblogs.asp.net/wallym`. Wally and coauthor Paul Glavich also co-host the ASP.NET Podcast. You can listen to it at `www.aspnet podcast.com`. In addition, Wally travels around the southeast United States doing user group talks and sessions at various CodeCamps.

When not working or playing with technology, Wally tries to spend time with his wife Ronda and their two children, Kirsten and Bradley. Occasionally, Wally plays golf and on July 30, 2005, broke par on a real golf course for the first time in his life. If he hadn't been there, he would not have believed it.

Scott Cate is the President of myKB.com, Inc., in Scottsdale, Arizona. myKB.com, Inc., is a technology company specializing in commercial ASP.NET applications. His product line includes myKB.com (knowledge base software), kbAlertz.com (Microsoft knowledge base notifications), and EasySearchASP.net (a pluggable search engine for ASP.NET sites). Scott also runs AZGroups.com (Arizona .NET user groups), one of the largest and most active user group communities in the country, and is a member of ASPInsiders.com, a group devoted to giving early feedback to the Microsoft ASP.NET team. In addition, Scott has coauthored the novel *Surveillance*, which can be found at `http://surveillance-the-novel.com`.

Paul Glavich is currently an ASP.NET MVP and works as a senior technical consultant for Readify. He has over 15 years of industry experience ranging from PICK, C, C++, Delphi, and Visual Basic 3/4/5/6 to his current specialty in .NET C++ with C#, COM+, and ASP.NET. Paul has been developing in .NET technologies since .NET was first in beta and was technical architect for one of the world's first Internet banking solutions using .NET technology. Paul can be seen on various .NET related newsgroups, has presented at the Sydney .NET user group (`www.sdnug.org`) and is also a board member of ASPInsiders (`www.aspinsiders.com`). He has also written some technical articles that can be seen on community sites, such as ASPAlliance.com (`www.aspalliance.com`).

On a more personal note, Paul is married with three children and two grandkids, and holds a third degree black belt in budo-jitsu.

Craig Shoemaker can't sit still. As the host of the Polymorphic Podcast (`polymorphicpodcast.com`), Craig teaches on topics as timely as software architecture and as cutting edge as the latest Ajax technologies. Whether he's writing for *CoDe Magazine*, ASPAlliance, or DotNetJunkies or speaking at local user groups, Southern California Code Camp, or VSLive!, Craig loves to share his passion for the art and science for software development. Craig is also a full-time software engineer for Microsoft Certified Partner PDSA, Inc. (`pdsa.com`) in Tustin, California.

About the Technical Editor

Steven A. Smith is president of ASPAlliance.com and DevAdvice.com. He is a Microsoft regional developer, a Microsoft ASP.NET MVP, and an ASPInsiders board member. He is an International .NET Association (INETA) Speaker Bureau member, and author of two books on ASP.NET. Steve is also an Army engineer officer and veteran of Operation Iraqi Freedom, where he spent 6 months locating and neutralizing munitions in 2004. He lives in Kent, Ohio, with his wife and business partner, Michelle, and their daughter, Ilyana. When he is not attached to a computer, Steve enjoys spending time with his family hiking, biking, and playing games.

Acknowledgments

It is truly interesting how writing projects get started and how ideas turn into books. I had seen the hidden frame trick for years (at least 1998), but I always felt that it was too hard to set up and keep running, so I just dismissed it in general. I saw my first formal Ajax application in the early part of 2003, though it wasn't called Ajax then. The application ran in Internet Explorer only and used the MSXML component. I remember sitting down with the person who had written it as we tried to debug the JavaScript that was necessary to get everything to work. Though it was only Windows/IE and debugging was very hard, I could see the potential of this type of development. I always kept it in the back of my mind. With the release of Google Suggest, Google Maps, and several other web sites and with Jesse James Garrett's essay on Ajax, where the coined term became public, Ajax has really taken off as far as developer mindshare. As I watched March 2005 turn into April 2005 and then into June 2005, I wondered if I was missing a an opportunity for a writing project on a killer technology. I started working with the Ajax library for ASP.NET in June 2005, and I wondered if the topic of Ajax on ASP.NET had enough meat to write about. With Scott Guthrie's announcement of Atlas near the end of June 2005, I knew that Ajax was something that I wanted to be involved with. I spoke with Bob Elliott of Wiley on the Tuesday of Scott Guthrie's announcement and probably every day through July 2005 regarding Ajax and writing a book on Ajax with ASP.NET. From there, things took off. I started talking a lot about Ajax in some online lists at aspadvice.com. Paul, Scott, and I immediately began talking about Ajax. Paul and I already worked together on the ASP.NET Podcast (at www.aspnetpodcast.com), and the three of us already knew each other from the ASPInsider and Microsoft MVP groups to which we belong. Given Scott and Paul's existing knowledge, it was not hard to convince them to come on board and work on this book.

Personally, I would like to thank Bob Elliott for keeping me focused on what was going on and working with us to develop this book. Our thanks also go out to the editorial staff at Wiley. Their help keeping us on track as "life happened" was appreciated. The work of our technical editor, Steven A. Smith, was impressive, and his attention to detail was great. Many other people behind the scenes have worked hard on the book. By pulling this group together, Wiley created a team that was dedicated to creating the best possible book on Ajax on ASP.NET. For that, we are truly appreciative.

~Wallace B. McClure and the author team

Contents

Contents

Contents

Contents

Contents

Contents

Introduction

Thank you for purchasing *Beginning Ajax with ASP.NET*. We know that you have a lot of options when selecting a programming book and are glad that you have chosen ours. We're sure you will be pleased with the relevant content and high quality you have come to expect from the Wrox Press line of books.

Ajax is a set of technologies that will revolutionize the way that web-based applications are designed. It revolutionizes the way that applications are used, provides users a responsive application, and provides developers with the alternatives for building their applications. We believe that this book will meet your needs regarding programming Ajax on the ASP.NET platform.

Who Is This Book For?

People interested in this book will be developers who are working in the ASP.NET environment and are looking to create a more responsive and modern application using technologies that are very similar to the desktop methodologies. Developers who are looking to improve the user experience of their existing applications, develop new applications, develop internal line-of-business applications, and those who want to bulk up with the latest technology that developers all over the world are talking about will find what they are looking for here.

This book is for programmers who use ASP.NET and are just starting to use Ajax technologies. This book will assist developers working on ASP.NET-based applications who want to improve their applications and skills, by providing a background in Ajax for them before delving into how to apply Ajax to their applications.

What You Need to Use This Book

To run the examples in this book, you will need the following items:

❑   Visual Studio .NET 2005

❑   Windows XP or Windows 2003 Server

❑   A modern web browser, such as the latest version of Internet Explorer, Mozilla Firefox, or Apple's Safari.

❑   Ajax.NET Pro addin—While not needed for all of the chapters, the chapters on Ajax.NET Pro will need the addin. For information on the addin, check out www.ajaxpro.info.

❑   Atlas addin—While not needed for all of the chapters, the chapters on Atlas will need the addin. For information regarding the addin and getting a copy, check out http://atlas.asp.net.

What Does This Book Cover?

This book is divided into 13 chapters as follows:

❑ **Chapter 1**, "Introduction to Ajax on ASP.NET," introduces the topic of Ajax with .NET. The chapter provides some background on development trends. We look at the parallels between PC development trends and web-based development trends.

❑ **Chapter 2**, "Introduction to DHTML," introduces the concept of Dynamic HTML. The ability to dynamically change the HTML within a page is a core piece of making Ajax work.

❑ **Chapter 3**, "JavaScript and the Document Object Model," talks about the role of JavaScript and the DOM.

❑ **Chapter 4**, "The XMLHttpRequest Object," discusses the `XmlHttpRequest` object and how it is used to communicate between the client web browser and the server. The `XmlHttpRequest` object is the object that makes Ajax really go.

❑ **Chapter 5**, "Data Communication: XML, XSLT, and JSON," presents an overview of XML, XSLT, and other ways to send data between the client and the server.

❑ **Chapter 6**, "What Is Built into ASP.NET," discusses the various Ajax-type features that are built into the ASP.NET 2.0 release.

❑ **Chapter 7**, "Ajax.NET Professional Library," introduces the Ajax.NET Pro library. This is an open source library that has garnered significant interest in the ASP.NET community.

❑ **Chapter 8**, "Anatomy of Ajax.NET Pro Library," takes a deep dive into the Ajax.NET Pro library and looks into how the library performs all of its magic.

❑ **Chapter 9**, "Other Ajax Libraries for .NET," introduces the reader to several other ASP.NET-oriented libraries.

❑ **Chapter 10**, "Atlas Client Script," introduces and discusses the client scripting environment in Microsoft's Atlas.

❑ **Chapter 11**, "Atlas Controls," discusses the building and using of controls in Microsoft's Atlas environment.

❑ **Chapter 12**, "Atlas Integration with ASP.NET Services," shows how to integrate Microsoft's Atlas with many of the services available in ASP.NET 2.0

❑ Debugging with Ajax can be problematic. That's why **Chapter 13**, "Debugging," discusses the options for debugging client-side Ajax applications.

Conventions

To help you get the most from the text and keep track of what's happening, we've used a number of conventions throughout the book.

> **Boxes like this one hold important, not-to-be forgotten information that is directly relevant to the surrounding text.**

Tips, hints, tricks, and asides to the current discussion are offset and placed in italics like this.

As for styles in the text:

❑   We *highlight* new terms and important words when we introduce them.

❑   We show keyboard strokes like this: Ctrl+A.

❑   We show filenames, URLs, and code within the text like so: `persistence.properties`.

❑   We present code in two different ways:

```
In code examples, we highlight new and important code with a gray background.
```

```
The gray highlighting is not used for code that's less important in the present
context, or has been shown before.
```

Source Code

As you work through the examples in this book, you may choose either to type in all the code manually or to use the source code files that accompany the book. All of the source code used in this book is available for download at `http://BeginningAjax.com`. You can link to that site directly or go through the book's Wrox web site found at `www.wrox.com`. Once at the Wrox site, simply locate the book's title (either by using the Search box or by using one of the title lists).

Because many books have similar titles, you may find it easiest to search by ISBN; this book's ISBN is 0-471-78544-X (changing to 978-0-471-78544-6 as the new industry-wide 13-digit ISBN numbering system is phased in by January 2007).

At the Wrox site, you can also go to the main Wrox code download page at `www.wrox.com/dynamic/books/download.aspx` to see the code available for all other Wrox books.

The code samples in the book are provided in C# on the server and JavaScript on the client.

Additionally, at both the `http://BeginningAjax.com` site and the book's Wrox site, you can find updated versions of the Atlas chapters of this book, written to the latest, most stable version of that product.

Errata

We make every effort to ensure that there are no errors in the text or in the code. However, no one is perfect, and mistakes do occur. If you find an error in one of our books, such as a spelling mistake or faulty piece of code, we would be very grateful for your feedback. By sending in errata, you may save another reader hours of frustration, and at the same time you will be helping us provide even higher-quality information.

To find the errata page for this book, go to `www.wrox.com` and locate the title using the Search box or one of the title lists. Then, on the book details page, click the Book Errata link. On this page, you can view all errata that has been submitted for this book and posted by Wrox editors. A complete book list, including links to each book's errata, is also available at www.wrox.com/misc-pages/booklist.shtml.

If you don't spot "your" error on the Book Errata page, go to www.wrox.com/contact/techsupport .shtml and complete the form there to send us the error you have found. We'll check the information and, if appropriate, post a message to the book's errata page and fix the problem in subsequent editions of the book.

p2p.wrox.com

For author and peer discussion, join the P2P forums at p2p.wrox.com. The forums are a web-based system for you to post messages relating to Wrox books and related technologies and interact with other readers and technology users. The forums offer a subscription feature to email you topics of interest of your choosing when new posts are made to the forums. Wrox authors, editors, other industry experts, and your fellow readers are present on these forums.

At http://p2p.wrox.com you will find a number of different forums that will help you not only as you read this book but also as you develop your own applications. To join the forums, just follow these steps:

1. Go to p2p.wrox.com, and click the Register link.

2. Read the terms of use, and click Agree.

3. Complete the required information to join as well as any optional information you wish to provide, and click Submit.

4. You will receive an email with information describing how to verify your account and complete the joining process.

> *You can read messages in the forums without joining P2P, but in order to post your own messages, you must join.*

Once you join, you can post new messages and respond to messages other users post. You can read messages at any time on the web. If you would like to have new messages from a particular forum emailed to you, click the Subscribe to this Forum icon by the forum name in the forum listing.

For more information about how to use the Wrox P2P, be sure to read the P2P FAQs for answers to questions about how the forum software works as well as many common questions specific to P2P and Wrox books. To read the FAQs, click the FAQ link on any P2P page.

Introduction to Ajax on ASP.NET

Over the years, we developers have seen many changes in terms of how development occurs. We have gone from terminal-based programming to PC-based programming to Windows-based programming to the web. Now we are on the verge of another programming revolution. This programming revolution will bring more interactive user interfaces to Web applications. This programming revolution is brought to developers courtesy of a set of technologies that are generally known as Ajax (Asynchronous JavaScript And XML). No longer will users see the annoying flash with the click of a button to submit data. No longer will users lose the context where they are located and be thrown back to the top of a page. With Ajax, developers can build applications that step out of the traditional postback model of the web, provide an improved user interface to users, and allow developers to develop applications that are much more user-friendly.

In this chapter, you are going to take a look at:

- ❏ ASP.NET development and how it led to Ajax
- ❏ What Ajax is and a high-level overview of some of its base technologies
- ❏ The advantages of Ajax
- ❏ Some things that it might not make sense to do with Ajax

Development Trends

If you have been developing for a while, like us old guys, you have gone through several iterations of development. Development has gone from terminals connected to mainframes and minicomputers to personal computers and then to client-server development. Client-server development allowed for the minimization of back-end resources, network resources, and the front-end PC by sending only the necessary data between back end and front end. Intelligent client-server development allowed for building applications that were responsive to the user and made efficient use of network and back-end resources. As the web development methodology took off in the late 1990s, we unfortunately returned to terminal-style development. In this methodology, any major operation between the client and server requires that all data be sent in what is called a *round trip*. With a round trip, all data from the form is sent from the client to the web server. The web server processes data, and then sends it back to the client. The result of a round trip is that lots of data is sent back and forth between the client and server. For example, form data, viewstate, and images may be sent back and forth without the need to be sent back and forth. Figure 1-1 shows how only a web browser is required at the client and how communications work with the web server being an intermediary between the client and any resources.

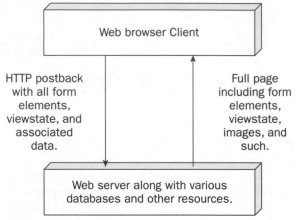

Figure 1-1

ASP.NET Development

ASP.NET is a set of web development technologies produced by Microsoft that is used to build dynamic web sites, web applications, and XML-based web applications. ASP.NET is a part of the .NET framework and allows developers to build applications in multiple languages, such as Visual Basic .NET, Jscript, and C#.

Design Methodology

ASP.NET attempts to make the web development methodology like the graphical user interface (GUI) development methodology by allowing developers to build pages made up of controls similar to a GUI. A server control in ASP.NET functions similarly to GUI controls in other environments. Buttons, textboxes, labels, and datagrids have properties that can be modified and expose events that may be processed. The ASP.NET server controls know how to display their content in an HTML page just like GUI-based user controls know how to display themselves in their GUI environment. An added benefit of ASP.NET is that the properties and methods of the web server controls are similar, and in some cases the same as, those of comparable controls in the Windows GUI/Winforms environment.

Problems ASP.NET Solves

Microsoft has released various web application development methodologies over the past 10 years. Why do developers need ASP.NET? What problems does ASP.NET solve that the previous development methodologies did not solve?

Microsoft's first popular web development technology was the Internet Database Connector (IDC). The IDC methodology provided only database access; it did not provide access to any other resource programmatically. There was no way to programmatically send email or do other nondatabase operations. Another issue was that it seemed to be somewhat different from the traditional programming languages that most developers were used to (Visual Basic and C++ being two popular ones). Along with this problem was the fact that the development experience was not very attractive within Microsoft FrontPage. Along with the development experience, IDC had no debugging experience worth mentioning. Overall, IDC was nothing more than a stopgap measure to get to an improved environment.

The next web development methodology from Microsoft was Active Server Pages (ASP). ASP was a scripting environment that allowed developers to work with a Visual Basic like or JavaScript type environment. Unfortunately, this type of environment came with several problems:

❑ **Prevalence of spaghetti code** — ASP code does not provide a structured development environment, often contributing to the creation of twisted and tangled "spaghetti code." ASP code is literally a file with some basic configuration information at the top of every page. Each page is executed from the top of the page to the bottom of the page. While it is possible to use Component Object Model (COM) objects to eliminate some of the spaghetti code, this introduces more complexity in the form of another development tool.

❑ **Lack of code separation** — The code tends to be intermixed with display code. Intermixing the code and the display logic requires that the tools that developers and designers use work well together. This was often not the case. For example, it was well known that various visual development tools could take a properly running ASP page, rearrange some of the code, and render the ASP page broken.

❑ **Lack of code reusability** — There is very little ability to reuse code within the ASP environment.

❑ **Lack of debugging support** — Debugging an ASP application typically involves the use of `Response.Write`. This is in sharp contrast to an integrated development environment (IDE) developed within a GUI environment.

❑ **Problems of COM** — ASP is based on the Component Object Model and suffers from many of the problems associated with COM. There were two major problems with COM.

   ❑ The first was that updating COM objects tended to overwrite one object with the new one. This could be problematic if a programming method call changed or any other new behavior was introduced.

   ❑ The second major problem with COM was that it was a binary standard. This binary standard was based on a 32-bit programming model. As a result, COM objects would not scale up to run natively within an environment that was an Intel-based 32-bit environment. While this might not have been a big deal in the early to middle 1990s when COM was designed and built, by the early 2000s and the introduction of inexpensive 64-bit systems, this was seen as a possible bottleneck.

❑ **Problems with being interpreted** — ASP is interpreted. Each time an ASP file is loaded, the ASP environment parses the ASP file, compiles the code, and then executes the file. This process is repeated on each call to an ASP file. The result is wasted processing on the server.

❑ **Presence of the statemachine** — ASP applications typically have a statemachine (in software code, a statemachine is a section of code that depends on both its direct inputs and inputs made during previous calls) at the top of every ASP page that processes the state of the user and then displays code. Given that most client-side applications are built based on events, which is a similar concept to a statemachine, this is an unfamiliar way to develop for developers not well versed in ASP.

Upon discovering these problems, Microsoft developed ASP.NET. ASP.NET greatly simplifies the web development methodology.

❑   Developers no longer need to worry about processing state. With ASP.NET, actions are performed within a series of events that provide statemachine-like functionality.

❑   With the use of code-behind/beside model, code is separated from display. By separating code and display files, there is less of a chance of designer and developer tools interfering with each other.

❑   A single development tool may be used for building the application and business logic. Having a single integrated development suite allows developers to more easily interact with the application logic. This results in more code reuse and fewer errors.

❑   With the Visual Studio .NET IDE, ASP.NET supports many methods to debug and track a running ASP.NET.

❑   Because ASP.NET is based on the common language runtime (CLR) and .NET, ASP.NET does not suffer from the problems of COM. The .NET framework allows for multiple versions of components to be on a system without interacting with each other.

❑   ASP.NET is compiled. The first time that a file is loaded, it is compiled and then processed. The compiled file is then saved into a temporary directory. Subsequent calls to the ASP.NET file are processed from the compiled file. The execution of the compiled file on requests is faster than the interpreted environment of Classic ASP.

All in all, ASP.NET is a dramatic improvement over ASP. It has become widely accepted in the development community.

So, What's the Problem?

Based on what you have just read regarding ASP.NET, it may sound really good to you. You may be asking yourself, "Why is there a need for something else? What's the problem?"

The truth is ASP.NET has several issues that need to be addressed:

❑   **Round trips** — The server events in ASP.NET require round trips to the server to process these events. These round trips result in all form elements being sent between client and server as well as images and other data files being sent back to the client from the server. While some web browsers will cache images, there can still be significant data transfer.

❑   **Speed/network data transfer** — Because of the VIEWSTATE hidden form element, the amount of data that is transferred during a postback is relatively large. The more data and controls on the page, the larger the VIEWSTATE will be and the more data that must be processed on the server and transmitted back to the client.

❑   **Waiting on the result** — When a user clicks on a button or some other visual element that posts data back to the server, the user must wait on a full round trip to complete. This takes time when the processing is done on the server and all of the data, including images and viewstate, are returned to the client. During that time, even if the user attempts to do something with the user interface, that action is not actually processed on the client.

❑ **User context**—Unless an application is able to properly use the SMARTNAVIGATION feature of ASP.NET, the user is redirected to the top of a page by default on a postback. Although there are ways around this issue, this is the default behavior.

❑ **Processing**—The number of server round trips, the amount of data that is transferred, and the VIEWSTATE element's size result in processing on the server that is not really necessary (Fig. 1-2).

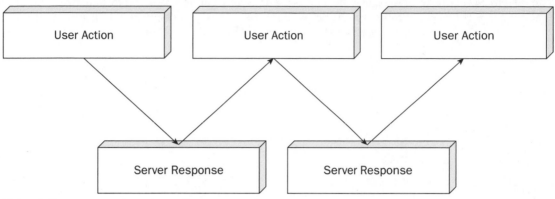

Figure 1-2

Improving the User Experience

Based on these issues, several options present themselves as available for improving the user experience:

❑ **Java**—Java applets are cross-platform applications. While being used as a cross-platform mechanism to display data and improve the user experience, Java development on the client has not been accepted with open arms into the development community and is primarily used for user interface gee-whiz features as opposed to improving the experience of the user application. (As a side note, Java has been widely accepted for building server-side applications.)

❑ **XML-based languages**—XML User Interface Language (XUL) and Extensible Application Markup Language (XAML) are two of several languages that can provide an improved user experience. The problem with XUL is that it has been used only in the Mozilla/Firefox line of browsers. XAML is not currently available as a released product. When it is, it will have the problem of being considered a Microsoft-only technology in spite of discussion items like XAML-lite, which has been stated as cross-platform.

❑ **Flash**—Although Flash has been used and there are cross-platform versions, the product has been used only in the area of graphic UI needs and has not been accepted by the development community as a whole for building line-of-business applications.

❑ **Ajax**—Ajax is a set of client technologies that provides for asynchronous communication between the user interface and the web server along with fairly easy integration with existing technologies.

Given the amount of recent discussion among developers regarding Ajax, it appears that Ajax has the greatest chance among these technologies of gaining market acceptance.

What Is Ajax?

So into this development environment comes a set of technologies that are collectively referred to as Ajax. If you are an "old guy" developer like us, then Ajax represents a similar concept to the client-server development we mentioned earlier in the chapter. With client-server development, the amount of data transferred is minimized over a terminal application by transferring only the necessary data back and forth. Similarly, with Ajax, only the necessary data is transferred back and forth between the client and the web server. This minimizes the network utilization and processing on the client. Figure 1-3 shows that typically Ajax operates with the assistance of some type of proxy.

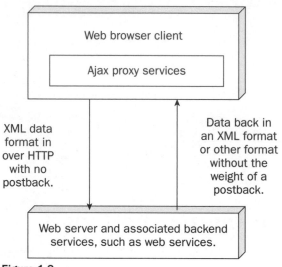

Figure 1-3

Advantages of Ajax

The advantages of Ajax over classical web based applications are:

- ❑ **Asynchronous** — Ajax allows for the ability to make asynchronous calls to a web server. This allows the client browser to avoid waiting for all data to arrive before allowing the user to act once more.

- ❑ **Minimal data transfer** — By not performing a full postback and sending all form data to the server, the network utilization is minimized and quicker operations occur. In sites and locations with restricted pipes for data transfer, this can greatly improve network performance.

- ❑ **Limited processing on the server** — With the fact that only the necessary data is sent to the server, the server is not required to process all form elements. By sending only the necessary data, there is limited processing on the server. There is no need to process all form elements, process the viewstate, send images back to the client, and no need to send a full page back to the client.

❑ **Responsiveness** — Because Ajax applications are asynchronous on the client, they are perceived to be very responsive.

❑ **Context** — With a full postback, the user may lose the context of where they are. The user may be at the bottom of a page, hit the Submit button, and be redirected back to the top of the page. With Ajax there is no full postback. Clicking the Submit button in an application that uses Ajax will allow the user to maintain their location. The user state is maintained, and the user is no longer required to scroll down to the location that he or she was at before clicking Submit.

Figure 1-4 shows how the user interface can still operate while using Ajax. The UI is not locked during the server processing.

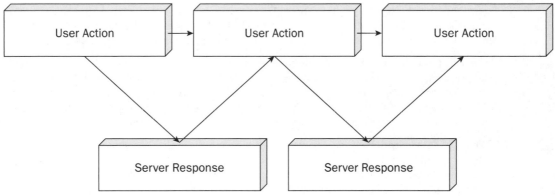

Figure 1-4

History of Ajax

For all of its perceived newness and sexiness, the technologies that make up Ajax are really not new. The ability to communicate back to the server through a hidden frame without posting the main page back to the server has been around for a long time. Communication between client and server has been available — back to the release of Internet Explorer's ability to script ActiveX controls on the client browser and to the MSXML component, both of which date back into the late 1990s. Personally, I saw the first formal usage of client script and MSXML in 2003. The problem with the technology at that time was the need to manually create the necessary client-side JavaScript. In 2003, there was too much code overall that had to be written and too much custom code that had to be written to get this to work. It has been only in the second half of 2005 that client-side libraries and server-side support for ASP.NET have started to make their presence felt and been used significantly.

The mainstream development community has only recently started using the technique. The release of Google's Suggest and Maps are what really opened the eyes of the users to the development technologies. These applications sent a shockwave through the development community.

Technologies That Make Up Ajax

Ajax is a general umbrella term. As mentioned earlier, Ajax itself stands for Asynchronous JavaScript And XML. The term *Ajax* was actually coined by Jesse James Garret of Adaptive Path in an essay that was published in February 2005 (`www.adaptivepath.com/publications/essays/archives/000385.php`) and was quickly accepted by the development community.

Based on this general umbrella term, take a look at the specific items that make up Ajax:

❑ **XmlHttpRequest** — `XmlHttpRequest` allows the browser to communicate to a back-end server. This object allows the browser to talk to the server without requiring a postback of the entire web page. With Internet Explorer, this capability is provided by the MSXML ActiveX component. With the Mozilla Firefox and other web browsers, this capability is provided by an object literally called `XmlHttpRequest`. The `XmlHttpRequest` object is modeled after the MSXML component. The client-side JavaScript libraries hide the differences between the various browser environments. Sometimes these communications are done through a hidden FRAME or IFRAME.

❑ **JavaScript** — JavaScript provides the capabilities to communicate with the back-end server. The JavaScript must be version 1.5 or later. Although JavaScript is not specifically required, it is needed from the standpoint that JavaScript is the only client-side scripting environment supported across the major modern web browsers. There are other client script languages; however, these are not supported across all browsers.

❑ **DHTML/DOM support** — The browser must support the ability to dynamically update form elements, and the ability to do this in a standard way comes through the support for the Document Object Model (DOM). By supporting the DOM, it becomes easy for developers to write a single piece of code that targets multiple browsers.

❑ **Data transport with XML or JSON** — Using XML allows for the ability to communicate with the web server in a standard mechanism. There are situations where the JavaScript Object Notation (JSON) is used as the communication notation instead of straight XML.

Running Ajax Applications

Unfortunately, not all web browsers ever produced will support Ajax. To run Ajax, a web browser must:

❑ Be relatively modern. Ajax style applications are not available in all versions of all web browsers. Whereas Internet Explorer version 6, Firefox version 1.5, and Opera 8.5 provide support for these applications, older versions may be problematic because of their support for different versions of the other requirements.

❑ Support DOM.

❑ Utilize JavaScript.

❑ Support Extensible Markup Language (XML) and Extensible Style Language Transformation (XSLT).

❑ Possibly have ActiveX enabled on the client. If you are using the Internet Explorer browser while running on Windows, you may have problems if ActiveX is not enabled.

Who's Using Ajax?

Great, now that you have seen that there is this technology called Ajax, are you alone in not having seen or talked about this before? Absolutely not! Ajax has just recently taken off in the second half of 2005 from a mindshare standpoint. As discussions have gone on with counterparts in the development community, many developers are just now looking to what Ajax can do for their applications and ultimately their customers. So, just who is using Ajax publicly?

- ❑ **Google Suggest** — Google Suggest features a dynamic drop-down list box that provides possible items to search on along with the approximate number of search results.

- ❑ **Google Maps** — The ability to grab a map and zoom around without requiring a postback is just amazing. This app/service took the development world by storm when it came out.

- ❑ **Google GMail** — Google GMail is a web-based email system available through Google.

- ❑ **Microsoft Hotmail Kahuna update** — At the time of this writing, the Hotmail upgrade that is referred to as Kahuna is in beta test. As a beta user of the application, I can testify to the improved user interface and responsiveness that this application provides.

- ❑ **Live.com** — The local.live.com service from Microsoft is actively using the Atlas framework, as is nearly the entire Live.com service.

- ❑ **Easy Search component** — The ASP.NET Easy Search Component provides support for searching a single web site similar to the Google Suggest service available through Google.

- ❑ **Other component vendors** — Component vendors such as ComponentArt, Dart, and others are providing controls that provide a rich user experience without forcing a full postback.

In addition to third-party interest, the amount of developer interest is tremendous. For example, one only has to put the word *Ajax* into a blog title to receive an increase in the number of web views. Given the amount of third-party support and the interest of developers, it is only a matter of time before everyone is using it.

Problems Ajax Won't Solve

Ajax is a great technology with a lot of help for typical application problems and a lot of general promise. It will help in areas like network load and user context by sending only the necessary data, creating less network traffic when processing a command. The user is not redirected to the top of a page when a command is sent the server. The problem is that to successfully run Ajax, a user needs to have the transport mechanism and JavaScript support mentioned previously. That sounds like something that any modern browser has, so what's the problem? Well, the problem is that many mobile browsers have support for neither. With many of Ajax solutions, you have limited or no downlevel support, so if you must support a mobile system, you may be limited to writing multiple versions of your application because Ajax may not be the right technology to include.

Summary

Ajax provides developers a foundation to build web-based applications that provide an improved user experience. In this introductory chapter, you have looked at:

- ❑ Development from a historical perspective
- ❑ Web development methodologies
- ❑ Some of the features that Ajax provides, such as improved user responsiveness and decreased load on the web server
- ❑ Multiple technologies that can improve the user experience
- ❑ Ajax, the problems that it solves, and who is using it

In the next chapter, you are going to examine Dynamic HTML (DHTML). Additional chapters will look at the other technologies that make up Ajax. After that you will examine the Ajax.NET library, Microsoft Atlas, and finally tips and tricks on debugging client-side applications.

Introduction to DHTML

Dynamic HTML (DHTML) is a combination of three technologies: Hypertext Markup Language (HTML), Cascading Style Sheets (CSS), and JavaScript. With these technologies, the content in a browser becomes dynamic, not having to rely on time-consuming updates from round trips back to the server. Additionally, finer control over the user experience is available by leveraging the various events inherent in HTML, such as playing a small sound when the mouse moves over an image or providing custom context menus instead of the standard one provided by the browser.

This chapter will introduce JavaScript, and then move into how it can interact with the browser environment to modify the HTML and CSS that make up the web page being displayed. Colors, images, text, and more can be modified, all through JavaScript code. In the next chapter, the coverage dives deeper, analyzing the nature of objects and continuing into the Document Object Model (DOM).

In this chapter, you take a look at:

❑ JavaScript basics

❑ The `alert`, `write`, and `loop` functions

❑ Modifying the status bar

❑ Getting input from the user with the `prompt()` function

❑ JavaScript events

❑ The `document.getElementById()` function

❑ The `innerHTML` property

What JavaScript Is, and What It Isn't

In the realm of computer languages and programs, there are two major types: compiled and interpreted.

❏ Examples of *compiled* programs are as simple as the Notepad application you'll be using to edit the samples shown in this chapter. Notepad was written in C++ and compiled to run specifically on 32-bit or 64-bit Intel hardware. Therefore, it is very specific as to what platform can run the code.

❏ JavaScript on the other hand is *interpreted*, meaning that any platform capable of interpreting the code can run it. For our purposes, this will mean virtually any web browser, from small handheld devices like web-enabled phones up to browsers available for mainstream operating systems like Internet Explorer, Opera, Safari, and Firefox. Some languages, such as .NET and Java, are actually hybrids, being both partially compiled and partially interpreted.

Although it's tempting to think that JavaScript is closely related to Java, because of its name, surprisingly that is not the case. The only real similarities between the two are that the structure of the code looks very similar, with the curly braces and semicolons, and they both provide an object-oriented programming experience. Java does this more elegantly and has established itself as a great academic tool to experiment with object-oriented code design. But the object model is very different from JavaScript.

General Rules of JavaScript

JavaScript code comprises a series of statements. And JavaScript statements are composed of either text that leads up to a semicolon or text that opens up a code block inside curly braces. Here's an example of a couple of statements that first declare a variable called message and then present it on the screen in a pop-up box:

```
var message="Hello, world!";
alert(message);
```

The computer determines the end of each of the statement simply by where it finds a semicolon. These two statements could have been placed on the same line with a semicolon separating them. But it is much clearer to put them on separate lines.

Most JavaScript interpreters will actually allow statements to exist without the semicolon appearing at the end of the line. But this is not in keeping with the specifications of other similar languages like Java, C++, and C#. So, it's recommended to keep the habit of using semicolons at the end of statements. All of the JavaScript examples in this book will do so, but when you delve into other samples from the Internet, you will undoubtedly find JavaScript code that omits the semicolons.

Now take a look at an example of a statement that opens a code block:

```
if(grade>=90)
{
  alert("You got an A!");
}
```

In this sample, the curly braces define a code block, and the single line of code found within runs only if the grade variable is greater than or equal to 90. There are two statements shown, if and alert, and there is no concluding semicolon required after the code block. In addition to having code blocks with an if statement, you'll see in upcoming samples that they are also found with the looping statement for and when functions get defined.

Writing Your First Block of JavaScript Code

So, now that you've seen JavaScript statements, you can write a few in order to create output in a web browser. Follow along by opening a copy of Notepad and typing in this sample or simply get all the code for the book from the download section of http://BeginningAjax.com. This sample is found in the file chapter_2_starter.htm.

In the example that follows you have a simple web page with some text, and in a `<script>` element, one line of JavaScript, an `alert` statement. You have already seen examples of some simple output operations using the `alert` function. The `alert` function is a method of the `window` object. The `window` object is present as part of every browser's object model.

Keep in mind that JavaScript code is case-sensitive, so if you do opt to type it all in, then pay particular attention to getting the casing on all JavaScript lines correct.

```
<html>
 <head>
 </head>
 <body>

 Some text before the Javascript<br />

 <script type="text/javascript">
  alert("Hello, world");
 </script>

 <br />
 Some text after the Javascript<br />

 </body>
</html>
```

Save the file as some name of your choosing with an .htm extension, and then when you open it with a web browser, you should see a pop-up appearing that presents "Hello, world," as shown in Figure 2-1.

Figure 2-1

The `alert()` function has produced a basic dialog box for the user to interact with, but as you can see, the user is allowed to acknowledge the prompt only by clicking the OK button.

If you are using either Internet Explorer 6.0 on a system that has Windows XP Service Pack 2 installed or Internet Explorer 7.0, then depending on your security settings you will probably be presented with an information bar explaining that Internet Explorer has restricted the file from showing active content. Simply click on the bar, select "Allow Blocked Content . . ." and select "Yes."

Notice that during the time the pop-up is showing, in the background, on the web page, only the line `Some text before the Javascript` has been rendered. Then after clicking OK to dismiss the pop-up text, the rest of the page is shown, and you see the line `Some text after the Javascript`. So, there is a sequence of events going on here. Because the JavaScript section was placed within the `<body>` element, it ran as the page was being rendered. You'll experiment a little more with this kind of JavaScript, which runs as the page is being rendered, and then move into JavaScript that sits dormant until an event, such as a button click, has occurred.

There are several places that JavaScript can be placed inside an HTML page. All of the code samples in this chapter will be placed, as was done in the first sample, within the `<body>` element. This is the same place that ASP.NET adds any JavaScript that is established using `Page.RegisterClientScriptBlock()`.

You can also place JavaScript in the `<head>` element. Another technique, described in the next chapter, is to place JavaScript in a separate code file, usually named with a `.js` extension, and then have a `<script>` element that includes the code file as if it were merged into the HTML at that point.

document.write()

You can see another way to create output by modifying this sample. Change the function `alert` to `document.write`, so the `<script>` element looks like this:

```
<script type="text/javascript">
  document.write("Hello, world");
</script>
```

Now the `"Hello, world"` text is placed right within the rendered page, just as if it was part of the HTML itself.

Using document.write() in Nested for() Loops

With `document.write`, you can have the client build calculated or repetitious HTML. As an example, you can put a few more lines of code in the `<script>` element to automatically build a 10×10 multiplication table:

```
<script type="text/javascript">
document.write('<table border="1">');
 for(y=1;y<=10;y++)
 {
  document.write("<tr>");
  for(x=1;x<=10;++x)
  {
   document.write("<td>"+(x*y)+"</td>");
  }
```

```
    document.write("</tr>");
  }
  document.write("</table>");
</script>
```

In this example, you see two `for` loops, each of which opens a code block and one of which is nested inside of the other. The innermost `document.write()`, which builds the `<td>` elements, is run 100 times and produces the output shown in Figure 2-2.

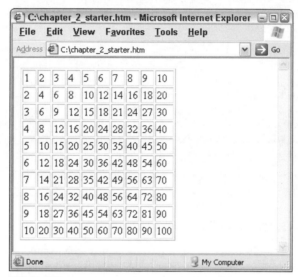

Figure 2-2

Notice that right after each of the `for` statements there is a somewhat cryptic set of code in parentheses, broken into three parts separated by semicolons. These are the parts that make up any `for()` loop. At the very least the semicolons need to be present to call out these three pieces, and the table that follows shows what each part does.

for (	x=1;	x<=10;	x++)
The keyword	A statement that is run before the looping begins. It is usually used to assign the starting value of a counter.	A condition to test if the looping should continue. As long as this is true, it keeps looping.	A statement that is run every time the loop reaches the end of the code block and iterates. This actually occurs before the condition to the left is tested.

The x++ and y++ portions of the for loop act to increment the value of x or y. Each time y is incremented by 1, the inner loop for x has gone through building a row of 10 cells. In this way, all the `<tr>` and `<td>` elements are built out properly inside the `<table>`, and it is all quickly rendered on the client.

It is possible to create long-running or endless loops in JavaScript, so be cautious. In such a circumstance, web browsers will often present a message asking the user if they want to continue running scripts on the page or not. You definitely want to carefully test any looping code that you write to avoid endless loops. You can read more about using loops in Chapter 3.

15

Single Quotation Marks and Double Quotation Marks in JavaScript

You have seen a couple of samples that use double quotation marks to surround the strings found in JavaScript. But in this example using those quotation marks would have confused the browser as to what should actually be included as part of the onload attribute. The start of a JavaScript string set up with double quotation marks would have looked to the browser just like the end of that onload attribute.

Fortunately, JavaScript lets you enclose strings with either double quotation marks or single quotation marks (apostrophes) so that you can work around this issue. So, that's exactly what you have done here.

Okay, so if apostrophes mark the start and end of your JavaScript string, what happens when you want to include an apostrophe as part of the string, such as with the word It's in this case? From the sample, you can see that it works if you precede that apostrophe with a backslash. This backslash is called an *escaping* character, which is a great trick, allowing us to put in double quotation marks and apostrophes wherever we need, as well as the actual backslash character itself. In a JavaScript string two backslashes in a row is interpreted as being a single backslash character. This whole business of escaping is a similar concept to using < in XML or HTML to represent the less than symbol.

You can read more about escaping characters in JavaScript in Chapter 3.

---

window.status and Events

Another way to present data is with custom text in the status area located at the bottom of the browser window. If you were to do this in the same <script> element used so far in the chapter, then the text would be changed very briefly while the page is being rendered but then overwritten by the browser with the text Done once the page is complete. So, instead you need to find a way to have this next piece of code run after the page has finished rendering. The perfect place is in something called an *event handler* on the <body> tag. There are several events you could trap in this way, and the one you want for this example is called onload.

You can find more information about event handlers in Chapter 3.

So, for this example, change the <body> tag to look like this:

```
<body onload="window.status='It\'s a beautiful day';">
```

This way, when the page is rendered, the actual document content is not affected at all; it looks the same. But once it is all rendered, then in the status area at the bottom of the window you find your custom text, as shown in Figure 2-3. If your browser is not currently configured to show the status bar, then in both Internet Explorer and Firefox, you can use View⇨Status Bar to turn it on.

Firefox users: In order for this example to work, you must tell Firefox it's okay for JavaScript to change the status bar text. This is done from Tools⇨Options⇨Content⇨Enable JavaScript⇨Advanced⇨ Change status bar text.

It's a beautiful day

Figure 2-3

Examine how this works — when the `<body>` of the document is fully loaded, the browser sees if any pieces of code out there care about that occurrence by searching for code that has registered for the `onload` event. The change made to the `<body>` tag was to include an inline event handler, effectively registering your code to be called when that event fired. So, when the browser finished rendering the page, this JavaScript code that was found within the double quotation marks was executed:

```
window.status='It\'s a beautiful day';
```

Getting Input from the User

Now that you've seen how to output information in a couple of ways, you need to see how to get some input with the `confirm()` and `prompt()` functions.

The `confirm` method is used to invoke a confirmation dialog box like this:

```
if (confirm("This is a confirmation box"))
    alert("You clicked OK");
else
    alert("You clicked cancel");
```

This produces the traditional OK/Cancel dialog box, as you'll see later in the chapter. The `confirm` method returns a value of `true` if the user clicks the OK button, and `false` if the user clicks the Cancel button.

The prompt dialog box is invoked by using the `prompt` method of the `window` object. So, suppose you would like to ask the user what his or her name is and then present that as text in the page. Here is some code you can put in your `<script>` element to make that happen:

```
<script type="text/javascript">
 var name=prompt("Please enter your name","");
 document.write("Welcome "+name);
</script>
```

In this case, you've declared a variable called `name` and assigned it to whatever string comes back from a pop-up textbox presented to the user. The box starts out blank because of the second parameter being passed into `prompt`, which is a blank string. In the next `document.write` statement, the text entered by the user is appended to a string in order to present some welcome text. The + operator is not just used for addition, but in this case, when working with strings, it concatenates one string on the end of another.

You will notice we have not prefixed any of the method calls with the window *object such as* window `.prompt("Please enter your name","");`*. This is because the* window *object is the root, or default, object within the browser. The* alert*,* confirm*, and* prompt *methods can be inferred to be a part of the* window *object, so prefixing the method call with* window*. is not necessary.*

17

Security Concerns When Getting Text Input

Because the name is written out exactly as it was entered, you want to be very careful when accepting any assorted text from the user because exactly what someone types in is presented on the screen, including any additional HTML or JavaScript. Try putting this in when prompted:

```
<script>location.href="http://www.wrox.com";</script>
```

When the page is rendered, the included script runs as part of the page and redirects the browser to the Wrox web site! Although we love the Wrox web site, this is probably not at all what you intended when you asked for the user's name. So, taking this example further, what if you blindly stored the text from the user in a database and then on the main page of your site presented a dynamic list of which users are currently online? When that user is online, suddenly anyone who visits your site is redirected to another page. This kind of attack is called HTML injection and is related to Cross Site Scripting (XSS). So to avoid this problem, you need to include code to filter out unintentional HTML elements and JavaScript. Conveniently, this kind of protection is intrinsic in Microsoft's ASP.NET environment when using the .NET Framework 1.1 or later.

Canceling the Normal Outcome of an Event

So, now you can look at another event handler called `onclick`. Every visible element found on an HTML page provides this event handler, even the `<body>` element. So, this really could be placed anywhere. But people are more accustomed to clicking hyperlinks, so for this example you are going to include this handler on an `<a>` element that is used to navigate to other pages. What if you wanted to confirm that people really wanted to navigate to another page when they clicked a link? Add this HTML at the end of your current `<body>` content to see how this is done:

```
<a href="http://mykb.com"
  onclick="return confirm('Really navigate away from this page?');">
Knowledge Base Software</a>
```

The `confirm()` function presents a pop-up with both OK and Cancel buttons, as shown in Figure 2-4. When a choice is made by the user, `confirm()` will equal `true` if the user clicks OK, or `false` if the user clicks Cancel or closes the pop-up. Returning this `true` or `false` in an `onclick` event handler determines if the handling of that event should continue or not.

Figure 2-4

The `return` keyword indicates that you're done with the piece of code that is running, and you can return a value back to the caller. So, in this case when someone clicks Cancel, a value of `false` is returned and whatever the `<a>` tag would normally do when clicked is cut short and does not happen. Hence, clicking Cancel has the effect of bypassing the actual navigation to another page.

There are other event handlers you can defer by returning false, such as the `onsubmit` event of a `<form>`.

You can find more information about event handlers in Chapter 3.

Causing an Event Not to "Bubble Up"

There is another concept related to using `return false` in an event handler. If you fully handle a given event in a contained control, you may not want that same event to "bubble up" to any parent controls it is within. For instance in the previous example, you may not want the `onclick` event on the `<a>` to be seen by an `onclick` handler for the `<body>` element. But by virtue of `<a>` being a child element under `<body>`, normally this `onclick` would bubble up. If you use only `return false`, then it will defer what would happen on the `<a>` but not what would happen in an `onclick` on the `<body>`. To keep this from happening, use this statement:

```
event.cancelBubble=true;
```

You must use this statement before any `return` because executing `return` indicates that you're done with the event handler code and want to return control to the browser.

Working with Images

By this point, you're probably starting to see that JavaScript can be a very handy way to enhance the user experience. But definitely the best is yet to come. Now you're going to see some "eye candy" types of examples, starting with images. You can begin by placing an image on your existing page by adding this line before the closing `</body>` tag:

```
<img src="images/ArrowLeft.gif" onclick="alert(this.src);">
```

Make sure that you have a folder called `images` and the GIF files in place before you render this sample.

When referring to the pathing of files on a Windows machine, backslashes are used to delimit each folder name found in the path. But in UNIX, which is the platform on which the Internet was born and pre-dominantly accessed, the forward slash is used instead. So, for all web development when providing pathing in a URL, make sure to use the forward slash.

The JavaScript in the `onclick` event handler says to bring up a pop-up with the `alert` statement. And shown in that pop-up will be whatever `this.src` is equal to. In event handlers, the keyword `this` is a reference to the object that experienced the event, which in this case is the actual image itself. By adding a dot and additional naming, you can then reference properties or methods of that object, such as `src` in this case being the URL from which the image data got loaded. Thus you can render the page and click the image to see its URL, as shown in Figure 2-5.

Figure 2-5

Working with the image src Attribute

Now what if you wanted to change the image when it is clicked? You can just assign a different URL to this.src, and it is then updated on the fly. Try that by changing the JavaScript in the event handler so that it now looks like this:

```
<img src="images/ArrowLeft.gif" onclick="this.src='images/ArrowRight.gif';">
```

Now when you click the first time on the image, this is the JavaScript that runs:

```
this.src= 'images/ArrowRight.gif';
```

Thus, as soon as the new image file loads, it is changed out to present the other arrow image.

The use of the src attribute with the <script> tag is discussed in Chapter 3.

Using Functions

Wouldn't it be nice to have the two images toggle with each click? How can you do this? It takes a little more code, and writing very much logic inside the double quotation marks of the onclick attribute starts to get a little obnoxious. So, this is the perfect point to introduce how to use a *function*. A function simply wraps up a bundle of useful code into a code block that can be called by name. In this case, the onclick code will call into a function called ChangeMe(), which will be defined in the <script> element.

```
<img src="images/ArrowLeft.gif" onclick="ChangeMe(this);">
```

You haven't deleted the <script> element that you were using before, have you? Hopefully not! But if so, then you can simply add one in again. It can exist anywhere in the <head> or <body> elements. It doesn't have to exist before the <img> element, since it is called after the page has fully loaded. Within that <script> element, add this:

```
var isArrowLeft=true;
function ChangeMe(target)
{
 isArrowLeft=!isArrowLeft;
 if(isArrowLeft)
  target.src = "images/ArrowLeft.gif";
 else
  target.src = "images/ArrowRight.gif";
}
```

After rendering the page, the isArrowLeft variable is initially set to true. And when the image is clicked, the ChangeMe() function is called with the image object being passed in. Within that function the image object is called as target. The isArrowLeft variable, which holds a boolean value, is set to its opposite with the first statement. Then that target image's src attribute is set based on what the isArrowLeft value holds.

A similar example to this is found at the start of Chapter 7, but it goes further to include more intricate string manipulation with the split() function and referencing an array member. It also uses the prototype keyword to add a method called substitute() to all strings. This more in-depth example will make better sense after you digest the next chapter, which has information about objects and more about functions.

Programmatically Populating the Options in <select>

When a choice is made in one drop-down list, it is often handy to populate a second drop-down list with appropriate choices. With Ajax, this is fairly straightforward, and this sample will show you how to implement the JavaScript side of things, dynamically adding new <option> objects to the contents of a drop-down list. The <select> element is what builds a drop-down list (or a list box if the size attribute has been set). This next Try It Out has you build a drop-down list by using <select>, and then add a textbox and button underneath. When you type some text and click the button, it will build a new option in the drop-down list.

Finding Objects with document.getElementById()

Before you go further, you need to know about an important tool at your disposal. In the last section, you worked with an image object by using the special this keyword available inside an event handler. It was convenient, but what if you wanted to find an existing object on the page and change its properties? This is where, historically, different browsers have had different approaches to get the job done. For example, Internet Explorer (IE) would use document.all, and Netscape would use document.layers. Fortunately, a common method on the document object now enables you to search through a web page and find any object by its ID anywhere on the page: getElementById(). To effectively use this, the elements being referenced must have id attributes applied. In the remaining samples in the chapter and in even more detail in the next chapter, you'll see the use of document.getElementById().

Dynamic Drop-Down Options

Begin with the following HTML:

```
<select id="mySelect"></select><br />
<input type="text" id="newOption" />
<input type="button" value="Add a new option to the drop-down"
  onclick="addOption(document.getElementById('newOption').value);" />
```

The onclick event handler for the button calls a function named addOption, using the getElementById() method in order to find the text value in the textbox named newOption.

Next, here is the addOption function that you should add:

```
<script type="text/javascript">
  function addOption(optionText)
  {
   var objSelect=document.getElementById("mySelect");
   objSelect[objSelect.length] = new Option(optionText);
  }
</script>
```

This function is a little different from the last one you saw: It accepts a parameter called optionText, called out in the parentheses after the name of the function. When called, this function expects a string value will be passed in for optionText. This is used later in the function to specify the text that should be associated with the new Option object being built.

A reference is obtained with document.getElementById() to the <select> element called mySelect. This reference, named objSelect, is used to update the contents of the options. The square brackets indicate that an array is being referenced, and in this case it's an array of options under the <select> element. The value inside the square brackets defines an index to which piece of the array is being modified. The new Option object is placed in as the very last piece of the array by having the index refer to the current length of the array. When this is added, the new option is immediately visible in the drop-down list, as shown in Figure 2-6. Notice how, in the top screen of Figure 2-6, the select box is empty. When you add the phrase "Who says HTML is boring" and click the "Add a new option to the drop-down" button, the bottom of Figure 2-6 shows the finished result.

If this <select> element were in an HTML form and was submitted to the server, the value posted back would be exactly the same as whatever text the user had typed.

If you want to have a different value posted back to the server, then you can specify two parameters when building out the new Option object, the first being the text to show the user and the second being the value that gets posted back to the server. To illustrate the importance of this concept, consider a drop-down list of states. You would want to display the state name to the user, but once it was posted back to the server, you would want your application to know about the state code. This is important because you are now associating what is important to the user, a friendly state name, with what is important to the computer, the unique state code.

Using the innerHTML Property

A very handy feature of `<span>` and `<div>` elements that first showed up in IE4 is the `innerHTML` property. This represents what the browser considers to be the actual HTML it will use to present the contents of the `<div>` or `<span>`. Although the `innerHTML property` is not officially a part of the World Wide Web Consortium (W3C) standard, it is still very useful, especially for Ajax — useful enough that it was also adopted by Netscape starting in version 6 of their browser.

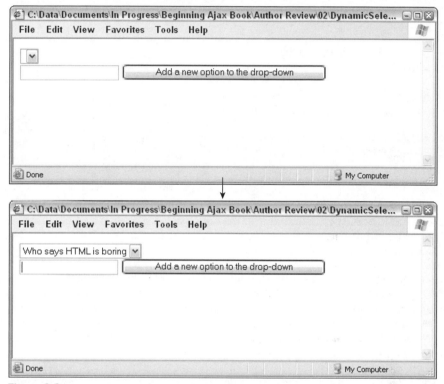

Figure 2-6

Try It Out   **Using the innerHTML Property**

To get a quick idea of what it can do, you can put a `<span>` on your page with `<textarea>` and `<input type="checkbox">` elements inside, and after the `<span>`, a button to present a pop-up showing what the browser sees inside the `innerHTML` of the `<span>`. Here's the code:

```
<span id="spanTxt">
 <textarea></textarea>
 <input type="checkbox" />
</span>
<input type="button" value="Show the innerHTML"
 onclick="alert(document.getElementById('spanTxt').innerHTML);" />
```

When you examine the contents of `innerHTML`, you'll find that things differ between different browsers. With the page loaded in Internet Explorer, try typing something in the `<textarea>`, and you'll find that when you click the button, the pop-up `alert()` shows exactly the HTML that would re-create the `<span>` in its current state. Click the checkbox as well, and then click the button to bring up the `alert()` again, and note that the CHECKED attribute then appears. See Figure 2-7 for a sample of what is shown. Unfortunately, in other browsers this nice dynamic reference to `innerHTML` doesn't happen; they simply show the page's source for what's inside the `<span>`.

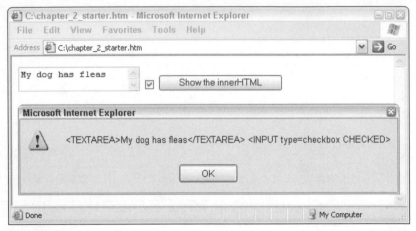

Figure 2-7

However, something that is possible with both Netscape and Firefox and IE is that you can change the `innerHTML` contents programmatically. Consider for a moment the potential. A `<div>` or `<span>` can be set up on a page, and with that page still showing, the browser can send an asynchronous request to the server, receive raw HTML data back, and conveniently place the result in the `innerHTML` property. That's the very basis of Ajax, dynamically updating only specific content on a page without having to refresh the whole thing.

Another way to place new content on a page dynamically is by using `createElement()` *and its relatives, which are discussed in the next chapter.*

Manipulating the Style Sheet

A primary feature of writing DHTML code is being able to dynamically change the style sheet. Using JavaScript you have the ability to manipulate the style sheet in a number of different ways. One of the ways to make these dynamic changes is to respond to user interaction on the page by hooking into element events. An example of one of these events is the `onclick` event of the anchor element.

Before making any changes to the style sheet, JavaScript must know what element on the page you want to affect. The most common way to find the element you are looking for on the page is to use the function `document.getElementById()`. A very useful attribute of the style sheet is the `display` attribute. The `display` attribute will determine how an element is displayed on the page. When the element is set to `display:block` the element will take up space on the page. When the element is set to `display:none` the element is removed from the elements displayed on the page.

To illustrate this behavior, the next Try It Out demonstrates how to build a panel for which you can toggle the display attributes. The result for the user is that it appears as if you are hiding the panel with one click and showing the panel with the next click.

Try It Out   **Showing and Hiding a DHTML Panel**

For this example, begin by adding the following HTML to your page:

```
<a href="javascript:void(0);"
    onclick="ShowHide('divDetails');UpdateText(this);">
    Show Details
</a>

<div id="divDetails" style="display:none;">
   Details Panel
</div>
```

This block has two sections. The first part of the HTML renders a link on the page that allows the user to click on an element to initiate the change to the style sheet. The next part of the code is the panel that is affected by the change. This is the panel that is hidden from and then displayed again to the user.

Next, add the following JavaScript to the page:

```
<script type="text/javascript">
function ShowHide(elementId)
{
   var element = document.getElementById(elementId);
   if(element.style.display != "block")
   {
      element.style.display = "block";
   }
   else
   {
      element.style.display = "none";
   }
}

function UpdateText(element)
{
   if(element.innerHTML.indexOf("Show") != -1)
   {
      element.innerHTML =
          "Hide Details";
   }
   else
   {
      element.innerHTML =
          "Show Details";
   }
}
</script>
```

The preceding JavaScript changes the web page in two ways. The ShowHide function does the work of finding the panel on the page, and then updating the style sheet's display property. If the element is not being shown to the user (display:block), then the settings are updated to display the panel. Alternatively, if the panel is being displayed, then the style sheet is updated to hide the panel.

The next function UpdateText uses the innerHTML property you learned about in the last section, to update the text in the link the user is clicking on. Notice in the HTML that when the function is called, a single argument of this is passed into the function. This element reference allows the function to know which element initiated the call to the function. With this reference, the function examines the innerHTML of the link and makes the appropriate changes to the text displayed to the user.

Creating a Context Menu

The last Try It Out in this chapter is for IE only and shows how to reference the various style properties on a <div> in order to make it visible or hidden and reposition it on the screen. You will use this <div> as a custom context menu that appears on the page when the right mouse button on a right-handed mouse is clicked (or whatever alternate mouse button is configured). The event that fires when this click is done is oncontextmenu. You will handle this event, first just showing the x and y position of the mouse in the status window and deferring the normal behavior of an alternate click: showing the browser's context menu.

Try It Out   Adding a Context Menu

If you've been working through all of the samples, then there is already an event handler in place on the <body> tag to handle onload. You'll keep that intact and add another event handler for oncontextmenu like this:

```
<body onload="window.status='It\'s a beautiful day';"
oncontextmenu="contextMenuClick(); return false;">
```

And as you may have guessed, the return false; statement bypasses the normal behavior of this event handler, which would bring up the browser's context menu. So, you can now add a function in the <script> tag called contextMenuClick(), which simply examines a couple of properties called clientX and clientY found on the event object:

```
function contextMenuClick()
{
  window.status=event.clientX+' '+event.clientY;
}
```

When you test this, you'll find that the event.clientX and event.clientY properties give the x and y coordinates of the exact location of the mouse during the click. So, when you render the page and right-click somewhere, the status menu shows those x and y coordinates. You can put that information to work by using the coordinates to place a <div>. Add this code anywhere in the body:

```
<div id="contextMenu"
  style="position:absolute; z-index:999;
  visibility:hidden; border:3px solid #000080;
  background-color:#4000C0; color:#FFFF00">
My excellent context menu
</div>
```

Now that you have this <div>, you can place it using its `style.left` and `style.top` properties. You also need to make it visible. Update the existing `contextMenuClick()` function with this code:

```
function contextMenuClick()
{
 var objContextMenu=document.getElementById("contextMenu");
 objContextMenu.style.left=event.clientX;
 objContextMenu.style.top=event.clientY;
 objContextMenu.style.visibility="visible";
}
```

In this case, you use that special method of the `document` object mentioned earlier in the chapter, `getElementById()`, to find the `contextMenu` object by its `id` and put that reference in a new variable called `objContextMenu`. This effectively gives you a handy pointer to the <div>, which you then use with the next three statements to update the position and visibility of the <div>. With that, wherever you right-click on the page the context menu is shown.

Summary

This chapter was designed to be an easy walkthrough to introduce you to some of the important concepts around DHTML, with most coverage given to JavaScript. At this point, you can take the principles you've learned and continue to experiment!

In this chapter, you looked at the following:

❑ Some quick coverage of JavaScript syntax and some examples of presenting data

❑ Retrieving data from the user

❑ Handling events with JavaScript functions

❑ Direct manipulation of HTML objects

These concepts will be essential as you learn more about Ajax. From here, you can dig deeper into how JavaScript objects work in the next chapter.

JavaScript and the Document Object Model

Hypertext Markup Language (HTML) is currently the language of the Internet. All browsers know how to parse and render HTML into a format that is easily viewed and understood by humans. When a browser is instructed to retrieve a page from a server, what is returned to the browser is a document that contains HTML. The browser can then interpret and render this HTML document for presentation to the user.

HTML documents are static representations of a user interface. Once this interface is presented to the user, the interface is typically unable to change without being re-sent to the server for processing, and another HTML document is returned to and rendered for the user. JavaScript and the Document Object Model (DOM) provide a way that you can change this rendered display programmatically and dynamically, according to events such as a user clicking the mouse, all from within the browser.

In this chapter, you take a look at:

- ❑ The development of JavaScript
- ❑ The basics of the language
- ❑ Advanced JavaScript features
- ❑ The HTML Document Object Model and associated standards
- ❑ Using JavaScript to programmatically and dynamically change rendered HTML documents with the Document Object Model

All the code samples for this chapter are available for downloading at http://beginningajax *.com. Just visit the site and download the samples for Chapter 3. They are provided as a Visual Studio .NET 2005 web site project. Simply load and execute each page as required.*

From Static to Dynamic — A Brief History

Approximately 10 years ago in 1995, almost a lifetime in computer industry terms, a man by the name of Brendan Eich developed a loosely typed scripting language intended to make Netscape Navigator's newly added Java support more accessible to non-Java programmers. On December 4, 1995, Netscape and Sun jointly announced the existence of the new JavaScript language to the world.

Although the original intent of JavaScript was to further the Java language, it soon took on a life of its own. JavaScript was commonly used to manipulate images and HTML documents' contents, instead of just manipulating and controlling Java applets. Although JavaScript retains the use of *Java* within its name, currently it bears no relationship to the core Java language other than the fact that Java was used to model the original language characteristics of JavaScript. This is often a source of confusion for developers, who assume JavaScript to be a subset of the Java core language. The development of JavaScript has taken on a life of its own.

Using JavaScript, previously static web content could now be dynamically manipulated. Web programmers the world over began to see enormous new potential in their web applications. Initially, a vast majority of web applications used JavaScript simply to change images in response to a mouse click by the user. JavaScript was not without its issues however. Browser compatibility issues and security issues plagued initial implementations, and it has undergone many revisions over the course of its lifetime. JavaScript has evolved into the primary way to control and extend the way in which document authors and web application designers can manipulate the client's browser experience.

Currently, JavaScript is the only way to achieve any sort of dynamic behavior on the client in a cross-browser-compatible way. Microsoft also attempted to address the issue of dynamic content and interaction on web pages by releasing VBScript, a scripting language closely resembling the Visual Basic syntax that was initially limited to the windows platform. Microsoft also released a port of JavaScript, called JScript in 1996. This fragmentation of scripting languages, the fact that Microsoft's scripting languages were not quite as powerful as JavaScript, and the fact that they were a revision or two behind led to JavaScript being the more popular choice for dynamic web content, in particular, the very popular image swapping effects.

Attempts at Standardization

As browsers evolved and dynamic web pages became more popular, differences in browsers and their implementations became apparent. Internet Explorer would implement a feature in one way, whereas Netscape would implement features in another (albeit often quite similar) way. The natural effect of this was to attempt to standardize the JavaScript language by submitting it to the European Computer Manufacturers Association (ECMA). JavaScript now had a new name: *ECMAScript*. ECMAScript was adopted in June 1997 by ECMA, and in 1998 by ISO (International Organization for Standardization).

While JavaScript was being standardized, browser vendors were releasing yet another version of their browsers. This was approximately around the time of the 4.0 release generation of browsers. With new abilities to dynamically update client-side content, browser vendors implemented object models within the browser to represent the documents they contained; each of these was known as the Document Object Model (DOM) by their respective browser vendor. Unfortunately, most vendors implemented different object models, making dynamic content difficult on browsers from different vendors.

Browser innovation continued at a rapid rate, and incompatibilities continued among different vendors' browsers. Many libraries were developed that attempted to provide a common application program interface (API) between the different browsers. These would typically enable a common way of developing Dynamic HTML (DHTML) applications across many browsers, but they were only moderately successful.

During this time, Microsoft, Netscape, and a number of other companies worked with the World Wide Web Consortium (W3C) to provide a consistent and standardized DOM. This was an attempt to remove the current complexity with developing DHTML applications across a variety of browsers.

The W3C develops interoperable technologies (specifications, guidelines, software, and tools) for all web-related technologies. You can visit their web site for more information at www.w3.org.

Throughout this chapter, you will look at the core components of JavaScript and methods of interacting with and manipulating the DOM. While still not fully realized, cross-browser compatibility with respect to the DOM is much improved and is much easier than it previously was. However, inconsistencies among vendor implementations still remain, and there are still many libraries and frameworks available to provide a common API across vendors' browser implementations. Some of these libraries are discussed in Chapter 9 of this book.

Today, JavaScript is the prevalent scripting language of browsers. It is the primary method of achieving dynamic client-side interactivity in web applications. Microsoft has already initiated work at integrating the powerful server-side programming environment of ASP.NET with JavaScript support. Technologies such as asynchronous client scripting and Atlas will also be discussed in later chapters of this book. All of these advanced technologies make use of the core components and features of JavaScript.

Digging into Some More JavaScript Basics

Chapter 2 started your introduction to JavaScript, particularly in showing how it can interact with the browser environment to modify the HTML and CSS that make up a web page. In this chapter, you will build on and extend what you learned in Chapter 2.

Take a look at the following simple JavaScript:

```
<!DOCTYPE html PUBLIC "-//W3C//DTD XHTML 1.0 Transitional//EN"
"http://www.w3.org/TR/xhtml1/DTD/xhtml1-transitional.dtd">
<html xmlns="http://www.w3.org/1999/xhtml" >
<head>
    <title>Basic Javascript</title>

    <script type="text/javascript">
        alert("Hi, I am some simple JavaScript");
    </script>

</head>
<body>
    <p>Simple Javascript Page</p>
</body>
</html>
```

Within the `<head>` section of the HTML document, you have a `<script>` tag that contains some basic JavaScript. In this case, a simple *alert* box is displayed with the text "Hi, I am some simple JavaScript."

`<script>` tags are the primary way of including scripted content in your HTML pages. You also have a `type` attribute on the `<script>` tag that has been set to `"text/Javascript"` to signify the type of script you will be including within the `<script>` tag. Current standards specify that you should use this `type` of script attribute setting for all JavaScript script and, additionally, place the `<script>` tag within the `<head>` section of the document (this is actually a semantic guideline and not a compliance requirement). Previously, this was not required, as shown in the following code:

```
<!DOCTYPE html PUBLIC "-//W3C//DTD XHTML 1.0 Transitional//EN"
"http://www.w3.org/TR/xhtml1/DTD/xhtml1-transitional.dtd">
<html xmlns="http://www.w3.org/1999/xhtml" >
<head>
    <title>Basic Javascript</title>
    <script type="text/javascript">
        alert("Hi, I am some simple JavaScript");
    </script>
</head>
<body>
    <script language="javascript">
        alert("Alert box 2");
    </script>
    <p>Simple Javascript Page</p>
    <script language="javascript">
        alert("Alert box 3");
    </script>

</body>
</html>
```

Although they are not strictly necessary, and despite the fact that many browsers will work fine without adhering to these standards, the recommended approach is to adhere to these standards for any current and future web development.

You will notice in the previous example, that we specified a `language` attribute with a value of `"javascript"` instead of a `type` attribute with a value of `"text/javascript"`. The script still works fine; however, this requires that each `<script>` tag have a `type` attribute with the specified MIME type to be contained within the `<script>` tag. There are some processing differences between the use of the `language` and `type` attributes; however, current standards dictate the use of the `type` attribute, and that's what will be used throughout this book.

> XHTML is the most recent version of HTML and describes or reformulates HTML elements more inline with XML semantics and form. It also enhances the separation of structure from presentation. More information can be found at www.w3.org/TR/xhtml1.

One of the most important attributes of a `<script>` tag is the `src` attribute. You may remember in the last chapter using the `src` attribute with the `<img>` tag. The functionality is similar here. This provides the ability to include JavaScript from external files and is a great way to centralize and share common JavaScript code.

```
<script type="text/javascript" src="BasicScripting_Script.js"></script>
```

The external file referenced in the preceding example contains some JavaScript code as follows:

```
document.writeln("I have been written by some javascript");
```

So, the page references the JavaScript file "BasicScripting_Script.js", which contains JavaScript code to output a string to the web page. The page then executes the JavaScript code as if it were declared directly within the page.

It is possible for a browser to have JavaScript disabled, and thus no script will be run when the page is loaded. On some browsers, when JavaScript is disabled, the script itself will be rendered to the page as it is written within the HTML page. To circumvent this side effect, developers often surround their script with comment tags that cause the script not to be rendered if JavaScript is disabled. Often, you will see this done with JavaScript libraries and frameworks. The following is an example:

```
<script type="text/javascript">
<!--
    alert("Hi, I am some simple Javascript");
-->
</script>
```

Functions and Syntax

Previous examples have shown the use of JavaScript that executes as the page loads, as it is encountered or parsed. However, you can also define functions to encapsulate blocks of functionality.

```
<script type="text/javascript">
function TestFunction()
{
    document.writeln("I have been written by some javascript");
}
</script>
```

Here you have defined a JavaScript function that outputs the specified text when it is called. As indicated in Chapter 2, a *function* is simply used to group a list of statements together. To call this function, you simply use the following script:

```
TestFunction();
```

You will notice the line is terminated with a semicolon (;). Again, as noted in Chapter 2, this is not strictly necessary. Each line can also be terminated with simply a carriage return.

```
function TestFunction()
{
    document.writeln("I have been written by some javascript")
    document.writeln("This is some more text")
    document.writeln("and yet some more")
}
```

However, to place more than one statement on a line, the statements must be separated with a semicolon.

```
document.writeln("<br />new line");document.writeln("<br />second new line");
```

Just a reminder of what was stressed in Chapter 2 — typically, for the sake of consistency and clarity, most developers will terminate each line with a semicolon regardless of whether there are multiple statements per line or not. This is the recommended approach for all JavaScript development.

Functions also require that the code block that comprises the function, or body of the function, be encased in curly braces ({ }). The opening and ending curly brace define the start and end of the code block, respectively. Code blocks defined within curly braces are not just used for functions. Other statements within JavaScript that require the grouping of more than one statement also use the curly brace syntax.

```
if (str == "something")
{
    document.writeln("str contains something");
    alert("Test evaluated");
}
```

Conditional statements and other core language features will be examined in detail later in this chapter.

Functions can accept arguments, or parameters, and return values. For example:

```
function ConstructMessage(msg)
{
    return "You Passed in the string: " + msg;
}
```

This function accepts a single argument and returns a string value that in part comprises the argument that was passed in. To use this function, the code would look like:

```
alert( ConstructMessage("Test Message") );
```

More than one argument can be specified for a function's input parameters by separating the arguments with a comma (,), for example:

```
function MethodWithParameters(arg1, arg2, arg3)
{
    // Do something with the values of arg1, arg2 and arg3
}
```

A function's arguments can be any primitive type or any type of object.

Event Handlers

You don't always want script to be executed as the page is loaded. Quite often you want script executed in response to events such as a user clicking a particular screen element or a mouse movement. (For example, you may recall that in Chapter 2, you used the `onload` event to insert custom text into the status area of a browser window once a page had fully rendered.) This activity is usually done by referencing either inline JavaScript or a function using an XHTML attribute. In the following examples, you are handling the `onclick` event of a button first using inline script:

```
<input type="button" value="Click Me (inline)" onclick="alert('I was clicked -
inline script');" />
```

and then using a `HandleClick()` function:

```
<input type="button" value="Click Me (function)" onclick="HandleClick();" />
```

The `onclick` event is probably one of the most familiar events to web developers and doesn't have to be applied only to obvious items such as buttons. It can be applied to other items such as paragraph tags, <p>, and most other items as well.

```
<p onclick="HandleParaTagClick();">This is some paragraph text</p>
```

XHTML requires that all event handler declaration be written in lowercase. Although case-sensitivity is not strictly required to be HTML-compliant, it is required for XHTML compliancy. For example, onClick, *ONCLICK, and* onclick *are all valid in HTML, but only the lowercase version is XHTML-compliant. For this reason, all event handlers used in this book will be written in lowercase.*

Many more event handling attributes are available that can be utilized by web developers, and these are discussed in detail later in this chapter.

Core Language

JavaScript is case-sensitive. This means that the case of a variable constitutes part of its name and that lowercase letters are different from uppercase letters. So, a function that has been named `getData()` is a different function to one named `GetData()`.

Variables

Variables are components that store data. A variable is defined in JavaScript by using the `var` keyword.

```
var str = "this is a string";
```

The preceding statement defines a variable called `str` that contains the string `this is a string`. The literal string value is surrounded by double quotation marks ("); however, you can use single quotation marks as well ('). These come in handy when specifying strings within JavaScript, which itself is encased in double quotation marks. This usually occurs when handling events.

```
<input type="button" value="Click Me (inline)" onclick="alert('I was clicked -
inline script');" />
```

Comments

Comments can be included in any JavaScript code in two ways. Using double forward slash characters (//) indicates that everything preceding the characters is a comment.

```
// This is a comment.
```

Additionally, an entire comment block can be defined by surrounding the comments with a /* to start the comment block and a */ to end the comment block.

```
/*
    These are some more comments. This is useful for a larger set of
    comments that is written in a paragraph like fashion.
*/
```

Datatypes

There are three basic, or primitive, datatypes in JavaScript: string, number, and boolean types. A boolean type can contain either a `true` or `false` value. Number types can contain either an integer or floating-point number.

```
var boolVar = true;
var numberVar = 8.13;
var stringVar = "This is a string";
```

The number datatype can have special values. These special values are `Infinity` and `NaN`.

❑   A number variable is given the value of `Infinity` when its maximum capacity is exceeded. Similarly, a number variable is given the value of `-Infinity` when its minimum value is exceeded.

❑   A number variable can also have a value of `NaN`, which stands for Not a Number, when the variable is assigned the value of an undefined operation, such as dividing zero by zero.

Infinity values can be compared, and all values that equate to infinity are equal — that is, any result of an operation that equals infinity is equal to any other operation that results in a value of infinity. Any operation involving a value of infinity causes the entire result to be equal to infinity. Unlike infinity, `NaN` must be explicitly tested for, using the `isNaN()` function.

Escape Codes

Strings can contain special characters such as backspaces, tabs, and carriage returns by "escaping" the characters, that is, by using an escape code to represent the character. Escape codes in strings are prefixed by a backslash. The list of escape codes is given in the following table.

Escape Code	Character or Value Represented
\b	Backspace
\r	Carriage return
\n	Linefeed or newline
\t	Horizontal tab
\v	Vertical tab
\f	Form feed
\"	Double quotation mark
\'	Single quotation mark

Escape Code	Character or Value Represented
\\	Backslash
\000	Latin-1 character represented by a three-digit octal value in the range 000–377, for example, \056.
\xHH	Latin-1 character represented by a two-digit hexadecimal number in the range of 00–FF, for example, \xA0.

The following is an example of using escape codes:

```
var s = "This is a tab\tThis is a newline\nI am on a new line";
```

Weak or Dynamic Typing

JavaScript supports the notion of *weak* typing, or *dynamic* typing. This means that the type of a variable is inferred from the data it contains. This is why there is only one way to declare variables — by using the var keyword.

Try this test:

```
var v = "Some String Data";
alert(typeof v);

v = 5;
alert(typeof v);
```

In the first instance, a message box will be displayed showing that the type of v is a string. In the second instance, the type of v is a number. The type of the v variable has been inferred, and in fact changed, according to what type of data it contains.

The typeof statement is an operator that returns the type of the variable being examined. This operator will return a value of object, boolean, number, string, function, and undefined depending on the argument specified.

Composite Types

JavaScript also has support for more complex datatypes known as *composite types*. Composite types can contain not only primitive types, such as a string or number, but also other composite types. The three composite types are arrays, objects, and functions. However, both the array and the function are really just special kinds of objects.

An easy way to think of a composite type is an object that can contain any other type of object or objects. An array is the typical composite type and will contain a list of other objects (which may be integers, strings, or custom objects) as a sequential list of elements. An array will typically contain a list of objects of the same type (all integers for example), but it is not limited to just that. Mixing datatypes within arrays can generally lead to confusing code, which may result in hard-to-track bugs. This practice is generally not recommended.

Composite types are required where there is a need for an object to contain or handle a logically grouped set of data. For example, an array might be used to store a list of countries or states.

Arrays are an ordered set of values and can be defined in a number of ways.

```
var array1 = [1,"string data",4,5,"6"];    // Mixing data types

var array2 = new Array(4);
array2[0] = "zero";
array2[1] = "one";
array2[2] = "two";
array2[3] = "three";

var array3 = new Array(1,"two",3,4);     // Mixing data types
```

You can access the values in an array by using an index value representing the element number contained at the position in the array:

```
var val1 = array1[0];
var val2 = array1[1];
```

Objects can contain any type of data and are the primary mechanism for data storage and browser interaction. Objects can contain data, which are referred to as *properties*, and functions, which are referred to as *methods*. Methods and properties are accessed on an object using dot notation in the format:

```
object.property;
```

or

```
object.method();
```

Browsers supply a rich set of objects so that developers can manipulate the browser programmatically. A popular object is the document object. This object has a write method, which outputs text to the browser window:

```
document.write("This is some text. ");
document.write("Some more text <br />");
```

To prevent your having to always specify the document object when using its properties and methods, you can use a with statement:

```
with (document)
{
    write("Some text again. ");
    write("some more text again. <br />");
}
```

Objects are typically created and allocated using the new keyword. Conversely, they are effectively destroyed by setting the object instance variable to null. JavaScript offers a delete keyword, and you might be tempted to think that this can be used to clear allocated objects; however, delete is used only to delete properties (more on this later) and array elements. The delete keyword is not like the delete keyword used in C++ and Java. Using delete to delete an object instance will simply fail silently.

```
var o = new Object();
delete o;

var array4 = new Array(5);
array4[0] = "something";
delete array4;
```

Operators and Expressions

For those familiar with C++ or Java, JavaScript will seem very familiar. JavaScript contains a standard set of operators and expressions for mathematical operations. The standard set of operators includes assignment (=), addition (+), subtraction (–), multiplication (*), division (/) ,and modulus (%). Some examples of these are shown in the following code lines:

Assignment/addition/subtraction:

```
y = x + 3 - 2;
```

Multiplication/division:

```
y = 2 * 4;
```

Modulus:

```
y = 8 % 3;
```

JavaScript also includes the standard set of bitwise operators for performing operations on data at the bit level. These include AND (&), OR (|), NOT (^), Exclusive OR ( ), left shift (<<), and right shift (>>) The result of using these operations is usually some value representing the bit pattern after the operation has been performed.

JavaScript also supports the standard shorthand notation for mathematical operations in the same way that C/C++ and Java do. Listed in the following lines are the shorthand versions of the mathematical operations and in comments their expanded equivalents:

```
var v = 3;
v++;      // v = v + 1;
v--;      // v = v - 1;
v *= 2;   // v = v * 2;
v /= 2;   // v = v / 2;
```

JavaScript also supports bitwise operators that provide the ability to perform operations on the bit representations of a set of arguments. These operators are the AND (&), OR (|), NOT (~), Exclusive OR (^), left shift (<<), and right shift (>>). These operators are rarely used within typical web applications using JavaScript because bit-level manipulation and comparison is normally out of the scope of typical web applications. Accordingly, they will not be discussed here.

However, it is important that these operators are not confused with, and in fact used in place of, logical operators that bear the same names. Logical operators only equate to a true or false value. These include the logical AND (&&), OR (||), and NOT (!).

These sets of operators are often used in conjunction with the relational operators, which are equal to (==), less than (<), greater than (>), not equal to (!=), less than or equal to (<=), and greater than or equal to (>=). So, the following expression:

```
5 < 11 && 10 > 20
```

equates to:

```
true && false
```

which ultimately equates to `false`. If you were to mistakenly substitute the bitwise AND (&) operator for the logical AND operator (&&) so that the expression looked like:

```
5 < 11 & 10 > 20
```

the expression would yield a result of 0, instead of the expected result of `false`. Clearly, this could lead to hard-to-track bugs, so it is important that logical operators be used. This mistake is quite often a source of frustration for beginners and seasoned developers alike.

If you utilize an `if` statement to create a more complex expression:

```
if ( ( (x > 1) && (y < 10) ) || x == 0)
```

where x = 0 and y = 5, the expression equates to:

```
if ( ( (false) && (true) || true)
```

which rationalizes to:

```
if (false || true)
```

and finally:

```
if (true)
```

Flow Control and Loops

Again, like C++ and Java, JavaScript contains a reasonably standard set of flow control statements, one of which you have seen previously, the `if-else` statement. This statement effectively is saying, if a condition is true, execute some code; otherwise, execute a different set of code. An example best illustrates this:

```
if (1 < 2)
{
    alert("the test is true");
} else
{
    alert("The test is false");
}
```

The `else` statement is not strictly required, so you can write the following:

```
var x = 2;
if (x < 5)
{
    document.write("value was less than 5");
}
```

In the case where multiple tests are required, you can use a `switch` statement. These provide a neat way of addressing multiple tests using the `case` keyword like this:

```
var z = 2;
switch (z)
{
    case 1:
        document.write("The value of z is 1");
        break;
    case 2:
        document.write("The value of z is 2");
        break;
    case 3:
        document.write("The value of z is 3");
        break;
}
```

In this example, the case statements are evaluated until a true equality test is found against the variable z and the corresponding value for the case statement. If no condition evaluates to `true`, the *default* condition is executed. Each case block is terminated with a `break` statement to exit the `switch` block. Failure to do this would cause evaluation to continue on down the `switch` block.

> The `switch` *statement is a relatively recent addition to the JavaScript language and wasn't introduced until version 1.2 of JavaScript. Some older browsers may not support this statement, so it should be used with care if older browsers need to be catered to.*

while and for Loops

Within JavaScript you have two main types of loops — `while` and `for` loops — with two variations on each. The `while` loop is used like this:

```
var x = 0;
while ( x < 3)
{
    x = x + 1;
    document.write("<br />Current Value of x = " + x);
}
```

This will execute the code within the code block, which increments the value of x until the value of x is greater than or equal to 3. That is, the condition within the parentheses must evaluate to `true` before the code block is executed. The test is performed before the code within the code block is executed. The variation on this is the `do`/`while` loop, which is used like so:

```
var y = 0;
do
{
    y = y + 1;
    document.write("<br />Current Value of y = " + y);
} while (y < 3);
```

The difference between the `while` loop and the `do/while` loop is that the `do/while` loop will execute the code block at least once, then the test is performed. The `while` loop will always evaluate the test before executing the code block.

The `for` loop, which you were introduced to in Chapter 2, is similar in function to the `while` loop; however, is a little more compact. Examine the following code example:

```
for (var i = 0; i < 3; i++)
{
    document.write("<br />Current Value of i = " + i);
}
```

The declaration of the variable, evaluation test, and variable increment are all performed in a single line. The code initializes a variable `i` to 0 and executes the code block only if the value of `i` is less than 3. The value of `i` is incremented on each iteration of the loop.

The variation on the `for` loop is the `for/in` loop. The `for/in` loop allows you to loop through the properties or members of an object. For example:

```
for (var member in document)
{
    document.write("<br />Document object has a member named: " + member);
}
```

This code will iterate over all the properties and events of the `document` object and write the name of those to the display.

Breaking or Continuing a Loop

In all examples of looping constructs shown so far, you can prematurely exit the loop by using the `break` statement. Issuing a `break` statement within a loop will cause program flow to exit the loop or code block, irrespective of whether the exit condition has been met.

```
var z = 0;
while ( z < 20 )
{
    z++;
    if (z > 5)
        break;
    document.write("<br />The value of z is : " + z);
}
```

This code example will exit the loop once the value of the variable z has exceeded a value of 5, even though the loop test will allow the value to only be less than 20. The if condition is evaluated to true once z is greater than 5, and the break statement is then executed.

Alternatively, the continue statement causes execution within a loop to immediately go to the next iteration in the loop and skip any intervening statements for that iteration only.

More on Objects and Functions

Almost everything in JavaScript that is not a primitive type is an object, including functions. Objects take full advantage of the dynamic nature of JavaScript, which is quite advanced, even compared to more traditional programming languages such as C#, C++, and Java.

Earlier in the chapter, you saw how you can create a new instance of an object using the new operator and how to clear that object instance by setting the object to equal null, which signifies that the object and anything it references are no longer required and the memory associated with that object can be released. The JavaScript interpreter present in the browser takes care of this process for you.

The dynamic nature of JavaScript allows you to create custom objects dynamically in code as you are executing it. Take the following code example:

```
function CreateCustomObject()
{
    var obj = new Object();
    obj.myCustomProperty = 1;
    obj.anotherProperty = "some data";
    return obj;
}

var o = CreateCustomObject();
alert("Property1: " + o.myCustomProperty);
alert("Property2: " + o.anotherProperty);
```

The CreateCustomObject function returns a custom object with two properties. The code then displays each property in an alert box. Within the CreateCustomObject function, you simply create a new generic object and assign values to two initially nonexistent properties. The JavaScript runtime infers the property types of each property from the data being assigned to it and also infers that you want to have these two properties available on your newly created object. You have just created a custom object with two properties by doing nothing other than assigning values to the properties. There was no need to explicitly define the properties themselves. Again, the JavaScript interpreter inferred the definition of these two properties on our behalf. You have dynamically created these two properties. This approach is vastly different from traditional languages, such as C#, C++, and Java, where typically a class definition is required that explicitly defines what properties are available on the class. However, this type of approach is still available, as we will examine later in this chapter.

You can also dynamically delete these instance properties from the object by using the delete keyword:

```
delete o.myCustomProperty;
alert("Property1: " + o.myCustomProperty);
```

Figure 3-1 shows the result that is displayed.

Figure 3-1

An interesting, but seldom used feature is the ability to reference properties using a weakly typed method. This means accessing the objects properties like a standard name/value pair. For example:

```
alert( o["anotherProperty"] );
```

is exactly the same as:

```
alert( o.anotherProperty );
```

Here, you will notice you are accessing the custom property as if it were an array element, except that the index used is the property name.

As already mentioned, this technique is seldom used within typical web applications. When developing frameworks for your own web applications, however, this technique can prove valuable due to the generic nature of frameworks. Often, the need to access an object property of which the name is not known at design time by using some string argument affords a degree of flexibility and generic operation to a framework where using the strongly typed mechanism could not normally be used.

Common Properties and Methods

All JavaScript objects have a common set of properties and methods. These properties and methods are relatively low level and not often used in your average web applications but are very important when dealing with your own custom objects. The common or basic set of properties available to all objects is listed in the following table:

Property/Method	Description
prototype	This property provides a reference to the object from which it inherits custom, "*non-instance*" properties. This feature is discussed later in this chapter.
constructor	Provides a reference to an object that acts as the objects constructor. A constructor is a function that is automatically executed when an object is first created.
toString()	Converts the object into its string representation.
toLocaleString()	Converts the object into its localized, or culture-specific string representation.
valueOf()	Converts the objects into an appropriate "primitive" type. This is normally a number.

Property/Method	Description
hasOwnProperty (nameOfProperty)	This method returns `true` if the instance property identified in the nameOfProperty argument exists; otherwise, it returns `false`.
isPrototypeOf(obj)	This method returns `true` if the objects acts as the prototype of the object passed in via the `obj` parameter; otherwise, `false` is returned.
propertyIsEnumerable (nameOfProperty)	This method returns `true` if the property specified in the nameOfProperty argument will be enumerated if the object is used in a `for/in` loop.

Custom Objects and Advanced Object Mechanics

The preceding section examined some properties and methods that are common to all JavaScript objects. Prior to that, the chapter examined how to define custom instance properties and create a customized form of a generic object. You can also dynamically add functions to objects, as shown in the following:

```
function someFunction()
{
    alert("You are in a function");
}

var newObj = new Object();
newObj.prop1 = true;
newObj.showMessage = someFunction;
```

Here you have created a generic object, assigned an instance property name prop1, and also assigned a function named someFunction to the showMessage method. To invoke the method on the object, you simply use:

```
newObj.showMessage();
```

Using Function Literals and Object Literals

You can make the preceding example even more compact by using function literals. A *function literal* is when a function is defined using the `function` keyword but is not given a function name. The example that follows demonstrates this:

```
var newObj = new Object();
newObj.prop1 = true;
newObj.showMessage = function() { alert ("You are in a function literal"); };

newObj.showMessage();
```

You can also pass in arguments to the function literal like so:

```
newObj.showMessage = function(msg)
        {
            alert ("You are in a function literal. Message was: " + msg);
        };

newObj.showMessage("my message");
```

This allows you to assign specific behavior to your object using the concept of function literals. In the preceding example, a custom function `showMessage` was defined that contained behavior to display a message. This could easily have been a much more complex function and represents part of the process in building a customized object with completely customized behavior.

Over the course of creating a web application, functionality can be grouped together within custom objects in the same way that traditional objects are created using server-side languages such as C# and VB.NET. *Encapsulation* is an object-oriented technique where logically grouped functionality is contained within singular components in order to reduce complexity within the greater application. Similarly, this technique can be applied to JavaScript, where you define your own custom objects with specialized behavior (using function literals to define your objects behavior) to logically group functionality and increase the manageability of your web application.

In addition to function literals, JavaScript (as of version 1.2 and above) also supports *object literals*. You use the standard set of curly braces to enclose a literal object definition of property value pairs and optionally function literals. Property names and values are separated by a colon, with each property/ value pair separated by a comma. The following code is the previous object example defined using an object literal:

```
var newObj = {
              prop1: true,
              showMessage: function(msg)
                     {
                            alert("You are in a function literal, which is inside
an object literal. Your message was: " + msg);
                     }
            };
// Invoke the method
newObj.showMessage("Another Message");
```

What you are seeing here is a way of completely describing an object's behavior in terms of properties and functions, without procedurally defining each property and function in code, as shown in previous examples. The objects functionality has been defined in a *declarative* manner.

Rather than having large sections of code that perform the task of creating your custom objects, an object definition using the object literal technique can be used to create your custom objects.

This technique is used throughout some of the custom frameworks and libraries available (which are discussed in detail in Chapter 9) to create a string representation of an object to transfer to a web application that uses JavaScript. Since the representation of an object literal is a simple string, this can be passed easily to other systems, or in fact, be generated *on the fly* (dynamically) by the server, for a client web application to use.

Using Prototypes

Ideally you want to be able to define an *object template* that can be used to create or instantiate custom objects in the same way that C#, C++, and Java programmers have class definitions. This is the function of the *prototype* feature in JavaScript.

Each object in JavaScript has a `prototype` property, which itself is an object. A `prototype` of an object can contain methods and properties that define the object to which the prototype belongs and are used when constructing a new object to give the object a default set of properties and methods. The prototype can be thought of as the blueprint of an object's properties and behavior when an object of that type is created. Custom instance properties and methods can still be defined on these objects and combined with the prototype-supplied properties.

Basically, the `prototype` property is a reference to an object that contains the initial structure and functionality of an object when first created. Further customization is possible via instance properties, as you have already seen. When you consider defining custom object structures, you have to grasp the concept of a constructor. A *constructor* is a method that is executed when an object is first created. As a web application developer, you do not need to explicitly call the constructor to have it executed. A constructor is implicitly executed when you create a *new* object. It is typically used to initialize any custom object data and prepare the object for use. A constructor is simply another function, and you can define it like this:

```
function Agent()
{
}

var agent1 = new Agent();
```

Here you have created a new `Agent` object. The `Agent` object has a constructor that doesn't really do anything special right now. You can use the constructor to add some instance properties to your `Agent` object, as follows:

```
function Agent()
{
    this.isActive - true;
    this.isSecret = false;
}

var agent1 = new Agent();
```

Here, you have added two instance properties to your `Agent` object. You no doubt noticed the use of the `this` keyword. The `this` keyword holds a reference to the object you are working within or basically a reference to your new object. Your object is now a customized object that can be used within your code. You can define a function to operate on your custom object:

```
function CheckIfActive(agentObject)
{
    if (agentObject.isActive)
        alert("The agent is currently active.");
    else
        alert("The agent is not active.");
}
```

And use that function in conjunction with the custom object like this:

```
var agent1 = new Agent();
CheckIfActive(agent1);
```

Because the constructor is just another function, you can also add parameters to the function:

```
function Agent(initiallyActive)
{
    if (initiallyActive == false)
        this.isActive = false;
    else
        this.isActive = true;
    this.isSecret = false;
}
```

This is known as a *parameterized constructor*.

Now, you can create a new instance of the object either using a parameter to specify an initial value or using the default constructor, as shown in the following:

```
var agent1 = new Agent();
var agent2 = new Agent(false);
CheckIfActive(agent1);
CheckIfActive(agent2);
```

You will notice that in the parameterized constructor, you explicitly check for a value of `false` and then set the instance property appropriately. It might seem redundant at first to check for a value of `false` and then set the value of the internal value `isActive` to `false`. Remember, though, that variables in JavaScript can be of any type based on what the value of that variable is that is being assigned.

When the `Agent` object is constructed using the parameterized constructor, the value of the `initiallyActive` argument is expected to be a boolean true/false value, but can in fact be any value, including `null`. The check to see if the `initiallyActive` variable is equal to `false` contains a fall-through condition to set the value of the internal variable `isActive` to `true` if anything but false is passed in. This ensures that the value of the internal variable `isActive` is only ever set to a boolean value of true or false and not a potentially incorrect or invalid value of null. This is known as *defensive programming*.

Try It Out   Creating a Prototype

So, now that you have seen how to customize an object using instance properties and also how to define a constructor for an object to perform some initialization within that constructor, you are ready to see how prototypes provide a flexible and powerful way to describe a "blueprint" of an object. To refactor the `Agent` example using prototypes, you would do the following:

```
function Agent(isUnderCover)
{
    if (isUnderCover)
        this.isSecret = true;
}

Agent.prototype.isSecret = false;
Agent.prototype.isActive = true;
Agent.prototype.checkIfActive = function()
    {
        if (this.isActive)
```

```
            alert("This agent is currently active. Is a Secret Agent?: " +
    this.isSecret);
            else
                alert("This agent is not active. Is a Secret Agent?: " +
    this.isSecret);
        };
```

What this example is doing is defining the properties and methods that exist on an object (in this case the `Agent` object) when a new object of that type is created. A "blueprint" of the object is defined by defining its prototype, and when a new object of that type is created, the prototype definition is automatically used to construct a new version of the object.

In the preceding example, the prototype contains two properties (`isSecret` and `isActive`, which are assigned initial values), a function named `checkIfActive()`, and a parameterized constructor. Contrast this to the previous example where a generic object is initially constructed, and then properties and functions are dynamically added through procedural code. In simple examples, using this procedural method of dynamically constructing an object may suffice; however, in more complex object definitions, providing prototype definitions allows greater flexibility in defining how your object will behave. This is particularly important when your object is part of a reusable framework or common library that can be reused within other applications.

Now to create and use your `Agent` object, you simply do the following:

```
var agent1 = new Agent();
agent1.checkIfActive();

var agent2 = new Agent(true);
agent2.checkIfActive();
```

Now you can see how you have defined the structure of the `Agent` object using the prototype feature and how easy it is to create objects based on the prototype definition. It is important to note that each object you create that is of type `Agent` shares the same prototype reference. That is, only one copy of the prototype is shared between all objects created from the prototype. This means that any change to the prototype is, in effect, made visible to all objects based on that prototype.

Modifying the prototype Property

As mentioned previously in this chapter, all objects have a `prototype` property, and it is possible to modify any object's `prototype` definition. This can be particularly useful for modifying the behavior of built-in objects. For example, if you want to enhance the built-in `String` object to include a method that prefixes a string with a particular set of characters, you can do the following:

```
String.prototype.addPrefix = function(prefix)
    {
        return prefix + this;
    }
```

You can then do the following:

```
var newString = "Some String".addPrefix("This is ");
alert(newString);
```

This produces the result shown in Figure 3-2:

Figure 3-2

As you can see, modifying an object's existing `prototype` definition or defining your own custom prototype provides a very powerful way to define the structure and behavior of your custom objects, as
well as the behavior of the existing built-in objects that JavaScript provides.

Inheritance and Prototype Chaining

You can extend this concept further by utilizing another object-oriented concept, that of inheritance. You
can *inherit* behavior and properties from an existing object and then build upon that to define your own
custom object. The obvious benefit of this is that you don't need to define all the object characteristics
you require. You can first inherit some characteristics from another object, and then provide additional
characteristics or selectively override the existing characteristics as required. The technique used to do
this is called *prototype chaining*.

To demonstrate this, you can inherit from the `Agent` object in the previous examples, as shown in the
following code block:

```
function SuperAgent()
{
}
SuperAgent.prototype = new Agent();
SuperAgent.prototype.secretAbility = "See through walls";

var superDude1 = new SuperAgent();
var superDude2 = new SuperAgent();
superDude2.secretAbility = "Super speed";

superDude1.checkIfActive();
superDude2.checkIfActive();
alert("SuperAgent1 is Active: " + superDude1.isActive.toString() + ", Secret
Ability: " + superDude1.secretAbility);
alert("SuperAgent2 is Active: " + superDude2.isActive.toString() + ", Secret
Ability: " + superDude2.secretAbility);
```

Here you have inherited characteristics from the `Agent` object that you defined earlier by chaining its
prototype to the `SuperAgent` object, using the line:

```
SuperAgent.prototype = new Agent();
```

This gives the `SuperAgent` object all the characteristics of the `Agent` object. From this, you can further supplement this behavior by continuing to define properties and methods using the standard prototype syntax. To override any of the behavior of the `Agent` object, simply define properties and/or methods of the same name as the inherited objects.

Summary of Material So Far

Up to this point, this chapter has covered some of the basics, core concepts, and advanced object concepts of JavaScript. You have learned the basic syntax of JavaScript, how to define arrays, functions, event handlers, basic flow control, operators, and basic input/output operations, and performed a whirlwind tour of object-oriented concepts like constructors and the more advanced concepts like object inheritance via prototype chaining.

One of JavaScript's main goals is to allow dynamic manipulation of HTML documents, that is, to act as the scripting engine for DHTML (Dynamic HTML) web applications. Now that you have the core concepts of JavaScript and its operation covered, you can delve into the world of the Document Object Model and how to manipulate it.

The Document Object Model

The Document Object Model, or DOM, is an object that provides access to all the elements within the HTML document or page, such as links, forms fields, anchors, and so on. There are, however, several object models that relate to the DOM as it stands today that warrant some discussion. Earlier in this chapter, we briefly discussed the evolution of the DOM by various browser vendors and touched upon the various incompatibilities that have occurred as the object models have evolved over time. This is both a good and a bad thing. On one hand, it means that the object models are constantly being reviewed and improved upon, with the ultimate goal to reach a level of standardization, or commonality, among all the major browser vendors. This is one of the major tenets of the W3C, which was also mentioned at the beginning of this chapter. On the other hand, it means that, over time, vendors have implemented browser features in different ways, which makes it hard for developers to implement functionality without ensuring that it works in browsers from various vendors, as well as different versions of browsers from the same vendor.

There are essentially three object models that form the primary pieces of the JavaScript object model set:

❑   The core JavaScript object library and language

❑   The Browser Object Model

❑   The Document Object Model

So far in the chapter, we have covered the first piece of the JavaScript object model set, and this is fairly consistent across browser vendors and the various browser versions.

The second piece represents the object model exhibited by the browser itself. This traditionally comprises a `window` object as the root object, which holds references to other objects contained within it such as the `document` object that contains the page elements. The `document` object is the reference to the standard DOM — the third of the primary pieces of the JavaScript object model set — and is the reference by which you can manipulate page elements dynamically using JavaScript. Figure 3-3 shows this relationship.

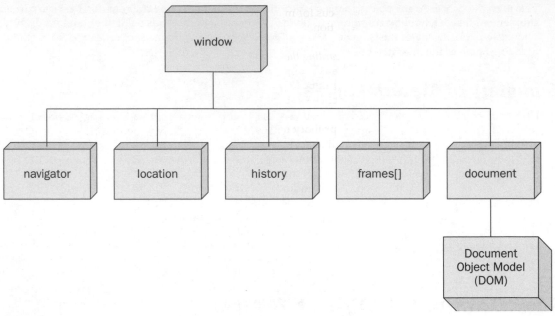

Figure 3-3

The distinction between the Browser Object Model and Document Object Model has always been a little blurred, especially in previous browser versions; however, this distinction is becoming more pronounced as the standards around them have matured and been more widely adopted.

The Browser Object Model really refers to the capabilities and characteristics of the browser itself. By interacting primarily with the window object, you can manipulate and control various aspects of the browser. Because the window object is the root object of the Browser Object Model, its use is often inferred. By this, we mean the following use of the alert function:

```
alert("We have inferred the use of the window object");
```

is equivalent to using the alert function in this manner:

```
window.alert("Directly referencing the window object");
```

with the latter version explicitly listing the window object. In contrast, the former version made use of the alert statement, which inferred the use of the window object. In other words, in that former case, the use of the window object was assumed. In the same way, you can write the following:

```
document.write("Some text");

window.document.write("Some text");
```

and both statements mean exactly the same thing. Inferring the use of the window object is a very common practice and will be used throughout the remainder of this book.

The document object is the primary focus for most web application developers and is used for almost all dynamic content within a web application.

> *For more information and details regarding the Browser Object Model, visit the URL* http://msdn
> .microsoft.com/library/default.asp?url=/library/en-us/dnproasp/html/
> thebrowserobjectmodel.asp *or* http://academ.hvcc.edu/~kantopet/old/
> javascript/index.php?page=the+js+bom&printme=true.

Since the document object will be the primary medium through which web application developers will operate, more time will be devoted to that subject than any other within this chapter. As with most elements of browser- and web-based application development, some history is involved. To fully describe the current DOM and to understand the fact that, as a web application developer, it is important to know what limitations your target customers or audience has, requires a knowledge of the various levels of DOM compliance, features, and acceptance.

As with any web application development, the fact that you are using the latest and greatest XHTML-compliant tool, does not mean that your users will be accessing this content using the latest and greatest set of browsers. Depending upon the nature of the business or the application, you may be required to cater for older browsers such as Internet Explorer 4 or Netscape 4. This is not particularly desirable due to the extra amount of work required to cater to these scenarios, but it is important to understand the limitations involved with these browsers, that is, the level of DOM that they provide access to.

Object Model Standardization (or Lack Thereof)

Early versions of the major browsers such as Netscape 2/3 and Internet Explorer 3 implemented object models that were similar in purpose, yet in some instances, quite different in implementation. They provided some rudimentary access to a document's elements but did not expose all of a document's elements and still lacked the mechanics to provide a truly dynamic experience.

Netscape 4 and Internet Explorer 4 laid the foundation upon which truly Dynamic HTML web pages (DHTML) could be created by exposing a far greater range of properties and elements to JavaScript, but they did so in a way that is different for each of those vendors.

Internet Explorer 5/5.5/6, Netscape 6+, and later Mozilla/Firefox have continued to build upon their object models, but with further guidance and standardization by the W3C, have slowly been coming together in terms of supporting a common API that can be utilized by JavaScript developers.

The DOM Levels

These three phases, or eras, of web development roughly correlate to the formation of, or compliance to, the "DOM Levels" that have been defined by the W3C. These have been introduced, or formalized, in order to help straighten out the various flavors of object models exhibited by earlier browsers, to unify the differences, and to bring a degree of commonality to browsers from different vendors and among browser versions from the same vendor. Even today, degrees of incompatibility exist between the latest versions of browsers from the major vendors, but these are much less prevalent than in previous versions, and the effort you need to expend to overcome these incompatibilities is significantly less compared to earlier efforts.

> *More detailed information on the Document Object Model and the standards that compose them is available at the W3C web site* www.w3.org/DOM.

There are four levels of the DOM, or more specifically, the standard Document Object Model. The first three levels (DOM Levels 0, 1, and 2) are what can be seen implemented in some browsers today at differing levels of completeness. The fourth level, DOM Level 3, is a relatively new level and has only recently been recommended by the W3C. As a result, no browsers currently implement anything more than a few features from this level, if any at all. Full support from the major browsers of this level will take some time. The four levels of the DOM are:

❑ **DOM Level 0** — This level is not a W3C specification, is often referred to as the classic or traditional JavaScript object model ,and is close to what Netscape 2/3 and Internet Explorer 3 offered. This level is more of a definition of the functionality provided, encompasses the limited exposure to the HTML document, and supports common object collections such as `forms[]`, `images[]`, and `anchors[]`.

❑ **DOM Level 1** — This level defines the ability to manipulate all elements in a document through a well-known or common set of methods and properties. This level is all about exposing all elements of a document and allowing them to be read, and written to, at all times. This level is composed of *DOM Core* and *DOM HTML* elements.

   ❑ The *DOM Core* refers to a set of interfaces that can represent any structured document, as well as an XML document and basic XML document support.

   ❑ *DOM HTML* refers to the higher-level interfaces that provide a more convenient way of viewing the document. DOM HTML refers to the lower-level interfaces of the DOM Core.

Support for this level within the current major browsers is very good. This level was approved as a recommendation by the W3C on October 1, 1998.

Although Internet Explorer 4 and above provide a `document.all` *property collection that exposes all elements of a document, this property is not part of the DOM Level 1 standard. The* `document.all` *property collection is specific to Internet Explorer 4 and above.*

❑ **DOM Level 2** — This level combines both DOM Levels 0 and 1, provides methods to access and manipulate style sheet elements, and provides further access to page elements relating to XML. There are other features that contribute to the DOM Level 2 standard that are lesser known; however, many of these features are not supported in common/major browsers. Even browsers that claim high standards compliance have yet to realize full DOM Level 2 support. Most major browsers tend to focus on the style sheet manipulation features advocated by DOM Level 2, but fail to implement the full set of DOM Level 2 features. This level is quite comprehensive and features six different recommendations — *DOM2 Core, DOM2 HTML, DOM2 Style/CSS, DOM2 Events, DOM2 Traversal and Range,* and *DOM2 Views.*

   ❑ The *DOM2 Core* and *DOM2 HTML* are extensions to the DOM Core and DOM HTML defined in the DOM Level 1.

   ❑ *DOM2 Style/CSS* provides interfaces for dealing with all aspects of style and cascading style sheets.

   ❑ *DOM2 Events* exposes a generic event system and introduces concepts such as event flow, bubbling, and cancellation.

   ❑ *DOM2 Traversal and Range* provides interfaces to allow scripts to dynamically traverse and identify a range of content in a document.

   ❑ *DOM2 Views* allows scripts to dynamically access and update the content of a representation of a document.

❏ This level was officially approved as a W3C recommendation on November 13, 2000, with the exception of DOM2 HTML, which was officially approved as a recommendation on January 9, 2003.

❏ **DOM Level 3** — This level represents the final evolution of the DOM standardization process. This level extends XML support to version 1.1 and other components of the XML Information Set specification, bringing DOM in line with XML Schema 1.0 and SOAP 1.2 W3C Recommendations. The new recommendation also makes full use of XML namespaces, which enables easier manip-ulation of Web Services Description Language (WSDL) descriptions. There are five different specifications within this level — *DOM3 Core, DOM3 Load and Save, DOM3 Validation, DOM3 Events,* and *DOM3 Xpath.*

    ❏ *DOM3 Core* is a further extension to DOM1 and 2 Core.

    ❏ *DOM3 Load and Save* refers to the ability to dynamically load the content of an XML doc-ument into a DOM document and serialize a DOM document into an XML document.

    ❏ *DOM3 Validation* provides method for dynamically updating a document and ensuring that the document and associated updates are valid.

    ❏ *DOM3 Events* is an extension of DOM2 events and mainly focuses on keyboard events.

    ❏ *DOM3 Xpath* provides interfaces to access a DOM tree using X Path 1.0 syntax.

❏ This level has only recently been officially recommended by the W3C, with DOM Core and DOM Load and Save being officially recommended on the April 7, 2004. DOM Validation, how-ever, was officially recommended on the January 27, 2004. Other parts of this level have yet to be officially recommended.

So, what does all this mean to you as a web application developer? These levels represent significant effort on the part of the W3C to define standards and specifications for all browsers to adopt. Those familiar with web development in the past know that trying to accommodate a majority of browsers required significant effort. These levels recommended by the W3C are a significant step forward in reducing the amount of effort required to create a truly cross-browser-compatible application.

Try It Out   Determining the Current Browser's DOM Level

The levels would not be of much use if there were not an easy way to determine what level the current browser supports and, therefore, what capabilities its DOM possesses. This can be achieved using the `document.implementation.hasFeatures()` method. This method accepts two strings — one for the feature to test for, such as `CORE`, and one for the version number, such as 1.0. For example, to determine if your browser supports DOM HTML Level 1 (or version 1.0), you can use the following JavaScript code:

```
document.implementation.hasFeature("HTML","1.0")
```

The `document.implementation.hasFeatures()` method returns a boolean value (true/false) that represents whether the specified feature is supported or not. In Internet Explorer v6.0, the following JavaScript code would write `true` to the browser window:

```
document.write(document.implementation.hasFeature("HTML","1.0"));
```

For something more comprehensive, the JavaScript code that follows displays a true or false value for the respective DOM feature and version.

```
var featuresLevel1 = ["HTML","XML"];
var featuresLevel2 =
["Core","HTML","XML","Stylesheets","CSS","CSS2","Views","Events","UIEvents","MouseE
vents","HTMLEvents","MutationEvents","Range","Traversal"];

document.write("<br />*** DOM Level 1 ***<br />");
showFeatureSupport(featuresLevel1,"1.0");

document.write("<br />*** DOM Level 2 ***<br />");
showFeatureSupport(featuresLevel2,"2.0");

// Generic function to loop through features and output feature support test result
function showFeatureSupport(featureArray,version)
{
    for (var featCnt=0; featCnt < featureArray.length; featCnt++)
    {
        var feature = featureArray[featCnt];

        var supportedFlag = document.implementation.hasFeature(feature,version);
        document.write("Feature '" + feature + "': " + supportedFlag);
        document.write("<br />");
    }
}
```

This example code simply uses the hasFeature method of the document.implementation object to determine if a particular feature is implemented. This method returns a true or false value, depending on whether the specified feature is available on the platform/browser the code is executing on. An array of features for each DOM level (1 and 2) is passed to the showFeatureSupport function to perform the test.

You will notice that you have an array of strings for the features that are relevant to DOM Level 1 and Level 2. These simple strings are named specifically for each feature, and it is important to specify the name of the feature exactly. Any incorrect spelling for the feature names will result in a false value being returned from the hasFeature method, when in fact the intended feature may be present.

The hasFeature method is an important method provided by the DOM to enable developers to test if specific features are implemented in the browser that their code is running on. Given the myriad combinations of browsers and DOM level support, it is necessary to be able to determine if a feature is present before using it.

Being able to perform this test means a more robust application for your users. If a specific feature that your site requires is not present, then you may be able to either inform the user in a graceful manner or possibly provide some workaround code to mitigate this issue. Without such a test, your site may generate errors when the specific feature is unavailable and may generally not be a good user experience.

It is interesting to note the different results that this code displays in different browsers. In arguably two of the most prevalent browsers today, Internet Explorer 6 and Firefox 1.5, this code produces the results shown if Figure 3-4.

Figure 3-4 clearly shows that even in the most current set of browsers DOM level support is inconsistent and varies across browsers. Even though standards do exist, the compliance of current browsers to these standards has a long way to go.

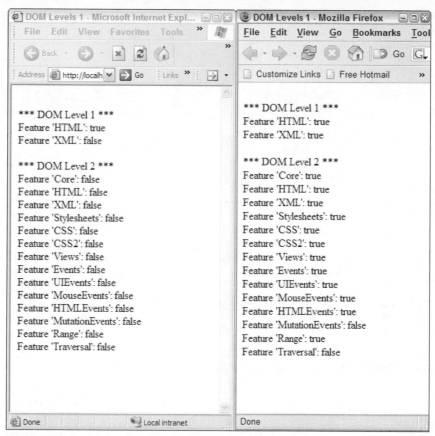

Figure 3-4

So, now you know that cross-browser support is difficult but is getting better. The DOMs in the past have been customized implementations by each browser vendor that sometimes looked similar but often had glaring differences that made web application development difficult. The move toward standardization with the various DOM levels is a slow, but eventual process. DOM Level 1 is relatively well adopted within the industry, so the remainder of this chapter will deal with components of DOM Level 1, namely DOM Core and DOM HTML.

Working with the DOM

Once you know the standard DOM, as defined by the W3C, is a workable model for today's web application, what are you really getting from that information? Essentially, when a (X)HTML page is loaded and rendered by a browser, a *document tree* is constructed in memory that represents the displayed document. The document tree provides an internal layout of the document that can be manipulated and updated. The document object displayed in Figure 3-3 earlier in the chapter is the reference to this internal document tree and itself implements a document interface defined by the W3C.

For a detailed description of the document interface provided by DOM Level 1 document *object, visit* www.w3.org/TR/REC-DOM-Level-1/level-one-core.html#i-Document.

Take a look at a simple example. The document that follows represents an extremely simplistic web page.

```
<!DOCTYPE html PUBLIC "-//W3C//DTD XHTML 1.0 Transitional//EN"
"http://www.w3.org/TR/xhtml1/DTD/xhtml1-transitional.dtd">
<html xmlns="http://www.w3.org/1999/xhtml" >
<head>
    <title>DOM Tree 1</title>
</head>
<body>
    <h1>This is the Header</h1>
    <p>This is a paragraph of text.</p>
    <ul>
        <li>List Item 1</li>
        <li>List Item 2</li>
    </ul>
</body>
</html>
```

When a browser loads and parses the preceding document, it builds a document tree and uses that for displaying the document. The document tree is equivalent to Figure 3-5.

Each box in Figure 3-5 represents a *node* in the document tree. The arrow-line above a node represents a parent-child relationship, with the node on the top being the parent and the node on the bottom being the child. Nodes that have the same parent are sibling nodes.

Try It Out   Modifying the Document Tree

The document tree as defined by DOM Level 1 is flexible and powerful enough that a document can be constructed from scratch using script code. Rarely is this necessary, however, with documents being defined with standard (X)HTML markup and the document trees being manipulated after being loaded and parsed by the browser. Any element within the document tree can be modified and manipulated using JavaScript at any time. For example, you might want to change the contents of the header, write more paragraph content dynamically, and also remove or delete the unordered list. Examine the JavaScript code that follows, which does just that:

```
// Get a nodelist with all the header elements
var headerNodeList = document.getElementsByTagName("h1");
// We know there is only 1, so get a reference to the 0th element
var hdr = headerNodeList[0];
// Use that reference to change the text/data
hdr.firstChild.data = "My Dynamically written Header Text";

// Get a nodelist with all the paragraph elements
var paragraphNodeList = document.getElementsByTagName("p");
// We know there is only 1, so get a reference to the 0th element
var paragraph = paragraphNodeList[0];
// Use that reference to change the text/data.
paragraph.firstChild.data = "This represents the new text of the first paragraph.";

// Get a nodelist with all the ul elements
var ulNodeList = document.getElementsByTagName("ul");
// We know there is only 1, so get a reference to the 0th element
```

```
var ul = ulNodeList[0];
// Using the parentNode (in this case the 'body' element), remove that child
element
paragraph.parentNode.removeChild(ul);

// create a new Text node for the second paragraph
var newTextNode = document.createTextNode("This text is the second set of paragraph
text");
// create a new Element to be the second paragraph
var newElementNode = document.createElement("p");
// put the text in the paragraph
newElementNode.appendChild(newTextNode);
// and put the paragraph on the end of the document by appending it to
// the BODY (which is the parent of para)
paragraph.parentNode.appendChild(newElementNode);
```

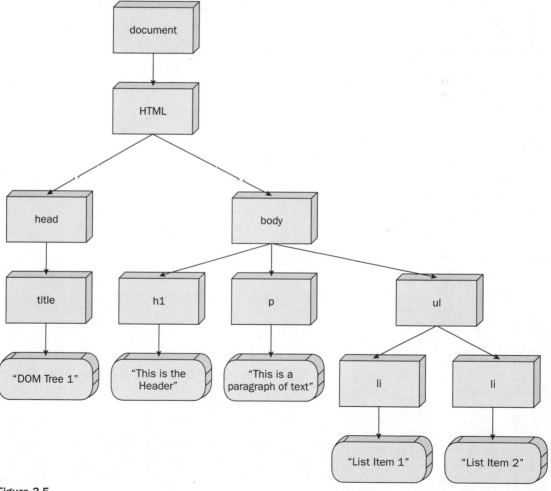

Figure 3-5

> For this particular example, it is important that the preceding script code be placed after the markup code in the document. If this code were placed in the `<head>` section for example, as most of the previous examples have done, the document tree would not have been constructed yet because the browser has not had a chance to parse those sections of markup and so the script code would fail.

As a matter of interest, you will note the use of an *index* to retrieve element number 0 in the node list, or the first element. The `getElementsByTagName()` method returns a node list, or an array of nodes, so you can use an array indexer to return a particular element in that array. Alternatively, you could use the `item` method to return a particular element number in that array list like this:

```
var hdr = headerNodeList.item(0);
```

The web page structure should look something like the document that follows (with the script code omitted for brevity):

```
<!DOCTYPE html PUBLIC "-//W3C//DTD XHTML 1.0 Transitional//EN"
"http://www.w3.org/TR/xhtml1/DTD/xhtml1-transitional.dtd">
<html xmlns="http://www.w3.org/1999/xhtml" >
<head>
    <title>DOM Tree 1</title>
</head>
<body>
    <h1>This is the Header</h1>
    <p>This is a paragraph of text.</p>
    <ul>
        <li>List Item 1</li>
        <li>List Item 2</li>
    </ul>

    <script type="text/javascript">

    alert("About to change the document.");

    // ... script code goes here ......

    </script>
</body>
</html>
```

Here you have dynamically manipulated the document tree, with the browser simply rendering the contents of that tree as they are changed.

In the previous example, you accessed elements using the `getElementsByTagName()` method, which returns a list of nodes (if any) of the specified element. Although this certainly works, you will more often use the `getElementById()` method that returns a reference to a specific element. You were first introduced to `getElementById()` in the last chapter, and while this method allows more immediate access to a particular element, it does require that elements be defined with a unique id attribute in the document itself. Consider the following:

```
<!DOCTYPE html PUBLIC "-//W3C//DTD XHTML 1.0 Transitional//EN"
"http://www.w3.org/TR/xhtml1/DTD/xhtml1-transitional.dtd">
<html xmlns="http://www.w3.org/1999/xhtml" >
<head>
    <title>DOM Tree 2</title>
</head>
<body>
    <h1 id="hdr1">This is the Header</h1>
    <p id="p1">This is a paragraph of text.</p>
    <ul id="ul1">
        <li>List Item 1</li>
        <li>List Item 2</li>
    </ul>

    <script type="text/javascript">

    alert("About to change the document.");

    // ... script code goes here ...

    </script>
</body>
</html>
```

This document is almost identical to the previous example except for the addition of id attributes to each of the elements you want to manipulate. The JavaScript code can then be simplified a little to make use of the getElementById() method, as shown in the following:

```
// Get a node reference to the header element
var hdr = document.getElementById("hdr1");
// Use that reference to change the text/data.
hdr.firstChild.data = "My Dynamically written Header Text";

// Get a node reference to the paragraph element
var paragraph = document.getElementById("p1");
// Use that reference to change the text/data.
paragraph.firstChild.data = "This represents the new text of the first paragraph.";

// Get a node reference to the ul element
var ul = document.getElementById("ul1");
// Using the parentNode (in this case the 'body' element), remove that child
element
paragraph.parentNode.removeChild(ul);

// create a new Text node for the second paragraph
var newTextNode = document.createTextNode("This text is the second set of paragraph
text");
// create a new Element to be the second paragraph
var newElementNode = document.createElement("p");
// put the text in the paragraph
newElementNode.appendChild(newTextNode);
// and put the paragraph on the end of the document by appending it to
// the BODY (which is the parent of para)
paragraph.parentNode.appendChild(newElementNode);
```

61

The method `getElementById()` allows immediate access to a node within the tree, whereas the `getElementsByTagName()` returns a list of nodes that you must examine further in order to ultimately retrieve the node object you require. Ultimately, you have a reference to a DOM node object within the document tree.

Manipulating Nodes

In the example in the preceding section, you saw a brief example of how to create an element, append a child node, and remove a node. The methods to manipulate nodes are simple yet extensive. You can construct the various types of elements, and either append or insert them into the document tree. You have seen how a reference to a node object can be retrieved, and with this information, you can also remove, replace, or copy the node. All of these methods are available as part of the `document` object that acts as the root object of the document tree. The sections that follow list the various node manipulation methods available.

Creating Nodes

The following table lists and describes node creation methods available.

Creation Methods	Description
`createAttribute( attributeName );`	Creates an attribute node with the given attribute name.
`createComment( commentString );`	Creates a comment node using the supplied string as the comment itself.
`createDocumentFragment();`	Creates a document fragment node that can be used to hold a collection of nodes for processing.
`createElement( tagName );`	Creates an element that is of the type specified by the `tagName` parameter.
`createTextNode( textString );`	Creates a text node with the supplied `textString` as the textual content.

Following are examples of using the node creation methods:

```
var attributeNode = document.createAttribute("width");
var commentNode = document.createComment("My Comment");
var docFragmentNode = document.createDocumentFragment();
var elementNode = document.createElement("H1");
var textNode = document.createTextNode("Some Simple Text");
```

In each case, a specific node object is returned by the method. Note that the statements in the preceding example do not affect the document in any way, but simply return a reference to a valid of object of the required type. For these to affect the document's content, the objects would typically have to be inserted into the document at some point. This is discussed in the following section.

Inserting and Appending Nodes

When using either the insert or append methods listed in the following table, usually you will obtain a reference to a parent node using the methods previously described in the chapter, with the method invoked from that node reference as you have already seen in previous examples. The inserted or appended node is now a child of that parent node that it was inserted into or appended to.

Insert/Append Methods	Description
`insertBefore( newChildNode, referenceNode );`	Inserts the node referenced by the `newChildNode` parameter before the node referenced by the `referenceNode` parameter in the document tree.
`appendChild( newChildNode );`	Appends the node referenced by `newChildNode` to the end of the list of child nodes for that parent node.

Removing, Replacing, and Copying Nodes

When you are removing a node, as seen in previous examples in the chapter, you need to obtain a reference to the node to be removed; and then using its parent, you call the `removeChild()` method. You use the `replaceChild()` method similarly; the parent node is used to invoke the method, passing a reference to the new node and a reference to the node to be replaced.

Copying a node is not quite as straightforward. You use the `cloneNode()` method of the node you want to copy/clone and also pass in a boolean value indicating whether a deep copy or a shallow copy should be performed. A value of true indicates the performing of a deep copy, which copies all children of the node in addition to the node being cloned/copied. A shallow copy simply copies the node itself.

Removal/Replacement/Copying Methods	Description
`removeChild( childNode );`	Removes the child node referenced by the `childNode` parameter from the list of children of the parent node invoking the method.
`replaceChild( newNode, nodeToReplace );`	Replaces the child node referenced by the `nodeToReplace` parameter with the node referenced by the `newNode` parameter.
`cloneNode( performDeepClone );`	Returns a reference to a copied or cloned version of the node on which this method was invoked. If the `performDeepClone` parameter is `true`, then a deep copy, meaning all the children are also included in the copy/cloning process, is performed.

Try It Out   Cloning a Node

Removing and replacing nodes is a relatively straightforward operation, and has been shown in previous examples; however, cloning is not quite as intuitive. Consider the web page and associated JavaScript code that follows:

```
<!DOCTYPE html PUBLIC "-//W3C//DTD XHTML 1.0 Transitional//EN"
"http://www.w3.org/TR/xhtml1/DTD/xhtml1-transitional.dtd">
<html xmlns="http://www.w3.org/1999/xhtml" >
<head>
    <title>Cloning a Node</title>
</head>
<body>
    <p id="p1">This is some text and here is an image <img src="Exclamation.bmp"
/></p>

    <div id="div1"></div>

    <script type="text/javascript">
    var node = document.getElementById("p1");
    var div = document.getElementById("div1");

    var nodeShallow = node.cloneNode(false);
    var nodeDeep = node.cloneNode(true);

    alert("About to append the shallow copied node");
    div.appendChild(nodeShallow);

    alert("About to append the Deep copied node");
    div.appendChild(nodeDeep);

    alert("Done");

    </script>
</body>
</html>
```

When this page is loaded and executed, initially it appears as though no node is added for the shallow cloned node, and then the deep cloned node is visibly added. In Figure 3-5, the document tree shows text content of the paragraph node as a child node of the paragraph node, and indeed JavaScript code examining the node properties confirms that. So, when you request a shallow copy/clone of the node, the textual content (and the image) is not cloned; therefore, nothing is displayed when this node is appended to the div element in the document.

Properties of a Node

The node object has a well-defined set of properties, which are listed in the following table:

DOM Node Object Properties	Description/Details
nodeName	Contains the name of the node.
nodeValue	Contains the value of the node but is generally applicable only to text nodes.
nodeType	This property contains a number corresponding to the type of node as listed in the table that follows this one.
parentNode	A reference to the parent node of the current node, if one exists.

DOM Node Object Properties	Description/Details
childNodes	A reference to a list of child nodes, if any exist.
firstChild	A reference to the first child node of the current object/node, if one exists.
lastChild	A reference to the last child node of the current object/node, if one exists.
previousSibling	A reference to the previous sibling node if one exists. This occurs if the parent node has multiple child nodes. This property will not have a valid reference if the node is the first child node.
nextSibling	A reference to the next sibling node if one exists. This occurs if the parent node has multiple child nodes. This property will not have a valid reference if the node is the last child node.
attributes	A list/array of attributes for the current node.
ownerDocument	A reference to the containing document, or the document object to which this node belongs.

The following table explains the numbers corresponding to the types of node, numbers used by the nodeType property.

Node Type Number	Type	Description	Comments
1	Element	Represents an XML or (X)HTML element	
2	Attribute	An XML or (X)HTML attribute	For example, class="light"
3	Text	Represents textual content contained within an element or attribute	
4	CDATA Section	Represents a block of text that may contain characters that would otherwise be treated as markup	XML-specific. Used to represent a literal section of text — that is, to tell the parser to NOT interpret this as markup
5	Entity Reference	Represents an entity reference	XML specific
6	Entity	Represents an entity	XML specific
7	Processing Instruction	Represents a processing instruction	XML specific. For example. The first line in an XML document: <?xml version="1.0" ?>
8	Comment	Represents a comment	For example: <!-- A comment -->

Table continued on following page

Node Type Number	Type	Description	Comments
9	Document	Represents a reference to the root object in the document tree, that is, a reference to the entire document	See previous detailed discussion in this chapter
10	Document Type	A Document Type Definition	For example, the DOCTYPE element in an HTML document: `<!DOCTYPE html PUBLIC "-//W3C//DTD XHTML 1.0 Transitional//EN" "http://www.w3.org/TR/xhtml1/DTD/xhtml1-transitional.dtd">`
11	Document Fragment	Represents a lightweight Document object, or a portion of a document	
12	Notation	Represents a notation declared in the DTD	DTD = Document Type Definition. An older form of defining an XML document structure

Try It Out   Using Node Properties

As an example of utilizing these properties, you can examine one of the paragraph (<p>) nodes from your previous example. You will add some further script code to the previous example, as shown in the following code block:

```
var node = paragraph;
var msg = "Node Name: " + node.nodeName;
msg += "\nNode Type: " + node.nodeType;
msg += "\nNode Value: " + node.nodeValue;
msg += "\nNode Child Name: " + node.firstChild.nodeName;
msg += "\nNode Child Type: " + node.firstChild.nodeType;
msg += "\nNode Child Value: " + node.firstChild.nodeValue;
alert(msg);
```

This will produce the dialog box shown in Figure 3-6.

Figure 3-6

You can see here that the paragraph node has a type of 1 and a name of *P*, and its child node, which represents the textual content of that paragraph node, has a type of 3 and a name of #text.

The attributes property of a node is convenient way of referencing or examining the attributes that accompany a particular element or node. As mentioned in the table listing properties earlier in this chapter, it is an array containing the attributes of the node. This array will contain a differing number of elements depending on which browser it is run within. To demonstrate this, examine the web page and associated script code that follows:

```
<!DOCTYPE html PUBLIC "-//W3C//DTD XHTML 1.0 Transitional//EN"
"http://www.w3.org/TR/xhtml1/DTD/xhtml1-transitional.dtd">
<html xmlns="http://www.w3.org/1999/xhtml" >
<head>
    <title>DOM Tree Attributes</title>
</head>
<body>
    <h1>Atrribute Listing</h1>
    <p id="p1" align="center" width="90%">This is some paragraph text</p>

    <script type="text/javascript">

    var p = document.getElementById("p1");
    var attrCnt = p.attributes.length;
    document.write("<br />Number of attributes: #" + attrCnt + "<br />");

    for (var cnt=0; cnt < attrCnt; cnt++)
    {
        var attr = p.attributes[cnt];
        var val;
        if (attr.value == "")
            val = "[EmptyString]";
        else
            val = attr.value;
        document.write("<br />Attribute: <i><b>" + attr.nodeName + "</b></i> has a
value of <b>" + val + "</b>");
    }
    </script>
</body>
</html>
```

This code has a very simple web page that contains a single header element (<h1>) and a paragraph (<p>) element. The JavaScript code obtains a reference to the paragraph element using the getElementById() method, displays the number attributes associated with that element, and then proceeds to list each attribute's name and its associated value.

When this page is rendered within Firefox, you get the expected result of three attributes and their associated values. The page output is shown in Figure 3-7.

However, when the web page and code is executed within Internet Explorer 6, you get a total of 83 attributes. This basically represents all the possible attributes that this element can have within Internet Explorer 6, whether defined or not. The screenshot in Figure 3-8 shows this output:

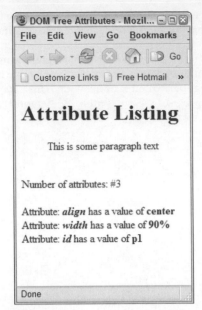

Figure 3-7

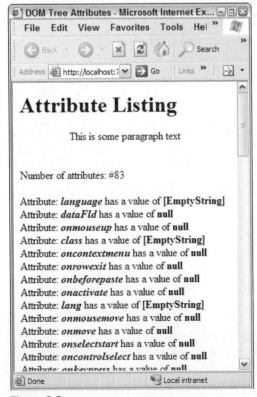

Figure 3-8

It is apparent that although the same script code executes without issue and the same basic properties are supported, still some degree of differences exists in the way that each DOM tree is represented within each different browser. As mentioned before in this chapter, when you are coding for cross-browser support, you need to be aware of all these discrepancies and consider how to work with them to achieve your desired outcome.

DOM Level 0 General Collections

To allow backward compatibility with older browsers, the DOM supports some object collections that are part of the DOM Level 0 specification. These collections allow indexed access to the various page elements suggested by the property names. The table that follows lists these collections.

Collection/Array Object	Description
document.anchors[]	An array or collection of all the anchor elements within the page represented by the anchor tag — that is, all the `<a name=". . .">` `</a>` tags
document.applets[]	An array or collection of all the java applets within the page
document.forms[]	An array or collection of all the form elements within the page
document.images[]	An array or collection of all the image elements in the page represented by the image tag — that is, all the `<img src=". . ." />` tags
document.links[]	An array or collection of all the link elements in the page represented by the link anchor tag — that is, `<a href=" . . .">` `</a>`

Using these collections is very simple and involves simply accessing each collection by an indexed value. If you have the simple example of a web page like the following:

```
<!DOCTYPE html PUBLIC "-//W3C//DTD XHTML 1.0 Transitional//EN"
"http://www.w3.org/TR/xhtml1/DTD/xhtml1-transitional.dtd">
<html xmlns="http://www.w3.org/1999/xhtml" >
<head>
    <title>DOM Level 0 Collections</title>
</head>
<body>
    <form id="form1" method="post" action="DOMLevel0Collections.htm">
        <a href="DOMLevel0Collections.htm">Links to this same page</a>
    </form>
</body>
</html>
```

you can access HTML elements using these level collections as shown in the following JavaScript code:

```
alert( document.links[0].nodeName );
alert( document.forms[0].nodeName );
```

The DOM, Styles, and CSS

So far you have seen how to manipulate the entities or nodes within a document tree. DOM Level 2 contains support for CSS (Cascading Style Sheets) and styles and enables you to manipulate these elements. Internet Explorer 6 does not contain complete support for DOM Level 2, but its DHTML model does contain support for setting styles per the DOM standard. One way to set an element's style is to manipulate the CSS styles for that element, that is, its inline style element. Suppose that you had the following paragraph element:

```
<p id="p1">Some Text</p>
```

When an inline style is used to modify the visual appearance of this element, the inline style attribute is added, as shown here:

```
<p id="p1" style="width:100%;text-align:left">Some Text</p>
```

To reference this inline style property, you use the style property of a node element within JavaScript.

The style Property and Naming Conventions

You will notice in the preceding example that the `text-align` style attribute is hyphenated (contains a - character). If you were to try and represent this literally in JavaScript, you would have a problem because the hyphen represents a minus operator. For this reason, style properties generally follow some naming guidelines. Any style property that is hyphenated has the hyphen removed and then capitalizes the following word — that is, it follows camel case naming convention. The *camel case naming convention* places the first letter of the first word in lowercase, with subsequent words starting with a capital, for example, *camelCase*. So, in the previous example, the style property `text-align` would be represented in JavaScript as `textAlign`. The example that follows demonstrates this:

```
<!DOCTYPE html PUBLIC "-//W3C//DTD XHTML 1.0 Transitional//EN"
"http://www.w3.org/TR/xhtml1/DTD/xhtml1-transitional.dtd">
<html xmlns="http://www.w3.org/1999/xhtml" >
<head>
    <title>DOM Styles - Example 1</title>
</head>
<body>
    <p id="p1" style="width:100%;text-align:left">Some Text</p>
    <hr />
    <script type="text/javascript">
    var para = document.getElementById("p1");
    if (para != null)
    {
        alert ("Changing the text alignment to 'center'");
        para.style.textAlign = "center";

        alert ("Changing the text alignment to 'right'");
        para.style.textAlign = "right";

        alert ("Changing the text alignment back to 'left'");
        para.style.textAlign = "left";
```

```
        }
        </script>

    </body>
    </html>
```

The only notable exception to the general *"remove hyphen, use camel casing"* rule is the `float` CSS style property. `float` cannot be literally represented in JavaScript because it is a reserved word. In this case, it becomes `cssFloat`. All other properties follow the general camel casing rule mentioned, which includes properties that normally have a capital. For example, `Top` becomes `top` and `Width` becomes `width` when accessing the style rules in JavaScript. Firefox, Internet Explorer 6, and other current major browsers support CSS1 for the most part (with some minor differences). CSS2 and CSS3 are less supported, particularly in Internet Explorer 6; however, this will change in time, and it is worth keeping abreast of the compliance levels of the various browsers. Mozilla/Firefox currently have the best support for these standards.

> *A full discussion of the various CSS levels, all the associated properties, and specific browser support is beyond the scope of this book. For detailed information on this, visit the W3C web site that hosts these standards at* www.w3.org/Style/CSS.

Modifying Style Sheets

Style sheets play an important part when defining CSS rules to be applied within your document. The DOM Level 2 supports a `styleSheets[]` collection that holds references to all the `<style>` elements within a document. As indicated by the `[]` of the `styleSheets[]` property, this is an array, with each element being a `CSSStyleSheet` object. This object contains methods and properties that allow a certain degree of manipulation; however, Internet Explorer does not conform to the standards in this case and uses a slightly nonstandard set of methods. The table that follows shows both the DOM standard methods and the Internet Explorer equivalents.

Method/Property	Description	Internet Explorer Equivalent
`insertRule( ruleText, ruleIndex );`	Inserts the CSS rule defined in the parameter `ruleText` at the specified index in the array	`addRule( ruleText, ruleIndex );`
`deleteRule ( ruleIndex );`	Deletes the specified rule contained at the specific `ruleIndex`	`removeRule( ruleIndex );`
`cssRules[]`	A property array that contains individual rules within the style block	`rules[]`

Care must be taken when using these properties in multiple browsers because of Internet Explorer's lack of standards support. When modifying a style, you must first check to see whether you have access to a specific property set.

Try It Out   Modifying a Style Sheet to Work in Both Firefox and IE

Consider the example that follows:

```
<!DOCTYPE html PUBLIC "-//W3C//DTD XHTML 1.0 Transitional//EN"
"http://www.w3.org/TR/xhtml1/DTD/xhtml1-transitional.dtd">
<html xmlns="http://www.w3.org/1999/xhtml" >
<head>
    <title>DOM Styles - Example 2</title>
    <style type="text/css">
        p { text-align: center; }
        body { color: blue; }
    </style>
</head>
<body>
    <p id="p1" >Some paragraph Text</p>
    <div>This is some body text</div>
    <hr />
    <script type="text/javascript">
document.write("Number of styleSheets: #" + document.styleSheets.length);

    var stylesheet = document.styleSheets[0];
    // Check to see if we are operating in Internet Explorer
    if (stylesheet.rules)
    {
        document.write("<br />Internet Explorer detected.<br />");

        // Map the standard DOM attributes and methods to the internet explorer
        // equivalents
        stylesheet.cssRules = stylesheet.rules;
        stylesheet.insertRule = function(ruleText, ruleIndex) {
this.addRule(ruleText, ruleIndex); };
        stylesheet.deleteRule = function(ruleIndex) { this.removeRule(ruleIndex);
};
    }

    // The 'p' style rule
    document.write("<br /><br /> 1st Style rule (text-Align) value: " +
stylesheet.cssRules[0].style.textAlign);
    // The 'body' style rule
    document.write("<br /> 2nd Style rule (color) value: " +
stylesheet.cssRules[1].style.color);

    alert("Deleting the 'body' color style rule.");
    stylesheet.deleteRule(1);
    </script>

</body>
</html>
```

The code in the example first checks to see if a `rules[]` collection exists, and if so, adds it to the stylesheets collection as a `cssRules` property. In addition, you also add the DOM standard `insertRule` and `deleteRule` methods and map them to the Internet Explorer equivalent methods. You are effectively adding the DOM properties and methods to Internet Explorer to mimic the required DOM Level 2 support. You can then develop against the standard DOM interface and ensure that your web page works in browsers that offer DOM Level 2 support, such as Firefox, as well as in Internet Explorer.

This type of code lends itself to reuse across all your web applications. For this reason, it is recommended that you put this reusable code in a script file that can be included and reused in all your web applications. To demonstrate this, the following code shows a revised version of the preceding example code:

```
<!DOCTYPE html PUBLIC "-//W3C//DTD XHTML 1.0 Transitional//EN"
"http://www.w3.org/TR/xhtml1/DTD/xhtml1-transitional.dtd">
<html xmlns="http://www.w3.org/1999/xhtml" >
<head>
    <title>DOM Styles - Example 3</title>
    <style type="text/css">
        p { text-align: center; }
        body { color: blue; }
    </style>

    <script type="text/javascript" src="DOMStyles3_Include.js"></script>
</head>
<body>
    <p id="p1" >Some paragraph text</p>
    <div>This is some body text</div>
    <hr />
    <script type="text/javascript">
    document.write("Number of styleSheets: #" + document.styleSheets.length);

    // The 'p' style rule
    document.write("<br /><br /> 1st Style rule (text-Align) value: " +
stylesheet.cssRules[0].style.textAlign);
    // The 'body' style rule
    document.write("<br /> 2nd Style rule (color) value: " +
stylesheet.cssRules[1].style.color);

    alert("Deleting the 'body' color style rule.");
    stylesheet.deleteRule(1);
    </script>

</body>
</html>
```

You will notice that the code now contains no logic to determine the browser type and the mapping of functions to DOM-compliant functions if required. The only addition is the line:

```
<script type="text/javascript" src="DOMStyles3_Include.js"></script>
```

which includes a script file to perform the browser-specific checks and mapping. This allows you to concentrate on the code relating to the functionality of your application and not worry about the code required to support multiple browsers. The include file can then be reused across your web applications as shown in the following example:

```
/****************************************************
** Include script that maps Internet Explorer methods
** to the DOM equivalents
****************************************************/

var stylesheet = document.styleSheets[0];
// Check to see if we are operating in Internet Explorer
if (stylesheet.rules)
{
    // Internet Explorer detected

    // Map the standard DOM attributes and methods to the internet explorer
    // equivalents
    stylesheet.cssRules = stylesheet.rules;
    stylesheet.insertRule = function(ruleText, ruleIndex) { this.addRule(ruleText,
ruleIndex); };
    stylesheet.deleteRule = function(ruleIndex) { this.removeRule(ruleIndex); };
}
```

This script include file can be built upon over time to act as a constantly evolving repository of utility code that saves you time and effort in all future web development applications.

Summary

This chapter has covered a lot of ground in a very short time, but it has exposed only the surface as far as possibilities go when developing web pages or applications. This is particularly true when dealing with the DOM interfaces and the varied support in different browsers. This itself can warrant an entire book. In this chapter you have:

❑   Covered the early and current development of JavaScript

❑   Examined the basics of the JavaScript language and associated concepts

❑   Learned advanced JavaScript features and how to use them within your web applications

❑   Examined the HTML Document Object Model and its significance to you — the web developer

❑   Examined how to dynamically change rendered HTML documents using the Document Object Model and JavaScript

The initial development of JavaScript provides insights into why JavaScript is the way it is today and serves to eliminate some confusion around its Java heritage. The basics of the JavaScript language were covered, and although the basics remain fairly consistent across browsers, different JavaScript version support can introduce further complexity and implementation differences. It cannot be stressed enough that when dealing with web pages or applications that can span browsers of different versions, and especially from different vendors, it pays to perform some investigation on the minimum levels of standard support that you need to comply with.

As you have seen, although JavaScript is a scripting language, it is extremely powerful, it has object-oriented methods, and it has very dynamic features. These features are often not found in more static languages such as C++, Java, and C#. JavaScript is the language of choice for dynamic web applications, and the current breed of highly interactive web sites rely heavily on JavaScript for their magic.

JavaScript and the Document Object Model go hand in hand when dealing with dynamic web applications. JavaScript provides the engine, while the DOM provides the vehicle. Many web application developers exist without knowing why something works in one particular browser and often resort to such rudimentary techniques as displaying disclaimers on their site that state that the web site will only work in browser version X. Not only does this limit the audience of the site, but it also displays the developer's inability to deal with cross-browser support and can leave a user feeling disgruntled because of this lack of support. Worse still, errors and unexpected behavior can leave a user feeling very frustrated, and it is unlikely that the user will visit your site again. Obviously, this is not desirable, and you need to determine what is the best way to achieve cross-browser support to address these issues. The DOM and its various standards can give us these answers. Knowledge of the DOM and the various capabilities of each level are important, but they can be complex. This chapter barely scratches the surface. Further investigation is recommended if you wish to truly utilize the advantages that the DOM has to offer.

Finally, both JavaScript and the DOM come with a lot of history. The development and progress of both has been fueled by the issues, problems and frustration faced over the years by many web developers trying to achieve what is substantially easier to do today. Both JavaScript and the DOM are the core of dynamic web applications and will act as core components for all future dynamic web content.

The XMLHttpRequest Object

The XMLHttpRequest object forms the main basis for most Ajax-style applications. It acts as the main component to facilitate asynchronous requests to the server and to perform server-side processing without a traditional postback. This is to avoid the traditional *postback delay* for the user and enhance the user experience dramatically.

There are other less traditional methods to achieve this behavior, but use of the XMLHttpRequest object is becoming the standard way in which this Ajax style functionality is achieved.

In this chapter, you take a look at:

❑   The XMLHttpRequest object — what it actually is and its history

❑   Synchronous and asynchronous requests

❑   Dealing with response data from the server

❑   Using web services

The use of these techniques causes a common usage pattern to emerge. So, it stands to reason that developers would want to factor out these common techniques and organize code into a library that they can reuse across many other projects. This would obviously save the time of recoding, redeveloping, and retesting similar functionality in the future, and this is exactly what is done throughout this chapter. At the end of this chapter, you will have the rudimentary basis of a reusable code library that you can carry across to all future projects.

Code Examples for This Chapter

All the code samples for this chapter are available for downloading at http://beginningajax.com. Just visit the site and download the samples for Chapter 4. They are provided as a Visual Studio .NET 2005 web site project. Simply load and execute each page as required.

Due to the project being a file-based web project, Visual Studio .NET will assign a random port number when you launch a web page in a browser. The port number will be apparent in the address bar of the browser. For example, if the address bar contains the following URL:

```
http://localhost:7615/XmlHttp_Chap4/Examples/SimpleAsyncResponseText.aspx
```

the web server is using a temporary port number of 7615. This port number needs to be used when any of the example code is accessing the site. It is for this reason that all the code samples that access a URL will utilize a dynamic way of determining the port number. The JavaScript location object contains a host property that will be used to specify the exact location to access. For example, the URL shown in the following example:

```
xmlHttpObj.open("GET","http://localhost/XmlHttp_Chap4/DataFile.xml", true);
```

would be changed to:

```
xmlHttpObj.open("GET","http://" + location.host + "/XmlHttp_Chap4/DataFile.xml",
true);
```

If the port number was 7615, then the location.host property would contain localhost:7615. The URL in the preceding example would be the correct host and location. All code samples in this chapter will utilize this method of accessing the resources required to correctly function.

What Is the XMLHttpRequest Object?

The XMLHttpRequest object is the heart of all asynchronous operations related to Ajax. It is the object responsible for providing the asynchronous behavior through which Ajax-style applications can interact.

XMLHTTP is a protocol that is designed to package data as XML and send it via the network to a specific destination, or endpoint. This information is typically processed in some way, and the result is returned to the caller. The XMLHttpRequest object is an object that is implemented by most modern browsers to facilitate this communication protocol.

A Little History

The techniques used by the XMLHttpRequest object have been in use since approximately 1998 and are not new. Microsoft was probably the first major player to make use of this technology in its Outlook Web Access product, which used an early form of the XMLHttpRequest object to implement the very functional interface of the web client application. It was available in a limited form within Internet Explorer 4.0 but really became usable as an ActiveX object within Internet Explorer 5.0.

Recently, companies such as Google have helped to popularize this technology with very effective implementations of asynchronous behavior in products such as Google Maps (http://maps.google.com) and GMail (www.gmail.com). Microsoft has also provided an excellent example with MSN Virtual Earth (http://virtualearth.msn.com).

Other browser vendors have noted the benefits of this approach and have provided their own implementation of this object to provide the same asynchronous capability. The current list of browsers that support this object are Internet Explorer 5.0 and above, Safari 1.2 and above, Mozilla 1.0/Netscape 7 and above, Opera 8.0 and above, and Firefox. Unfortunately, the support across different browsers is not seamless, but neither is it a major obstacle. To use this object in the Safari, Mozilla, and some other non-Microsoft browsers, you can create an object using JavaScript with the following syntax:

```
var xmlHttpObj = new XMLHttpRequest();
```

Creating the same object in Microsoft Internet Explorer requires creating an ActiveX object, as shown here:

```
var xmlHttpObj = new ActiveXObject("Microsoft.XMLHTTP");
```

or

```
var xmlHttpObj = new ActiveXObject("Msxml2.XMLHTTP");
```

depending on which version of the Microsoft XML parser is installed.

The terms JavaScript *and more recently* ECMAScript *in this context both refer to the same thing, which is the Java-like scripting language available in modern browsers. The remainder of this chapter will refer to this scripting language as JavaScript.*

The usage of the XmlHttpRequest object is the same across the different browsers; it is only the construction of the object that differs. For this reason, it is necessary to either check for the browser type to determine how to construct the object.

Try It Out   Checking Browser Type to Determine How to Construct the XMLHttpRequest Object

A simple way of doing this is shown in the following JavaScript code:

```
if (window.XMLHttpRequest)
   xmlHttpObj = new XMLHttpRequest();
else
{
   try
   {
      xmlHttpObj = new ActiveXObject("Microsoft.XMLHTTP");
   } catch (e)
   {
      xmlHttpObj = new ActiveXObject("Msxml2.XMLHTTP");
   }
```

This checks to see if the browser supports standard object construction; if it doesn't, the code defaults to creating an ActiveX object. An alternative approach is:

```
if (window.ActiveXObject)
{
   try
   {
      xmlHttpObj = new ActiveXObject("Microsoft.XMLHTTP");
   } catch (e)
   {
      xmlHttpObj = new ActiveXObject("Msxml2.XMLHTTP");
```

```
        }
    }
    else
        xmlHttpObj = new XMLHttpRequest();
```

This version does the reverse check in that the code checks to see if ActiveX Objects are supported. If so, then the ActiveX object is created; otherwise, the code will default to standard object creation.

It is highly likely that the creation of the XmlHttpRequest object will be required many times in current and future web applications. Therefore, it is a good idea to separate out this code into a reusable script library that can be included in any future pages that are developed. This has the advantage of reusing working and tested code, as well as reducing the amount of work you would normally have to do by recoding this logic in each and every application. Further, because script files are cached locally by most browsers, placing common script logic in separate script files reduces the amount of data that must be sent between the web server and the browser across subsequent requests.

The preceding example, which created the XmlHttpRequest object in a cross-browser fashion will be encapsulated in a function called CreateXmlHttpRequestObject() and included in a script file named CommonAJAXLibrary.js.

The following code fragment shows how to include the file for use within your applications, and you will see this library referenced in upcoming samples:

```
<head runat="server">
    <title>AsyncHandlerSimpleExample</title>

    <script type="text/javascript" src="CommonAJAXLibrary.js"></script>

    <script type="text/javascript">

    // A "global" variable that is our XMLHttpRequest object reference.
    var xmlHttpObj = CreateXmlHttpRequestObject();
```

As can be seen from the previous code sample, a <script> tag is included within the <head> section of the page with the src attribute specifying the script file to include, in this case, the CommonAJAXLibrary .js that you have created. From that point, it is possible to call the function within that file as if it were a part of the existing page.

Traditional web-based browser applications capture user interactions and send the results of that to the server via a synchronous HTTP request. The user is typically forced to wait while the request is initiated by the browser and the response is received by the browser from the server. This is the nature of a synchronous request and is what the Internet-using world is very familiar with.

In concept, the XMLHttpRequest object operates no differently from a typical web browser. Data is captured or packaged in some way; that data is sent via the network to a server, or endpoint; the result is sent back to the client or caller that initiated the request. A standard browser form posts the data to the server; the XMLHttpRequest object sends the data using the XMLHTTP protocol. Both methods can be scripted, that is, both methods can be initiated and manipulated using a scripting language such as JavaScript. The main difference between a standard HTTP post and an XMLHTTP request is that the XMLHTTP request can operate in an asynchronous manner. This means that an XMLHTTP request can be initiated in parallel with the current browser operation, in effect, acting like a background request while the user is still manipulating the information within the browser. This represents the heart of Ajax and is the core advantage that it represents within traditional browser applications. A user can continue to work within the browser application uninterrupted, while in the background a request is sent and a response that contains the result of some server-side processing is received.

Synchronous Requests

Take a look at a following simple code example of a synchronous operation and then take a look at the explanation of exactly what is occurring that follows. Note: The code for the inclusion of the script include file mentioned previously has been omitted for brevity.

Try It Out   A Synchronous Operation

```
function MakeXMLHTTPCall()
{
   var xmlHttpObj;
   xmlHttpObj = CreateXmlHttpRequestObject();

   if (xmlHttpObj)
   {
      xmlHttpObj.open("GET","http://" + location.host +
"/XmlHttpExample1/DataFile.xml", false);
      xmlHttpObj.send(null);
      alert("Request/Response Complete.");
   }
}
```

How It Works

The preceding code sample is very simple, however it does show the basic usage of the XMLHTTP object. If you examine the code in detail, you'll see the following:

1. First you create a new XMLHTTP object and assign it to a variable.

2. After checking if the object is not null, that is, that the object creation in Step 1 was successful, you execute the open method passing in three parameters:

    ```
    xmlHttpObj.open("GET","http://" + location.host + "/XmlHttpExample1/DataFile.xml",
    false);
    ```

    ❑   The first parameter, "GET", is the type of request to make (this can be any of the standard HTTP verbs "GET", "POST", "PUT", or "HEAD")

    ❑   The second parameter is the server address, or endpoint, to make the request to. In this case, it's an XML file located at http://localhost/XmlHttpExample1DataFile.xml.

    ❑   The third parameter, false, indicates whether a synchronous or asynchronous request should take place. In this case, false indicates that a synchronous request should occur.

3. The send method is executed on the XMLHTTP object instance to perform the actual request.

    ```
    xmlHttpObj.send(null);
    ```

4. Since you specified that a synchronous operation should occur, the next `alert` statement to display a message box is not shown until the request has completed executing and returns from the server.

```
alert("Request/Response Complete.");
```

As already mentioned, the previous example shows a synchronous operation that offers no real change from the standard request/response paradigm that is prevalent in web applications. A request is issued, the user waits until a response is received, and the user can continue. Now, we can change this to be asynchronous.

Asynchronous Requests

Examine the code that follows, which performs exactly the same operation as the previous example, but operates in an asynchronous manner. Note: The code for the inclusion of the script include file mentioned previously has been omitted for brevity.

Try It Out   **An Asynchronous Operation**

```
function MakeXMLHTTPCall()
{
    var xmlHttpObj;

    xmlHttpObj = CreateXmlHttpRequestObject();

    if (xmlHttpObj)
    {
       xmlHttpObj.open("GET","http:// " + location.host +
"/XmlHttpExample1/DataFile.xml", true);
       xmlHttpObj.onreadystatechange = function()
       {
         if ( xmlHttpObj.readyState == READYSTATE_COMPLETE )
         {
             alert("Request/Response Complete");
         }
       }
       xmlHttpObj.send(null);
    }
}
```

How It Works

There are two main differences in this example as compared to the initial synchronous example:

```
xmlHttpObj.open("GET","http://" + location.host +
"/XmlHttpExample1/DataFile.xml", true);
```

The first difference is the use of the `true` parameter as the last argument to the `open` method to indicate that the request should be executed in an asynchronous manner.

The second difference is the use of the `onreadystatechange` event and the `readyState` property value. The code:

```
xmlHttpObj.onreadystatechange = function()
```

assigns a function or *event handler* to the `onreadystatechange` event. When the state of the object changes, this event is triggered and the function is executed. The code:

```
if ( xmlHttpObj.readyState == READYSTATE_COMPLETE )
```

checks the state of the object to determine if any action should be taken. The ready state of the `XMLHttpRequest` object actually contains a numeric value representing its state. The numeric value being checked for in the preceding example is a value of 4, which is represented by the variable `READYSTATE_COMPLETE`. The valid list of `XMLHttpRequest` ready states is listed in the following table:

Value	Description
0	Uninitialized
1	Loading
2	Loaded
3	Interactive
4	Complete

A convenient place to put the values of the `XMLHttpRequest` ready states is in the library that was defined earlier to house the function that created an `XMLHttpRequest` object. This makes it possible to add meaning to what appears to be an arbitrary value. The following code:

```
/* Common values for the ReadyState of the XMLHttpRequest object */
var READYSTATE_UNINITIALIZED = 0;
var READYSTATE_LOADING = 1;
var READYSTATE_LOADED = 2;
var READYSTATE_INTERACTIVE = 3;
var READYSTATE_COMPLETE = 4;
```

has been added to the JavaScript common library defined earlier in the chapter. This means that the previous example, showing an asynchronous call, equates to the following line:

```
if ( xmlHttpObj.readyState == 4 )
```

However, the line currently is written as:

```
if ( xmlHttpObj.readyState == READYSTATE_COMPLETE )
```

which makes it much more readable and adds clarity as to what is being tested in the code fragment.

So, the JavaScript code in the example simply checks the ready state of the object to determine if the asynchronous request has completed. If the ready state is complete, then you continue processing your response data (if any).

So far, you have seen to how to perform an asynchronous request to the server and wait for the response by assigning an event handler. This forms the basis of all asynchronous request functionality, and you will use this as the foundation for more complex examples as you progress.

Dealing with Response Data

In most scenarios, you will want to retrieve and process some response data from the server as part of your asynchronous call. In the previous examples, you have requested an XML data file but have not attempted to process the data returned. You have simply indicated the request has completed.

To retrieve data from the response stream once the request is completed, you can use the following properties:

❑ `responseText` — This property returns the response data as a string.

❑ `responseXML` — This property returns the response data as an XML document object. This object can be examined and parsed using the standard methods and properties available from the W3C Document Object Model (DOM) node tree in a read-only (cannot be updated) fashion.

A Note on Security

It is worth noting at this point that there are security restrictions that are placed on the use of the `XMLHttpRequest` object. All browsers that implement the `XMLHttpRequest` object implement a security policy called the "same origin" policy. This means that a request issued using an `XMLHttpRequest` object must be to a server of the same origin from which it was loaded.

For example, if a web page were loaded from `www.yourserver.com/somepage .aspx`, then all requests issued using the `XMLHttpRequest` must be serviced by the same host, that is, `www.yourserver.com`. Any deviation to the server/host name, protocol, or the port will break the security policy. For example, given the previous example server, if a subsequent `XMLHttpRequest` were issued to `www.anotherserver .com/anotherpage.aspx`, then this would fail the security policy. Similarly, trying to access `www.yourserver.com/somepage.aspx` will also fail because the protocol is specified as `https:` whereas previously the code originated from an `http:` address.

This policy makes sense because it means that web pages cannot simply issue requests to any server they choose and potentially become yet another client capable of initiating denial-of-service attacks to servers (that is, flooding the servers with requests in order to bring down or disable the service/server).

Unfortunately, different browsers implement the "same origin" security policy differently. Most will fail in some way if a request is issued to a server that is not deemed the origin, and it is very hard to accommodate all browsers when performing these types of requests and handling the errors. The recommended practice is simply to not use requests that break the same origin policy. Issue a request back to the originating server as already discussed and let the server make any cross-domain/nonoriginating server calls on your behalf using standard server-based programming techniques.

Using the responseText Property

The `responseText` property is the simplest of the methods to utilize data from the response. All data that is part of the response is returned as a single string. This property is useful for simple operations where only a singular piece of data is returned and manipulated or displayed by the page. Alternatively, the data returned may be in a proprietary format that requires specialized parsing by the client. To have a look at how you use this property in code, you can enhance the existing sample to display data returned from the asynchronous call on the web page.

Try It Out   **Returning Response Data As a String**

This web page will be a very simple page with a button and a section to display the response data. The HTML fragment that follows shows the "body" section of the HTML page.

```
    <body>
      <form id="Form1" method="post" runat="server">
          <input type="button" onclick="MakeXMLHTTPCall();" value="Test XMLHTTP Call"
 />
          <br />
          <br />
          <div id="divResults">{no results}</div>
      </form>
    </body>
```

The example JavaScript code will now look like the fragment that follows. The emphasized text shows what has been added compared to the previous examples:

```
        <script type="text/javascript" src="CommonAJAXLibrary.js"></script>

        <script type="text/javascript">
        function MakeXMLHTTPCall(){

            var xmlHttpObj = CreateXmlHttpRequestObject();


            if (xmlHttpObj)
            {
                xmlHttpObj.open("GET","http://" + location.host +
    "/XmlHttpExample1/DataFile.xml", true);

                xmlHttpObj.onreadystatechange = function() {
                    if ( xmlHttpObj.readyState == READYSTATE_COMPLETE )
                    {
                        // Extract the response text here and place in the div element.
    document.getElementById("divResults").childNodes[0].nodeValue =
    xmlHttpObj.responseText;
                    }
                }

                xmlHttpObj.send(null);
            }
        }

        </script>
```

The code sets the value of the text property of the page's single `div` element to the `responseText` of the returned data. For this simple example, the `DataFile.xml` file that is requested using the `XMLHttpRequest` object contains the following:

```xml
<?xml version="1.0" encoding="utf-8" ?>
<Customers>
    <Customer>
        <Firstname>Joe</Firstname>
        <Lastname>Bloggs</Lastname>
        <email>joe@bloggs.com</email>
    </Customer>
    <Customer>
        <Firstname>Alan</Firstname>
        <Lastname>Anonymous</Lastname>
        <email>anon@ymous.com</email>
    </Customer>
    <Customer>
        <Firstname>Marvin</Firstname>
        <Lastname>Martian</Lastname>
        <email>marvin@mars.com</email>
    </Customer>
</Customers>
```

When the page executes, and the button is clicked, the web browser displays the result shown in Figure 4-1.

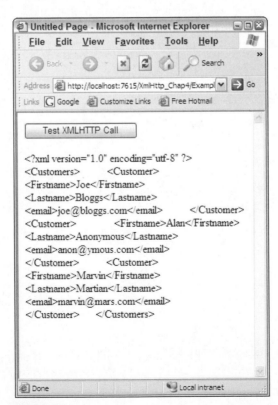

Figure 4-1

As you can see, the data contained within the XML file is rendered in the page in exactly the same way it is stored within the file.

As mentioned previously, this might be okay for simple scenarios that require only a single unit of data or data that is in a proprietary format, but for more complex scenarios you'll want to use the `responseXML` property.

Using the responseXML Property

In a majority of scenarios, you will want to return multiple result items. This might be a list of names to display in a drop-down list, a list of customers, or an object representation. The XML format is ideally suited to this, and direct support for this format is provided by the `responseXML` property of the `XMLHttpRequest` object. This property is a standard XML document object that can be examined and parsed using W3C DOM node tree methods and properties.

> *For detailed reference material on the XML Document Object Model, visit* `http://msdn` `.microsoft.com/library/en-us/xmlsdk30/htm/xmmscxmlreference.asp`.

Try It Out   Returning Response Data As an XML Document Object

You can continue to modify the code example to extract values from the XML data that was retrieved and displayed in the previous example. Rather than reproduce the entire previous code sample, we will show only the modified section that replaces the added code from the previous example that used the `responseText` property. Examine the following code:

```
if ( xmlHttpObj.readyState == READYSTATE_COMPLETE )
{
    var doc = xmlHttpObj.responseXML;
    var node = doc.selectSingleNode("//Customers/Customer/Firstname/text()");
    document.getElementById("divResults").childNodes[0].nodeValue = node.nodeValue;
}
```

Instead of simply displaying the entire set of returned data, you are extracting the text value of the first instance of the `<Firstname>` node. You do this by utilizing the `selectSingleNode` method, which takes an X Path expression as an argument and returns an XML node object if one is found or `NULL` if the X Path query is unsuccessful. With the returned node object, you assign the `nodeValue` property of the first element of the `childNodes` property, which itself is a property of the `divResults` element to the text value of the node.

> *For those unfamiliar with the X Path language, you can think of it as a dynamic query language for XML documents that operates in a similar way to ANSI SQL for databases. Nodes, elements, and data can be queried and returned using X Path expressions. X Path expressions can contain conditional expressions and be quite complex. For a detailed reference on X Path expressions and the associated syntax, visit the W3C site at* `www.w3.org/TR/xpath`, *or for something a little more readable, try* `www.topxml.com/xsl/XPathRef.asp`.

This example is still fairly simplistic, though. Now, you're going to take your newfound knowledge and apply this by creating a simple web page that allows you to make a selection from a list of customers and display the fullname and email address by doing a server-side lookup into your XML data file asynchronously.

> Firefox does not currently support the use of the `selectSingleNode()` and `selectNodes()` methods to access data within an XML document. To address this, the script include library includes some JavaScript code to enable this support. The code included was taken from the site `http://km0ti0n.blunted.co.uk/mozXPath.xap`. A full explanation of the details of this support is beyond the scope of this chapter; suffice it to say that it allows support of the `selectSingleNode()` and `selectNodes()` methods in the same way that Internet Explorer does.

Enhancing Usability

One of the primary reasons that the asynchronous capability of the `XMLHttpRequest` object has received so much attention lately is that it can remove the interruption of the user experience that would normally occur when a postback, or server-side call, is required to gather some server-side data.

In the example that follows, you will provide a list of names via a drop-down list gathered from the XML data file. When the user selects a name, a server call is issued to retrieve that data and extract the email address. Without using the asynchronous capability of the `XMLHttpRequest` object, this would require a postback, and the user would be forced to wait while the request was sent to the server and processed, and the results returned and displayed on the browser. Now that you have the ability to perform a server request asynchronously, the call to retrieve data can be performed without interrupting the user interaction on the browser. It is, in effect, an *invisible postback* — a server request that is executed behind the scenes and in parallel to any user interface interaction.

Try It Out   Performing a Server Request Asynchronously

Examine the code that follows, which is a fragment listing of a web page:

```
<body onload="LoadCustomers();">
    <form id="form1" runat="server">
    <div>
        <select id="ddlCustomers" onchange="DisplayCustomerDetails();">
            <option value="">- Select a Customer -</option>
        </select>
        <hr />
        <div>
            <p>Details:</p>
            <span id="spnDetailDisplay">(You have not made a selection yet.)</span>
        </div>
    </div>
    </form>
</body>
</html>
```

Within the ASP.NET form element `<form id="form1" runat="server">` is a `<select>` element that acts as your customer drop-down list and a `<span>` element where you can display the customer details. You will also notice that the `onload` event of the document has a `LoadCustomers()` function assigned to it to initially load in the list of customers and that the `onchange` event of the `<select>` item has a `DisplayCustomerDetails()` function assigned to it to display the selected customers details once a selection is made.

Next listed in the following code blocks are the JavaScript functions that accompany the page listing. The first function is a generic function to simply create an `XMLHttpRequest` object that you can use:

```
<!DOCTYPE html PUBLIC "-//W3C//DTD XHTML 1.0 Transitional//EN"
"http://www.w3.org/TR/xhtml1/DTD/xhtml1-transitional.dtd">

<html xmlns="http://www.w3.org/1999/xhtml" >
<head runat="server">
    <title>Untitled Page</title>

    <script type="text/javascript">

    // A "global" variable that is our XMLHttpRequest object reference.
    var xmlHttpObj = CreateXmlHttpRequestObject();
```

The next function is what is called when the document first loads and deals with loading the customer data from the server using the `XMLHttpRequest` object:

```
// Function to load the customer selection data into the <SELECT> drop list control
function LoadCustomers()
{
    if (xmlHttpObj)
    {
        // We want this request synchronous
        xmlHttpObj.open("GET","http:// " + location.host +
"/XmlHttp_Chap4/DataFile.xml", false);

        // Execute the request
        xmlHttpObj.send(null);

        // If the request was ok (ie. equal to a Http Status code of 200)
        if (xmlHttpObj.status == 200)
        {
            var xmlDoc = xmlHttpObj.responseXML;
            // Our list of <CUSTOMER> nodes selected using the X Path argument
            //var nodes = xmlDoc.selectNodes("//Customers/Customer");
            var nodes = xmlDoc.selectNodes("//Customers/Customer/Lastname/text()");
            // Obtain a reference to the <SELECT> drop list control.
            var ctrl = document.getElementById("ddlCustomers");

            for (var i=0; i < nodes.length; i++)
            {
                // Get the lastname element from our XML data document
                var lastName = nodes[i].nodeValue;
                // Create a new <OPTION> node.
                var htmlCode = document.createElement('option');
                // Add the new <OPTION> node to our <SELECT> drop list
                ctrl.options.add(htmlCode);
                // Set the <OPTION> display text and value;
                htmlCode.text = lastName;
                htmlCode.value = lastName;
            }
        } else
```

```
        {
            alert('There was a problem accessing the Customer data on the
server.!');
        }
    }
}
```

In the preceding code, you will notice the use of a literal number 200 in the following line of code:

```
if (xmlHttpObj.status == 200)
```

This is another perfect candidate to place into the common script include file. The code can be defined in the following manner:

```
/* Common values for HTTP status codes */
var HTTPSTATUS_OK = 200;
```

which means that any code comparing the HTTP status codes as in the previous example can be replaced with the following line of code:

```
if (xmlHttpObj.status == HTTPSTATUS_OK)
```

This makes the code much easier to read and maintain.

Finally, you have the JavaScript function that deals with displaying a customer's details once a selection is made from the drop-down list:

```
function DisplayCustomerDetails()
{
    if (xmlHttpObj)
    {
        // We want this request asynchronous
        xmlHttpObj.open("GET","http:// " + location.host +
"/XmlHttp_Chap4/DataFile.xml", true);

        xmlHttpObj.onreadystatechange = function()
        {
            if ( xmlHttpObj.readyState == READYSTATE_COMPLETE )
            {
                var ctrl = document.getElementById("ddlCustomers");
                var doc = xmlHttpObj.responseXML;
                var lastName = ctrl.options[ctrl.selectedIndex].value;
                var node = doc.selectSingleNode("//Customers/Customer[Lastname='" +
lastName + "']");
                var details = 'Fullname: ' +
node.selectSingleNode('Firstname/text()').nodeValue +
                    ' ' + lastName + '. Email: ' +
node.selectSingleNode('email/text()').nodeValue;
                document.getElementById("spnDetailDisplay").childNodes[0].nodeValue
= details;
            }
```

```
            }

        // Execute the request
        xmlHttpObj.send(null);
    }
}
    </script>
</head>
</head>
```

Here, you have opted to define the XMLHttpRequest object as a "global" variable xmlHttpObj, rather than redeclaring and creating this object in each function. The function to assign a valid XMLHttpRequest instance to the variable is separated into its own discrete function. This might typically be included as part of your common script library rather than having to rewrite this in every page.

Using a "global" object to hold a reference to your XMLHttpRequest object can expose your client-side application to a potential bug or flaw in its operation if a subsequent request is issued using the same XMLHttpRequest object before the first request has completed.

In addition, since the LoadCustomers() function is executed as part of the load event of the page, and the page is not usable until this function has executed, you make the server call in a synchronous manner using the false parameter, as shown in the line below:

```
// We want this request synchronous
xmlHttpObj.open("GET","http://" + location.host + "/XmlHttp_Chap4/DataFile.xml",
false);
```

You execute the call, and then you check the status of the call by examining the status property of the XMLHttpRequest object. This property contains the standard HTTP status code returned by the server as a result of the request being made. In this example, you check to ensure that a status code of 200 was returned as part of the call:

```
// If the request was ok (ie. equal to a Http Status code of 200)
if (xmlHttpObj.status == 200)
{
    // rest of function . . .
```

The status code of 200 returned from the server indicates a successful server request has been made. Because you have defined this literal value in the script include file, the code would read:

```
// If the request was ok (ie. equal to a Http Status code of 200)
if (xmlHttpObj.status == HTTPSTATUS_OK)
{
    // rest of function . . .
```

For a list of all the valid HTTP status codes defined by the W3C, see www.w3.org/Protocols/ rfc2616/rfc2616-sec10.html.

You then use the XML DOM method selectNodes to execute an X Path expression over the XML data to find each Lastname node for each Customer node and return a list of matching nodes:

```
var nodes = xmlDoc.selectNodes("//Customers/Customer/Lastname/text()");
// Obtain a reference to the <SELECT> drop list control.
var ctrl = document.getElementById("ddlCustomers");

for (var i=0; i < nodes.length; i++)
{
    // rest of function . . .
```

You iterate over the list of `Lastname` nodes, adding each customer's last name to the drop-down list.

Within the `DisplayCustomerDetails()`, you define a function that is executed when the appropriate `readystate` of the request has been reached (`readystate == READYSTATE_COMPLETE`). You then use an X Path expression to locate the node matching your selected customer, extract the details of the customer from the XML data file using the `selectSingleNode` method, and display those details within the `<span>` element.

The previous example introduced the `status` property that is part of the `XMLHttpRequest` object. The `XMLHttpRequest` object does not have an extensive list of properties and methods and is relatively simple and straightforward. The two tables that follow are, respectively, a reference table of the methods and one of properties available for the `XMLHttpRequest` object.

Method	Description
`abort()`	Cancels the current request.
`getAllResponseHeaders()`	Returns the complete set of HTTP headers as a string.
`getResponseHeader("headername")`	Returns the value of the specified HTTP header.
`open("method","URL", "async", "uname","pswd")`	Specifies the method, URL, and other optional attributes of a request. The method parameter can have a value of GET, POST, or PUT (use GET when requesting data and use POST when sending data — especially if the length of the data is greater than 512 bytes). The URL parameter may be either a relative or complete URL. The `async` parameter specifies whether the request should be handled asynchronously or not. `true` means that script processing carries on after the `send()` method, without waiting for a response. `false` means that the script waits for a response before continuing script processing.
`send(content)`	Sends the request.
`setRequestHeader("label","value")`	Adds a label/value pair to the HTTP header to be sent.

Property	Description
onreadystatechange	An event handler for an event that fires at every state change. (Read/Write)
readyState	Returns the state of the object: (read-only) 0 = uninitialized 1 = loading 2 = loaded 3 = interactive 4 = complete
responseText	Returns the response as a string (read-only)
responseXML	Returns the response as XML. This property returns an XML document object, which can be examined and parsed using W3C DOM node tree methods and properties (read-only)
status	Returns the status as a number (e.g., 404 for "Not Found" or 200 for "OK", 500 for "Server Error") (read-only)
statusText	Returns the status as a string (e.g., "Not Found" or "OK") (read-only)

Passing Parameters to the Server

Obviously, there are going to be times when you need to pass some parameters to the server-side request. One traditional way is to use query string arguments as part of the XMLHttpRequest. An example follows where the parameter arg is being passed with a value of 123.

```
xmlHttpObj.open("GET","http://" + location.host +
"/XmlHttpExample1/WebForm1.aspx?arg=123", true);
```

This method of passing arguments to the server is typically used with a "GET" request (or the "GET" verb) as shown in the preceding code; however, it can also be used with "POST" requests as well as shown in the following example:

```
xmlHttpObj.open("POST","http://" + location.host +
"/XmlHttpExample1/WebForm1.aspx?arg=123", true);
```

The page that receives and processes this request (in this example, WebForm1.aspx) can extract the query string arguments from the URL and use this to return the appropriate data back to the client. A simple example of extracting query string arguments using server-side code is shown here:

```
private void Page_Load(object sender, System.EventArgs e)
{
   if (Request.QueryString.Count > 0)
   {
```

```
        string queryArg = Request.QueryString["arg"];
        switch (queryArg)
        {
            case "123":
                Server.Transfer("DataFile1.xml");
                break;
            case "456":
                Server.Transfer("DataFile2.xml");
                break;
            default:
                Server.Transfer("DataFile1.xml");
                break;
        }
    }
}
```

Using a traditional web page to act as the receiver for an XMLHTTP request is not the most efficient way of performing this type of operation. A page is typically suited to rendering HTML, and you typically want to respond with some customized data, quite often in the form of a custom XML document. While the preceding example does achieve that, you also don't want to have to worry about what ASP.NET may add to the response as part of its page-processing pipeline. Not only does this add unnecessary processing overheard but in some instances may also cause issues with the response data and the way it's handled. Ideally, instead of using a standard page, it would be better to have ASP.NET hand off the request to a custom piece of code that can be specifically dedicated to the task of producing the customized response that your web application requires.

HTTP Handlers

A more typical approach to handling these requests is to use an HTTP handler. A *handler* has the ability to respond to requests with more direct control over the response data. Essentially, an HTTP handler exists very early in the ASP.NET processing pipeline and can deal directly with requests without having to worry about HTML data being generated by the page and the unnecessary burden of the entire page lifecycle. Additionally, the handler need not be concerned with having the initial request be a properly formed page but can instead have it be a custom formatted message that has meaning within the context of your application. Often, this is an XML document used to transfer data between the client and the server.

> *HTTP handlers are a way to hook into the early stages of the ASP.NET processing pipeline before any actual page processing is performed. For more information on developing custom HTTP handlers, please see the MSDN reference at* `http://msdn.microsoft.com/library/en-us/cpguide/ html/cpconhttphandlers.asp.`

Try It Out   **Using a HTTP Handler**

To demonstrate the use of a HTTP handler to accept arguments sent from an `XMLHttpRequest` object, you first define the user interface within the web page, as shown in the following code. This simply shows a drop-down list with a list of three customers. When one of the customers is selected, that customer ID is used as part of the asynchronous request to request a specific set of data pertaining to that customer's details only:

```
<form id="form1" runat="server">
<div>
    <select id="ddlCustomers" onchange="LoadCustomer();">
```

```
        <option value="">- Select a Customer -</option>
        <option value="1">Customer 1</option>
        <option value="2">Customer 2</option>
        <option value="3">Customer 3</option>
    </select>
    <hr />
    <div>
        <p>Details:</p>
        <span id="spnDetailDisplay">(You have not made a selection yet)</span>
    </div>
  </div>
  </form>
```

You also provide an implementation of the JavaScript function named LoadCustomer() referenced in the onchange attribute of the select element as follows:

```
function LoadCustomer()
{
    if (xmlHttpObj)
    {
        // Obtain a reference to the <SELECT> drop list control.
        var ddlCtrl = document.getElementById("ddlCustomers");
        var disp = document.getElementById("spnDetailDisplay");

        var custNumber = ddlCtrl.value;
        // We want this request synchronous
        xmlHttpObj.open("GET","http:// " + location.host +
"/XmlHttp_Chap4/AsyncRequestHandler.ashx?arg="+custNumber, true);

        xmlHttpObj.onreadystatechange = function()
        {
            if (xmlHttpObj.readyState == READYSTATE_COMPLETE)
            {

                // If the request was ok (ie equal to a Http Status code of 200)
                if (xmlHttpObj.status == HTTPSTATUS_OK)
                {
                    var xmlDoc = xmlHttpObj.responseXML;
                    // Our list of <CUSTOMER> nodes selected using the X Path
argument
                    var name =
xmlDoc.selectSingleNode("//root/Customer/name/text()");
                    var email =
xmlDoc.selectSingleNode("//root/Customer/email/text()");
                    alert(name);
                    disp.childNodes[0].nodeValue = "Name: " + name.nodeValue + " -
Email: " + email.nodeValue;
                }
            }
        }
        // Execute the request
        xmlHttpObj.send("SomeDataToSend");

    }
}
```

You will notice the use of a handler when defining the URL for making the asynchronous request and appending the value for the arg parameter based on the drop-down list selection.

```
xmlHttpObj.open("GET","http://" + location.host + "/XmlHttp_Chap4/AsyncRequest
Handler.ashx?arg="+custNumber, true);
```

Finally, the implementation of the server-side HTTP handler itself is shown in the following code block. This is the handler that receives the asynchronous call from your XMLHttpRequest object, extracts the customer number or ID, and then uses that to return an XML document containing only that customer's name and email address. This code resides within the AsyncRequestHandler.ashx file.

```csharp
<%@ WebHandler Language="C#" Class="AsyncRequestHandler" %>

using System;
using System.Web;
using System.Data;

public class AsyncRequestHandler : IHttpHandler {

    public void ProcessRequest (HttpContext context) {
        // Grab the URL parameters
        string param = context.Request.QueryString["arg"];

        const string xmlData = @"<?xml version=""1.0"" encoding=""utf-8"" ?>
            <root><Customer><name>{0}</name><email>{1}</email></Customer></root>";

        string returnXML = null;

        switch (param)
        {
            case "1":
                returnXML = string.Format(xmlData, "Big Bob", "big@bob.com");
                break;
            case "2":
                returnXML = string.Format(xmlData, "Small Sammy",
"small@sammy.com");
                break;
            case "3":
                returnXML = string.Format(xmlData, "Large Larry",
"large@larry.com");
                break;
        }

        context.Response.ContentType = "application/xml";
        context.Response.Write(returnXML);
    }

    public bool IsReusable {
        get {
            return false;
        }
    }
}
```

In addition to using query string arguments, as shown in the previous example, you can also utilize the `send` method of the `XMLHttpRequest` object to specify some data to be sent with the server request as part of the request body.

Previous examples have used the syntax:

```
xmlHttpObj.send(null);
```

to initiate a request, specifying `null` as the method argument. This argument represents the content to be sent along with the request as part of the request body. To indicate the data to be sent with the request, you simply specify it as the method argument:

```
xmlHttpObj.send("MyDataToSend");
```

To extract this data from the request body within your HTTP handler, you can add the code that follows following to your handler implementation:

```
byte[] data = new byte[context.Request.ContentLength];
context.Request.InputStream.Read(data, 0, context.Request.ContentLength);
string body = System.Text.UTF8Encoding.UTF8.GetString(data);
```

Once you have extracted the data from the body of the request, you can then extract the relevant information. Typically, this means that you load the data into an `XMLDocument` object, and extract the data required to perform your server-side work.

What about Web Services?

.NET contains extensive support for web services and is the preferred mechanism for exposing server-side functionality or providing entry points to your server-side processes. Accessing these services or entry points in an asynchronous manner is an obvious step in achieving a marriage of the best technologies on both the client and server when developing .NET web-based applications.

Web services do require some extra information to be passed as part of the client request to ensure that a valid call is recognized. The example that follows contains a web service named `Adder` that will calculate the result of the addition of two integer arguments that are passed to the service from the client.

Try It Out   **Accessing Web Services**

First you construct a simple user interface to facilitate this:

```
<form id="form1" runat="server">
    <div>
        <input type="text" id="val1" />
        <input type="text" id="val2" />
        <input type="button" value="Calculate" onclick="ExecWebService();" />
        <hr />
        <div>
            <p>Details:</p>
            <span id="spnDetailDisplay">(You have not made a selection yet)</span>
        </div>
    </div>
</form>
```

This HTML document simply contains two text fields that accept the integer arguments and a button to calculate the result of the addition of the two arguments. The button contains an `onclick` handler, which points to a JavaScript function. This function will execute your asynchronous call to your web service.

Next, have a look at the code of your web service, which is extremely simple and should be very familiar to all developers who have created web services. The web service itself was created using the endpoint of `AsyncService.asmx` and contains a method, more specifically a `WebMethod`, called `Adder`:

```
[WebService(Namespace = "http://tempuri.org/")]
[WebServiceBinding(ConformsTo = WsiProfiles.BasicProfile1_1)]
public class AsyncService : System.Web.Services.WebService {

    public AsyncService () {
    }

    [WebMethod]
    public int Adder(int arg1, int arg2) {
        return arg1 + arg2;
    }
}
```

Finally, examine the client-side code to call the web service shown previously:

```
function ExecWebService()
{
    if (xmlHttpObj)
    {
        var disp = document.getElementById("spnDetailDisplay");
        var ctlVal1 = document.getElementById("val1");
        var ctlVal2 = document.getElementById("val2");

        // We want this request synchronous
        xmlHttpObj.open("POST","http://" + location.host +
"/XmlHttp_Chap4/AsyncService.asmx/Adder", true);

        xmlHttpObj.onreadystatechange = function()
        {
            if (xmlHttpObj.readyState == READYSTATE_COMPLETE)
            {
                // If the request was ok (ie equal to a Http Status code of 200)
                if (xmlHttpObj.status == HTTPSTATUS_OK)
                {
                    var xmlDoc = xmlHttpObj.responseXML;
                    var result = xmlDoc.lastChild.childNodes[0].nodeValue;
                    disp.childNodes[0].nodeValue = "Result: " + result;
                } else
                {
                    var fault = xmlHttpObj.responseText;
                    alert("Error Occurred! \n\n" + fault);
                }
            }
        }
        // Execute the request
        xmlHttpObj.setRequestHeader("Content-Type","application/x-www-form-
urlencoded");
```

```
        xmlHttpObj.send("arg1=" + ctlVal1.value + "&arg2=" + ctlVal2.value);

    }
}
```

How It Works

This client-side code is very similar to previous examples but does have some important differences to facilitate calling the web service.

First, when specifying the endpoint to your web service, the URL follows a slightly different convention than that of previous requests:

```
xmlHttpObj.open("POST","http://" + location.host + "/XmlHttp_Chap4/AsyncService
.asmx/Adder", true);
```

You will notice that the URL contains the location to the web service asmx file, with the web service method or operation to be called, appended to the URL /Adder. You have also specified that a "POST" operation should be performed.

If some data is specified as part of the content to be sent using the XMLHttpRequest.send *method, a* "POST" *operation is always performed due to the fact that a* "GET" *operation does not send data as part of the content or HTTP request body.*

Prior to executing the request to call the web service, you set a particular header value named "Content-Type" to a value of "application/x-www-form-urlencoded". The "Content-Type" attribute specifies the encoding type for the form. The default value for a form is "application/x-www-form-urlencoded"; however, this is not included by default as part of the XMLHttpRequest and must be specified manually as shown in the preceding code.

In actually executing the "send" method of the XMLHttpRequest object, you construct the list of arguments required in a similar fashion to the way you would specify these arguments as a URL query string.

```
xmlHttpObj.send("arg1=" + ctlVal1.value + "&arg2=" + ctlVal2.value);
```

Notice how the "arg1" parameter and "arg2" parameter are separated by an ampersand (&) in much the same way URL query strings are constructed. This would result in a string equating to:

```
arg1=1&arg2=2
```

where the value of "arg1" is 1 and the value of "arg2" is 2. This string would be sent as part of the request body and is automatically parsed and handled by the web service so that the correct values are assigned to the correct web service parameters on the server side. Again, this is similar to the way query strings are specified in "GET" requests in the browser. A similar request using a query string might look like:

```
http://www.somesite.com/SomePage.aspx?arg1=1&arg2=2
```

Finally, the code to extract the result is as follows:

```
var xmlDoc = xmlHttpObj.responseXML;
var result = xmlDoc.lastChild.text;
```

The code extracts the text value of the last child node of the response. The response to the web service request, using the previous set of arguments, would look like:

```
<?xml version="1.0" encoding="utf-8"?>
<int xmlns="http://tempuri.org/">3</int>
```

The first child node of this XML document would equate to the initial processing instruction line, so you must extract the last child node in this XML response, which equates to the line representing the integer result. This method of value extraction is fairly simplistic but should work in most cases; however, this does not take into account whether an error is generated by the web service.

For this example, you can generate two different types of errors that must be handled in different ways:

❑ One type of error can be generated by removing the method specification from the URL passed into the open method (that is, removing the /Adder from the URL) or by passing in blank or invalid arguments to the request.

❑ Another type of error can be generated by forgetting to specify the "Content-Type" in the request header.

For both types of errors, you are returned a status code of 500 representing a server error. However, in the first instance, you are returned the following as the body of the response:

```
System.InvalidOperationException: Request format is invalid: .
    at System.Web.Services.Protocols.HttpServerProtocol.ReadParameters()
    at System.Web.Services.Protocols.WebServiceHandler.CoreProcessRequest()
```

In the second instance, you are returned the following in the body of the response:

```
<?xml version="1.0" encoding="utf-8"?><soap:Envelope
xmlns:soap="http://www.w3.org/2003/05/soap-envelope"
xmlns:xsi="http://www.w3.org/2001/XMLSchema-instance"
xmlns:xsd="http://www.w3.org/2001/XMLSchema"><soap:Body><soap:Fault><soap:Code><soa
p:Value>soap:Receiver</soap:Value></soap:Code><soap:Reason><soap:Text
xml:lang="en">System.Web.Services.Protocols.SoapException: Server was unable to
process request. ---&gt; System.Xml.XmlException: Data at the root level is
invalid. Line 1, position 1.
    at System.Xml.XmlTextReaderImpl.Throw(Exception e)
    at System.Xml.XmlTextReaderImpl.Throw(String res, String arg)
    at System.Xml.XmlTextReaderImpl.ParseRootLevelWhitespace()
    at System.Xml.XmlTextReaderImpl.ParseDocumentContent()
    at System.Xml.XmlTextReaderImpl.Read()
    at System.Xml.XmlTextReader.Read()
    at System.Web.Services.Protocols.SoapServerProtocol.SoapEnvelopeReader.Read()
    at System.Xml.XmlReader.MoveToContent()
    at
System.Web.Services.Protocols.SoapServerProtocol.SoapEnvelopeReader.MoveToContent()
    at System.Web.Services.Protocols.SoapServerProtocolHelper.GetRequestElement()
    at System.Web.Services.Protocols.Soap12ServerProtocolHelper.RouteRequest()
    at
System.Web.Services.Protocols.SoapServerProtocol.RouteRequest(SoapServerMessage
message)
    at System.Web.Services.Protocols.SoapServerProtocol.Initialize()
```

```
    at System.Web.Services.Protocols.ServerProtocolFactory.Create(Type type,
HttpContext context, HttpRequest request, HttpResponse response, Boolean&amp;
abortProcessing)
    --- End of inner exception stack trace ---</soap:Text></soap:Reason><soap:Detail
/></soap:Fault></soap:Body></soap:Envelope>
```

In most cases, simply capturing the fact an error has occurred via the status code will be sufficient. However, determining a more specific nature of the error requires specific processing and will require specific parsing of the responseText property of the XMLHttpRequest object. To illustrate this, the code that follows shows an enhanced version of the function to deal with responses from the web service call.

```
if (xmlHttpObj.status == HTTPSTATUS_OK)
{
    var xmlDoc = xmlHttpObj.responseXML;
    var result = xmlDoc.lastChild.childNodes[0].nodeValue;
    disp.childNodes[0].nodeValue = "Result: " + result;
} else
{
    var fault = xmlHttpObj.responseText;
    alert("Error Occurred! \n\n" + fault);
}
```

In the event of an error, an alert box will be displayed to the user, with the specific error response text that was generated by the server.

Invoking Web Services — A Few Caveats

It should be noted that the method of invoking a web service shown in the preceding code is not a standard way of invoking a web service. Web services message format is typically in an XML format known as SOAP (Simple Object Access Protocol) and is far more complex to construct than the simplistic HTTP body used in the previous example. Constructing a properly formatted SOAP message to access web services in a standard way is certainly possible but is far more complex than the previous example and requires considerable effort to implement a SOAP protocol stack to ensure any messages are constructed in a valid "SOAP envelope."

The method shown in the previous example to pass arguments to a web service is not guaranteed to work on other web service implementations. Part of the interoperability features of web services are achieved by using the SOAP message format, and because you are not using that format to call the web service, calling non-.NET web services is not guaranteed to be successful.

For more information on the SOAP format in relation to web services, visit www.w3.org/TR/soap.

Nevertheless, the method of accessing a .NET web service as described previously will be sufficient to invoke a .NET web service using the default and most basic implementation of a web service. Services that have the "GET" and "POST" verbs disabled or disallowed for web service content may cause errors and not function as expected.

Additionally, previously we stated that the Content-Type needs to be specified to ensure that the web service call works. On occasion, it may be also necessary to specify an additional header attribute, the SOAPAction HTTP header attribute, setting it to the name of the *Action* or method to be executed.

Although this is not strictly required in the trivial examples shown so far, it adds an extra level of compliance to the web service call and is worthwhile doing to make your web service clients work better with your services. This can be achieved by using the following code:

```
xmlHttpObj.setRequestHeader("SOAPAction","{your_action}");
```

where "{your_action}" specifies the service method or *action* to execute. Short of implementing a full SOAP implementation, this is all you need to do to call .NET web services. Again, this does depend entirely on the configuration of the service itself. The more complex the requirements, configuration and parameters of the service, the more likely you are to experience difficulty in effectively crafting a client side proxy to call it. Some of the frameworks described later in the chapter provide a full SOAP implementation and are a much easier alternative to writing your own implementation.

Summary

In this chapter, you have had a look at how to construct an XMLHttpRequest object in a cross-browser friendly way and how to utilize the asynchronous and synchronous request capabilities of this object. We examined the object's properties in detail and had a look at how to utilize this object to make server-side requests to access:

❑   A specific file

❑   A page

❑   A request against a .NET HTTP handler

❑   A request against a .NET web service

You have also had a look at how to extract the response from these requests, and deal with errors when they occur. This provides a general overview of the majority of ways you can use the XMLHttpRequest object and bend it to your will. Using these techniques, you can develop your own custom methods and common routines for accessing and manipulating asynchronous requests.

The XMLHttpRequest object is really the core of Ajax. Building upon this, you have examined how to perform the typical functions a web developer might need to implement asynchronous features of the XMLHttpRequest object. Accessing server-side functionality without browser interruption or disruption to the user is the key, and as already mentioned, this may be performed by simple HTTP GET requests all the way through to the use of HTTP handlers and web services.

In addition, you have been able to slowly build a reusable script library to factor out common functions such as the creation of the XMLHttpRequest object in a cross-browser way and to identify commonly used constants such as HTTP status codes. All this can save time in any future development and can form the basis of any custom library that you wish to develop further.

Using the knowledge learned from this chapter and the code library you have developed, you are well armed to begin developing Ajax-style applications. The information presented in this chapter forms the basis for almost all libraries and applications that utilize Ajax-style functionality.

Data Communication: XML, XSLT, and JSON

An important part of any type of distributed application is how data is pushed around between tiers or layers of the application. Additionally, with Ajax, several concepts are fairly important to know and understand, concepts involved with building distributed heterogeneous environments. Accordingly, in this chapter, you are going to look at:

❑ **XML** — XML is Extensible Markup Language. It is primarily used for data interchange.

❑ **XSLT** — XSLT is Extensible Stylesheet Language Transformations. XSLT is designed to take XML data from one format and put it into another format.

❑ **JSON** — JSON is the JavaScript Object Notation. JSON is a lightweight data interchange format.

When tied together with web services, XML and JSON allow for data interchange between different operating systems and also across the Internet. This is a major change from systems that are heavily tied together and require that each system run a specific operating system merely because of the format the data is communicated in. Another advantage web services provide these data interchange formats is that web services typically run on HTTP. HTTP runs on port 80. Port 80 is a very widely used port and is not blocked, unlike many other ports and protocols, such as Microsoft's Distributed Component Object Model (DCOM) objects.

> *Trying to put all information about XML, XSLT, and JSON into one chapter will not do any of the subjects justice. This chapter attempts to cover enough information regarding these products so that the reader will have a basic understanding of these technologies as they relate to data communication. However, these topics can each fill a thousand-page book and not completely cover the subject. Wrox offers several good, complete books on the subject of XML and XSLT, including* Beginning XML, *Third Edition (Wiley, 2004),* XSLT 2.0 Programmer's Reference, *Third Edition (Wiley, 2004),* X Path 2.0 Programmer's Reference *(Wiley, 2004). You can find these and other titles at* www.wrox.com.

> *This chapter assumes that you are using Visual Studio 2005 and .NET 2.0. Also, you can download the code samples for this chapter (Chapter 5) at* http://beginningajax.com.

XML

I won't bother you with all of the grand hoopla (and already well covered) talk about how XML will do this or that. Suffice it to say, it is fairly widely used. XML work began at the level of the W3C in 1996. It was formally introduced in February 1998. XML won't wax your floors, and it is not a dessert topping; however, take a quick look at what XML really is and what features it has that are well designed for data transfer and storage:

❑ **XML is based on Standard Generalized Markup Language (SGML)** — Having a format based on existing international standards, such as SGML, which has been used since 1986, means that you have an existing body of knowledge to draw upon.

❑ **It has a self-describing format** — The structure and field names are well known.

❑ **It has textual representation of data** — This textual representation of data allows computer science data structures to be represented textually. These data structures include trees, lists, and records.

❑ **It is both human- and machine-readable** — This is an improvement over binary/machine data because humans can read it, which allows for simple visual inspection of the data.

❑ **It has multiple-language support** — It supports information in any human language as well as ASCII and Unicode.

❑ **It is efficient and consistent** — Its strict syntax and parsing requirements allow the parsing algorithms to perform efficiently and consistently.

❑ **It is widely applicable** — The hierarchical structure of XML is appropriate for many types of documents.

❑ **It is platform-independent** — By being text-based, XML is relatively platform-independent and relatively immune to changes in technology.

All that said, XML is not the best solution for everything. XML has several weaknesses that programmers need to be aware of. These are:

❑ **XML is fairly verbose** — In some cases, an XML representation of data may be redundant. The result may be higher bandwidth and CPU processing needs. With compression, the storage cost and bandwidth needs may be negated; however, the cost may be increased storage CPU processing requirements. In addition, by compressing the data, the advantage of XML being human readable is almost certainly lost.

❑ **Data storage requirements do not support a wide array of datatypes.** The result is that the numeric e value of 2.781828 may not easily be identified as a floating-point value or a string with a width of eight characters. XML Schema and validation routines provide this support; however, XML does not natively provide this information.

❑ **Mapping to a relational database model may be difficult** — Complex XML layouts may not easily map to a relational database model.

History of XML

XML can trace its heritage back to the mid 1960s with roots in Generalized Markup Language (GML) from IBM. SGML is based on the GML work done at IBM. SGML is a metalanguage that was standardized in

1986 by ISO standard "ISO 8879:1986 Information processing—Text and office systems—Standard Generalized Markup Language (SGML)." After that there were several modifications of the standard to correct some omissions and clear up some loose ends.

In mid-1996, work began on integrating SGML and the web. During the working time, the group had various names for the specification until it finally decided on Extensible Markup Language (XML). This group worked throughout 1997, and on February 10, 1998, the W3C approved the result as a W3C recommendation. This is sometimes referred to as XML 1.0.

Minor revisions of XML 1.0 have taken place. The current revision is known as XML 1.0 Third Edition. This revision was published on February 4, 2004.

The XML 1.1 version was published on February 4, 2004, the same day as the XML 1.0 Third Edition. XML 1.1 has been primarily designed to assist those with unique needs, such as mainframe/host developers. XML 1.1 is not widely implemented at this time.

There is talk and discussion regarding future versions of XML. There is some talk regarding XML 2.0 that would have it eliminate Document Type Definitions (DTDs) from syntax, integration of namespaces, and the addition of other features into the XML standard. In addition, the W3C has had some preliminary discussion regarding the addition of binary encoding into the XML feature set. There is no official work to include binary encoding, merely discussion and investigation, at the time of this writing.

XML Documents

Take a look at what a simple valid XML document looks like:

```
<?xml version="1.0" encoding="UTF-8"?>
<menu>
    <menuitem>
        <item>Hamburger</item>
        <item>French Fries</item>
        <item flavor="Chocolate">Milk Shake</item>
        <cost>4.99</cost>
    </menuitem>
</menu>
```

The first line of the file is the *XML declaration*. This line is optional. It contains information regarding the version of XML, typically version 1.0, character encoding, and possibly external dependencies. Next, with XML, there must be one *root element*. In the preceding example, the <menu> tag is the root element.

The rest of the document contains a set of nested elements, which can be further divided into attributes and content. An *element* is typically defined with a start tag and an end tag. In the preceding example, you have a start tag of <item> and an end tag of </item> for your list of menu items. The end tag can be omitted if the start tag is defined as <item />. The content of the item is everything that is between the start and end tags. Elements may also contain attributes. *Attributes* are name/value pairs included within the start tag and after the element name. Attribute values must be quoted with a single or double quotation mark. Each attribute name should occur only once within an element. In the preceding code, the item with value of Milk Shake has an attribute. The name of the attribute is flavor and the value is "Chocolate". In addition to text, elements may contain other elements. In the preceding code example, the <menuitem> element contains three individual <item> elements.

XML Document Correctness

For an XML document to be considered to be correct, it must meet two requirements. It must be:

❑ **Well formed** — A *well-formed* document meets all of the XML syntax rules. A parser must refuse to process a document that is not well formed. A well-formed document must conform to the following rules:

    ❑ XML declaration, processing instructions, encoding, and other information may exist in the XML document.

    ❑ Only one root element is specified in the XML document.

    ❑ Elements that are not empty are defined with both a start tag and an end tag.

    ❑ Empty elements may be marked with the empty element tag. An example is `<item />`.

    ❑ Attributes must be enclosed in single or double quotation marks. Attribute names are case-sensitive.

    ❑ Tags may be nested but must not overlap.

    ❑ The document must use the specified encoding. UTF-8 is the default.

    ❑ Elements names are case-sensitive.

❑ **Valid** — A *valid* document has data that conforms to a set of content rules. These rules describe correct data values and document organizational structure. (For example, the datatypes in an element must match.)

❑ XML documents that comply with a defined schema are defined as valid. An *XML Schema* is a description of a type of XML document. The schema is typically expressed as constraints on the structure and content of the document. This is above and beyond the basic constraints imposed by XML. You will find out more about schemas a bit later in this chapter.

Try It Out   Creating Valid and Well-Formed XML

XML requires that elements be properly next and not overlap. The following example shows invalid XML because of the overlapping of tags with the `<item>` tag. In the example that follows, a tag is open, then a second tag of the same type is opened, the first `<item>` tag is closed, and then the second `<item>` tag is closed.

```
<?xml version="1.0" encoding="UTF-8"?>
<menu>
    <menuitem>
       <item>Hamburger<item></item>
             French Fries</item>
       <item flavor="Chocolate">Milk Shake</item>
    </menuitem>
</menu>
```

Consider the following code sample that is not well formed. This example contains no root element.

```
<?xml version="1.0" encoding="UTF-8"?>
<item>Hamburger</item>
<item>French Fries</item>
<item flavor="Chocolate">Milk Shake</item>
```

For this example to be well formed, a root element must be added. Now this document is set up so that multiple menu items may be created and is more along the lines of what is desired:

```
<?xml version="1.0" encoding="UTF-8"?>
<menu>
    <menuitem>
        <item>Hamburger</item>
        <item>French Fries</item>
        <item flavor="Chocolate">Milk Shake</item>
    </menuitem>
</menu>
```

Figure 5-1 shows a simple XML example after it has been parsed and displayed in Internet Explorer v6.

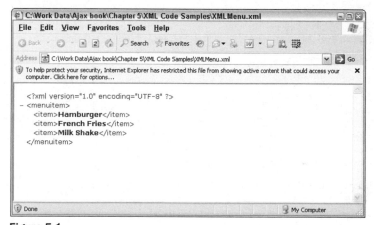

Figure 5-1

Now compare the previous example to the following invalid XML:

```
<?xml version='1.0' encoding='UTF-8'?>
<menu>
    <menuitem >
        <item>Hamburger</item>
        <item>French Fries</item>
        <item>Milk Shake</item>
    </MenuItem> <!- Note the capital M and I -->
</menu>
```

Figure 5-2 shows the result in Internet Explorer. In this example, the closing `</MenuItem>` does not match the opening `<menuitem>` because the opening and closing tags do not match from the standpoint of case.

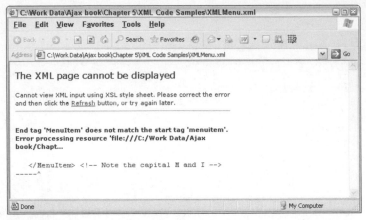

Figure 5-2

Entity References and Numeric Character References

Within XML is the need to store special characters. These special characters are entity characters and numeric character references.

An *entity* in XML is body of data, typically text, which contains unusual characters. An *entity reference* in XML is a placeholder for an entity. XML contains several predefined entities The entity's name is prefixed with an ampersand (&) and ends with a semicolon (;). The following is a full list of redefined entities:

❑   The ampersand character (&) is defined as `&amp;`.

❑   The left bracket, or less than, character (<) is defined as `&lt;`.

❑   The right bracket, or greater than, character (>) is defined as `&gt;`.

❑   The single quote, or apostrophe, character (') is defined as `&apos;`.

❑   The double quote character (") is defined by `&quot;`.

Additional entities may be defined in a document's DTD — see the next section for more on DTDs.

Numeric character references are similar to entities. Instead of merely the & followed by the entity name and ending with the semicolon, a & and a # character are followed by a decimal or hexadecimal character representing a Unicode code point and a semicolon. For example, the & character may also be defined as `&#038;`.

DTD

A Document Type Definition (DTD) is the original syntax for XML. A DTD is inherited from SGML. Although a DTD is defined in the XML 1.0 standard, its use is limited for several reasons:

❏ DTDs lack support for new features of XML. For example, there is no support for namespaces.

❏ Not all parts of an XML document can be expressed within a DTD.

❏ DTDs use a syntax inherited from SGML, as opposed to an XML syntax.

XML Schema

The successor to DTDs is XML Schema. Another term for XML Schemas is XML Schema Definition (XSDs). XSDs are better suited for describing XML languages than DTDs. XSDs have some of the following features:

❏ Have datatyping support

❏ Allow for detailed constraints on a document's logical structure

❏ Are required for using XML in validation framework

❏ Use an XML-based format

Here is an example XML document for a test. In this example, the MenuSchema will be used to validate the menu XML document.

```
<?xml version="1.0" encoding="UTF-8"?>
<menu xmlns="http://my-example.com/menus"
xmlns:xsi="http://www.w3.org/2001/XMLSchema-instance"
xsi:schemaLocation="http://my-example.com/menus Menu2.xsd">
    <menuitem>
        <item>Hamburger</item>
        <cost>1.99</cost>
    </menuitem>
    <menuitem>
        <item>Drink</item>
        <cost>.99</cost>
    </menuitem>
    <menuitem>
        <item>Fries</item>
        <cost>.49</cost>
    </menuitem>
</menu>
```

Here is an example XSD file that will validate that document:

```
<?xml version="1.0" encoding="UTF-8"?>
<xs:schema xmlns="http://my-example.com/menus"
xmlns:xs="http://www.w3.org/2001/XMLSchema" targetNamespace="http://my-
example.com/menus" elementFormDefault="qualified"
attributeFormDefault="unqualified">
<xs:element name="menu">
    <xs:annotation>
        <xs:documentation>Menu is the root element</xs:documentation>
    </xs:annotation>
    <xs:complexType>
        <xs:sequence>
            <xs:element name="menuitem" maxOccurs="unbounded">
```

```
                    <xs:complexType>
                        <xs:sequence>
                            <xs:element name="item" type="xs:string"/>
                            <xs:element name="cost" type="xs:decimal"/>
                        </xs:sequence>
                    </xs:complexType>
                </xs:element>
            </xs:sequence>
        </xs:complexType>
    </xs:element>
</xs:schema>
```

In this example code, the menuitem is validated. The <item> tag is validated as a string, which is fairly easy to validate, and the <cost> tag is validated as a decimal. Within the <menu> tag, there are multiple copies of the <menuitem> tag that are allowed. Above the <menuitem> tag is the <menu> tag.

Try It Out   Validating XML

Given that there is some XML and the need to validate the XML, take a look at some code to validate the XML in a .NET 2.0 application. In this example, the code creates an XmlSchemaSet object. This object holds the contents of the XML Schema file. An XmlReaderSettings object is created. This object holds the XML Schema and any other settings necessary for reading the XML feed. The XmlReader document is created from XML feed and the XmlReaderSettings object. Once the XmlReader object is created, any errors that occur when reading the XML document are raised and passed to the XmlReaderSettings' ValidationEventHandler method. In this example, the user is notified in a label.

ASPX page
```
<form id="form1" runat="server">
<div>
Load Result: <asp:Label ID="lblLoadResult" runat="server" Text=""></asp:Label>
</div>
</form>
```

Code-Behind
```
protected void Page_Load(object sender, EventArgs e)
{
    System.Xml.XmlReaderSettings xmlRDS = new System.Xml.XmlReaderSettings();
    System.Xml.Schema.XmlSchemaSet sc = new System.Xml.Schema.XmlSchemaSet();
    sc.Add("http://my-example.com/menus", Server.MapPath("Menu2.xsd"));
    xmlRDS = new System.Xml.XmlReaderSettings();
    xmlRDS.ValidationEventHandler += new
System.Xml.Schema.ValidationEventHandler(xmlRDS_ValidationEventHandler);
    xmlRDS.ValidationType = System.Xml.ValidationType.Schema;
    xmlRDS.Schemas.Add(sc);
    System.Xml.XmlReader xmlRd =
System.Xml.XmlReader.Create(Server.MapPath("Menu2.xml"), xmlRDS);
    while (xmlRd.Read())
    {
    }
}
private void xmlRDS_ValidationEventHandler(object sender,
System.Xml.Schema.ValidationEventArgs e)
```

```
{
    this.lblLoadResult.Text = "Validation Error: " + Convert.ToString(e.Message) +
"<br />";
}
```

The `XmlReaderSettings` object specifies the settings used in reading in some XML. This object is used with the static `.Create()` method when an `XmlReader` object is created. The properties to note are the `ValidationType`, which is set from an enumeration, and the `Schemas` property, which is based on the `SchemaSet` object. The `XmlSchemaSet` object contains a set of XML Schemas to validate against. If the XML is not valid based on the schema, an `XmlSchemaException()` is generated.

Parsing XML

Two popular types of XML processing exist — the Document Object Model (DOM) and the Simple API for XML (SAX). The key difference between these two approaches is that the first loads the entire XML document into an in-memory data structure, whereas the latter iterates over the XML document one piece at a time in a forward-only, read-only fashion.

DOM Parsing

The Document Object Model (DOM) is an API that allows access to XML and HTML documents and their elements. The DOM is programming-language- and platform-independent.

Typically, XML parsers have been developed that must make use of a tree structure will all elements fully loaded into the parser before any operations occur. As a result, DOM is best used for applications where the document elements are randomly accessed and manipulated.

There are several levels of DOM specification. These specification levels are:

❑ **Level 0** — A Level 0 DOM contains all of the vendor-specific DOMs that existed before the W3C standardization process.

❑ **Level 1** — A Level 1 DOM allows for the navigation of documents and modification of their content.

❑ **Level 2** — A Level 2 DOM contains support for XML namespaces, filtered views, and events.

❑ **Level 3** — A Level 3 DOM consists of support for:

    ❑ DOM Level 3 Core

    ❑ DOM Level 3 Load and Save

    ❑ DOM Level 3 XPath

    ❑ DOM Level 3 Views and Formatting

    ❑ DOM Level 3 Requirements

    ❑ DOM Level 3 Validation

For further information on the DOM, please refer to Chapter 3.

SAX Parsing

Simple API for XML (SAX) parsing is another form of processing of XML files. A SAX-based parser handles XML as a single stream of data that is available only unidirectionally. As a result, accessing previously used data will result in the XML stream being reread and reparsed.

SAX processing is based on asynchronous events. In this model, as the XML document is read and parsed, events are fired as set up by the program. This is believed to result in faster XML processing than the DOM, because of a much smaller memory footprint compared to using a fully loaded and parsed DOM tree. Truthfully, the speed comparison should be based on a specific program, so generalities like this do not hold up in all situations. The other problem with SAX, which is more significant than the unidirectional issues, is the event-driven programming model. Accurately creating an event-driven program can be very complicated and frustrating.

XML Summary

As you have noticed, XML can be a very complicated topic. In this section, we have attempted to cover the basic topics that you need regarding what XML is, but this is not meant to be a complete reference for XML, just a set of basic information. For more complete information, please reference the books mentioned at the beginning of the chapter. In the next section, we will look at the processing XML with a technology referred to as XSLT.

XSLT

Extensible Stylesheet Language Transformations (XSLT) is an XML-based language used to convert XML from one format to another. These other formats may be a different XML Schema, HTML, plain text, PDF, or some other format. XSLT grew out of the Extensible Stylesheet Language (XSL) development effort within the W3C. The XSLT specification was first published by the W3C as a recommendation on November 16, 1999.

How Processing Occurs

The XSLT language is declarative. Being declarative means that the XSLT stylesheet is made up of a set of templated rules. Each rule in the collection specifies what to add to the resulting output, and the result is then sent to the output. Once an XSLT processor finds a node that meets the processing conditions, instructions within the template rules are processed sequentially.

The XSLT specification defines a transformation in terms of source and results. This keeps from locking a developer into a set of system specific APIs.

XSLT uses the X Path language for identifying the appropriate data in the source tree. X Path also provides a range of functions that assist XSLT processing.

Now take a look at some example XSLT coding. First, consider the following sample XML:

```
<?xml version="1.0" encoding="UTF-8" ?>
<menuitem xmlns:xsi="http://www.w3.org/2001/XMLSchema-instance"
xsi:noNamespaceSchemaLocation="MenuSchema.xsd">
    <item>Hamburger</item>
    <item>French Fries</item>
    <item>Milk Shake</item>
    <cost>4.99</cost>
</menuitem>
```

Suppose that from this code you want to pull out the elements within the `<item>` tags. The following XSLT code will pull out a list of items.

```
<?xml version="1.0" encoding="UTF-8" ?>
<xsl:stylesheet version="1.0" xmlns:xsl="http://www.w3.org/1999/XSL/Transform"
xmlns="http://www.w3.org/1999/xhtml">
    <xsl:template match="/item">
        <xsl:apply-templates />
    </xsl:template>
    <xsl:template match="item">
        <xsl:value-of select="." />
        <br />
    </xsl:template>
    <xsl:template match="cost" />
</xsl:stylesheet>
```

This code works by looking for the matches for the `<item>` tag, pulling them out, and sending them to the output stream. With the .NET Framework, there is an XML Transform control. By setting the control's `DocumentSource` and `TransformSource` properties, the control may be used to easily output the results of an XML file being transformed by an XSLT file. The result of this XML file being transformed by the XSLT file is Figure 5-3.

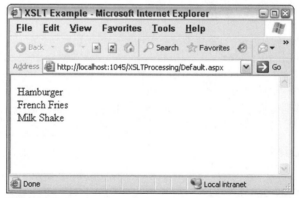

Figure 5-3

Figure 5-4 shows how XSLT processing occurs at a high level.

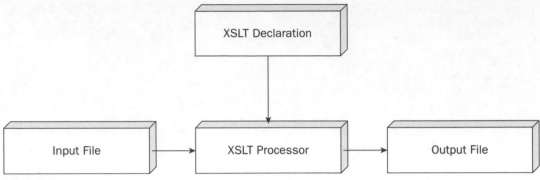

Figure 5-4

XSLT processing occurs in the following steps:

1. The XSLT stylesheet is loaded by the XML parser.

2. The XSLT stylesheet is converted into a tree of nodes. These nodes are also referred to as a *stylesheet tree*.

   a. XSLT stylesheet errors are detected.

   b. `Include` and `import` commands are handled.

3. The XML input is loaded by the parser and converted into a tree of nodes.

4. Whitespace only text nodes are removed from the stylesheet tree.

5. Whitespace-only text nodes are removed from the source tree.

6. The stylesheet tree is supplemented with built-in template rules for default processing.

7. The root node of the source tree is processed along with child nodes.

   a. The template rule that best matches a node is processed.

   b. Template rules are created. Elements are treated as instructions and their semantics are interpreted. Elements and text nodes in the template rules are copied specifically into the result tree.

8. The result tree is serialized, if necessary, according to any provided `xsl:output` instructions.

Built-In Functions

Like many of programming languages, XSLT provides a set of built-in commands. These commands range from string processing to date processing and looping operators, such as a `for` loop structure. In this section, we will look at some of the functions built into XSLT processors. These functions provide the basics upon which many XSLT operations are built.

XSLT <template>

The `<xsl:template>` element is used along with the `match` attribute to build templates and to associate them with XML elements.

```
<xsl:template match="item" />
```

In this example function, the XSLT processor will search for the node named `"item"`. If a match is made, then additional functionality is performed.

XSLT <value-of>

The XSLT `<xsl:value-of>` element is used to extract the value of an XML element. The extracted value is then added to the output's stream of the transformation. Consider the following example:

```
<xsl:value-of select="item" />
```

This code will pull the data from the `item` element of an XML file, and then add that value to the stream of the transform's output.

XSLT <for-each>

The XSLT `<xsl:for-each>` element is used to provide looping support in XSLT. Take a look at the following example:

```
<xsl:for-each select="item" />
    <xsl:value-of select="." />
</xsl:for-each>
```

This example will pull all the `item` nodes from the specified node set and return the value of the current node to the XSLT stream.

XSLT <sort>

The XSLT `<sort>` element is used to assist the `<xsl:for-each>` element in sorting the node set produced by the `<xsl:for-each>` element.

XSLT <if>

The `<xsl:if>` element is used to test the content of an XML file, much like the `if/endif` of a traditional computer programming language. Take a look at the following example:

```
<xsl:if test="cost &gt; 1.00">
..........
</xsl:if>
```

This `if/endif` are often used for conditional tests. With these tests, program execution can be altered based on these tests. If the condition is true, the commands within the `<xsl:if></xsl:if>` are executed. In this example, if the cost node has a value of greater than `1.00`, the code between the `<xsl:if>` and `</xsl:if>` is executed.

XSLT <choose>

The `<xsl:choose>` element is used along with `<xsl:when>` and `<xsl:otherwise>` to perform multiple conditional tests. Consider the following code:

```
<xsl:choose>
    <xsl:when test="expression">
    ..........
    </xsl:when>
    <xsl:otherwise>
```

```
          . . . . . . . . . . .
        </xsl:otherwise>
    </xsl:choose>
```

In this example, the expression is tested. When the `expression` is true, the code within the `<xsl:when></xsl:when>` tags is executed. If not code is executed, the processing will drop out to the `<xsl:otherwise></xsl:otherwise>` tags and execute within those tags.

Processing with XSLT

Now that you have looked at some of the main XSLT directives, take a look at some more complicated examples of processing XSLT. In this example, you are going to perform some string processing, conditional processing, and mathematical processing in some examples.

String Processing

String processing is something that is very common to modern programming languages, and XSLT is no different. It has a number of built-in string processing commands. These commands allow for the searching of strings, returning the location of characters within strings, and other processing functions. You will use the following XML file:

```
<?xml version="1.0" encoding="UTF-8"?>
<employees xmlns:xsi="http://www.w3.org/2001/XMLSchema-instance">
    <Name>John Jones</Name>
    <Name>Mike Smith</Name>
    <Name>William Skakespeare</Name>
    <Name>Wally McClure</Name>
</employees>
```

You need to perform several operations on this XML code. These operations include getting the length of the name, parsing for the first name of the employee, and parsing for the last name of the employee. The following XSLT file will perform these operations:

```
<?xml version="1.0" encoding="UTF-8" ?>
<xsl:stylesheet version="1.0" xmlns:xsl="http://www.w3.org/1999/XSL/Transform"
xmlns="http://www.w3.org/1999/xhtml">
    <xsl:template match="/">
        <table border='1'>
            <tr>
                <th>
                    Employee Name:
                </th>
                <th>
                    Length of Name:
                </th>
                <th>
                    First Name:
                </th>
                <th>
                    Last Name:
                </th>
```

```
            </tr>
            <xsl:apply-templates />
        </table>
    </xsl:template>
    <xsl:template match="Name">
        <tr>
            <td>
                <xsl:value-of select="." />
            </td>
            <td>
                <xsl:value-of select="string-length(.)" />
            </td>
            <td>
                <xsl:value-of select="substring-before(., ' ')"/>
            </td>
            <td>
                <xsl:value-of select="substring-after(., ' ')"/>
            </td>
        </tr>
    </xsl:template>
</xsl:stylesheet>
```

The XML and XSLT file can be processed by using an XML control like this:

```
<asp:Xml ID="XMLStringExample" runat="server" DocumentSource="XMLStringTest.xml"
         TransformSource="XMLStringTest.xslt">
```

In this example, a table is created. Each row contains four columns.

❑   The first column is the name of the employee. This is pulled straight from the <name> tag.

❑   The second column contains the length of the employee's name.

❑   The third column contains all of the employee names before the first space.

❑   The final column contains all of the employee names after the first space.

This example assumes that the format for the names is first name, space, and then last name.

Figure 5-5 displays the output of the example XML file being processed by the XSLT file.

Employee Name:	Length of Name:	First Name:	Last Name:
John Jones	10	John	Jones
Mike Smith	10	Mike	Smith
William Skakespeare	19	William	Skakespeare
Wally McClure	13	Wally	McClure

Figure 5-5

For a listing of the methods available for string processing in XSLT, review Appendix A.

Try It Out   Numeric Processing

XSLT also possesses the ability to perform standard mathematical operations like many other programming languages. These operations can range from the simple addition and subtraction to ceiling, floor, and rounding.

Take a look at the following XML file:

```
<?xml version="1.0" encoding="utf-8" ?>
<numbers xmlns:xsi="http://www.w3.org/2001/XMLSchema-instance">
   <a>9</a>
   <b>24.6</b>
   <c>-1</c>
   <d>4.3</d>
   <e>5</e>
</numbers>
```

You are going to process the numbers in this set and perform several operations on them — displaying data, performing a sum on the nodes, performing a modulo operation, and finally running through a conditional to output a string depending on whether or not the processed value is negative. The XSLT file that follows will process the preceding numeric XML file and output the numeric values.

```
<?xml version="1.0" encoding="UTF-8" ?>
<xsl:stylesheet version="1.0" xmlns:xsl="http://www.w3.org/1999/XSL/Transform"
xmlns="http://www.w3.org/1999/xhtml">
   <xsl:template match="/">
      <table border='1'>
         <tr>
            <th>
               a
            </th>
            <th>
               b
            </th>
            <th>
               c
            </th>
            <th>
               d
            </th>
            <th>
               e
            </th>
            <th>
               sum of numbers
            </th>
            <th>
               a mod e
            </th>
            <th>
               Is (a-b) negative or positive
            </th>
         </tr>
         <xsl:apply-templates />
```

```
            </table>
        </xsl:template>
        <xsl:template match="numbers">
            <tr>
                <td>
                    <xsl:value-of select="a" />
                </td>
                <td>
                    <xsl:value-of select="b" />
                </td>
                <td>
                    <xsl:value-of select="c" />
                </td>
                <td>
                    <xsl:value-of select="d" />
                </td>
                <td>
                    <xsl:value-of select="e" />
                </td>
                <td>
                    <xsl:value-of select="sum(*)"/>
                </td>
                <td>
                    <xsl:value-of select="a mod e"/>
                </td>
                <td>
                    <xsl:choose>
                        <xsl:when test="(a - b) &gt; 0">
                            positive
                        </xsl:when>
                        <xsl:when test="(a - b) &lt; 0">
                            negative
                        </xsl:when>
                        <xsl:otherwise>
                            0
                        </xsl:otherwise>
                    </xsl:choose>
                </td>
            </tr>
            <br />
        </xsl:template>
    </xsl:stylesheet>
```

The XML and XSLT file may be processed by using an XML control like this:

```
<asp:Xml ID="XmlNumericExample" runat="server"
DocumentSource="XMLNumericExample.xml"
            TransformSource="XMLNumericExample.xslt">
```

Figure 5-6 shows the output of the numeric XML file after it has been processed by the numeric XSLT file.

- ❑ The first five columns display the values from the XSLT file.

- ❑ The sixth column displays the sum of the numbers.

- ❑ The seventh column displays a modulo e.

119

❑ The last column shows a combination of conditional tests, `<xsl:choose>` and `<xsl:when>` tags, as well as testing using less than and greater than commands.

a	b	c	d	e	sum of numbers	a mod e	Is (a-b) negative or positive
9	24.6	-1	4.3	5	41.9	4	negative

Figure 5-6

For more information on the processing functions built into XSLT, please refer to Appendix A on XSLT elements.

Writing Functions in XSLT

The XSLT processor in the .NET Framework and MSXML component support only the XSLT version 1 standard. This standard version makes it a little bit hard to write functions within XSLT. However, these components support the ability to write custom business logic. The ability to write these custom business objects is provided by extending XSLT, using traditional programming languages, such as VBScript, JavaScript, or any .NET-support language. Given the widespread acceptance of JavaScript, these examples use JavaScript to extend XSLT.

XSLT extensions are mostly specific to a given processor. For more comprehensive examples, please refer to the documentation provided by the XSLT processor that is being used.

XSLT 1.0 provides two types of extensions.

❑ **Extension elements**, which include such things as `xsl:transform`, `xsl:template`, and the like.

❑ **Extension functions**, which include `string`, `substring`, and the like.

XSLT 1.0 has a template base model. XSLT processors need information to distinguish between static content and extension elements. This can be accomplished by some commands that the processor recognizes. The code that follows shows an example:

```
<xsl:transform version"1.0" xmlns:xsl=http://www.w3.org/1999/XSL/Transform
xmlns:out=http://www.w3.org/1999/xhtml
xmlns:ext=http://exampleurl/extension
extension-element-prefixes="ext">
<xsl:template match="/">
   <out:html>
      <ext:ExampleFunction/>
   </out:html>
</xsl:template>
</xsl:transform>
```

This example shows the very basics of calling an external function in XSLT. The `xml` namespace for output is defined by the `xmlns:out` attribute and the extension's namespace is added through the `xmlns:ext` attribute. The output is formatted for HTML through the `<out:html>` tag, and a call is made to the external `ExampleFunction` through the `<ext:ExampleFunction/>` tag. This example calls out to an external function using the MSXML calling convention.

X Path

The XML Path Language (X Path) is a non-XML syntax for addressing parts of an XML document. X Path has been adopted by developers as a simple query language. X Path is a sequence of steps to get from one set of nodes to another set of nodes. The steps are separated by a slash (/) character. Each step is made up of the following parts:

- ❑ **Axis Specifier** — The Axis Specifier indicates a navigation direction. The axes available are:
  - ❑ child
  - ❑ attribute
  - ❑ descendant-or-self
  - ❑ parent
  - ❑ ancestor
  - ❑ ancestor-or-self
  - ❑ following
  - ❑ precending
  - ❑ following-sibling
  - ❑ self
  - ❑ namespace
- ❑ **Node Test**
- ❑ **Predicate**

In X Path:

- ❑ The root element is defined by /*.
- ❑ All elements are defined as //*.
- ❑ All top-level elements are defined as /*/*.

Therefore, an example X Path expression can look like /CustomerOrder/Item. This will select all of the nodes that are named Item and a child of CustomerOrder.

A more complex expression might be specified as: /CustomerOrder/Item/following-sibling::*[1]. This expression selects all elements that are below the Item node and indicates the Item node is a child of the CustomerOrder node.

In X Path, the expression @ can be used to get at the attribute axis. For example, the expression //Item[@price > 2] selects the Item nodes that have an attribute of price that is greater than the value of 2.

Try It Out   X Path Example

In this Try It Out, you take a look at X Path processing using one of the menu examples. In this example, you are going to search for the <item> tag of one of the Menu2.xml file's menuitems. Take a look at the example code in C# and ASP.NET:

```
System.Xml.XPath.XPathDocument document = new
System.Xml.XPath.XPathDocument(Server.MapPath("Menu2.xml"));
System.Xml.XPath.XPathNavigator navigator = document.CreateNavigator();
System.Xml.XPath.XPathNodeIterator nodes =
navigator.Select("//menu/menuitem[cost=.49]/item");
while (nodes.MoveNext())
{
    Response.Write(nodes.Current.Value);
}
```

In this code, the `item` tag of the `menutitem` will be returned if the cost of the item is set to `.49`. The code works by creating an X Path DOM document and loading it with the contents of the `Menu2.xml` file. The next step is to create the `XPathNavigator` object. The X Path expression is passed though the `XPathNavigator`'s `.Select()` method and returns a collection of nodes that can then be iterated through.

Now, take a look at the XML file that you are working with for this example:

```
<?xml version="1.0" encoding="UTF-8"?>
<menu>
    <menuitem>
        <item>Hamburger</item>
        <cost>1.99</cost>
    </menuitem>
    <menuitem>
        <item>Drink</item>
        <cost>.99</cost>
    </menuitem>
    <menuitem>
        <item>Fries</item>
        <cost>.49</cost>
    </menuitem>
</menu>
```

From the XML feed, you can see that the only `menuitem` that matches the cost of `.49` is the `Fries` item and that is the only result that is returned from the sample X Path code.

Integrating XML and Ajax

Now that we've covered XML, we come to the inevitable question — how do we integrate this with Ajax? It's actually a fairly simple process if your development team has its own library or needs to debug something that is occurring in an existing library.

Take a quick look at some code. In this example, you are using the Sarissa client-side library to perform the communication back to the server. For the callback to the server, you get a list of people in an XML format. This is put within an XML `DomDocument`. In this example, the code is loaded synchronously, but it could be loaded asynchronously with a callback. You have created a string holding the XSLT commands. This string is put within an `XSLTProcessor()` object. The final steps are to use the XSLT object to transform the XML `DomDocument` and to then output the data to the browser.

```
<script language="javascript" src="SarissaLibrary.js">
<script language="javascript">
var xsltProc = new XSLTProcessor();
var xsltDoc = Sarissa.getDomDocument();
var xsltStr = "<?xml version=\"1.0\" encoding=\"UTF-8\" ?>" +
    "<xsl:stylesheet version=\"1.0\"
xmlns:xsl=\"http://www.w3.org/1999/XSL/Transform\"
xmlns=\"http://www.w3.org/1999/xhtml\">" +
    "<xsl:template match='/'>" +
        "<table border='1'>" +
            "<tr>" +
                "<th>" +
                    "Employee Name:" +
                "</th>" +
            "</tr>" +
            "<xsl:apply-templates />" +
        "</table>" +
    "</xsl:template>" +
    "<xsl:template match=\"Name\">" +
        "<tr>" +
            "<td>" +
                "<xsl:value-of select=\".\" />" +
            "</td>" +
        "</tr>" +
    "</xsl:template>" +
    "</xsl:stylesheet>";
xsltDoc = (new DOMParser()).parseFromString(xsltStr, "text/xml");
xsltProc.importStylesheet(xsltDoc);
function SimpleExample() {
    var xmlDoc = Sarissa.getDomDocument();
    xmlDoc.async = false;
    xmlDoc.load("XMLStringTest.xml");
    var newDocument = xsltProc.transformToDocument(xmlDoc);
    document.write(Sarissa.serialize(newDocument));
}
SimpleExample();
```

Figure 5-7 shows the output of the preceding example.

Figure 5-7

JSON

As indicated earlier in the chapter, JSON is the JavaScript Object Notation, and it is a lightweight data interchange format. JSON's chief advantage over XML is that the data may be parsed fairly easily using JavaScript's built-in `eval()` method. And although JSON has JavaScript in the name, it may actually be used by various languages.

Layout of JSON

JSON's usefulness is in the area of data interchange, and in some ways it is similar to XML. However, there are some key conceptual differences. Whereas XML is conceptually similar to working with databases and is designed to primarily work with sets of data, JSON is conceptually similar to arrays and collections in procedural programming languages. That means JSON is designed to be easily usable from within a procedural programming language.

JSON is built on the following data structures:

❑   **Name/value pairs** — This may be called an object, record, structure (struct), HashTable, keyed list, or associated array.

❑   **List of values** — This list of values is referred to an array in most programming languages.

Take a look at the specific layout of JSON in the following table.

Name	Description
object	`{ }`
	`{ members }`
members	`string : value`
	`members , string : value`
array	`[ ]`
	`[ elements ]`
elements	`value`
	`elements , value`
value	`string, number, object, array, boolean, null`

With JSON, these items take on the following forms:

❑   An object is a set of name/value pairs. An object begins with a left brace (`{`) and ends with a right brace (`}`). Names are followed by a colon (`:`). Name/value pairs are separated by a comma (`,`).

❑   An array is a collection of values. Arrays start with a left bracket (`[`) and end with a right bracket (`]`). Values within an array are separated by a comma (`,`).

❑ A value may be one of several datatypes. If it is a string, it will be contained within double quotation marks. Other datatypes supported within an array are numbers, booleans, null, objects, and arrays.

❑ A string is a collection of Unicode characters wrapped within double quotation marks. Characters may be escaped by using the forward slash character (/).

JSON Example

Take a look at some data encoded in JSON:

```
{'Tables':[{
'Name':'Table1','Rows':[
{'tblStateId':1,'State':'Tennessee'},
{'tblStateId':2,'State':'Alabama'}]}],
'getTable':function(n){return _getTable(n,this);}}
```

This example text displays the textual representation of an ADO.NET dataset. In this JSON object, there is a table with two rows. There are two columns. These columns are tblStateId and State. Row 1 contains tblStateId:1 and State:Tennessee. Row 2 contains tblStateid:2 and State:Alabama.

Now you can look at the JavaScript code to actually use a JSON object. This JavaScript code runs in Internet Explorer and uses the Sarissa client-side JavaScript library. It will pull data from a local web server and then create an object based on a JSON object.

```
var xmlhttp = new XMLHttpRequest();
function clickme(){
    xmlhttp.onreadystatechange= myHandler
    xmlhttp.open("GET", "GetData.aspx", true);
    xmlhttp.send(null);
}
function myHandler() {
    if ( xmlhttp.readyState == 4 ) // READYSTATE_COMPLETE is 4
    {
    var strObj = xmlhttp.responseText;
    var obj;
    eval("obj=" + strObj);
    for(m in obj)
        alert(m);
    }
}
```

In this example, an XMLHTTP object is created and a request is sent to the web server. When the request comes back, an object is created from the returned data and the properties of that object that are available are displayed in a pop-up window to the user.

The example that is shown uses the Sarissa library. This library is discussed in Chapter 9.

Summary

In this chapter, you examined several topics related to data communication.

- ❑ **XML** — XML contains the raw data of a data transfer. It is human- and computer-readable in a language-independent format.

- ❑ **XSLT** — XSLT is used to transform information from one XML format into another.

- ❑ **X Path** — X Path is used to navigate within an XML/XSLT document.

- ❑ **JSON** — JSON is a human- and computer-readable data interchange format that is less complex then XML.

These topics form an important basis for heterogeneous communications, such as that used in Ajax and between a web client and a web server. Knowing how XML, XSLT, and JSON are structured can be very valuable as a basis of a custom Ajax library, for getting data between a web client and a web server, or for being able to diagnose a problem in an existing library.

You can find more on the topics discussed in this chapter at the following sites:

- ❑ **Wikipedia** — `http://en.wikipedia.org/wiki/XML`

- ❑ **"SGML Source" by Charles F. Goldfarb** — `www.sgmlsource.com`

- ❑ **World Wide Web Consortium (W3C)** — `www.w3c.org`

- ❑ **W3 Schools web site** — `www.w3schools.org`

- ❑ **JSON web site** — `www.crockford.com/JSON`

What Is Built into ASP.NET

ASP.NET 2.0 contains an incredible amount of enhancements over ASP.NET 1.0 and 1.1. The ASP.NET team has attempted to address various areas that required improvement in previous versions, and the inclusion of Ajax-style functionality is one of those areas.

ASP.NET 2.0 contains a technology called Asynchronous Client Script Callbacks, or simply *callbacks* for a shortened name. As the name suggests, this offers the ability for ASP.NET to directly support the inclusion of JavaScript code that enables asynchronous calls to the server for processing — that is, to execute a server method asynchronously from within the browser and have ASP.NET instruct the browser to execute a JavaScript *callback* method when the server method completes.

In this chapter, you take a look at:

❑ Server controls included with ASP.NET V2.0 that support asynchronous callback functionality

❑ Enabling your pages to support asynchronous behavior using callbacks in ASP.NET V2.0

❑ Using advanced techniques to develop controls that support asynchronous behavior, using client callbacks

Out-of-the-Box Controls

Before you delve into the fundamentals and implementation of these features, it is important to note that some web controls that ship with ASP.NET come with the ability to support callback functionality. Specifically, these controls are the:

❑ `TreeView`

❑ `GridView`

❑ `DetailsView`

These controls come with simple boolean properties that enable the use of asynchronous callbacks in a browser-friendly way, without the need to know or write any JavaScript at all.

Again, before the chapter gets too technical, have a look at how easy it is to make use of Asynchronous Client Script Callbacks by using some of the controls that support this technology natively.

TreeView Control

The TreeView control allows hierarchical navigation over any datasource. A very common use of this control is to act as a navigation control for web sites. This is easily achieved by binding the TreeView control to a SiteMapDataSource control. However, for the purposes of this example you are interested in the built-in ability to provide asynchronous callback functionality to your applications. Examine the following simple ASP.NET page:

Try It Out   **TreeView Control Utilizing Asynchronous Client Script Callback Support**

```
<%@ Page Language="C#" AutoEventWireup="true"  CodeFile="TreeView.aspx.cs"
Inherits="_Default" %>

<!DOCTYPE html PUBLIC "-//W3C//DTD XHTML 1.0 Transitional//EN"
"http://www.w3.org/TR/xhtml1/DTD/xhtml1-transitional.dtd">

<html xmlns="http://www.w3.org/1999/xhtml" >
<head runat="server">
    <title>Treeview Asynchronous Example</title>
</head>
<body>
    <form id="form1" runat="server">
    <div>
         <asp:XmlDataSource ID="XmlDataSource1" runat="server"
DataFile="TestXMLFile.xml">
        </asp:XmlDataSource>
        <asp:TreeView ID="TreeView1" runat="server" DataSourceID="XmlDataSource1"
ExpandDepth="1">
        </asp:TreeView>
    </div>
    </form>
</body>
</html>
```

This page contains a TreeView control and an XmlDataSource control. The XmlDataSource control provides data from an XML file named TestXMLFile.xml. This file has the following contents:

```
<?xml version="1.0" encoding="utf-8" ?>
<root>
    <Node1>
        <Data1>
            <MoreNodes1 />
            <MoreNodes2 />
            <MoreNodes3 />
            <MoreNodes4 />
        </Data1>
        <Data2 />
    </Node1>
    <Node2>
        <Data3>
```

```
                <More1 />
                <More2 />
                <More3 />
                <More4 />
                <More5 />
            </Data3>
            <Data4 />
        </Node2>
        <Node3>
            <Data5 />
            <Data6 />
        </Node3>
        <Node4>
            <Data7 />
            <Data8 />
        </Node4>
    </root>
```

How It Works

From the example data shown in the preceding block, the nodes Node1, Node2, Node3, and Node4 will be displayed by the TreeView control. When one of these nodes is clicked or selected, the TreeView requests the subnodes for the selected node from the datasource. By default, when the TreeView control is dropped onto a page using Visual Studio .NET 2005, asynchronous callback functionality is enabled. The EnableClientScript property determines this behavior and is set to true by default. The effect that this has is that when a node within the TreeView is clicked and that node has some subnodes within it that need to be loaded from the datasource, an asynchronous callback is performed to retrieve the data or list of subnodes in this case. The user does not see the web page postback to the server. If you were to change the preceding web page code so that the markup for the TreeView control looked like:

```
<asp:TreeView ID="TreeView1" runat="server" DataSourceID="XmlDataSource1"
ExpandDepth="1" EnableClientScript="False"></asp:TreeView>
```

this would then tell the TreeView control to *not* attempt to use client script to retrieve the extra data it requires. Each time a node is expanded in this case, you would notice that the browser performs a post-back. Obviously, causing a postback is not as seamless an experience as performing a callback, where no user experience interruption is seen.

All the JavaScript required to invoke the necessary asynchronous callback method is controlled via the use of the EnableClientScript boolean property. No JavaScript knowledge or effort is required on the part of the developer.

Code samples for this chapter are available for download at http://beginningajax.com.

GridView Control

The GridView control has its roots in the DataGrid control in ASP.NET 1.0/1.1 that was used extensively to render tabular data. The GridView control is still used to render tabular data but has some more advanced features and makes extensive use of ASP.NET 2.0 new features and functionality.

Again, for purposes of this example, you are concerned with the asynchronous behavior that this control provides for you. Unlike the `TreeView` control, which had asynchronous callback functionality enabled by default, the `GridView` control does not have asynchronous behavior enabled by default. You will have a look at why this is the case after examining a simple Try It Out. Consider the code that follows.

Try It Out   **GridView Control Utilizing Asynchronous Client Script Callback Support**

```
<%@ Page Language="C#" AutoEventWireup="true" CodeFile="GirdView.aspx.cs"
Inherits="GridViewAsyncExample_GirdView" %>

<!DOCTYPE html PUBLIC "-//W3C//DTD XHTML 1.0 Transitional//EN"
"http://www.w3.org/TR/xhtml1/DTD/xhtml1-transitional.dtd">

<html xmlns="http://www.w3.org/1999/xhtml" >
<head runat="server">
    <title>GridView Asynchronous Example</title>
</head>
<body>
    <form id="form1" runat="server">
    <div>
        <asp:GridView ID="GridView1" runat="server" AllowPaging="True"
AutoGenerateColumns="False"
            DataSourceID="XmlDataSource1" EnableSortingAndPagingCallbacks="True">
            <Columns>
                <asp:BoundField DataField="BookTitle" HeaderText="BookTitle"
SortExpression="BookTitle" />
                <asp:BoundField DataField="Description" HeaderText="Description"
SortExpression="Description" />
                <asp:BoundField DataField="Comment" HeaderText="Comment"
SortExpression="Comment" />
            </Columns>
        </asp:GridView>
        <asp:XmlDataSource ID="XmlDataSource1" runat="server"
DataFile="~/GridViewAsyncExample/XMLFile.xml">
        </asp:XmlDataSource>
          

    </div>
    </form>
</body>
</html>
```

The simple page contains a `GridView` control and an `XmlDataSource`, which the `GridView` control uses to retrieve and manipulate its data to render. The data is again stored in an XML file, this time with the following contents:

```
<?xml version="1.0" encoding="utf-8" ?>
<rootNode>
  <data1 BookTitle="Some Interesting stuff" Description="Lots of interesting stuff"
Comment="Sort of interesting" />
  <data1 BookTitle="More Interesting stuff" Description="Even more interesting
stuff" Comment="Much more interesting" />
  <data1 BookTitle="Less Interesting stuff" Description="Less interesting stuff"
Comment="Not as interesting" />
```

```
   <data1 BookTitle="Big book" Description="A very big book" Comment="Too big" />
   <data1 BookTitle="Small Book" Description="A very small book" Comment="Too small"
/>
   <data1 BookTitle="Medium Book" Description="A medium sized book" Comment="Just
right" />
   <data1 BookTitle="Truthfull stories" Description="Its the truth!" Comment="You
know its true" />
   <data1 BookTitle="Lies, and why I never tell them" Description="Its all lies"
Comment="I dont believe any of it" />
   <data1 BookTitle="Fun stories" Description="Lots of fun" Comment="Heaps of fun"
/>
   <data1 BookTitle="Horror stories" Description="Very scary" Comment="I was too
scared to finish it" />
   <data1 BookTitle="Detective Stories" Description="Who dunnit?" Comment="Its a
real mystery" />
   <data1 BookTitle="Fantasy stories" Description="Its a real fantasy" Comment="Its
like living in a dream" />
   <data1 BookTitle="Drama stories" Description="Dramatic" Comment="I was riveted"
/>
   <data1 BookTitle="Action Stories" Description="Its all about action"
Comment="Heart pounding" />
</rootNode>
```

How It Works

Here you have a list of books, their descriptions, and a comment associated with each one. The GridView will render the list of books for the user to browse through. By default, sorting and paging is not enabled on the GridView control, so all the book entries are displayed on the web page. In many cases, paging is enabled to allow a smaller list of content to be displayed at any one time, but also to allow the user to advance that window or page to view more entries within the list. In this example, you have enabled paging by setting the AllowPaging property of the control to true. The GridView control also contains a PageSize property that determines how many entries are displayed per page when paging is enabled. By default this is 10, which is what this example uses.

When paging is enabled, the GridView displays a paging navigation bar at the bottom of the control to allow the user to select a different page to view. By default, when a new page is selected by the user, the GridView causes a postback to occur, so that the data for the next page can be retrieved by the server.

In the example, you will note that you set the EnableSortingAndPagingCallbacks property to true, and this is what is required to enable asynchronous callbacks for the GridView control. With this property enabled, each time the user clicks on the paging navigation bar to view a different page of data, *no* postback occurs, but rather an asynchronous callback is executed to perform this work on the server and return the results. The new page is then dynamically updated within the GridView control on the browser.

It may now be more apparent why this property is not enabled by default. The EnableSortingAnd PagingCalbacks property is applicable only if paging and/or sorting is enabled within the GridView control, and this functionality is *not* enabled by default. Therefore, enabling the EnableSortingAnd PagingCalbacks property by default would make no sense.

DetailsView Control

The DetailsView control also has very similar functionality to the GridView control. As with the GridView control, client-side callback functionality for the DetailsView control is initially disabled. If paging is enabled on the control, then the AllowPagingCallbacks property can be set to true to cause the control to execute its server-side paging functionality asynchronously from the browser.

Browser Compatibility

Microsoft has learned from its lessons of the past, and good cross-browser compatibility is one of the main goals of ASP.NET 2.0. All of the samples shown previously work across a majority of fifth genera-tion browsers, such as Internet Explorer 5.*x* and above, Mozilla/Netscape 6.*x* and above, Safari 1.2*x*, Opera 7.*x*, and Firefox.

From an application development perspective, it is also very easy to check whether the browser cur-rently accessing your application supports asynchronous client-side callbacks. There are two new boolean properties of the Browser object that are part of the request. These are the SupportsCallback and SupportsXmlHttp properties, and they indicate if the requesting browser supports asynchronous client callbacks and use of XMLHttpRequest object, respectively. They are part of the property collection of the Browser object, which itself is part of the Request object, and so can be accessed using the syntax Request.Browser.SupportsCallback and Request.Browser.SupportsXmlHttp. The properties can be easily examined to determine if the requesting browser supports the desired functionality, as shown in the following Try It Out.

Try It Out   Determining Client-Side Callback Support Using Server-Side Code

```
protected void Page_Load(object sender, EventArgs e)
{
    if (Request.Browser.SupportsCallback)
        lblCallbackMsg.Text = "This browser supports client side callbacks.";
    else
        lblCallbackMsg.Text = "This browser DOES NOT support client side
callbacks.";

    if (Request.Browser.SupportsXmlHttp)
        lblXmlHttpMsg.Text = "This browser supports XmlHttp (receiving XML over
HTTP).";
    else
        lblXmlHttpMsg.Text = "This browser DOES NOT XmlHttp (receiving XML over
HTTP).";
}
```

How It Works

The Request object (which is of type System.Web.HttpRequest) that is available to all pages has a Browser property (which is of type System.Web.HttpBrowserCapabilities) where you access the boolean properties SupportsCallback and SupportsXmlHttp.

❑ The `SupportsCallback` property checks for explicit support of the callback functionality used by ASP.NET 2.0 and looks for advanced script support such as the ability to invoke scripts upon completion of an asynchronous operation (that is, in callback mode).

❑ The `SupportsXmlHttp` property will return `true` only if the browser supports sending XML content over the HTTP channel.

The combination of asynchronous callbacks and the sending of well-formed XML content over HTTP provides a powerful method of communication when dealing with complex data, as you will see later in this chapter.

The Framework

So, you have seen some of the controls that natively support Asynchronous Client Script Callbacks, and you have seen how you can detect the support of this feature programmatically, but how do you customize it for use in your own applications and really harness its potential? The answer is twofold.

❑ First, there is a newly introduced interface named the `ICallbackEventHandler` interface. There is another interface called the `ICallbackContainer` interface that indicates that a class can generate its own script to invoke a callback, but it is not the primary interface used when dealing with Asynchronous Client Script Callbacks and will be detailed later in this chapter.

❑ Second, in a change from ASP.NET 1.0/1.1, all client scripting functions are now housed in a client script object (which is of type `System.Web.UI.ClientScriptManager`) that exists as a member within every ASP.NET page object. This houses the required functions to support the client-side generation and manipulation of JavaScript code, in particular to work in conjunction with your server-side methods to be called asynchronously.

ICallbackEventHandler Interface

The `ICallbackEventHandler` interface is the primary mechanism for enabling pages or controls to participate in the Asynchronous Client Script process. By implementing this interface within a control or page, server code can generate the relevant JavaScript code that allows asynchronous interaction between the client browser and the server. This interface has two methods associated with it:

Interface Method	Description
`string GetCallbackResult( );`	This method returns the result of the callback event/asynchronous call to the client browser.
`void RaiseCallbackEvent(string eventArgument);`	The method that is called asynchronously to handle the callback event. The `eventArgument` parameter contains any data passed in via the callback event/method.

A web control or web page that intends to provide support for Asynchronous Client Script Callbacks needs to implement this interface and provide implementations for the two interface methods described in the preceding table.

The reason there are two methods is to provide support for asynchronous datasources, a new feature in .NET 2.0. An asynchronous datasource will typically initiate a request to get data and then, at some later stage, process the results of the initial call when they become available. Having two methods to deal with asynchronous callbacks from the client provides this server-side support for asynchronous datasources.

These events are central to all callback events. This means that if a page implements this interface in order to act as the recipient for Asynchronous Client Script Callback events, the `RaiseCallbackEvent` method will be invoked for all client script callbacks defined within the page, whether one or one hundred. This has implications for complex situations where you have multiple ways of triggering a callback method from the client and multiple types of data associated with each event that are passed with each call. This will become more apparent as you examine some more complex scenarios that utilize Asynchronous Client Script Callback functionality.

Page.ClientScript — System.Web.UI.ClientScriptManager

In order for the server methods of the `ICallbackEventHandler` interface to be invoked on the server, a callback event must first be triggered by the client, which is the browser. Since almost everything dynamic on the browser is performed using JavaScript, you need to provide a method or register a method to perform this function.

One of the changes that ASP.NET 2.0 introduced was the centralization of all script-based management functions into a client script management object that is available to all ASP.NET pages. This includes client script registration functions that were present in ASP.NET 1.0/1.1 such as the `RegisterStartupScript` and `RegisterClientScriptBlock` method. These functions now exist as part of the `ClientScript` object that is now a member of the `Page` object. Previously, in ASP.NET 1.0/1.1, you accessed the client script functions as part of the `Page` object:

```
private void Page_Load(object sender, System.EventArgs e)
{
    Page.RegisterStartupScript("MyScript","<script
type='text/javascript'>alert('This is some Javascript');</script>");
}
```

With ASP.NET 2.0, this functionality is now accessed through the `ClientScript` object, which is part of the `Page` object. The `ClientScript` object is of type `System.Web.UI.ClientScriptManager`. The syntax differences are shown in the following example:

```
protected void Page_Load(object sender, EventArgs e)
{
    Page.ClientScript.RegisterStartupScript(this.GetType(), "MyScript",
"alert('This is some Javascript');", true);
}
```

Page.ClientScript.GetCallbackEventReference

In addition to the ASP.NET 1.0/1.1 script management functions, the asynchronous client script management functions also exist as part of this object. Of particular note is the `GetCallbackEventReference` method. This method allows a developer to obtain a reference to the JavaScript method that will trigger the asynchronous callback event. The method allows you to specify the name of the variables used to pass in event data and contextual data, as well as what client-side JavaScript methods to call when the asynchronous callback event completes. This method will throw an exception if the control or page in which it is executing does not implement the ICallbackEventHandler interface described in the previous section. The following code shows an example of using this method:

```
string js = Page.ClientScript.GetCallbackEventReference(this,
        "arg", "OnServerCallComplete", "ctx", true);
```

The first argument represents the object used to act as the recipient of the callback event. The arg parameter represents the name of the parameter used to pass the result of the callback event to the client-side JavaScript method. The OnServerCallComplete argument represents the name of the client-side JavaScript method that is called when the asynchronous callback event has completed execution. The ctx parameter represents the name of the context parameter that is passed to the client-side method (in this case OnServerCallComplete) when the asynchronous callback event completes. Finally, the true parameter indicates that the callback event reference returned should be executed in an asynchronous manner. The js string parameter holds a reference (in actual fact a block of JavaScript code) that is used to invoke the asynchronous client callback given the parameters specified. Given the preceding example, the js parameter would contain the following:

```
WebForm_DoCallback('__Page',arg,OnServerCallComplete,ctx,null,true);
```

Making All the Moving Parts Work Together

So far, you know that in order for a web page or control to participate in, or support, Asynchronous Client Script Callbacks, the ICallbackEventHandler interface must be implemented. In addition to implementing the two server-based methods of the ICallbackEventHandler interface, the page or control must utilize the script management functionality of the ClientScript object, which is part of every Page object, to register the requisite JavaScript that will trigger the asynchronous callback event. This initiates the asynchronous callback process.

Once the process has been initiated, client-side methods (JavaScript methods that exist within the web page) need to be supplied to act as the final endpoint where the asynchronous process returns its results for displaying or manipulation by the JavaScript code.

This process can be quite hard to grasp and that complexity contributes to the difficulty in being able to develop and debug applications that utilize asynchronous client scripting. It is important to be able to fully understand the entire process. As you proceed to integrate all the parts of the asynchronous process, it helps to visualize the flow of functionality. This is shown in Figure 6-1, which appears shortly in the chapter. Constant reference to this diagram as you proceed through the code samples can help in being able to follow the steps in the process flow.

Obtaining a Callback Reference

The first part of this process, as you have already seen, is retrieving a reference to a callback event within the browser to trigger the asynchronous call:

```
string js = Page.ClientScript.GetCallbackEventReference(this,
        "arg", "OnServerCallComplete", "ctx", true);
```

In order to make use of this to invoke a callback event, you must register it as a script block on the client. Although it is possible to register this block explicitly, it is generally better practice to encapsulate this script block in a simplified function to allow easy use by your client-side code. Consider the server-side code in the following example:

```
protected void Page_Load(object sender, EventArgs e)
{
    // Get our callback event reference
    string js = Page.ClientScript.GetCallbackEventReference(this,
        "arg", "OnServerCallComplete", "ctx", true);

    // Create a simplified wrapper method
    StringBuilder newFunction = new StringBuilder();
    newFunction.Append("function StartAsyncCall(arg, ctx) ");
    newFunction.Append("{ ");
    newFunction.Append(js);
    newFunction.Append(" } ");
    // Now register it
    Page.ClientScript.RegisterClientScriptBlock(this.GetType(), "NewAsyncMethod",
        newFunction.ToString(), true);
}
```

Using the preceding code, you have explicitly defined a JavaScript function called `StartAsyncCall` that accepts two parameters named `arg` and `ctx`. This function will invoke the JavaScript event generated by the call to the `GetCallbackEventReference` method, which itself invokes the asynchronous event.

Implementing the ICallbackEventHandler Interface

As already mentioned, you need to provide implementation for the methods defined in the `ICallback` `EventHandler` interface. For a simple implementation, consider the following implementation of the `ICallbackEventHandler` interface methods:

```
public string GetCallbackResult()
{
    return "Server method completed at: " + DateTime.Now.ToLongTimeString();
}

public void RaiseCallbackEvent(string eventArgument)
{
    System.Threading.Thread.Sleep(2000);
}
```

This simple example waits a period of 2 seconds before returning a string containing the date and time of the server.

This takes care of providing a way of initiating the asynchronous event (through getting a callback reference) and also providing an implementation for your asynchronous operation to execute on the server side, but this is only half of the picture. You need a way to handle the result of this asynchronous event or process. To illustrate what the chapter has covered so far by way of implementation, Figure 6-1 shows the entire asynchronous callback process, with the specific areas that have already been covered indicated by shaded areas:

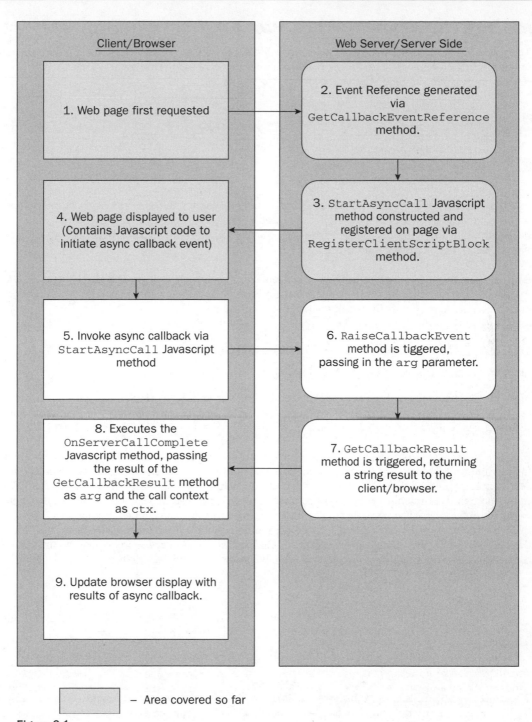

Figure 6-1

Initiating the Asynchronous Process from the Browser

The web page itself needs to initiate the asynchronous callback using the JavaScript method that has been constructed and registered using the asynchronous client script framework. This is easily accomplished in the following HTML fragment:

```
<form id="form1" runat="server">
<div>
    <input type="button" onclick="StartAsyncCall('some text','my context');"
value="Initiate Async Call" />
</div>
</form>
```

In the preceding code, the onclick event of the button is executing the StartAsyncCall method passing in 'some text' as an argument to the function and a string 'my context' to represent the contextual data of the call. The StartAsyncCall method is the method you constructed and registered using the Page.ClientScript object methods earlier.

At this stage, the asynchronous call has now been executed and will trigger the RaiseCallbackEvent method on the server (which was defined earlier). Shortly thereafter, the GetCallbackResult method is also executed and the result is sent back to the client/page.

Handling the Result of Asynchronous Server-Side Call on the Client

Now that the asynchronous call has been executed, the server-side processing has been performed, and the results have been sent back to the client browser, you must have a way of receiving and processing those results. This represents the final step in the asynchronous process, as shown in Figure 6-2.

In the earlier server-side code, you used the Page.GetCallbackEvenReference method to obtain the JavaScript event that triggers the asynchronous event, but that also provided the ability to specify the name of a JavaScript method that receives the result of the asynchronous call. This event is automatically called upon successful completion of the asynchronous server-side process. In the earlier example, this method was named OnServerCallComplete. This method simply needs to be defined (with a corresponding implementation) within the web page. This is the method that processes the result of the server-side call on the client and typically updates the web page or performs some other action in response to this data. A simple example implementation of this method is shown in the following example:

```
<script type="text/javascript">
function OnServerCallComplete(arg,ctx)
{
    alert("Async Call completed. Returned: [" +arg+"] Context Value: [" + ctx +
"]");
}
</script>
```

The preceding example simply displays a dialog box showing the result of the server-side call, as passed in via the arg parameter, and also the context data passed with the server-side operation, passed in the via the ctx parameter. These parameter names were also registered through the Page.GetCallback EvenReference method shown earlier.

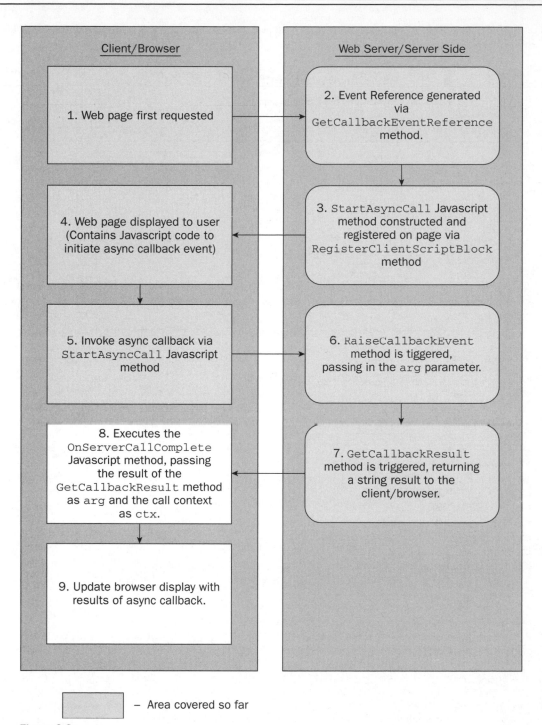

Figure 6-2

This completes this simplistic asynchronous callback process. To bring this all together, the complete listing of the web page and the associated server-side code is shown in the following code listing.

Simple Asynchronous Client Script Callback Example

Web Page (GetCallbackEventReferenceExample.aspx):

```
<%@ Page Language="C#" AutoEventWireup="true"
CodeFile="GetCallbackEventReferenceExample.aspx.cs"
Inherits="GetCallbackEventExample_GetCallbackEventExample" %>

<!DOCTYPE html PUBLIC "-//W3C//DTD XHTML 1.0 Transitional//EN"
"http://www.w3.org/TR/xhtml1/DTD/xhtml1-transitional.dtd">

<html xmlns="http://www.w3.org/1999/xhtml" >
<head runat="server">
    <title>GetCallbackEventReference Example Page</title>

    <script type="text/javascript">
    function OnServerCallComplete(arg,ctx)
    {
        alert("Async Call completed. Returned: [" +arg+"] Context Value: [" + ctx +
"]");
    }
    </script>
</head>
<body>
    <form id="form1" runat="server">
    <div>
        <input type="button" onclick="StartAsyncCall('some text','my context');"
value="Initiate Async Call" />
    </div>
    </form>
</body>
</html>
```

Server-Side Code (GetCallbackEventReferenceExample.aspx.cs):

```
using System;
using System.Data;
using System.Configuration;
using System.Collections;
using System.Web;
using System.Web.Security;
using System.Web.UI;
using System.Web.UI.WebControls;
using System.Web.UI.WebControls.WebParts;
using System.Web.UI.HtmlControls;
using System.Text;

public partial class GetCallbackEventExample_GetCallbackEventExample :
System.Web.UI.Page, ICallbackEventHandler
{
    protected void Page_Load(object sender, EventArgs e)
    {
```

```
            // Get our callback event reference
            string js = Page.ClientScript.GetCallbackEventReference(this,
                "arg", "OnServerCallComplete", "ctx", true);

            // Create a simplified wrapper method
            StringBuilder newFunction = new StringBuilder();
            newFunction.Append("function StartAsyncCall(arg, ctx) ");
            newFunction.Append("{ ");
            newFunction.Append(js);
            newFunction.Append(" } ");
            // Now register it
            Page.ClientScript.RegisterClientScriptBlock(this.GetType(),
"NewAsyncMethod",
                newFunction.ToString(), true);
        }

        #region ICallbackEventHandler Members

        public string GetCallbackResult()
        {
            return "Server method completed at: " + DateTime.Now.ToLongTimeString();
        }

        public void RaiseCallbackEvent(string eventArgument)
        {
            System.Threading.Thread.Sleep(2000);
        }

        #endregion
    ]
```

So, now you have a fully functional, albeit very simple, implementation of Asynchronous Client Script Callbacks. The server-side methods in this example are extremely simple and would not normally have any problems or generate any exceptions, but in a normal application where complexity is much higher, this is a very real consideration. Luckily, the asynchronous client script framework provides a mechanism for handling this.

Handling Errors in the Asynchronous Process

When an error occurs on the server, this usually means an exception has been thrown. Obviously, some way of identifying when an exception has occurred and dealing with this on the client browser is required. In the same way that you defined a JavaScript method that is called on completion of the asynchronous process, you can define a JavaScript method that is called when an exception is raised on the server during your asynchronous callback. This is specified as an additional parameter in the call to the GetCallbackEventReference method, which is shown in the following example:

```
    string js = Page.ClientScript.GetCallbackEventReference(this,
            "arg", "OnServerCallComplete", "ctx","OnServerCallError", true);
```

The parameter that contains OnServerCallError identifies the name of the JavaScript method that is called when an exception occurs on the server. The number of parameters that this method requires is

almost identical to the method defined previously to cater for a successful call. The JavaScript implementation for the `OnServerCallError` method is shown here:

```
function OnServerCallError(err,ctx)
{
    alert("An error occurred! [" + err + "] Context passed in was [" + ctx + "]");
}
```

The first parameter `err` represents the message of the exception that was generated, and the `ctx` parameter represents the same context defined in previous examples.

To demonstrate this, the implementations of the server-side methods have been altered to explicitly
throw an exception in order to simulate an error condition. In the following example, the
`GetCallbackResult` method has been modified to throw an exception:

```
public string GetCallbackResult()
{
    throw new Exception("Whoa! This is a server side exception from
'GetCallbackResult'");
    return "Server method completed at: " + DateTime.Now.ToLongTimeString();
}
```

This time, when the button on the web page is clicked, the asynchronous process is initiated as expected.
However, the JavaScript error routine is now invoked, with the exception message being displayed,
along with the context data you defined earlier. This, the definition of JavaScript handler methods for
both a successful and an unsuccessful call, would typically be basic requirements for any production
system using the Asynchronous Client Script Callback techniques.

> *Although the preceding code example allows an exception to be handled by the browser for the purpose
> of demonstration, it is important that you properly handle all exceptions in your callback code. Normal
> exception-handling techniques should be used with a* try...catch *syntax. This way, only exceptions
> that are meant to be flowed and handled by the browser are allowed by your code. In addition, your
> server- side code can take action to prevent data corruption or undesired behavior before allowing the
> exception to be passed up to the client-side code.*

In the preceding example, the exception was generated from the `GetCallbackResult` method. The
JavaScript error handler method displayed the message of the exception as expected, but what if the exception were generated by the companion `RaiseCallbackEvent` server-side method? In the following example, the generation of the exception has been moved to the `RaiseCallbackEvent` method and removed
from the `GetCallbackResult` method. To aid this example and prevent confusion, the entire server-side
code listing is shown:

```
using System;
using System.Data;
using System.Configuration;
using System.Collections;
using System.Web;
using System.Web.Security;
using System.Web.UI;
using System.Web.UI.WebControls;
```

```csharp
using System.Web.UI.WebControls.WebParts;
using System.Web.UI.HtmlControls;
using System.Text;

public partial class
GetCallbackEventWithErrorHandlingExample_GetCallbackEventWithErrorHandlingExample :
System.Web.UI.Page, ICallbackEventHandler
{
    protected void Page_Load(object sender, EventArgs e)
    {
        // Get our callback event reference
        string js = Page.ClientScript.GetCallbackEventReference(this,
            "arg", "OnServerCallComplete", "ctx","OnServerCallError", true);

        // Create a simplified wrapper method
        StringBuilder newFunction = new StringBuilder();
        newFunction.Append("function StartAsyncCall(arg, ctx) ");
        newFunction.Append("{ ");
        newFunction.Append(js);
        newFunction.Append(" } ");
        // Now register it
        Page.ClientScript.RegisterClientScriptBlock(this.GetType(),
"NewAsyncMethod",
            newFunction.ToString(), true);
    }

    #region ICallbackEventHandler Members

    public string GetCallbackResult()
    {
        return "Server method completed at: " + DateTime.Now.ToLongTimeString();
    }

    public void RaiseCallbackEvent(string eventArgument)
    {
        System.Threading.Thread.Sleep(2000);
        throw new Exception("Whoa! This is a server side exception from
'RaiseCallbackResult'");
    }

    #endregion
}
```

The results from this are not what you might expect and are shown in Figure 6-3.

Figure 6-3

Here you can see that the exception message has been displayed, *in addition* to the result of the GetCallbackResult method. Both of the messages have been aggregated together, but separated by a pipe (|) character. What is happening is that the asynchronous client script framework is still calling both of the required methods of the ICallbackEventHandler interface, even though one of the methods generated an exception. The fact that one of the methods generates an exception does not preclude the execution of the other method. This is an important point because the GetCallbackResult method needs to be aware of any errors that have occurred during the execution of the RaiseCallbackEvent method and not blindly execute assuming that if execution reaches that method, then all previous program execution has occurred without error.

Dealing with Complex Data

In the previous examples, the result of the asynchronous callback server-side methods has been only a simple singular textual string result. The needs of applications are many, and the need to deal with more complex data is a common scenario, particularly where there is a need to return more than one result. As an example, suppose that you wanted to load the values of a drop-down list from a potentially long-running server-side query or operation. There might be many items to load into the drop-down list, and each item will typically have a value associated with it, which is returned when the user selects a particular option from the drop-down list.

To illustrate this scenario, the following web page contains a simple drop-down list and a span area that will contain the selected value from the drop-down list:

```
<%@ Page Language="C#" AutoEventWireup="true"
CodeFile="AsyncDropDownListExample.aspx.cs"
Inherits="AsyncDropDownListExample_AsyncDropDownListExample" %>

<!DOCTYPE html PUBLIC "-//W3C//DTD XHTML 1.0 Transitional//EN"
"http://www.w3.org/TR/xhtml1/DTD/xhtml1-transitional.dtd">

<html xmlns="http://www.w3.org/1999/xhtml" >
<head runat="server">
    <title>Asynchronous Drop Down List Example</title>

    <script type="text/javascript">
    function LoadListItems()
    {

    }
    </script>

</head>
<body onload="LoadListItems();">
    <form id="form1" runat="server">
    <div>
        <select id="ddlList" disabled="true">
            <option>(Loading values from the Server)</option>
        </select>
    </div>
    <hr />
```

```
      <div>
          <label>Value Selected: </label><span id="msg">{none}</span>
      </div>

      </form>
  </body>
  </html>
```

As already mentioned, the web page contains a drop-down list and an area to display the selected value, but it also contains a `LoadListItems` JavaScript method that is called when the page loads, via the `onload` event defined in the `body` element. This will be where the asynchronous server-side call is initiated to retrieve the items to be loaded in the drop-down list.

The initial state of the drop-down list will be disabled. This is because there will be no items to select until the list has been populated by your asynchronous operation.

Enabling the Page for Asynchronous Callbacks

The web page must be enabled for Asynchronous Client Script Callback support by implementing the `ICallbackEventHandler` interface and also by getting a callback event reference (in the form of a JavaScript method call) to initiate the request to the server side.

To obtain a callback event reference, you can use exactly the same mechanism and code that was listed previously. It is the implementation of the `ICallbackEventHandler` interface that will differ. The code for the server-side page implementation is shown in the following listing:

```csharp
using System;
using System.Data;
using System.Configuration;
using System.Collections;
using System.Web;
using System.Web.Security;
using System.Web.UI;
using System.Web.UI.WebControls;
using System.Web.UI.WebControls.WebParts;
using System.Web.UI.HtmlControls;
using System.Text;

public partial class AsyncDropDownListExample_AsyncDropDownListExample :
System.Web.UI.Page, ICallbackEventHandler
{
    private DataSet lookupData = null;

    protected void Page_Load(object sender, EventArgs e)
    {
        // Get our callback event reference
        string js = Page.ClientScript.GetCallbackEventReference(this,
            "arg", "OnServerCallComplete", "ctx", "OnServerCallError", true);

        // Create a simplified wrapper method
        StringBuilder newFunction = new StringBuilder();
```

```
            newFunction.Append("function StartAsyncCall(arg, ctx) ");
            newFunction.Append("{ ");
            newFunction.Append(js);
            newFunction.Append(" } ");
            // Now register it
            Page.ClientScript.RegisterClientScriptBlock(this.GetType(),
    "NewAsyncMethod",
                newFunction.ToString(), true);


        }

        #region ICallbackEventHandler Members

        public string GetCallbackResult()
        {
            // nothing to return yet
            return null;
        }

        public void RaiseCallbackEvent(string eventArgument)
        {
            // no implementation yet
        }

        #endregion
    }
```

You will notice that this code listing is almost identical to the previous example. An important difference at this point is the inclusion of the declaration of a private member variable of type `DataSet` named `lookupData`.

```
    private DataSet lookupData = null;
```

This is important because it will be used to store the lookup data across the two methods of the `ICallbackEventHandler` interface. However, the implementation of the interface methods will contain the majority of the custom code and be radically different from previous examples.

Obtaining the Data — Implementing the ICallbackEventHandler Interface

This example will attempt to simulate obtaining lookup values from a database, with associated ID values, for populating the drop-down list. Obtaining this data will be implemented in the `RaiseCallbackEvent` method. The `RaiseCallbackEvent` method is the first method that is invoked on the server side during the asynchronous callback process, and it makes sense to initiate the data retrieval request as soon as possible. The formatting and returning of that data will be implemented in the GetCallbackResult method. The separation of process into the two methods also separates the discrete process of data retrieval and formatting into more manageable units.

When you are dealing with data from a database, a common technique is to use a `DataSet` object to encapsulate that data. For this example, a `DataSet` will be used as the object returned from your database call. For simplicity, the data retrieval code will not actually query a database, but rather manually construct a

`DataSet` object with some data and simulate a lengthy database query. The implementation details of this method are not important and can be easily changed to match what is required in different applications. The following is the listing of the method itself:

```
private DataSet GetLookupValuesFromDatabase()
{
    DataSet ds = new DataSet();
    DataTable dt = new DataTable();

    DataColumn idCol = new DataColumn("ID", typeof(int));
    DataColumn nameCol = new DataColumn("Name", typeof(string));
    dt.Columns.Add(idCol);
    dt.Columns.Add(nameCol);
    dt.AcceptChanges();

    DataRow newRow = null;
    newRow = dt.NewRow();
    newRow[idCol] = 1;
    newRow[nameCol] = "Joe Bloggs ID#1";
    dt.Rows.Add(newRow);

    newRow = dt.NewRow();
    newRow[idCol] = 2;
    newRow[nameCol] = "Mr A. Nonymous ID#2";
    dt.Rows.Add(newRow);

    newRow = dt.NewRow();
    newRow[idCol] = 3;
    newRow[nameCol] = "Mrs N. Extdoorneighbour ID#3";
    dt.Rows.Add(newRow);

    newRow = dt.NewRow();
    newRow[idCol] = 4;
    newRow[nameCol] = "Mr. Pea Body ID#4";
    dt.Rows.Add(newRow);

    ds.Tables.Add(dt);
    ds.AcceptChanges();
    return ds;
}
```

The implementation of the `RaiseCallbackEvent` method may now look like the following:

```
public void RaiseCallbackEvent(string eventArgument)
{
    System.Threading.Thread.Sleep(2000);  // Simulate a delay
    lookupData = GetLookupValuesFromDatabase();
}
```

Notice how the results of the data retrieval routine `GetLookupValuesFromDatabase` are assigned to the private member variable `lookupData`.

With this in place, you can now utilize the returned data from the GetCallbackResult routine. Examine the following implementation of this method:

```csharp
public string GetCallbackResult()
{
    StringBuilder ids = new StringBuilder();
    StringBuilder names = new StringBuilder();

    int rowCnt = 0;
    int numRows = lookupData.Tables[0].Rows.Count;

    foreach (DataRow row in lookupData.Tables[0].Rows)
    {
        rowCnt++;

        ids.Append(row["ID"].ToString());
        if (rowCnt < numRows)  // Only append a separator if its NOT the last
element
            ids.Append("|");  // Include a data element separator character

        names.Append(row["Name"].ToString());
        if (rowCnt < numRows)   // Only append a separator if its NOT the last
element
            names.Append("|");  // Include a data element separator character
    }

    // Make one big string, separating the sets of data with a tilde '~'
    string returnData = string.Format("{0}~{1}", ids.ToString(), names.ToString());

    return returnData;
}
```

The preceding code loops through each row in the DataSet object that was previously assigned from the RaiseCallbackEvent method. The code then extracts each ID field value, adds it to a string (implemented by using a StringBuilder object for speed), and separates each value with a *pipe* (|) character. The code also does the same for the Name field values, but adds the pipe-separated values to a different string. Once this process is complete, and all values have been assigned to separate StringBuilder objects, there is a final step — that of creating a string that contains all of the pipe-separated ID values and pipe separated Name values, but with each set of data separated by yet another character, this time a *tilde* (~) character.

The reason the data is separated by these characters is that when this data is returned to the browser, JavaScript can easily split this string data into separate element arrays so that you can iterate over the array and load this data into your drop-down list. All that is required is explicit knowledge of what characters are used to delimit this data.

The pipe (|) and tilde (~) characters themselves are not important and were simply chosen because they are typically not used in string data. They can, however, be any character you choose.

The data that is returned to the browser, looks like the following:

```
1|2|3|4~Joe Bloggs ID#1|Mr A. Nonymous ID#2|Mrs N. Extdoorneighbour ID#3|Mr. Pea
Body ID#4
```

Dealing with the Returned Data on the Client

Now that the server side has been fully implemented, you must provide a way for the client routines to parse the string *blob* of data that is returned.

As in the previous examples, when the callback event reference was obtained during the `Page_Load` event on the server, the `OnServerCallComplete` and `OnServerCallError` JavaScript routines were specified as the recipient for the result of the successful and unsuccessful asynchronous calls, respectively. Consider the following implementations of these methods:

```
function OnServerCallComplete(arg, ctx)
{
    var idsAndNames = arg.split("~");
    var ids = idsAndNames[0].split("|");
    var names = idsAndNames[1].split("|");

    var htmlCode;
    var ddl = document.getElementById("ddlList");

    for (var i=0; i < ids.length; i++)
    {
        htmlCode = document.createElement('option');

        // Add the new <OPTION> node to our <SELECT> drop list
        ddl.options.add(htmlCode);

        // Set the <OPTION> display text and value;
        htmlCode.text = names[i];
        htmlCode.value = ids[i];
    }

    // Enable our drop down list as it
    // should have some values now.
    ddl.disabled = false;
}

function OnServerCallError(err, ctx)
{
    alert("There was an error processing the request! Error was [" + err + "]");
}
```

The `OnServerCallComplete` method first uses the `split` method, which is available as part of all JavaScript string objects, to separate the single string into a string array, using the specified character as the delimiter to denote the separation between elements. The `ids` string array contains all the `id` values of the data to select, and the `names` string array contains the corresponding textual descriptions to display in the drop-down list. These arrays are identical in length.

The code then obtains a reference to the control, as shown in the following line:

```
var ddl = document.getElementById("ddlList");
```

Using a *for loop* to iterate over each element of the ids array, you create a new selection option using the following line:

```
htmlCode = document.createElement('option');
```

This creates something like the following markup:

```
<option></option>
```

This is then added to the list of options for the drop-down list, and the corresponding id and textual display values are then assigned to this newly added drop-down list option. Once all the options have been added, the drop-down list is enabled by setting the disabled flag to false:

```
ddl.disabled = false;
```

The drop-down list is now populated with values from your asynchronous server-side call and ready for selection. To illustrate that the drop-down list has been populated correctly, the drop-down list has had its onchanged event assigned a JavaScript method to display the selected value, or ID of the textual selection element. The following is the complete code listing for both web page and server-side code.

Try It Out   A More Complex Asynchronous Client Script Callback Example

Web Page (AsyncDropDownListExample.aspx):

```
<%@ Page Language="C#" AutoEventWireup="true"
CodeFile="AsyncDropDownListExample.aspx.cs"
Inherits="AsyncDropDownListExample_AsyncDropDownListExample" %>

<!DOCTYPE html PUBLIC "-//W3C//DTD XHTML 1.0 Transitional//EN"
"http://www.w3.org/TR/xhtml1/DTD/xhtml1-transitional.dtd">

<html xmlns="http://www.w3.org/1999/xhtml" >
<head runat="server">
    <title>Asynchronous Drop Down List Example</title>

    <script type="text/javascript">
    function LoadListItems()
    {
        StartAsyncCall(null,null);
    }

    function OnServerCallComplete(arg, ctx)
    {
        var idsAndNames = arg.split("~");
        var ids = idsAndNames[0].split("|");
        var names = idsAndNames[1].split("|");

        var htmlCode;
        var ddl = document.getElementById("ddlList");

        for (var i=0; i < ids.length; i++)
        {
            htmlCode = document.createElement('option');
```

```
            // Add the new <OPTION> node to our <SELECT> drop list
            ddl.options.add(htmlCode);

            // Set the <OPTION> display text and value;
            htmlCode.text = names[i];
            htmlCode.value = ids[i];
        }

        // Enable our drop down list as it
        // should have some values now.
        ddl.disabled = false;
    }

    function OnServerCallError(err, ctx)
    {
        alert("There was an error processing the request! Error was [" + err +
"]");
    }

    function OnDropListSelectChanged()
    {
        var ddl = document.getElementById("ddlList");

        // Display selected value
        var msg = document.getElementById("msg");
        msg.firstChild.nodeValue=ddl.value;


    }
    </script>

</head>
<body onload="LoadListItems();">
    <form id="form1" runat="server">
    <div>
        <select id="ddlList" disabled="false"
onchange="OnDropListSelectChanged();">
            <option>(Loading values from the Server)</option>
        </select>
    </div>
    <hr />
    <div>
        <label>Value Selected: </label><span id="msg">{none}</span>
    </div>

    </form>
</body>
</html>
```

Server-Side Code (AsyncDropDownListExample.cs):
```
using System;
using System.Data;
using System.Configuration;
```

```
using System.Collections;
using System.Web;
using System.Web.Security;
using System.Web.UI;
using System.Web.UI.WebControls;
using System.Web.UI.WebControls.WebParts;
using System.Web.UI.HtmlControls;
using System.Text;

public partial class AsyncDropDownListExample_AsyncDropDownListExample :
System.Web.UI.Page, ICallbackEventHandler
{
    private DataSet lookupData = null;

    protected void Page_Load(object sender, EventArgs e)
    {
        // Get our callback event reference
        string js = Page.ClientScript.GetCallbackEventReference(this,
            "arg", "OnServerCallComplete", "ctx", "OnServerCallError", true);

        // Create a simplified wrapper method
        StringBuilder newFunction = new StringBuilder();
        newFunction.Append("function StartAsyncCall(arg, ctx) ");
        newFunction.Append("{ ");
        newFunction.Append(js);
        newFunction.Append(" } ");
        // Now register it
        Page.ClientScript.RegisterClientScriptBlock(this.GetType(),
"NewAsyncMethod",
            newFunction.ToString(), true);

    }

    #region ICallbackEventHandler Members

    public string GetCallbackResult()
    {
        StringBuilder ids = new StringBuilder();
        StringBuilder names = new StringBuilder();

        int rowCnt = 0;
        int numRows = lookupData.Tables[0].Rows.Count;

        foreach (DataRow row in lookupData.Tables[0].Rows)
        {
            rowCnt++;

            ids.Append(row["ID"].ToString());
            if (rowCnt < numRows)  // Only append a separator if its NOT the last
element
                ids.Append("|");  // Include a data element separator character

            names.Append(row["Name"].ToString());
            if (rowCnt < numRows)  // Only append a separator if its NOT the last
element
```

```
                    names.Append("|");   // Include a data element separator character
        }

        // Make one big string, separating the sets of data with a tilde '~'
        string returnData = string.Format("{0}~{1}", ids.ToString(),
names.ToString());

        return returnData;
    }

    public void RaiseCallbackEvent(string eventArgument)
    {
        System.Threading.Thread.Sleep(2000);   // Simulate a delay
        lookupData = GetLookupValuesFromDatabase();
    }

    #endregion

    #region GetLookupValuesFromDatabase helper method

    private DataSet GetLookupValuesFromDatabase()
    {
        DataSet ds = new DataSet();
        DataTable dt = new DataTable();

        DataColumn idCol = new DataColumn("ID", typeof(int));
        DataColumn nameCol = new DataColumn("Name", typeof(string));
        dt.Columns.Add(idCol);
        dt.Columns.Add(nameCol);
        dt.AcceptChanges();

        DataRow newRow = null;
        newRow = dt.NewRow();
        newRow[idCol] = 1;
        newRow[nameCol] = "Joe Bloggs ID#1";
        dt.Rows.Add(newRow);

        newRow = dt.NewRow();
        newRow[idCol] = 2;
        newRow[nameCol] = "Mr A. Nonymous ID#2";
        dt.Rows.Add(newRow);

        newRow = dt.NewRow();
        newRow[idCol] = 3;
        newRow[nameCol] = "Mrs N. Extdoorneighbour ID#3";
        dt.Rows.Add(newRow);

        newRow = dt.NewRow();
        newRow[idCol] = 4;
        newRow[nameCol] = "Mr. Pea Body ID#4";
        dt.Rows.Add(newRow);

        ds.Tables.Add(dt);
        ds.AcceptChanges();
```

```
            return ds;
    }

    #endregion
}
```

Limitations on Returning Complex Data in XML

The previous example demonstrates one way to deal with multiple elements of return data. Ultimately, any situation that demands that you return multiple elements of data must somehow be packaged and represented in a string format. One of the major limitations of asynchronous callbacks is the fact that all data returned from the server-side call must be packaged into a string.

In the previous example, which consisted of textual display elements and corresponding ID values, the elements were separated by special characters acting as data delimiters. An alternate way of representing data is, of course, using an XML document. XML is good at representing complex data structures, in particular hierarchical data structures. .NET has many ways to construct an XML document, and it is beyond the scope of this book to illustrate these techniques; however, DataSets can easily be represented as XML by using the WriteXML method of the DataSet object. Alternatively, the XMLDocument object can be employed to create an XML document from scratch.

Parsing XML data on the browser/client can be a little more work. DOM support for manipulation of XML documents is still not properly supported in all browsers and quite often, third-party libraries are required to properly support parsing of XML document, using such tools as X Path.

See Chapter 4 for more details on DOM XML support and handling XML data in the browser.

The main point to be aware of is that the nature of the data to be returned will play a huge part in dictating how the data should be formatted and packaged into a string for return to the client browser, where it is parsed and "unpacked."

ICallbackContainer Interface

This interface is a "companion" interface to the previously detailed ICallbackEventHandler interface and is for more advanced scenarios, typically where a custom control is required that supports asynchronous callback. An example is the GridView control that was detailed at the beginning of this chapter. For asynchronous callback operations, the ICallbackEventHandler interface is implemented in all cases; however, the ICallbackContainer interface is typically used only by controls that support asynchronous callbacks (although this is not strictly mandatory).

The ICallbackContainer interface has only one method, which has the following signature and parameters:

❑   **Method**—string GetCallbackString(IButtonControl control, string argument);

❑   **Description**—Creates a script for initiating a client callback to a web server. Essentially, this method returns a string that contains a JavaScript method or script that will initiate the asynchronous callback to the server when executed.

❑ **Parameters** —

    ❑ `IButtonControl control` — A reference to the control initiating the callback request.

    ❑ `string argument` — The arguments that are used to build the callback script. This parameter is passed to the `RaiseCallbackEvent` method that handles the callback and is part of the `ICallbackEventHandler` interface discussed previously. This essentially represents any context data that the caller wishes to pass to the method to aid in creation of the final output or return data.

As mentioned previously, this interface is typically implemented by control developers who are authoring controls that utilize the asynchronous callback functionality. This interface acts as a complement to the `ICallbackEventHandler` interface and actually makes use of the same techniques to emit the required script to initiate a callback.

The following code shows a sample implementation of this interface for a control that supports asynchronous callbacks.

Try It Out   **Implementing the ICallbackContainer Interface**

```
public string GetCallbackScript(IButtonControl buttonControl, string argument)
{
    // Prepare the input for the server code

    string arg = "ControlArgument";

    string js = String.Format("javascript:{0};{1};{2}; return false;",
        "__theFormPostData = ''",
        "WebForm_InitCallback()",
        Page.ClientScript.GetCallbackEventReference(
            this, arg, "MyControl_Callback", "null"));
    return js;
}
```

How It Works

To illustrate a complete server control design is an advanced scenario and is beyond the scope and intention of this book; however, an explanation of this implementation is warranted — in particular, the formatting of the JavaScript method. The following code:

```
javascript:{0};{1};{2}; return false;
```

effectively executes the JavaScript code that will be placed in the placeholder positions {0}, {1}, and {2}, until finally returning a `false` value. The `false` value being returned ensures that no further JavaScript processing takes place as a result of the event raised. For each placeholder element, a section of JavaScript is embedded.

First, the {0} placeholder represents the:

```
"__theFormPostData = ''"
```

JavaScript code, which simply resets a hidden variable to an empty value.

The {1} placeholder represents the:

```
"WebForm_InitCallback()"
```

JavaScript code, which collects and prepares the form data to post to the server for the callback to the server to be correctly interpreted and trapped by the ASP.NET runtime engine. This is crucial so that the correct server-side methods are executed in response to the callback event as expected.

Finally, the {2} placeholder represents the code:

```
Page.ClientScript.GetCallbackEventReference(
            this, arg, "MyControl_Callback", "null"));
```

This code should look familiar, and is the same method used to obtain a callback event reference in the initial page-centric examples detailed previously in the discussion of the `ICallbackEventHandler` interface. It is used for exactly the same purpose here, as the final step to initiate the asynchronous callback request to the server.

To summarize, the implementation of the `ICallbackContainer` method first constructs the arguments to send to the server-side callback request and returns a JavaScript block that first clears the posted data, initializes the collection of the posted data in the HTTP request (via `WebForm_InitCallback()`), and finally initiates the callback request by obtaining the callback event through the `Page.GetCallbackEventReference` method.

This section is not intended as a complete discussion on the specifics of implementing asynchronous callback functionality within your custom controls, but merely serves as an introduction on how to begin such a task with asynchronous callbacks in mind. The reader is encouraged to perform further investigation in this advanced topic area and in particular in the creation of custom controls.

Summary

This chapter has introduced the concept of Asynchronous Callback Client Scripts that are provided with ASP.NET 2.0. This feature allows a developer to utilize Ajax-like functionality within ASP.NET in a number of ways.

You looked at how you could include asynchronous callbacks in your applications by:

❑   Using "out-of-the-box" server controls that come included with ASP.NET

❑   Implementing the requisite interfaces to enable your pages to support asynchronous behavior using callbacks

❑   Working with advanced techniques to develop controls that support asynchronous behavior using client callbacks

By far the easiest way to do this is to use the existing controls shipped with ASP.NET 2.0 that support this functionality, such as the `GridView`, `DetailsView`, and `TreeView` controls. No JavaScript or explicit server-side coding is required to utilize asynchronous callbacks. Simply set some properties and let the controls do the rest.

For any custom behavior, the most common application will be implementing the `ICallbackEvent` `Handler` interface and crafting it to meet your applications requirements. In the examples shown in this chapter, you explored various ways to interact with the client-side code and server-side code, and in particular, examined ways of packaging custom data to transfer between the client and server side.

Finally, you engaged in a brief examination of the `ICallbackContainer` interface that is used for more advanced scenarios in the creation of custom controls that support asynchronous client script callback functionality.

Asynchronous Client Script Callbacks provide a framework to utilize Ajax-like functionality that is integrated with the server-side-centric development nature of ASP.NET. It is a powerful framework that is flexible, but does require some manual effort to customize to meet your applications requirements. Experimentation is the key to becoming adept at making this powerful feature set work the way you want it to.

It is worth mentioning here that the future of asynchronous client script callbacks actually lies in a technology that Microsoft is currently developing, code named Atlas. Atlas will make the implementation of asynchronous functionality on the client as well as the server significantly easier. It will consist of a vastly enhanced client-side framework, as well as tightly integrated server controls to make what has been demonstrated in this chapter achievable with far less effort and complexity.

Atlas technology will be covered in detail later in this book starting at Chapter 10.

Ajax.NET Professional Library

Every once in a while, a technology is extremely simplified with the introduction of new wrapper libraries. These libraries use existing technologies but make the development process easier to use by wrapping the sometimes difficult concepts into easier-to-use, more simplified concepts. So, the term *wrapper library* comes from having a library of code wrapped around existing technology. You can tell when a great wrapper library is released because of its instant popularity.

This chapter covers one such wrapper library known as the Ajax library for .NET. In this chapter and the next, we will show off the simplicity of talking back and forth between client browsers and your application server without page postbacks. We'll also dig a little under the hood of the library to show you how and why the library works.

This chapter shows you how to get started using the Ajax.NET Pro library. To get started, you'll set up a simple example and get it working. The following topics will be covered:

- ❑ Acquiring Ajax.NET Pro
- ❑ Adding a reference to the Ajax.NET Pro assembly
- ❑ Setting up the `Web.Config` to handle Ajax requests
- ❑ Registering the `page` class
- ❑ Writing methods in code-behind to be accessible on the client
- ❑ Examining the request
- ❑ Executing the Ajax method and getting a server response
- ❑ Digging into callbacks and context
- ❑ Trapping errors

When you have finished these examples, you will have completed your first implementation of the Ajax.NET Pro library. You will have successfully set up an ASP.NET page that uses the library to refresh parts of your page with data from the web server.

Acquiring Ajax.NET Pro Version 6.4.16.1

In Chapters 7 and 8, we're using and talking about Ajax.NET Pro version 6.4.16.1. As with all software, this library is evolving and continually being added to and upgraded. We've made the version 6.4.16.1 library available to you for downloading on our web site, http://BeginningAjax.com. You can download the version in one of two ways:

❑   *Compiled Library*, ready to use

❑   *Library Source Code*, must be compiled first

I would recommend that first you download the Compiled Library. This is a simple zip file that contains a single file named Ajax.NET. This is the already compiled library that is ready for you to start using as a reference in the next section. If you would like to have access to the source code, you can download the Library Source Code, which has all the source code files needed for you to do the compiling yourself; then the code can be embedded into your application.

Preparing Your Application

In order to prepare your application to use Ajax.NET Pro, follow these two steps:

1.   Add a reference to the Ajax.NET Pro library.

2.   Wire up the Ajax.NET Pro library in the Web.Config file so that your application can process the special requests created by the Ajax.NET Pro library.

Try It Out   **Preparing Your Application to Use Ajax.NET Pro**

1.   To use the Ajax.NET Pro library, your first step is to set a reference to the library. This allows you to use library functionality inside your application. Create a new web site in Visual Studio. Visual Studio 2005 automatically creates a Bin folder for you. Right-click on this folder and select Add Reference. Figure 7-1 shows the Add Reference dialog box. Select the Browse tab, and navigate to the AjaxPro.dll file that you downloaded (or compiled from the Library Source Code). Once this is selected, click the OK button, and you will have successfully referenced the Ajax.NET Pro library from your application.

2.   The Ajax.NET Pro library uses a page handler to process requests that come into the server from your client application. This page handler needs to be wired up to your application, and this is done by an inserting it into your Web.Config file. This code should be inserted in the <system.web> section of Web.Config:

```
<httpHandlers>
  <add verb="POST, GET" path="AjaxPro/*.ashx"
type="AjaxPro.AjaxHandlerFactory,AjaxPro" />
</httpHandlers>
```

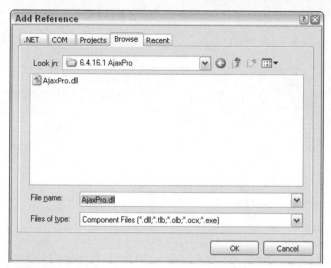

Figure 7-1

If you don't fully understand what an HTTP handler is, you're not alone. This code basically tells ASP.NET to take ownership of all requests that come into your web site with the path of /AjaxPro/ and have a file extension of .ashx, and then process that request with the Ajax.NET Pro library. Later you'll see JavaScript that is loaded dynamically from these *.ashx paths. When you see URLs like this, remember that they're being processed by the Ajax.NET Pro library.

You'll examine what is happening with those requests later in this chapter.

Using the Ajax.NET Pro Library

Now that your application is set up to use the Ajax.NET Professional library, you are ready to benefit from the ease of use the library offers. In Chapter 2, you saw how a JavaScript method could be used to change an image. In the first example here, you'll perform that same functionality, but instead of changing the image client side from left to right and back again, you'll ask the server for an image to display.

There are three steps required to use the Ajax.NET Pro library in your application:

1. First, you write the code that is going to be used in your image switching routine.

2. Second, you wire up that code to be used by the Ajax.NET Pro library.

3. Third, you execute that code from JavaScript.

So, your goal in this example is to switch an image by using JavaScript as you did in Chapter 2. However, the major difference will be that you ask the server for an image name, and the response from the server will become the src attribute of your image.

The server-side code that is responsible for switching the image looks like this:

ChangeImage Method for Code-Behind Page

```
public string ChangeImage(string input, string left, string right)
{
    //Get the image filename without the file extension
    string filename = System.IO.Path.GetFileNameWithoutExtension(input);
    //Check if the strings match, ignoring case
    if (string.CompareOrdinal(filename, left) == 0)
    {
        //if the strings match then send back the 'right' string
        return input.Replace(filename, right);
    }
    //strings did not match, send back 'left' string
    return input.Replace(filename, left);
}
```

The `ChangeImage` method accepts three parameters; an `input` string, which is the path of the current image that is loaded; a `left` string, which defines what the Left image `src` should be; and a `right` string, which defines the Right image `src`. Calling this method in code would look something like this:

```
MyImage.ImageUrl = ChangeImage(MyImage.ImageUrl, "ArrowLeft", "ArrowRight");
```

This is straightforward code that switches the image.

Try It Out   Placing the Image-Switching Code in Your Page

1. Create a page in the root of your web site called `ImageSwitcher.aspx`.

2. Right-click on this file, and select Use as Default, so that when you run your application, this is the page that will be shown in your browser. By default, Visual Studio creates an `ImageSwitch.aspx.cs` file for you.

3. Add `using AjaxPro;` with all the other using statements at the top of your page.

4. Open this file, and insert the `ChangeImage()` method just below your `Page_Load` method. Compile your project.

At this point, your project should compile with zero errors. If you do have compile errors, it's most likely because you haven't referenced the `AjaxPro` assembly correctly, as shown in Figure 7-1. If you run your project, you will not see any page output because you haven't done any UI work just yet. That will come later.

You have completed Step 1 in using the Ajax.NET Pro library in your application. However, the real magic in this example is in Step 2 — making that code accessible using JavaScript so that you can access this functionality in the client browser. This is very simple to do using the Ajax.NET Pro library, and that is just where you're going with this example. One of the nicest features of the Ajax.NET Pro library is that you can easily adapt your existing code without rewriting it. Yes, you read that correctly — you do not have to rewrite any of your code to make it available in your JavaScript. All you have to do is register your code with the Ajax.NET Pro library. That sounds kind of strange — register your code — doesn't it? The first two of the three steps in using the Ajax.NET library are the easiest to implement. And if your code is already written, this next step should take you only about 2 minutes. To make your code accessible using JavaScript, you first register your page class with the Ajax.NET Pro library. This class has method(s) on it that you want to expose to JavaScript. Then, you register the method you want to expose. This is all explained in the next two sections.

Registering Your Page for Ajax.NET Pro

Registering your page class with the Ajax.NET Pro library is what activates the library. This is the command that generates a JavaScript object that you can use on the client browser. Registering your page class is very simple and is done with just one line of code. This single line of code needs to be executed somewhere in the page's lifecycle and is generally inserted into the Page_Load method.

```
protected void Page_Load(object sender, EventArgs e)
{   AjaxPro.Utility.RegisterTypeForAjax(typeof(Chapter7_ImageSwitcher));
}
```

By default, your page class is the same as the page name that you assigned to the .aspx file, preceded by any folder structure that the file is in. In this case, the file ImageSwitcher.aspx is in a /Chapter7/ folder, so the name is automatically created as Chapter7_ImageSwitcher. This can get out of sync if you've used the rename function in Visual Studio. You can confirm your page class name in two places if your application is compiling.

❑   At the top of the .aspx page in the page directive, you'll see an Inherits attribute. This is your page class name.

```
<%@ Page Language="C#" Inherits="Chapter7_ImageSwitcher" %>
```

❑   The second place you can check your page class name is in the .cs file. The .cs file actually defines a partial class that is shared with the same class your .aspx page is inherited from. The class signature is the class name.

We bring this up only because if you rename an .aspx page, Visual Studio will rename the actual files, but it will not rename the page class.

```
public partial class Chapter7_ImageSwitcher: System.Web.UI.Page
```

Remember that C# is a case-sensitive, so imageswitcher is different from ImageSwitcher is different from imageSwitcher. If you've incorrectly cased the name, your application shouldn't compile.

Registering Your Methods for Ajax.NET Pro

Now that you've registered your page, the next step is to register your page methods. You can't have one without the other. You have to register a class that has Ajax.NET Pro method(s) on it. You've already added the ChangeImage() method to your ImageSwitch.aspx.cs file. Remember, I said you can call this code in JavaScript without rewriting any of it. Here is the magic of the library. Simply mark your method with an AjaxPro.AjaxMethod() attribute. If you've never used attributes before you're in for a great surprise. This is a simple way of decorating your existing code. Just add the following line preceding your ChangeImage() method:

```
[Ajax.AjaxMethod()]
```

So, your entire server-side `ImageSwitch.aspx.cs` code file should look like this:

Server Side — Chapter7_ImageSwitcher.aspx.cs

```
protected void Page_Load(object sender, EventArgs e)
{
    AjaxPro.Utility.RegisterTypeForAjax(typeof(Chapter7_ImageSwitcher));
}

[AjaxPro.AjaxMethod()]
public string ChangeImage(string input, string left, string right)
{
    //Get the image filename without the file extension
    string filename = System.IO.Path.GetFileNameWithoutExtension(input);
    //Check if the strings match, ignoring case
    if (string.CompareOrdinal(filename, left) == 0)
    {
        //strings match == send back 'right' string
        return input.Replace(filename, right);
    }
    //strings did not match, send back 'left' string
    return input.Replace(filename, left);
}
```

Violà! Step 2 of using the Ajax.NET Pro library in your application is done. You've now registered your `page` class, and that class has an `AjaxMethod()` in it. You can now access this method in JavaScript with a very standard syntax. Your JavaScript is going to be as simple as the following:

```
Chapter7_ImageSwitcher.ChangeImage(img.src, "ArrowLeft", "ArrowRight");
```

This line of code returns a `response` object that has a value of the URL that you want to set as the source of your image, pointing to either the left or the right image. Now you're ready to start writing the UI and the JavaScript, which is the last step in the three-step process to use the Ajax.NET Pro library.

Examining the Request Object

In the coming pages, you'll execute the preceding JavaScript line and work with the `response` object you'll get back from the JavaScript call. This object is very simple to work with and has only five properties: `value`, `error`, `request`, `extend`, and `context`. These are defined in the table that follows. All of these properties have a default value of null, so if they are never populated, you will get a client-side error if you try to use them. This is usually the culprit for the famous ever-so-unhelpful `undefined` error, as seen in Figure 7-2. It's good practice to check for null values just about everywhere. You'll see more of this as you move on, specifically under the section about trapping errors later in the chapter.

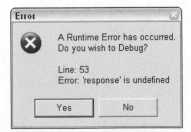

Figure 7-2

Property	Default Value	Description
response.value	null	The value is populated with what is returned from the server.
response.error	null	The error value is either null or the error string that was returned from the server. Normally you want this to be null, although, as you'll see, it can be a nice way to provide information to yourself about the client.
response.request	null	This is a copy of the original `request` object that was used to issue the request back to the server. This contains two very helpful properties: `method` and `args`. `method` is the original method name that was called, and `args` is an object describing all of the values passed into the method.
response.extend	null	The `extend` property is a JavaScript prototype that is added to all Ajax.NET Pro objects. It is used internally by the library to bind events and is not normally used.
response.context	null	The `context` is optional and can be used in certain situations to pass data along from one point to another. You'll see this in use later in the chapter, where it'll be easier to understand.

Executing Your Ajax on the Client

Building on the concept you learned from Chapter 2, you'll start this example with very similar HTML, as you see in the code that follows. The HTML preloads both the left and the right image. This is simply to make the switch faster once you get a response from the server. If you didn't preload these images in a hidden `<div>` tag, the end user would have to wait while the new image was downloaded from the server. You also have a `ChangeMe()` JavaScript function that does the work of actually changing the image. So, how does this `ChangeMe()` function get fired?

Client Side — Chapter7/ImageSwitcher.aspx

```
<script type="text/Javascript" language="Javascript">
function ChangeMe(target, leftName, rightName) {
    var response = Chapter7_ImageSwitcher.ChangeImage(target.src, leftName,
rightName);
    target.src = response.value;
}
</script>

<div style="DISPLAY:none;VISIBILITY:hidden">
    <!-- preload images -->
    <img src="images/ArrowLeft.gif" border="0" runat="server" ID="ImgPreload1">
    <img src="images/ArrowRight.gif" border="0" runat="server" ID="ImgPreload2">
</div>
<img onclick="ChangeMe(this,'ArrowLeft','ArrowRight')" src="images/ArrowLeft.gif"
border="0">
```

What Is a Language Proxy?

The term *proxy* is used when one language represents an object that has all the same properties (and sometimes method calls) as an object in another language. So, a JavaScript proxy object will mimic all the properties of the .NET object. This means you can easily use the same syntax in JavaScript that you would use in .NET. It is the job of the proxy object to talk back and forth between JavaScript and .NET. Proxy classes make your programming life easier because you don't have to worry about communication between the two languages or systems.

Think of a proxy class as a language interpreter, allowing you to communicate easily in your native language, while the proxy does all the interpreting for you to the other language.

Notice that the `<img>` tag has a JavaScript `onclick` attribute that points to your `ChangeMe()` function. You pass in three values: first, the `<img>` tag represented by the keyword `this`, followed by the left and right image names, `ArrowLeft` and `ArrowRight`.

The first line of the function calls into the Ajax.NET Pro library with the `Class.Method` naming convention. Remember, you registered your `page` class, which was named `Chapter7_ImageSwitcher`, and then you attributed your server-side `ChangeImage()` method with the `AjaxPro.AjaxMethod()` attribute. The Ajax.NET Pro library now makes a JavaScript object for you that is a proxy object used to communicate with your ASP.NET application.

This proxy object makes it possible for you to simply call the `Chapter7_ImageSwitcher.ChangeImage()` method, which looks like it's executing your server-side code right inside your JavaScript. What's actually happening is that the proxy object uses the same signature and naming conventions that your server-side code uses, making it look transparent when you call your server code from JavaScript.

When the end user clicks the image, the `ChangeMe()` function is called. The first thing you do is build a response variable that will hold the return value of your `Chapter7_ImageSwitcher.ChangeImage()` method. Notice that you also pass in the appropriate parameters to your server-side method to the proxy. Finally, you get back a value from the server in the `response.value` property, and that becomes the new source value of the image, which is the new URL of the image to be used.

This is the same client-side effect that you saw in Chapter 2, changing the image from left to right when the user clicked the image. However, this time the value came from the server. Although this example is pretty basic, it is very important because what you've really built so far is the ability to use Ajax.NET Pro between the client browser and your ASP.NET server to return a single string from the server and then update the client page.

Imagine the possibilities here. You could return the HTML of an entire datagrid and update the `innerHTML` of a `div` tag. With a little Dynamic HTML (DHTML) you can change the style of a `div` or `span` tag and create some very powerful features using just what you've learned so far.

Digging into response.value

In the first example, you received a string in the `response.value` property. This was the string name of the image `LeftArrow` or `RightArrow` that you used to set the image source to change the image from right to left. Strings can be very helpful and are a very common datatype to be passed back to the client from the server. Imagine using HTML in your return strings. What if you rendered an entire control, such as a datagrid, to its HTML and then returned that HTML as your string value. With this logic, it's pretty easy to magically load a datagrid client side. The code that follows is used to render a control to HTML. The next example then builds a datagrid, and you can easily adapt these examples to any control to get its rendered HTML. The reason that this works is that all controls have a `RenderControl()` method.

RenderControlToHtml() — Getting the HTML String from a Control

```
public string RenderControlToHtml(Control ControlToRender)
{
    System.Text.StringBuilder sb = new System.Text.StringBuilder();
    System.IO.StringWriter stWriter = new System.IO.StringWriter(sb);
    System.Web.UI.HtmlTextWriter htmlWriter = new
System.Web.UI.HtmlTextWriter(stWriter);
    ControlToRender.RenderControl(htmlWriter);
    return sb.ToString ();
}
```

Rendering a Datagrid

```
[AjaxPro.AjaxMethod()]
public string CreateNewDataGrid()
{
    DataGrid myDataGrid = new DataGrid();
    myDataGrid.ShowHeader = false;
    myDataGrid.DataSource = BuildMultiplicationTable();
    myDataGrid.DataBind();
    return RenderControlToHtml(myDataGrid);
}

public DataTable BuildMultiplicationTable()
{
    //Build a Data Table with 11 cells
    DataTable myTable = new DataTable();
    for (int i = 1; i < 11; i++)
        myTable.Columns.Add(new DataColumn(i.ToString()));

    //Populate 10 rows with a 10X10 multiplication chart
    for (int i = 1; i < 11; i++)
    {
        DataRow row = myTable.NewRow();
        for (int j = 1; j < 11; j++)
        {
            row[j-1] = i*j;
        }
        myTable.Rows.Add(row);
    }

    return myTable;
}
```

Using strings will get you moving quickly on your project. After all, just about anything can be converted to a string, but as you'll see in the next section, it's also nice to be able to return custom objects. Ajax.NET Pro has support out of the box for the following .NET types. Any type on this list can be returned from your server side function to your client side call with no additional programming.

❑   Strings

❑   Integers

❑   Double

❑   Boolean

❑   DateTime

❑   DataSet

❑   DataTable

All the types in this list are pretty easy to understand with exception of the last two items. What would you do with a DataSet in JavaScript on the client? What about a DataTable? Well, it turns out that you would do pretty much the same thing as you would on the server. You do not have Databind() operations as you would on the server, but you do have a DataTable.Tables array, each table has a Rows array, and finally, each row has properties that are inline with the original table column names.

Try It Out   **Building an HTML Table from a DataTable Object**

The following code gets a DataTable, server side, and draws an HTML table on the client.

Client Code — Building an HTML Table from a DataSet

```
<script type="text/javascript" language="javascript">
function BuildHtmlTable() {
    var response = Chapter7_BuildHtmlTable.BuildMultiplicationTable();
    if(response.value != null && response.value.Rows.length>0) {
        var datatable = response.value;
        var table = new Array();
        table[table.length] = '<table border=1>';
        for(var r=0; r<datatable.Rows.length; r++) {
            var row = datatable.Rows[r];
            table[table.length] = '<tr>';
            for(var c=0; c<datatable.Columns.length; c++) {
                table[table.length] = '<td valign=top>' + row[c+1] + '</td>';
            }
            table[table.length] = '</tr>';
        }
        table[table.length] = '</table>';
        document.getElementById("DynamicTable").innerHTML  = table.join('');
    }
}
function ClearHtmlTable() {
    document.getElementById("DynamicTable").innerHTML = '';
}
//-->
</script>
<form id="form1" runat="server">
```

```
<p>Chapter 7 :: Build Html Table.<br />
    <a href="#" onclick="ClearHtmlTable()">Clear Html Table</a><br />
    <a href="#" onclick="BuildHtmlTable()">Build Html Table</a>
</p>
<div id="DynamicTable"></div>
</form>
```

Server Code — Returning a DataTable

```
protected void Page_Load(object sender, EventArgs e)
{
    AjaxPro.Utility.RegisterTypeForAjax(typeof(Chapter7_BuildHtmlTable));
}


[AjaxPro.AjaxMethod()]
public DataTable BuildMultiplicationTable()
{
    //Build a Data Table with 11 cells
    DataTable myTable = new DataTable();
    for (int i = 1; i < 11; i++)
        myTable.Columns.Add(new DataColumn(i.ToString()));

    //Populate 10 rows with a 10X10 multiplication chart
    for (int i = 1; i < 11; i++)
    {
        DataRow row = myTable.NewRow();
        for (int j = 1; j < 11; j++)
        {
            row[j - 1] = i * j;
        }
        myTable.Rows.Add(row);
    }
    return myTable;
}
```

Notice that the last line in the client code block is an empty <div> tag named DynamicTable. When the hyperlink "Build Html Table" is clicked, the JavaScript function BuildHtmlTable() is called. In the server-side code, the page class name is Chapter7_BuildHtmlTable, and the server side method that returns a DataTable is BuildMultiplicationTable(). So, inside the JavaScript function BuildHtmlTable(), you can call Chapter7_BuildHtmlTable.BuildMultiplicationTable(). Then in the response.value, you'll get back an object that is very similar to a server-side DataTable, with Rows and Columns properties. As with the DataTable object, Ajax.NET Pro also has a DataSet object that can be used just as easily.

Returning Custom Objects

So, what about custom objects? Suppose that you have a person class, and the person has name, street, city, state, zip, and phone number properties. Can you return this person from your function and have it magically converted for you? Luckily, the answer is yes — but there is a catch. The custom class that you're returning needs to be registered, just like the page class needed to be registered (you'll see why this needs to happen in Chapter 8), and the custom class needs to be marked with a Serializable() attribute. The code block in this section shows the partial code for the custom person class, just showing the name and street properties. To use this class as a return type, it would need to be registered, and the proxy class will automatically be processed by the Ajax.NET Pro library.

```
Ajax.Utility.RegisterTypeForAjax(typeof(Person));
```

The only down side to this is that the automatic conversion is one-way. It allows for you to serialize your .NET objects to JavaScript Object Notation (JSON as described in Chapter 5) for use in JavaScript, but it does not allow you to use the `Person` class as an input value from JavaScript back to .NET. It is possible to send this `Person` class back to .NET (maybe as a parameter), but it's not automatic. You'll look at how to get a custom class back to .NET form JavaScript in Chapter 8.

A Simple Person Class Marked with [Serializable()] Attribute

```
[Serializable()]
public class Person
{
    public Person()
    { }

    private string _Name;
    public string Name
    {
        get { return _Name; }
        set { _Name = value; }
    }

    private string _Street;
    public string Street
    {
        get { return _Street; }
        set { _Street = value; }
    }
}
```

More Advanced Callbacks and Context

The preceding method of using the Ajax.NET Pro library is great, but it's worth going to the next step here. Did you notice that the way the response is requested was inline in your code? What if it took 10 seconds to execute your method and get a response back to the client? That means your browser would be locked and waiting for the response to come back, and nothing else could happen while you were waiting. This, as you've encountered previously in this book, is called *synchronous* execution. There is a very simple way to make this code execute *asynchronously*, which is to say that the request will be fired, but you're not going to wait for the response. Instead you're going to tell the Ajax.NET Pro library what to do with the response once it is returned. This is accomplished with a callback routine. A *callback* is simply another function that can be called where the response can be passed in.

Take a look at a minor difference in this JavaScript `ChangeMe()` function, and compare it to the one earlier in the chapter in the "Executing Your Ajax on the Client" section.

```
function ChangeMe(target, onName, offName) {
    Chapter7_ImageSwitcherCallback.ChangeImage
            (target.src, onName, offName, ChangeMe_Callback, target);
}
```

Notice the number of parameters that you're passing into the `ImageSwitcher.ChangeImage()` method. There are now five parameters, where before there were only three. The server-side method accepts only three, so how can this work? Remember that this is actually a JavaScript proxy object that is created by the Ajax.NET Pro library for you to use. Every proxy object that is created is created with a couple of overloads. An *overload* is a variation of a method using the same method name but with a unique set of parameters known as a *signature*. The signature is defined as the order and types of the parameters the method accepts. The proxy object `Chapter7_ImageSwitcher.ChangeMe()` gets created with the following signatures.

❑   `Chapter7_ImageSwitcher.ChangeImage(string, string, string)`

❑   `Chapter7_ImageSwitcher.ChangeImage(string, string, string, callback)`

❑   `Chapter7_ImageSwitcher.ChangeImage(string, string, string, callback, context)`

Notice the last two parameters, `callback` and `context`. `callback` is the name of the method that you want the response to be sent to. In this example, you would have a problem if all you could work with in the callback method was the response from the server. You'd have a problem because you need to set the value of the image tag, and you wouldn't know what that image tag was. So, Ajax.NET Pro has a last parameter called `context`. Whatever object you pass in as the `context` parameter will be returned in the response object as its `context` property. Remember, the `response` object has five properties, `value`, `error`, `request`, `extend`, and `context`. Now you see where the `context` is helpful. The `context` basically gets a free ride from your execution point (where you ask for the server method to be called) into your callback method.

It is common to name the callback function the same as the original function name, with the `_Callback` appended to it. Take a look at this callback function.

```
function ChangeMe_Callback(response) {
    if(response.error != null)
        alert(response.error.name + ' :: ' + response.error.description);
    else
        response.context.src = response.value;
}
```

Notice that the callback method takes only one parameter. It's common to call this parameter `response`, or `res`. The `response` object's context parameter is populated with the image tag because you sent that tag in as the context when you executed this line.

```
Chapter7_ImageSwitcherCallback.ChangeImage
        (target.src, onName, offName, ChangeMe_Callback,target);
```

In the JavaScript, you can reference the `response.context` as if it's the image. You set its source equal to the value that was returned from the server. To get the value returned from the server, you look in the `response.value` property. The entire HTML + JavaScript now should look like this.

Client Side — Chapter7/ImageSwitcherCallback.aspx
```
<script type="text/Javascript" language="Javascript">
<!--
function ChangeMe(target, leftName, rightName) {
    alert(response.value);
```

```
      Chapter7_ImageSwitcherCallback.ChangeImage(target.src, leftName,
rightName,ChangeMe_Callback,target);
}
function ChangeMe_Callback(response) {
    if(response.error != null)
        alert(response.error.name + ' :: ' + response.error.description);
    else
        response.context.src = response.value;
}
//-->
</script>

<div style="DISPLAY:none;VISIBILITY:hidden">
  <!-- preload images -->
  <img src="images/ArrowLeft.gif" border="0" runat="server" ID="ImgPreload1">
  <img src="images/ArrowRight.gif" border="0" runat="server" ID="ImgPreload2">
</div>
<img onclick="ChangeMe(this,'ArrowLeft','ArrowRight')" src="images/ArrowLeft.gif"
border="0">
```

In the preceding code, you're now executing the image changer in an asynchronous manner. This means that you don't have to wait for the server to return a response. The code can continue to execute and do other functions. When the server does return a response, the Ajax.NET Pro library will receive that response and execute the callback method, sending in the response as its object. This is a much more fluid style of programming, and you'll enjoy the benefits of not having your code bottlenecked because of a long-running process on the server.

Ajax.NET Pro Request Events — Keeping Your Users Updated

The `AjaxPro.Request` object has several placeholder events that you can set up JavaScript functions against. These event placeholders are `onLoading`, `onError`, `onTimeout`, and `onStateChanged`. I call them placeholders because they're null unless you assign a function to them. In this section, we're going to look at the `onLoading` event and how it can be used to let your users know that something is happening in the background. For example, the user might have just clicked a button that loads a large set of data and takes 5 seconds to execute. During this 5 seconds (which seems like forever) if nothing updates to let the user know something is happening, they might get antsy and press the button again, and again, and again — which we know just further delays the problem.

The following example uses the `onLoading` event from the class object that was registered using the `Utility.RegisterTypeForAjax` call (probably in your page load event). This `onLoading` event is called by the Ajax.NET Pro library before and after all calls are made to `AjaxMethods` on your registered class. The code-behind page for this example has a simple method on it called `WaitXSeconds`. Its job is to simply wait for a given number of seconds and then return true. In a real application, this might be your database call or some other routine that might take a while. While this code is working, you can let your users know the code is busy with a little DHTML. When the text button is clicked, a red "Loading . . ." box will show in the top-left corner of the window. When the method is done, the "Loading . . ." box is hidden.

Chapter7_Onloading.aspx.cs Example

```
protected void Page_Load(object sender, EventArgs e)
{
    Utility.RegisterTypeForAjax(typeof(Chapter7_OnLoading));
}
[AjaxPro.AjaxMethod()]
public string WaitXSeconds(int SecondsToWait)
{
    System.Threading.Thread.Sleep(SecondsToWait*1000);
    return string.Format("{0} seconds have passed",SecondsToWait.ToString());;;
}
```

The onLoading event in this example will get assigned to a function that you create. The onLoading function takes a single parameter, which is true or false, and lets you know if the onLoading function is being called at the beginning of the request (true) or at the end of the request (false). You use this parameter to set the visible property of an absolute positioned div tag named "loading". When it's true, you set the visibility to visible, and when it's false (the end), you set its value to hidden.

Chapter7_Onloading.aspx Example

```
<form id="form1" runat="server">
<div id="loading"
style="visibility:hidden;position:absolute;top:0px;left:0px;background-
color:Red;color:White;">Loading...</div>
<div>
    <A href="#" onclick="javascript:ShowLoading(4);void(0);">Click Here</A>
    to run a 4 second process, and let the user know with a "Loading..."
    tag in the top left corner of the window.
</div>
</form>
<script language="javascript" type="text/javascript">
    Chapter7_OnLoading.onLoading = function(currentVis) {
        var loadingDiv = document.getElementById("loading");
        if(loadingDiv != null) {
            loadingDiv.style.visibility = currentVis ? "visible" : "hidden";
        }
    }
    function ShowLoading(seconds) {
        Chapter7_OnLoading.WaitXSeconds(seconds,WaitXSeconds_Callback);
    }
    function WaitXSeconds_Callback(response) {
        alert(response.value);
    }
</script>
```

A nice feature of the way the onLoading event works is that it's tied to the class object. So, if your registered class (in this case the Page class) has many AjaxMethods on it, the onLoading event will be fired at the beginning and the end of every method that is called. And remember, you had to program this only once!

Errors, Errors, Errors. They Happen, You Trap 'em.

So far you've covered the response's value, request, and context properties. Last, and maybe most important, is the error property. When Ajax.NET Pro processes your request, if all goes as planned and no error occurs, this property will have a null value. If any unhandled error is thrown during the Ajax.NET

Checking for Null Values

If the `error` property is null, there is no error, at least not one that was sent back with the response object. If the `value` property is null, the server didn't return any values, and if the `context` is null, no context was originally set up. But no matter what they mean, usually you account for these nulls with a simple `if()` statement in your code, as demonstrated in code earlier in the chapter using this line:

```
if(response.error != null)
```

This line lets you know if an error was returned. In the sample, you coded that if there is an error, the error is shown to the user, and the value of the image source tag is not set. But you can choose to handle the error however you want.

Pro request, the string value of that error is returned. The `response.error` object has three properties — name, description, and number.

Property	Description
`response.error.name`	The name of the error, usually the namespace of the error that was thrown.
`response.error.description`	This is the equivalent of the `Exception.Message` in the .NET Framework.
`response.error.number`	If the exception thrown has an error number, it is populated here.

Notice that the last code block in the preceding section contains code to check the `response.error` property to see if it is null. If it is found not to be null, then you know you have an error, and you display the error message to the user. This will probably not be what you want to do in your real-world application. You would probably check the error number, and then handle the error appropriately, according to what caused the error.

Using the Ajax.NET Pro Library — Looking under the Hood

So, in summary, preparing your application to use the Ajax.NET Pro library requires the following steps:

1. First, you have to set up your ASP.NET application to be Ajax.NET Pro–enabled. This is done with the reference being set to the `AjaxPro.dll` assembly.

2. Second, you must modify your `Web.Config` file to register the `AjaxPro.AjaxHandlerFactory` to process all the `AjaxPro/*.ashx` requests.

3. Now that your application is Ajax.NET Pro–enabled, you're ready to build some Ajax functionality into your pages. On the page level, register your `page` class with the `AjaxPro.Utility.RegisterTypeForAjax()` method.

4. Then decorate your methods with the `AjaxPro.AjaxMethod()` attribute.

5. Finally, the Ajax.NET Pro library will create a JavaScript proxy object for you that follows the `ClassName.MethodName()` naming convention. Just add a little client UI and JavaScript to activate your server response, and your application is running on Ajax fuel.

You also now know how to trap errors, check for those errors, and check for null values.

However, although you now know the steps to make this all happen, you may have some questions about what's really happening under the hood to make this functionality work. The next few sections answer some of the common questions you may have about how all this functionality is really working.

When Is the Proxy JavaScript Created?

Remember preparing your page to be enabled with the Ajax.NET Pro library? This involved two steps. The first was registering your `page` class, with a line like the following:

```
AjaxPro.Utility.RegisterTypeForAjax(typeof(Chapter7_ImageSwitcher));
```

The second was attributing your public method with the `AjaxPro.AjaxMethod()` attribute:

```
[AjaPro.AjaxMethod()]
```

If you set a breakpoint on the `RegisterTypeForAjax` call and walk through the code, you'll find that this part of the library is doing something very simple. It's creating JavaScript tags that will be inserted at the top of your page with source values that point back to the `AjaxPro/*.ashx` page handler. When you set up your `Web.Config` file, you registered the page handler so that these types of calls are processed by the Ajax.NET Pro library. So, the entire job of the `RegisterTypeForAjax` method is to write `<script>` tags to the page. If you view source on the ASPX page from the browser, look towards the top of the page scripts that match this format.

```
<script type="text/javascript" src="/ajaxpro/prototype.ashx"></script>
```

```
<script type="text/javascript" src="/ajaxpro/core.ashx"></script>
```

```
<script type="text/javascript" src="/ajaxpro/converter.ashx"></script>
```

```
<script type="text/javascript" src="/ajaxpro/Chapter7_BuildHtmlTable,App_Web_it-_kzny.ashx"></script>
```

The first three tags point to `/AjaxPro/common.ashx`, `core.ashx`, and `converter.ashx` files. These are JavaScript files that contain some general housekeeping helpers for Ajax.NET Pro (you'll look at this in the next chapter).

The fourth script source has a little more interesting name. The `RegisterTypeForAjax` created this script source, and the format is:

```
ClassName,AssemblyName.ashx
```

But this file doesn't exist—how does it get processed? Remember the `/AjaxPro/*.ashx` mapping to the Ajax page handler in the `Web.Config`? Because of that, any requested file path in the `/AjaxPro/` directory that ends with `.ashx` will be processed by the Ajax.NET Pro library. This URL is parsed, and from the named assembly that is found and the named class, the library is able to create the JavaScript proxy objects.

How does it know what proxy objects to create? It knows by using something in the .NET Framework called reflection. *Reflection* allows you to use code to inspect other code. So, the Ajax.NET Pro library creates a page class instance, in the example, a `Chapter7_ImageSwitcher.aspx` page, and then inspects that page class for any methods that are marked with the `AjaxPro.AjaxMethod()` attribute. Any methods that are found will automatically have JavaScript proxy objects created for them. These proxy objects are generated on demand and are written as the source of the `AjaxPro/Chapter7_ImageSwitcher,` `App_Web_it-kzny.ashx` request.

Why the funky assembly name `App Web it-kzny`? This is a framework-generated assembly where the page class `Chapter7_ImageSwitcher` lives. The .NET framework uses these unique names to keep separate versions of the page when it shadow compiles them, so it's helpful to the framework to have a set of random characters added to the assembly name. These unique assembly names are generated by the framework, and the Ajax.NET Pro library is smart enough to figure this out for you. So luckily, you don't ever have to know or care where the page class lives. The `RegisterTypeForAjax` call does this for you.

What Does the JavaScript Do?

When the browser requests a URL, the server (in this case your ASP.NET application server) returns to it a bunch of HTML. You can easily see this HTML with a view source in your browser. As soon as this HTML is received, it has to be parsed. You don't ever see the raw HTML (unless you do a view source) because the browser actually renders that HTML into a web page. When the `<script>` tag that has a source attribute is loaded, the browser will make another request back to the server to get that data. It's important to realize that these are loaded as separate requests. The same thing is done for images; that is they are loaded in separate synchronous requests one right after the other.

What Happens on the Server after the Proxy JavaScript Has Been Fired?

When the JavaScript source is called on the server, based on the URL, you know that these script files are going to be processed by the Ajax.NET Pro library. The JavaScript that is created, creates the proxy objects that enable you to call the `PageClassName.MethodName()` JavaScript function calls. These are called proxy objects because they don't actually do any of the work; they simply proxy the call through an Ajax protocol to the server.

How Is the Method in the Code-Behind Actually Executed and How Is the Page Actually Created?

You'll see how this is done in detail in the next chapter. Essentially, this is where the reflection is done, the page class is created in code, and then the method is executed with the parameters that were sent in from the JavaScript call.

What Is Really Being Sent Back to the Client

In an earlier example, you read about a string being sent back to the client. Remember `response.value`? `response.value` can hold any value or object, or even stay null. When a simple type is sent back (such as `String` or `Integer`), the actual value is what is stored. When something like a `DataSet` is returned, because there is no such thing as a `DataSet` object in JavaScript, the `DataSet` is converted into a JavaScript Object Notation (JSON) object (JSON is discussed in Chapter 5) that holds much of the same data that a `DataSet` holds. But understand, you're not dealing with a full ADO.NET `DataSet`, you're dealing with a JSON object that has simply been populated with data that matches the data in the `DataSet` you were expecting. This was shown earlier in the chapter when you dynamically created an HTML table from an Ajax.NET Pro call that returned a `DataTable`. Once you know that JSON objects can be held in the `response.value` property, the question to answer is this — "Can I return my own custom types?" Absolutely, you can. In fact if your custom type is a simple type, you can simply mark you class with the `[Serializable()]` attribute, and the Ajax.NET Pro library will do the rest. You'll look more into this functionality when you look at extending the Ajax.NET Framework in Chapter 8.

Summary

In this chapter:

- ❑   You were given an introduction to the Ajax.NET Pro library.

- ❑   You were able to download the code from `www.BeginningAjax.com` and reference the Ajax.NET Pro library.

- ❑   And once you had the project set up, you were able to create a client/server conversation, and updated your web page with the server content Ajax style.

In Chapter 8, you'll look under the hood of the Ajax.NET library and see more about how the magic is happening. You'll walk through the code that comes with the library and show what's happening when and why. Remember, the idea of a wrapper library is to make life easier, which hopefully the simplicity of the code in this chapter has shown. Chapter 8 is a little more advanced. If you're interested in extending the library with custom objects, then Chapter 8 will be a good read for you.

Anatomy of Ajax.NET Pro Library

There are many different levels of learning a specific technology. Sometimes, just knowing that a technology works and how to use it is good enough. You know how to use the technology well enough to get what you need out of it, and it doesn't really matter how it works. Let's talk about Microsoft Excel as an example. You're probably pretty good at using Excel. You can color-code cells, create formulas, print spreadsheets, and probably accomplish hundreds of other somewhat complicated tasks. You accomplish these simply by using the technology. Do you really truly understand what happens in Excel to make all those features work? A better question might be — do you really care how anything works "under the hood" of Excel? My guess is probably not. In Chapter 7, you were given an introduction to using the Ajax.NET Pro library, which brings you up to speed on how to use the library.

Now that you're comfortable using the library, you can look at how the magic happens. There is a difference between understanding that something just works and understanding the fundamentals of why it works. In this chapter, you're opening the hood to check what's inside the Ajax.NET Pro library to better understand why it works the way it does. And unlike Excel, you'll want to know how this works because that's what makes it very easy for you to extend the library or modify it for your own usage.

This chapter covers a code walk-through of the library. You'll use the steps that you took in Chapter 7 as a guide to this chapter. That is to say, you will duplicate the examples in Chapter 7, only this time, you're going to walk into the library and examine what happens when and why.

In this chapter, the following topics will be covered:

- ❏ Getting the Ajax.NET Pro C# Code library running on your machine
- ❏ The Ajax.NET Pro Web.Config settings and what they accomplish
- ❏ Registering the page class
- ❏ The role of the `AjaxPro.AjaxMethod()` attribute

Chapter 8

❑   How the JavaScript call gets to the server and back

❑   Ajax.NET Pro converters

When you understand the mechanics of these examples, you will have a great foundation for extending the Ajax.NET Pro library for use in your application.

Getting the Ajax.NET Pro Code

In Chapter 7, you were given two options to prepare your application to use the Ajax.NET Pro library. You can either download the Ajax.NET Pro code library and compile it as a project, or you can choose to download the Ajax.NET Pro assembly and simply set a reference to it. Because this chapter is doing a walk-through of the code, it's not a requirement, but it will be more helpful to have the code local on your machine; therefore, it is highly suggested. If you want the code, then you'll need to grab the code library from the http://BeginningAjax.com web site. Two versions of the library are available, one for ASP.NET 1.1 and another for ASP.NET 2.0.

ASP.NET Version	URL for Ajax.NET
ASP.NET 1.1	http://BeginningAjax.com/Downloads/ ASP1-Ajax-6.4.16.1.zip
ASP.NET 2.0	http://BeginningAjax.com/Downloads/ ASP2-Ajax-6.4.16.1.zip

Download and extract the zip file for the version of the ASP.NET framework you're working with. You'll have all the code necessary to follow along in this chapter. The zip file contains a Visual Studio project file named AjaxPro.csproj. Open the Ajax application you've been working with, and add this project to your solution.

Figure 8-1 shows an easy way to add a project to your already open solution. Right-click on the Solution, and select Add⇨Existing Project. This will bring up an open file dialog box that you can point to the Ajax.csproj file.

There's another way to get this code to compile within your solution. The first example assumes that you want to add a new project to your solution. (See Fig. 8-2) However, if you already have a project in your solution that you want to add this code to you can do that by simply dragging/dropping the files from the file system into your chosen project. If you choose this route, then you need to be aware of the build action for several files. By default when you drop a file into your project, the build action of the file is Compile. This is great for all the files, except core.js and prototype.js. These two files are embedded resources and need to have the default Build Action changed from Compile to Embedded Resource. To do this, simply click each file once to select it. If the properties window is not already displayed, you can right-click the file and select properties. Figure 8-3 shows the properties for core.js and that the Build Action should be set to Embedded Resource.

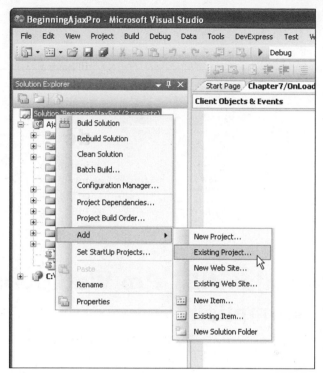

Figure 8-1

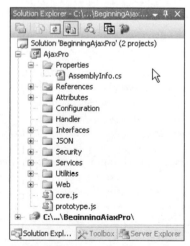

Figure 8-2

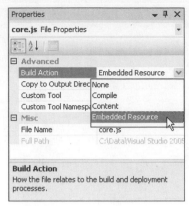

Figure 8-3

What Do the Ajax.NET Pro Web.Config Settings Accomplish?

When you prepare your application to use the Ajax.NET Pro library, one of the first steps is to create a `Web.Config` entry to wire up the Ajax.NET Pro HTTP page handler.

```
01.<system.web>
02.  <httpHandlers>
03.    <add verb="POST,GET" path="ajaxpro/*.ashx"
                          type="AjaxPro.AjaxHandlerFactory,AjaxPro" />
04.  </httpHandlers>
05.</system.web>
```

This `Web.Config` modification tells ASP.NET that all requests that come in for the AjaxPro directory with ASHX file extensions should be processed by the Ajax.NET Pro library. What this allows you to do is have a page request, with a page name, that doesn't exist in the file system. This is done with the use of a page handler. When you create an ASPX page, this is done for you automatically. If your page is named `Default.aspx`, you can request `Default.aspx`, and ASP.NET will serve you back that content.

But what happens if you want to be able to dynamically generate page names and parse the page names during the request to use those newfound values to serve content to do something in your application? You use an `HttpPageHandler` like the Ajax.NET Pro library does. If you examine the `<add />` on line 3 of the preceding code block, you'll notice a few attributes. Take a look at the `path` attribute. You might remember from the old DOS days, that the * symbol is a wildcard character. This path is not case-sensitive, but is usually written in lowercase. As you'll see in the next few sections, the Ajax.NET Pro library will be creating requests using this path structure. The type attribute's value is broken into three pieces of useful formatted data. The first part is the namespace, followed by the class name, followed by the assembly that this class can be found in (without the `.dll` extension). So, the type in the preceding example says find the `AjaxHandlerFactory` in the `AjaxPro` namespace in the `AjaxPro.dll` assembly.

Mastering the concept of `HttpPageHandler` is outside the scope of this book, but I would like to dive in just a little more and show you what's happening with an example. Remember the proxy classes that were magically created for you in Chapter 7?

Listing 8-1 shows two examples that will end up being processed by the Ajax.NET Pro library.

Note that in this chapter, some code blocks contain listing numbers and line numbers to aid reference.

Listing 8-1: Creating a Request, Matching Your PageHandler Path

```
01. <script type="text/javascript"
          src="/BeginningAjaxPro/ajaxpro/core.ashx"></script>
02. <script type="text/javascript"
          src="/BeginningAjaxPro/ajaxpro/Chapter7_OnLoading,
          App_Web_rjv9qbqt.ashx"></script>
```

These are JavaScript tags with `src` attributes that call back into your application. `BeginningAjaxPro` is the application name, `ajaxpro` is the pseudo-folder, and the page name is `Chapter7_OnLoading_App_Web_rjv9qbqt_ashx`. You know that this file doesn't exist; in fact, the `ajaxpro` folder doesn't even exist in your application. But, because you have the `HttpPageHandler` wired up in `Web.Config`, the Ajax.NET Pro library is able to process these files for you. When these requests come in, the class name `Chapter7_OnLoading` is loaded from the automatically named `App_Web_rjv9qbqt` assembly. This is a quick introduction to the page handler; later in this chapter, you'll look deeper into how this really works, but for now the concept is what's important.

What Happens When You Register the Page Class?

Once your application is set up to work with the Ajax.NET Pro library and you've made your `Web.Config` modification, you're ready to start using the library. When you're serving a page from ASP.NET that has code-behind methods that you want to be able to access, there are two steps the library requires. First, register the page class, and second, mark the method with an `AjaxPro.AjaxMethod()` attribute. This was demonstrated several times in Chapter 7. Take a look at what happens when you register the page class.

```
01. protected void Page_Load(object sender, EventArgs e)
02. {
03.     AjaxPro.Utility.RegisterTypeForAjax(typeof(Chapter7_Onloading));
04. }
```

The page class name here is `Chapter7_OnLoading`. You'll notice that you're sending in a `type` as the parameter to the `AjaxPro.Utility.RegisterTypeForAjax()` method. Using the `typeof()` method, you can get the `type` of the class, in this case the page you're using, and send that as your parameter. So, take a peek into the `AjaxPro.Utility.RegisterTypeForAjax()` method. Listing 8-2 is the code that gets run for the `RegisterTypeForAjax()` method. This method has two jobs. First, to make sure that the `Common.ashx` has already been rendered to the page, and second, to render the proper script tag to the page for the type that is being registered. This is the HTML code rendered in Listing 8-1.

Listing 8-2: RegisterTypeForAjax Definition in /Ajax/Utility.cs

```
01.  public static void RegisterTypeForAjax(Type type)
02.  {
03.      System.Web.UI.Page page =
              (System.Web.UI.Page)System.Web.HttpContext.Current.Handler;
04.      RegisterTypeForAjax(type, page);
05.  }
06.
07.  public static void RegisterTypeForAjax(Type type, System.Web.UI.Page page)
08.  {
09.      RegisterCommonAjax(page);
10.      string path = type.FullName + "," + type.Assembly.FullName.Substring(0,
             type.Assembly.FullName.IndexOf(","));
11.      if(Utility.Settings.UseAssemblyQualifiedName) path =
             type.AssemblyQualifiedName;
12.
13.      if(Utility.Settings != null &&
             Utility.Settings.UrlNamespaceMappings.ContainsValue(path))
14.      {
15.          foreach(string key in Utility.Settings.UrlNamespaceMappings.Keys)
16.          {
17.              if(Utility.Settings.UrlNamespaceMappings[key].ToString() == path)
18.              {
19.                  path = key;
20.                  break;
21.              }
22.          }
23.      }
24.
25.      RegisterClientScriptBlock(page, "AjaxType." + type.FullName,
             "<script type=\"text/javascript\" src=\"" +
             System.Web.HttpContext.Current.Request.ApplicationPath +
             (System.Web.HttpContext.Current.Request.ApplicationPath
             .EndsWith("/") ? "" : "/") + Utility.HandlerPath + "/" +
             GetSessionUri() + path + Utility.HandlerExtension + "\"></script>");
26.  }
```

The first thing that happens in the `RegisterTypeForAjax()` method is that the `Utility.Register CommonAjax()` method is called on line number 09. The `RegisterCommonAjax()` method is responsible for adding script references to the `prototype`, `core`, and `converter` files. This method makes sure to register these files only once per page, even if you're registering multiple types. You'll see how this is done shortly with the inspection of the `Settings` object.

At this point, you know that the `prototype`, `core`, and `converter` scripts have been registered, and you're ready to move on and create a reference to your own type. Line 10 creates a string that consists of the type's fully qualified name and the assembly that the type is in. This results in the `/Chapter7_OnLoading`, `App_Web_rjv9qbqt` found in line 2 in Listing 8-1. This value is checked against a HashTable named `Utility.Settings.UrlNamespaceMappings`. If the value is found, line 20 calls `break`, and the method replaces the type name with the mapped name. You'll take look at this `UrlNameSpaceMappings` shortly. If the value is not found, then you know to simply use the type name as the script source.

Line 25 creates the actual JavaScript tag that renders on the page. This is the entire line number 2 entry from Listing 8-1. Also, line 25 uses the `RegisterClientScriptBlock` method to inject this JavaScript call onto the page that is being rendered.

Listings 8-2 and 8-3 make common references to the `Utility.Settings` class. This class is populated with several properties that all have default values.

Listing 8-3: RegisterCommonAjax in /Ajax/Utility.cs

```
01.   internal static void RegisterCommonAjax(System.Web.UI.Page page)
02.   {
03.     if(page == null)
04.       return;
05.
06.     // If there is a configuration for this fileName in
07.     // web.config AjaxPro section scriptReplacements we will
08.     // redirect to this file.
09.
10.     string rootFolder = System.Web.HttpContext.Current.Request.
               ApplicationPath + (System.Web.HttpContext.Current.
      Request.ApplicationPath.EndsWith("/") ? "" : "/");
11.
12.     string prototypeJs = rootFolder + Utility.HandlerPath +
               "/prototype" + Utility.HandlerExtension;
13.     string coreJs = rootFolder + Utility.HandlerPath + "/core" +
               Utility.HandlerExtension;
14.     string convertersJs = rootFolder + Utility.HandlerPath +
               "/converter" + Utility.HandlerExtension;
15.
16.     if(Utility.Settings != null)
17.     {
18.       if(Utility.Settings.ScriptReplacements.
               ContainsKey("prototype"))
19.       {
20.         prototypeJs = Utility.Settings.ScriptReplacements["prototype"];
21.         if(prototypeJs.Length > 0 && prototypeJs.StartsWith("~/"))
22.           prototypeJs = rootFolder + prototypeJs.Substring(2);
23.       }
24.       if(Utility.Settings.ScriptReplacements.ContainsKey("core"))
25.       {
26.         coreJs = Utility.Settings.ScriptReplacements["core"];
27.         if(coreJs.Length > 0 && coreJs.StartsWith("~/"))
28.           coreJs = rootFolder + coreJs.Substring(2);
29.       }
30.       if(Utility.Settings.ScriptReplacements.ContainsKey("converter"))
31.       {
32.         convertersJs = Utility.Settings.ScriptReplacements["converter"];
33.         if(convertersJs.Length > 0 && convertersJs.StartsWith("~/"))
34.           convertersJs = rootFolder + convertersJs.Substring(2);
35.       }
36.     }
37.
```

(continued)

Listing 8-3: (continued)

```
38.    if(prototypeJs.Length > 0)
39.      RegisterClientScriptBlock(page, Constant.AjaxID + ".prototype",
40.        "<script type=\"text/javascript\" src=\"" +
            prototypeJs + "\"></script>");
41.
42.    if(coreJs.Length > 0)
43.      RegisterClientScriptBlock(page, Constant.AjaxID + ".core",
44.        "<script type=\"text/javascript\" src=\"" +
            coreJs + "\"></script>");
45.
46.    if(convertersJs.Length > 0)
47.      RegisterClientScriptBlock(page, Constant.AjaxID + ".converters",
48.        "<script type=\"text/javascript\" src=\"" + convertersJs +
            "\"></script>");
49.
50.
51.    if(Settings.TokenEnabled)
52.    {
53.      RegisterClientScriptBlock(page, Constant.AjaxID + ".token",
54.        "<script type=\"text/javascript\">AjaxPro.token = \"" +
            CurrentAjaxToken + "\";</script>");
55.    }
56.  }
```

Being as flexible as possible, the library allows you to set these property values with additional
Web.Config entries. The only thing you've done so far in the Web.Config is to wire up the Ajax Pro
page handler. The library has defined a custom section that you can use in your Web.Config. This is
processed by the AjaxPro.AjaxSettingsSectionHandler, found in the /Configuration/
AjaxSettingsSectionHandler.cs file.

Try It Out	Adding Custom Sections to Your Web.Config File

Fortunately, ASP.NET has framework calls that make it really easy to add custom sections to your
Web.Config file. Listing 8-4 shows a sample entry in your Web.Config to override the several default
property and actions of the Ajax.NET Pro library. Listing 8-5 shows how the library reads those overridden
values.

Listing 8-4: Web.Config configSections Sample

```
<configuration>
...
01. <configSections>
02.   <sectionGroup name="ajaxNet">
03.     <section name="ajaxSettings"
               type="AjaxPro.AjaxSettingsSectionHandler, AjaxPro"
04.            requirePermission="false"
05.            restartOnExternalChanges="true" />
06.   </sectionGroup>
07. </configSections>
08.
```

```
09. <ajaxNet>
10.   <ajaxSettings>
11.     <urlNameSpaceMappings>
12.       <add namespace="Namespace.ClassName,AssemblyName" path="MyPath" />
13.     </urlNameSpaceMappings>
14.     <jsonConverters>
15.       <!--  <remove type="Namespace.Class1,Assembly"/>
16.             <add type="Namespace.Class2,Assembly"/>
17.         -->
18.     </jsonConverters>
19.     <debug enabled="false" />
20.     <token enabled="false" sitePassword="password" />
21.     <!-- <scriptReplacements>
22.             <file name="core" path="~/scripts/debugcore.js" />
23.             <file name="prototype" path="~/scripts/debugprototype.js" />
24.             <file name="converter" path="~/scripts/debugconverter.js" />
25.         </scriptReplacements>
26.       -->
27.   </ajaxSettings>
28. </ajaxNet>
...
</configuration>
```

How It Works

❑   The first custom setting in Listing 8-4 is the `urlNameSpaceMappings` on line 11. This setting allows you to mask your JavaScript calls so that you do not expose the class name and assembly names in your application. You may or may not be able to use this, depending on the version of ASP.NET and Visual Studio that you are using. If you know the name of your final assembly, then you can add this masking. If you're using dynamic compiling, as you did in Listing 8-1, then you can't use this mask because you don't know the assembly name beforehand. The benefit to masking your class and assembly names is that this removes the ability of someone to discover the internal knowledge of your application.

❑   Next is `jsonConverters`. This is the section that enables you to instruct Ajax.NET Pro to load your JavaScript JSON converters. In the commented section, on lines 15 and 16, you can see the format of loading these converters. Converters can be removed and added with the standard `<remove />` and `<add />` nodes.

   Debugging can also be turned on or off in this section. If debugging is turned on, and an exception returned in the `Response.Error` object, then the exception will contain more information than just the exception text, such as `Stack`, `TargetSize`, and `Source` information.

❑   Ajax.NET Pro supports a token concept that tries to confirm that requests are coming from clients that you originally served content to. This is to help eliminate spoofing of your site. Because the calls back into the server are simple JavaScript calls, it's possible to execute JavaScript from other pages against your site. If the token is enabled and the password is set, then a security token is placed in the head of the page that is rendered.

```
<script type="text/javascript">AjaxPro.token =
                "f5274a7d77bc2a417b22efb3dfda9ba8";</script>
```

This token is a hash that is made up of several parameters about the user, including IP address, the site being visiting, the browser being used, and the password you supplied. This makes it much more difficult to try hacking routines from another machine against your site.

> **The token should be enabled in all cases. It's a very nice feature that makes hacking your site more difficult.**

❑ Refresh your memory with Listing 8-1, specifically with the line number 1. Script replacements allow you to use scripts other than the default scripts that were installed with Ajax.NET Pro. Maybe you have a static file that you've added some debugging code to that you'd like to use while you're debugging your application, but not once you deploy your application. Having these replacement script options in Web.Config is great because you can switch it without recompiling your application. How would you create an overridden core, prototype, or converter file? Don't you still need all the base functionality that the original files offer? The answer is yes, you do, but that doesn't mean that you can't add you own debugging or other code into that script. Open your browser and point it to your web application, /AjaxPro/core.ashx. Do a view source, and you now have a copy of the core.ashx JavaScript file. Save this in your application as /scripts/debugcore.js. You might play with simply adding an alert() method in a few places, just to see it work. Now to try that debugcore.js in your application, add Listing 8-4 line 22 to your Web.Config. Set the path of the core to "~/scripts/debugcore.js". Save and run your application, and view the source of the page. Notice that the listing for the Core.ashx shown in Listing 8-1 has changed to your /scripts/debugcore.js file.

Listing 8-5 shows the code for Ajax/AjaxSettingsSectionHandler.cs that makes all of these configuration settings possible. If you're new to Web.Config section handlers, this code is a great read. It's pretty simple to follow and might introduce you to a few new XML tricks.

Listing 8-5: /Ajax/AjaxSettingsSectionHandler.cs

```
01. namespace AjaxPro
02. {
03.    internal class AjaxSettingsSectionHandler :
                    IConfigurationSectionHandler
04.    {
05.      #region IConfigurationSectionHandler Members
06.      public object Create(object parent, object configContext,
                        System.Xml.XmlNode section)
07.      {
08.        AjaxSettings settings = new AjaxSettings();
09.
10.        foreach(XmlNode n in section.ChildNodes)
11.        {
12.          if(n.Name == "coreScript")
13.          {
14.            if(n.InnerText != null && n.InnerText.Length > 0)
15.            {
16.              settings.ScriptReplacements.Add("core", n.InnerText);
17.            }
18.          }
```

```
19.          else if(n.Name == "scriptReplacements")
20.          {
21.            foreach(XmlNode file in n.SelectNodes("file"))
22.            {
23.              string name = "";
24.              string path = "";
25.              if(file.Attributes["name"] != null)
26.              {
27.                name = file.Attributes["name"].InnerText;
28.                if(file.Attributes["path"] != null) path =
                     file.Attributes["path"].InnerText;
29.               if(settings.ScriptReplacements.ContainsKey(name))
30.                  settings.ScriptReplacements[name] = path;
31.               else
32.                  settings.ScriptReplacements.Add(name, path);
33.              }
34.            }
35.          }
36.          else if(n.Name == "urlNamespaceMappings")
37.          {
38.            settings.UseAssemblyQualifiedName =
               n.SelectSingleNode("@useAssemblyQualifiedName[.='true']") !=
               null;
39.           XmlNode ns, url;
40.           foreach(XmlNode e in n.SelectNodes("add"))
41.            {
42.              ns = e.SelectSingleNode("@type");
43.              url = e.SelectSingleNode("@path");
44.             if(ns == null || ns.InnerText == "" || url ==
                  null || url.InnerText == "")
45.                continue;
46.             if(settings.UrlNamespaceMappings.Contains(url.InnerText))
47.                throw new Exception("Duplicate namespace mapping '"
                            + url.InnerText + "'.");
48.             settings.UrlNamespaceMappings.Add
                        (url.InnerText, ns.InnerText);
49.            }
50.          }
51.          else if(n.Name == "jsonConverters")
52.          {
53.            XmlNodeList jsonConverters = n.SelectNodes("add");
54.           foreach(XmlNode j in jsonConverters)
55.            {
56.              XmlNode t = j.SelectSingleNode("@type");
57.             if(t == null)
58.                continue;

59.              Type type = Type.GetType(t.InnerText);
60.             if(type == null)
61.              {
62.                // throw new ArgumentException("Could not find type "
63.                // + t.InnerText + ".");
64.                        continue;
65.              }
```

(continued)

Listing 8-5: *(continued)*

```
66.                    if (!typeof(IJavaScriptConverter).
                          IsAssignableFrom(type))
67.                       {
68.                           // throw new ArgumentException("Type " +
69.                           //   t.InnerText + " does not inherit from
70.                           // JavaScriptObjectConverter.");
71.                           continue;
72.                       }
73.
74.                 IJavaScriptConverter c =
                        (IJavaScriptConverter)Activator.CreateInstance(type);
75.                 c.Initialize();
76.                 settings.JavaScriptConverters.Add(c);
77.               }
78.             }
79.         else if(n.Name == "encryption")
80.         {
81.           string cryptType = n.SelectSingleNode("@cryptType") !=
                      null ? n.SelectSingleNode("@cryptType").InnerText
                      : null;
82.           string keyType = n.SelectSingleNode("@keyType") !=
                      null ? n.SelectSingleNode("@keyType").InnerText
                      : null;
83.           if(cryptType == null || keyType == null)
84.               continue;
85.
86.           AjaxEncryption enc = new AjaxEncryption(cryptType, keyType);
87.           if(!enc.Init())
88.               throw new Exception("Ajax.NET Professional
                      encryption configuration failed.");
89.           settings.Encryption = enc;
90.         }
91.         else if(n.Name == "token")
92.         {
93.           settings.TokenEnabled = n.SelectSingleNode("@enabled") !=
                      null && n.SelectSingleNode("@enabled")
                      .InnerText == "true";
94.           settings.TokenSitePassword =
                      n.SelectSingleNode("@sitePassword") != null ?
                      n.SelectSingleNode("@sitePassword").InnerText :
                      settings.TokenSitePassword;
95.         }
96.         else if (n.Name == "debug")
97.         {
98.           if (n.SelectSingleNode("@enabled") != null &&
                  n.SelectSingleNode("@enabled").InnerText == "true")
99.             settings.DebugEnabled = true;
100.        }
101.        else if (n.Name == "oldStyle")
102.        {
103.          if (n.SelectSingleNode("objectExtendPrototype") != null)
104.          {
```

```
105.              if (!settings.OldStyle.Contains("objectExtendPrototype"))
106.                settings.OldStyle.Add("objectExtendPrototype");
107.            }
108.          }
109.        }
110.
111.      return settings;
112.    }
113.    #endregion
114.  }
115. }
```

What Role Does the Ajax.AjaxMethod() Attribute Play?

As far as the library goes, at this point, you've registered a type with the AjaxPro.RegisterType ForAjax() method, which in turn sent multiple <script> tags to the browser. These are seen in Listing 8-1. Now it's time to examine the request that is generated because of the src of the script. In the example, the source of the registered type rendered as /BeginningAjax/ajaxpro/Chapter7_OnLoading, App_Web_rjv9qbqt.ashx. Remember that Chapter7_OnLoading is the page class name, and App_Web_rjv9qbqt is the dynamic assembly that the page class is compiled into.

The first code in the library to get this request is the AjaxHandlerFactory, which is assigned to catch all incoming requests for /AjaxPro/*.ashx. The AjaxHandlerFactory is in charge of looking at the incoming URL, creating a new AjaxPro.Request object, and then handing off that request to an AjaxProcessor, which is run. This is all pretty standard and happens on every request. Remember, one of the ideas of using a page handler is to handle dynamically generated requests. The library does this so that you can ask for the class and assembly that you want a JavaScript proxy for. Once you've supplied this information (class name and assembly), the library is smart enough to figure out what you're looking for.

How is it smart enough, you ask? Well, truthfully, it's not without another piece of information that you've already supplied. That piece of information is the AjaxPro.AjaxMethod() attribute that you placed over the signature of the public method that you wanted to make available to the AjaxPro.NET library. So, we'll fast forward a little bit and talk about what the library does. A request comes in, and the library is able to parse the class name and the assembly name from the URL. If you're using the urlNameSpaceMappings, then the library is still able to figure out the class name and the assembly; it just has to look in this mappings' HashTable first. Once the library has these two crucial pieces of information, it's able to use a .NET Framework technology called reflection to inspect or, as it's appropriately named, reflect upon the class that you've supplied. Reflection really is an aptly named portion of the .NET Framework. Something already exists, a compiled class in this example, and you wish to reflect upon that class. So, reflection has its own great support that is native in the .NET Framework, and it allows you to find everything you want to know about that class. The library at this point is interested in finding all the methods in the class that have been marked with the AjaxPro.AjaxMethod() attribute. Once the library finds a method that has been marked with that attribute, it knows that a JavaScript proxy is going to need to be built. This is, in fact, done for all the methods on the class that are marked with the `AjaxPro.AjaxMethod()` attribute. The proxy classes are all created sequentially and sent back to the browser as the source of your JavaScript call.

You'll look at the code in a minute, but it should all be coming into focus now, and to drill it in, consider the following quick review.

1. When you register a page class, the register utility is responsible for writing the `<script>` tag with a source that will call into the library and tell the library the class name and the assembly name to find that class in.

2. Once this call comes into the library, it uses reflection to load that class and find all the methods marked with the `AjaxPro.AjaxMethod()` attribute.

3. For each method it finds, a JavaScript proxy class is created, and this final result is sent back to the browser as the source of the `<script>` tag.

Now all this JavaScript is loaded into the browser memory and is ready for you to make the JavaScript calls (as you did in Chapter 7) that use the proxy classes created to communicate back to the server.

How Does the JavaScript Call Get to the Server and Back?

So now you know how the framework creates the proxy classes. This is typically never seen by the developer, or anyone, because the view source just shows a URL as the `src` attribute pointing into the library. Listing 8-6 shows the rendered code from the `Chapter7_OnLoading` JavaScript source page. This is what's returned to the browser as a result of the `<script>` having a URL pointing to `AjaxPro/Chapter7_ OnLoading,App_Web_rjv9qbqt.ashx`.

Listing 8-6: JavaScript Source from AjaxPro/Chapter7_OnLoading,App_Web_rjv9qbqt.ashx

```
01. addNamespace("Chapter7_OnLoading");
02. Chapter7_OnLoading_class = Class.create();
03. Object.extend(Chapter7_OnLoading_class.prototype,
                 Object.extend(new AjaxPro.AjaxClass(), {
04.   WaitXSeconds: function(SecondsToWait) {
05.     return this.invoke("WaitXSeconds", {"SecondsToWait":SecondsToWait},
            this.WaitXSeconds.getArguments().slice(1));
06.   },
07.   initialize: function() {
08.     this.url =
        '/BeginningAjaxPro/ajaxpro/Chapter7_OnLoading,App_Web_ao7bzzpr.ashx';
09.   }
10. }));
11. Chapter7_OnLoading = new Chapter7_OnLoading_class();
```

Notice that the end of line 3 is a call to return a `new AjaxPro.AjaxClass` function. This function is calling into the source returned by the `Core.ashx` request. Remember that this is the code that is coming back from only one of the two requests you made. This is specific to the `Chapter7_OnLoading` request, but there is also an `/AjaxPro/Core.ashx` request.

What Is an Ajax.NET Pro Converter?

You now should have a great fundamental understanding of the Ajax.NET Pro library and how it works inside and out. You know how to register classes that create <script> tags with src values that will build and dynamically generate JavaScript proxy classes of your AjaxPro.AjaxMethod() methods. You also know how these methods get called in the proxy classes, and the return values processed with the sync request or async callback methods. There is only one thing that you have missed, and that's dealing with parameter mismatching.

The JavaScript language is not a part of the .NET Framework, and obviously it's true that .NET is not part of the JavaScript language. One of the consequences of communicating between two different platforms is making sure that both platforms understand each other's data types. The Ajax.NET Pro converters have the sole job of converting objects between .NET and JavaScript Object Notation (JSON). These converters make it possible to have access to objects and their properties in a similar fashion on both platforms, and lucky for us all, part of the Ajax.NET Pro library already defines a nice set of the converters for us. Once both platforms can understand each other's data types, the types can be passed around, and interchanged more easily on both platforms. Think of the converters as language interpreters. They're the man in the middle, communicating back and forth to both platforms.

In the following example, you'll look at the System.Data.DataTable converter that is built into the Ajax.NET Pro library. The example shows the JSON converter for a DataTable. You may recognize this format from the basic DataTable sample in the introduction to JSON in Chapter 5.

```
01:  public override string Serialize(object o)
02:  {
03:      if(!(o is DataTable))
04:          throw new NotSupportedException();
05:
06:      StringBuilder sb = new StringBuilder();
07:      DataTable dt = (DataTable)o;
08:
09:      DataColumnCollection cols = dt.Columns;
10:      DataRowCollection rows = dt.Rows;
11:
12:      bool b = true;
13:
14:      sb.Append("new ");
15:      sb.Append(clientType);
16:      sb.Append("([");
17:
18:      foreach(DataColumn col in cols)
19:      {
20:          if(b){ b = false; }
21:          else{ sb.Append(","); }
22:
23:          sb.Append('[');
24:          sb.Append(JavaScriptSerializer.Serialize(col.ColumnName));
25:          sb.Append(',');
26:          sb.Append(JavaScriptSerializer.Serialize(col.DataType.FullName));
27:          sb.Append(']');
28:      }
29:
```

```
30:        sb.Append("],[");
31:
32:        b = true;
33:
34:        foreach(DataRow row in rows)
35:        {
36:            if(b){ b = false; }
37:            else{ sb.Append(","); }
38:
39:            sb.Append(JavaScriptSerializer.Serialize(row));
40:        }
41:
42:        sb.Append("])");
43:
44:        return sb.ToString();
45:    }
```

This converter allows you to work with a .NET `DataTable` in JavaScript. If you look back at the Try It Out "Building an HTML Table from a DataTable Object" section in Chapter 7, you'll see how this `DataTable` is used in action on the JavaScript side.

You have the ability to create custom converter classes for your objects as well. A custom converter class is needed only if you need to expose additional functionality in JavaScript. Most of the time, simply marking your custom class with a `[Serializable()]` attribute will be sufficient. Remember, if your class is marked with the `[Serializable()]` attribute, then Ajax.NET Pro will automatically create a JavaScript proxy class for that object and pass all the data back for you.

Summary

In this chapter, you took a deep dive into the Ajax.NET Pro library. You should now have a great understanding of the library and the entire process taken to communicate with the library from the client browser using JavaScript to the server-side code behind. Specifically, in this chapter, you looked at:

❑   Ajax.NET Pro library C# source code

❑   Custom Setting through the `Web.Config`

❑   Ajax.NET Pro converters

Now, in the next chapter, you will turn your attention to other Ajax libraries for .NET.

Other Ajax Frameworks for .NET

Ajax.NET is certainly the most popular of the open source Ajax frameworks for ASP.NET, but the following material will give you a working knowledge of additional frameworks that aid in Ajax development.

This chapter is broken up into two parts. The first part provides a high-level review of three client-side Ajax frameworks: Sarissa, HTMLHttpRequest, and MochiKit. The second part of the chapter features more in-depth explanations and examples of three server-side frameworks: ComfortASP.NET, MagicAjax, and Anthem.NET.

> *Throughout this chapter the terms* framework *and* library *will be used interchangeably to describe third-party assemblies referenced in your project to provide Ajax functionality.*

In this chapter, you will learn about:

- ❏ How client-side only Ajax frameworks operate
- ❏ The difference between returning data structures and using the changed-HTML architecture of server-side frameworks
- ❏ Integration methods of a library: custom controls and panels
- ❏ Different configuration options among the Ajax frameworks
- ❏ Implementing real-world scenarios using three different server-side Ajax frameworks

Client-Side Frameworks

Ajax development is about seamlessly integrating communication between the client and the server for the user. Although there may be times when you have full control over how data is presented in an application, at times you may encounter a situation where you have no control over what the server makes available to the client. In these situations, a client-side-only Ajax framework is a great asset to your toolkit. The following section will introduce you to three frameworks that abstract Ajax functionality on the client.

Sarissa

URL: http://sarissa.sourceforge.net/doc/

Sarissa is an entirely client-side library written in JavaScript that provides a programming layer, or application program interface (API) that abstracts a majority of implementation details away from the web developer. Specifically, Sarissa can be used to perform the following tasks:

- ❑ XML DOM (Document Object Model) manipulation and document loading (both synchronous and asynchronous)
- ❑ XMLHttpRequest functionality
- ❑ XSLT (Extensible Stylesheet Language Transformations)
- ❑ X Path document navigation
- ❑ Object serialization and deserialization

Some browsers natively support some of the functionality provided by the Sarissa framework, but Sarissa provides a common layer for access to all these functions, regardless of which browser you are developing for. This means that a developer using this library can develop code using the same method calls and objects regardless of the type of browser it is operating under. The Sarissa framework will take care of translating those method calls and object creation in a way that is suitable for or specific to that browser.

Creating an XMLHttpRequest Using the Sarissa Framework

The following is an example of using the Sarissa framework to create a new XMLHttpRequest object in a way that is supported across all the browsers previously listed and to use the object to perform an asynchronous request:

```
var xmlhttp = new XMLHttpRequest();
xmlhttp.open("GET", "http://www.YourServer.com/DataDocument.xml", true);
xmlhttp.onreadystatechange = function()
  {
    if(xmlhttp.readyState == 4)
      alert("Finished loading!");
  }

xmlhttp.send(null);
```

As you can see from the preceding code, creating the XMLHttpRequest is extremely simple. Creating the object in specific ways across all the supported browsers is taken care of for you by the Sarissa framework. Once you have an XMLHttpRequest object, you manipulate it in exactly the same way you would a normal XMLHttpRequest.

Testing for Features Using the Sarissa Framework

There is provision within the framework to test for the existence of various features. Sarissa provides a utility object called `Sarissa` with some properties that make it easy to determine the capabilities of the browser your application is running under. This is a very useful feature because it ensures that you don't have to be overly concerned with what browser your code is running under. The code can simply test for the existence of a particular feature and make use of that feature if it exists or take corrective action. Two primary examples are the `IS_ENABLED_SELECT_NODES` and `IS_ENABLED_XMLHTTP` properties.

❑ The `IS_ENABLED_SELECT_NODES` property is a boolean value that is `true` if the `selectNodes`/`selectSingleNode` functionality is available. The `selectNodes`/`selectSingleNode` methods are used to perform X Path queries over an XML document. Currently, this functionality is available in Internet Explorer but not available in Firefox. In Chapter 4, the script library that was developed contains functionality to add this capability into Firefox. The `IS_ENABLED_SELECT_NODES` property is a static boolean property and accessing it does not require the creation of an object instance. See the example that follows shortly.

❑ The `IS_ENABLED_XMLHTTP` property is a boolean value that is `true` if the `XMLHttpRequest` (or equivalent) functionality is available. This is the central object around which asynchronous request functionality is made available. This is a static property, and accessing it does not require the creation of an object instance.

To use these properties in your application, you can do the following:

```
<script type="text/javascript">
function TestPageProperties()
{
    if (Sarissa.IS_ENABLED_SELECT_NODES)
        alert("selectNodes/selectSingleNode functionality is supported in this
browser");
    else
        alert("selectNodes/selectSingleNode functionality is NOT supported in this
browser");

    if (Sarissa.IS_ENABLED_XMLHTTP)
        alert("Asynchronous functionality using XMLHTTP is supported in this
browser.");
    else
        alert("Asynchronous functionality using XMLHTTP is NOT supported in this
browser.");
}
</script>
```

As shown in the previous example, simple one-line checks can be performed to determine if a feature exists. This makes catering to features in different browsers very easy and straightforward. Normally, intricate knowledge of a browser is required, and checking for a particular feature can be often be done in many different ways, according to what browser is running your web applications. These simple one-line checks can be performed within the page or be embedded with an `include` script to allow for seamless detection of a browsers features.

Using Sarissa Framework for Asynchronous XML Document Loading

In addition to providing an easy way of creating the XMLHttpRequest object, you can also use the XML document asynchronous loading capabilities of Sarissa, as shown in the following example:

```html
<!DOCTYPE HTML PUBLIC "-//W3C//DTD HTML 4.0 Transitional//EN">
<html>
    <head>
        <title></title>
        <meta name="GENERATOR" content="Microsoft Visual Studio .NET 7.1">
        <meta name="vs_targetSchema"
content="http://schemas.microsoft.com/intellisense/ie5">
        <script type="text/javascript" src="sarissa.js"> </script>

<script type="text/javascript">
function TestDocLoad()
{
    var oDomDoc = Sarissa.getDomDocument();
    oDomDoc.async = true; // this line can be ommited - true is the default
    // we add a listener for the load event to know when loading is finished


    oDomDoc.onreadystatechange = function() {
        if(oDomDoc.readyState == 4)
            document.getElementById("mySpanElement").firstChild.nodeValue
=Sarissa.serialize(oDomDoc);
    };
    oDomDoc.load("someXMLDocument.xml");

}
</script>
    </head>
    <body>

    <form>
        <input type="button"  onclick="TestDocLoad()" name="tstButton"
id="tstButton" value="Run Test Function" /><br />
        <hr />
        <span id="mySpanElement">{nothing to display}</span>
     </form>
    </body>
</html>
```

Again, the Sarissa framework has made the task of asynchronously requesting a document from the server a trivial task. The code is clean and self-explanatory, making it easy to maintain and debug. The code is still quite similar to the original code shown in Chapter 4 to achieve the same functionality using the XMLHttpRequest object directly.

Effectively, the creation of the XMLHttpRequest object has been masked for you with the code:

```
var oDomDoc = Sarissa.getDomDocument();
```

Attaching an event to check for the completion of the document load is exactly the same as if you were dealing with an XMLHttpRequest object directly, as shown in the following sample:

```
oDomDoc.onreadystatechange = function() {
        if(oDomDoc.readyState == 4)
```

Initiating the request is slightly different but very easy and intuitive:

```
oDomDoc.load("someXMLDocument.xml");
```

From the previous examples, it is easy to see how Sarissa simplifies the task of dealing with asynchronous or Ajax-like functionality but more important, Sarissa extends that simplicity to be a common factor across all supported browsers.

You will also notice a line in the preceding code that reads:

```
ctrl.firstChild.nodeValue=Sarissa.serialize(oDomDoc);
```

This illustrates the ability of the Sarissa framework to cater to custom document and object serialization. The serialization process caters to nonstandard JavaScript objects (that is, custom defined) and will convert these objects to an XML string representation and back again into an object with a very simple single method call. Because Sarissa is a completely client-side/JavaScript-only library, no server type object support is included.

Included in the downloadable package for Sarissa is a complete set of unit tests to run against the framework. Unit tests are a way of testing and verifying that each individual component of an application or library works as expected. If a unit test is run and fails, then some part of the code is broken and needs to be rectified. If all unit tests are run and passed, then the code should work as expected. Unit tests also provide a form of documentation, showing how a library's methods are expected to be used. These unit tests were written using another freely available and open source tool known as ECMAUnit. ECMAUnit is a specific framework that allows the writing of unit tests for ECMAScript or JavaScript code.

For more information on ECMAUnit or to download a copy of ECMAUnit, please visit the web site at http://kupu.oscom.org/download/ecmaunit-0.3.html. *Currently this unit test framework is version 0.3.*

Overall, the Sarissa framework is a reasonably comprehensive programming interface. Its adoption rate or usage within the industry is low; however, it is a relatively new framework and worth investigation.

HTMLHttpRequest

URL: www.twinhelix.com/javascript/htmlhttprequest/

The HTMLHttpRequest library is a JavaScript client script framework that does not contain as much functionality as some other libraries or frameworks, such as Sarissa, but does provide a unique way of asynchronously loading content and issuing requests.

It should be noted that as of this writing, this library is currently only in the beta 2 stage.

Like many other Ajax-style libraries and frameworks, this library provides a layer of abstraction around the XMLHttpRequest object and shields the developer from having to know any intricate details about coding against that specific object. The purpose of this library is somewhat different and more focused than some other libraries available. Most other frameworks and libraries provide generic mechanisms around construction and manipulation of the XMLHttpRequest object and manipulation of various aspects or functionality surrounding that object, such as "supporting" technologies like X Path, XSLT, and the like. This framework is specifically geared at the asynchronous loading and displaying of HTML content, hence, the name HTMLHttpRequest. HTML content is the focus, and various mechanisms make the loading and displaying of that content very easy, and make it occur in an asynchronous manner.

One of the major differentiators that this library offers is the unique way of invoking an asynchronous request. A direct method call is not required (although this can be used) to load a remote document. Instead, decorating <a href="...." /> tags in the document with a specific class style reference cause an asynchronous load of the referenced document to occur and place it in a predefined location, dynamically within the HTML document. An example demonstrates this best:

```
/*
HTMLHttpRequest v1.0 beta2
(c) 2001-2005 Angus Turnbull, TwinHelix Designs http://www.twinhelix.com
Licensed under the CC-GNU LGPL, version 2.1 or later:
http://creativecommons.org/licenses/LGPL/2.1/
This is distributed WITHOUT ANY WARRANTY; without even the implied
warranty of MERCHANTABILITY or FITNESS FOR A PARTICULAR PURPOSE.
*/
<a class="loadinto-displayDocument" href="SomeDirectory/SomePage.html">My HTML
Content Document</a>

<div id="displayDocument">
 Area to have document loaded into
</div>
```

The preceding code example asynchronously loads in the SomePage.html HTML file from the SomeDirectory directory and dynamically places that content inside the <div> element, which has an id of displayDocument. Notice that this code contains no JavaScript at all, yet the asynchronous loading behavior of the XMLHttpRequest object is being utilized. The magic is in the naming system of the class attribute of the <a href="..." /> element and the <div> element.

An element with a class attribute that contains the loadinto-{control_id} text, indicates that when this element receives a mouse click, the underlying framework should create an XMLHttpRequest object and use it to perform an asynchronous request for the document specified in the href attribute. Once the document is received, the framework then locates the control that has an id attribute that matches the second part of the loadinto-{control_id} class attribute (that is, the {control_id} portion of that attribute). In the preceding example, the control ID to search for is displayDocument. The document that has been loaded is then assigned to the .innerHTML property of the control.

Additional functionality includes creating a "blind" toggle where a link is clicked and toggles the display of a content section, which is often used on sites that display articles and contain a *Read More* link to expand the entire article. This also utilizes a similar method to that described previously with specific class attribute definition to achieve this dynamic behavior.

The framework contains supporting code to trap events where the user clicks on a link that points to another HTML document on the server. The click event is interrogated by the custom method, and if it contains a "class" attribute that matches the format described previously (that is, `loadinto-{control_id}`), then an asynchronous operation is invoked to perform the document loading and subsequent dynamic displaying on the web browser display.

Currently, this framework is ideally suited to constructing HTML pages using multiple content sources located on a server and loaded in asynchronously so that links never actually cause a postback to occur. As of this writing, experimental modifications allow `post`-ing a form asynchronously to a server and receiving a result, which is also dynamically displayed. This is, however, not fully tested and is a work in progress.

If the display of an HTML file using dynamic and asynchronous behavior is desired, then this library can be easily and effectively used to achieve that. If access to specific server-side services is required above and beyond that of simple HTML document display, then this library may not be the ideal choice. If nothing else, the ability of this library to capture events easily can be used to perform any number of tasks not currently offered by the framework.

MochiKit

URL: `http://mochikit.com`

MochiKit is a client-side JavaScript framework or more specifically, a suite of JavaScript libraries. MochiKit is described as (taken from the web site itself) a suite of JavaScript libraries that "make JavaScript suck less." The aim of the MochiKit framework is to make programming in JavaScript a lot easier and, like many of the other client-side-only libraries, provide a layer of abstraction between raw coding details that are specific to each browser. This allows a common method of accessing objects and functions, such as Ajax asynchronous functionality, without having to code specific implementations for all the browsers you are required to support in your development efforts.

MochiKit is quite a comprehensive framework and contains a large amount of functionality that extends asynchronous behavior. Broadly speaking, MochiKit covers the following areas:

❑ Asynchronous requests

❑ Low-level functional and comparison features

❑ DOM manipulation

❑ Color and style manipulation with CSS3 (Cascading Style Sheets) support

❑ Date and time formatting and parsing routines

❑ String formatting routines

❑ Logging features and supporting an API

❑ Specialized Logging Pane to aid in tracing and debugging

❑ Visual effects library

❑ Iteration support API

Each one of the areas listed is contained within a separate module of the MochiKit framework. Simplicity is a key goal with this framework and some examples best demonstrate this:

```
var x = getXMLHttpRequest();
```

The preceding code will simply return an object that is the equivalent XMLHttpRequest object for the particular platform (that is, browser type):

```
var d = loadJSONDoc(url):
```

This code will perform an asynchronous request to the specified URL location and retrieve the response as a JSON-formatted document. JSON is an acronym for the JavaScript Object Notation and is a standard, lightweight way of representing objects using a string format. JavaScript natively understands this format and can evaluate a string that is in JSON format using the eval method to return a valid object.

The loadJSONDoc method shown in the preceding code line returns an object that is of type Deferred. The Deferred object is a special type provided by the MochiKit library. Deferred type objects are a way of abstracting nonblocking events, such as the final response to an XMLHttpRequest. These allow the addition of callback functions to the Deferred objects collection that are called when an asynchronous operation completes. The complete code might look like this:

```
var d = loadJSONDoc("http://www.yourhost.com/somedocument.json");
var gotMetadata = function (meta) {
    alert("JSON document loaded ok.");
};
var metadataFetchFailed = function (err) {
  alert("The document could not be fetched.");
};
d.addCallbacks(gotMetadata, metadataFetchFailed);
```

The first line of the preceding example:

```
var d = loadJSONDoc("http://www.yourhost.com/somedocument.json");
```

simply instructs the MochiKit library to asynchronously load the document specified and returns an instance of an object that is of type Deferred. The next two lines define functions that you want to be called when the document loads successfully and when an error occurs, respectively.

```
var gotMetadata = function (meta) {
    alert("JSON document loaded ok.");
};
var metadataFetchFailed = function (err) {
  alert("The document could not be fetched.");
};
```

It is then a matter of attaching these functions to the Deferred object that is returned using the syntax:

```
d.addCallbacks(gotMetadata, metadataFetchFailed);
```

The Deferred object is a fundamental part of the MochiKit framework and provides much more extensive functionality than what has been listed here to support a wide variety of asynchronous operations, locking, synchronization, callbacks, and so on. In many ways, the `Deferred` object provides similar features, or at least provides a similar function, to delegates within the .NET framework.

In addition to support for asynchronous behavior, MochiKit also contains support for some basic visual effects. At this time, MochiKit provides one visual effect: rounded corners for your HTML elements. These rounded corners are created completely through CSS manipulations and require no external images or style sheets. This is performed by calling either of the two methods, `roundClass` or `roundElement`. The former rounds all of the elements that match the supplied `tagName` and `className` arguments, and the latter immediately rounds the corners of the specified element.

MochiKit provides a good abstraction around some of the complexities and drudgery of JavaScript coding and is continually undergoing enhancement and change. It is a well-documented library, with provision for unit tests and extensive API reference documentation. This alone makes it a framework worth considering and evaluating for client-side development that seems to succeed in its mission of "making JavaScript suck less."

Server-Side Frameworks

While the client side frameworks have their obvious advantages as an ASP.NET developer you may find yourself wanting to work with a framework that is tailor-made for the ASP.NET world. The following discussion will briefly explain the differences between three server-side frameworks and give you an opportunity to work directly with each one.

Architectural Distinctions

Every software architect tries to solve the same problems using a different approach. An Ajax-enabled page will not only use the `XmlHttpRequest` object but will also need to alter the rendered page to update the user interface. Each library highlighted in this section is chosen for the varying ways the framework developers tried to create an abstraction layer around the lower-level Ajax technologies.

Creating Ajax applications can be taxing on a developer. JavaScript is an integral part of Ajax development and is not supported in the same way as server-side languages. While some programmers have limited skills in JavaScript, even seasoned developers do not have the luxury of full integrated development environment (IDE) integration, powerful debugging tools, and unit-testing support. The creators of the various Ajax frameworks have addressed this challenge by architecting their frameworks to minimize the need for manual JavaScript coding. In fact, some frameworks allow you to develop full Ajax applications without writing one line of JavaScript; while this is attractive, each benefit comes with its own tradeoff.

Some frameworks require you to inherit from a base class; others give you the option or have no requirement at all. Some frameworks wrap up Ajax functionality by abstracting all JavaScript calls to the server; others allow you to use JavaScript to directly invoke server methods.

How do you remove JavaScript from the equation? Ajax is dependent on the `XmlHttpRequest` object, which exists only on the web browser, so how is this possible?

The answer lies in how the application deals with data and how the user interface is updated.

Data Structures versus Changed HTML

Ajax frameworks may be categorized in many ways, but one way to distinguish them is to look at what type of data is returned to the browser. Some Ajax frameworks will return data structures and others will return only changed HTML.

> **Anthem.NET is unique in this regard because you have the option of returning data structures or changed HTML.**

The idea behind the two different approaches lies in the use of JavaScript. A framework that returns data structures to the client will require the browser to "do something" with that data. Often the browser will glue the data to the existing HTML structure on the page using the DOM.

Some developers would rather stay away from working with JavaScript directly and return to the browser only the changes in HTML. This technique removes the need for intensive JavaScript parsing of the DOM and the need to write JavaScript manually. Another benefit of this approach is that the standard ASP.NET page event lifecycle may be preserved.

Ajax.NET and Atlas return JavaScript Object Notation (JSON) data structures to the client, whereas ComfortASP.NET and MagicAjax return only changed HTML. Anthem.NET gives you the option working manually with JSON objects or simply serving back to the browser what is changed in the HTML.

Benefits

The benefit of working with data structures is that you have complete power and control over your data. Should you choose to return a block of data to the client and render the same information a number of different ways, you may do so. The availability of data structures also allows you to manipulate data in ways that are not available to you in a strict code-behind setup. If you want to make an Ajax call when the focus is lost on a control, having a package that returns data structures where you can write custom functions to manipulate your data is not only desirable but also required.

HTML-only solutions are nice because they truly make Ajax development effortless. When all you have to do is define some controls on your page and then in code-behind manipulate the controls the same way you would if there was a postback, the learning curve is drastically shortened. Solutions that will return changed HTML to the browser also often do not require the writing of any manual JavaScript. This is desirable because now you do not have to worry about maintaining client-side code.

Drawbacks

The drawbacks may seem obvious, but when you have a framework that returns data structures you will often have to write and maintain your own JavaScript code.

The disadvantage to frameworks that offer a changed HTML-only architecture is that should you need to manipulate your data in such a way that is not native to an ASP.NET control, you will have no way to hook into the framework. For example, in ComfortASP.NET there is no way for you to call a server-side method when the focus leaves a control. The architectural structure of this library is designed to keep development as close to the way you would code if the page were still operating under the traditional ASP.NET postback model.

Panels versus Custom Controls

Once the server has finalized its processing and has returned a response to the client, the application must have a way of determining what part of the HTML page to update. The two methods you find in the frameworks in this section use either panels or custom controls.

When you think of an "Ajax panel" think along the same lines as the ASP.NET `Panel` control. When using this control, you create a container on the page where other controls placed inside the container may be dealt with as a group. For example if you make the panel invisible, all the child controls are invisible.

The panels used in the Ajax libraries function in much the same way. When you define an Ajax panel on your page, you are automatically given the ability to update the panel's child control attributes without requiring the page to conduct a full postback. All three frameworks feature panels in their architecture.

The other method of letting the browser know what to update is to use custom controls. Instead of wrapping your controls in some sort of container, you may declaratively add Ajax controls to the page. These controls are then recognized by the host framework and are given the Ajax capabilities. Custom controls are an integral part of the Anthem.NET framework.

Benefits

The benefits of a paneled architecture are most apparent in ease of use. When using panels, most of the hard work of creating Ajax solutions is managed by the code the panel creates for a developer. Perhaps the greatest benefit to using panels is that you may deal with controls as a group; you are not required to touch each control just to give it the behavior you desire. Panels bring flexibility to your page.

Custom controls bring an alternate set of benefits. Since a custom control is specific for each control on the page, you will have a richer set of features available to you. Anthem.NET adds a variety of custom properties, events, and methods to its custom controls. The primary benefit of custom controls is the fine-grained control over a page.

Drawbacks

The downside to using panels is that you will not have as much control over the controls on your page. This method's advantage may be a disadvantage, depending on your situation.

The disadvantages of using custom controls are twofold:

❑ The first drawback is that there is sometimes not a one-to-one relationship between ASP.NET controls and the custom controls of the framework. For instance, as of this printing Anthem.NET does not feature an equivalent control for the ASP.NET 2.0 `DetailsView` control.

❑ The other disadvantage is that when using custom controls you are, by nature, forced to replace the native ASP.NET controls with your library's controls. This may or may not be a problem depending on your situation.

Configuration Options

Each framework requires you to configure your application a little bit differently. The different configuration approaches found among the featured frameworks include using `httpHandlers` or `httpModules`, inheriting your ASP.NET page from the library's base page class, or using page control directives.

❑ The use of an `httpHandler` or `httpModule` is similar in the respect that ASP.NET will process the requests through either the handler or module before allowing the page to execute. To signify this distinction, from now on we will refer to the use of either an `httpHandler` or `httpModule` as "preprocessing." Preprocessing provides a layer where the application will examine requests coming to the server to determine if any Ajax support is required to render to the page. Preprocessing configuration options are not enough alone to grant a page Ajax support, but less work is required on a page level.

❑ Some frameworks have a base page class that you inherit your ASP.NET web forms from instead of the traditional `System.Web.UI.Page` class. The custom base class will encapsulate the required plumbing that your page needs to handle Ajax interaction between the client and server.

❑ The final option is to use a page control directive. These directives allow you to declaratively add Ajax support to a page at design time. The page control directive can supersede the need for preprocessing or the use of a base page class.

You will see each of these options implemented in coming examples.

Benefits

Preprocessing allows each page in your application the ability to cycle through your Ajax engine. This can make turning on Ajax features of a page easier because there is less code you must write on the page level.

Base classes give you all the benefits of inheritance by giving your page Ajax processing support "for free." The base class will often include useful services that make coding easier, but the true benefit is found in ease of use. Often frameworks that provide a base class require very little extra coding to create an Ajax experience. Another benefit to using a base class lies in the fact that you may inherit from the class. This extra layer of abstraction allows you to make changes and provide services to your Ajax pages in one place.

Page control directives perhaps give you the best of both worlds, because you will avoid the disadvantages (stated in the following section) of the preprocessing and base class options, while still giving your page full Ajax support.

Drawbacks

In some experiments with frameworks that use preprocessing, we have found a few cases where the Ajax `httpHandler` or `httpModule` interfered with applications that used their own custom handler or module. The preprocessing configuration may not be the best option for you if you are working on a project that already employs its own handlers or modules. Test rigorously to ensure a true working solution.

The drawbacks to base classes are classic in object-oriented development. If want to use a solution that *requires* you inherit from the base class, you may run into a few problems. What if you are already inheriting from your own base class? The .NET runtime does not support multiple inheritances, so you must then make a choice; do you keep your base class or go with the base class from the third-party framework? Other questions you might pose to yourself are: What if I change Ajax libraries? What will that to do my inheritance structure? Although base classes at first may seem attractive, implementation by inheritance, rather than composition may often architecturally limit you in the end.

Page control directives are nice because they are a light-touch addition to your page. However, since you are not inheriting from the control, making global changes becomes more difficult. If you wanted to add custom logic to the directive control, you would have to inherit from the Ajax control and create your own control exposing it as a page directive control.

Creating Your Resource Data File

Before you begin implementing the coming examples, there is a file you must create that will give your applications some sample data. This file is an XML structure that will allow you to conduct data binding without having to worry about connecting up to a database.

1. Open Visual Studio.NET 2005.

2. Press *Ctrl+N* to display the New File dialog box.

3. Click XML file template.

4. Click the Open button.

5. Enter the following code:

Resources.xml
```xml
<?xml version="1.0" encoding="utf-8"?>
<resources>
  <resource>
    <title>Polymorphic Podcast</title>
    <url>http://polymorphicpodcast.com/</url>
    <author>Craig Shoemaker</author>
  </resource>
  <resource>
    <title>ASP.NET Podcast</title>
    <url>http://aspnetpodcast.com/</url>
    <author>Wally McClure</author>
  </resource>
  <resource>
    <title>Glavs Blog : The dotDude of .Net</title>
    <url>http://weblogs.asp.net/pglavich/</url>
      <author>Paul Glavich</author>
  </resource>
  <resource>
    <title>Scott Cate Weblog</title>
    <url>http://scottcate.mykb.com/</url>
    <author>Scott Cate</author>
  </resource>
</resources>
```

6. Press *Ctrl+S* to save the file.

7. Save the file to `C:\BeginningAJAX\Chapter9\Resources.xml`.

Introduction to the Frameworks

The following examples will highlight different features from the ComfortASP.NET, MagicAjax, and Anthem.NET frameworks. While learning about each framework, keep in mind the type of development that you do and which solution best fits your needs.

Each library employs a number of the architectural distinctions presented earlier in this section. The introductory sections will familiarize you with the framework and describe the options available in each framework. The examples begin with the traditional "Hello World" implementation, and then proceed to more in-depth samples. Some demonstrations are repeated between the frameworks. The repetition is included by design to illustrate how the same problems are addressed by the different libraries.

ComfortASP.NET

URL: www.comfortasp.de

ComfortASP.NET is a framework that allows you to quickly Ajax-enable any ASP.NET page. A demo version of the software is all that is needed for the following examples. You may download ComfortASP.NET from http://beginningajax.com/chapter9/ComfortASPNET. For more information about ComfortASP.NET, please visit the official web site at www.comfortasp.de.

ComfortASP.NET's architecture is flexible and gives a developer a number of different ways to configure the application. The framework employs a changed HTML-only architecture, uses panels, and gives you the option of either using preprocessing or a base page class.

In the coming examples, you will use ComfortASP.NET's base page class. When the base class is configured properly, you may code your page normally, and the framework will worry about the Ajax implementation details. What's surprising about this framework is that the only configuration required of the base class is to set the `HiddenFormPostBack` property to `true`.

Optionally, ComfortASP.NET will save the page and `ViewState` information in session. Using session state allows the framework to quickly serve pages back to the client because it uses the information persisted in session rather than asking the server to build up the page again. Session use is optional and may or may not be desirable, depending on the application you are building.

Data transferred between the client and server may also be compressed by ComfortASP.NET. The `CompressionLevel` property of a ComfortASP.NET `Manager` control determines the amount of compression applied to the transporting data. The compression scale ranges from 1 to 9. At the low end of the spectrum, there is little compression with higher transfer speeds. The higher end of the spectrum is more data compression, resulting in lower transmission speeds.

Setup

Before you begin using the ComfortASP.NET framework, you must first download the files and then reference them in a web project. The following steps help you build a solution that houses all the samples you create for the ComfortASP.NET framework.

Downloading Files

1. Download the zip file containing the `ComfortASP.NET DLL` file from `http://beginning ajax.com/downloads/chapter9/Chapter9-Framework DLLs.zip`.

2. Extract the files and place them in a convenient location.

Creating the Solution

1. Open Visual Studio 2005.

2. Click File⇨New⇨Website.

3. Select the ASP.NET Website template.

4. Choose File System under location.

5. Set the path to `c:\BeginningAJAX\Chapter9\ComfortASPDemo`.

6. Choose C# as the language.

7. Click OK.

Referencing ComfortASP.NET

1. In the Solution Explorer, right-click on the project name and select Add ASP.NET Folder.

2. Choose `App_LocalResources` to create the ASP.NET folder.

3. Copy `ComfortASP.dll` (from the zip file you extracted) to the `App_LocalResource` folder.

4. Create a reference to `ComfortASP.dll`.

Copying the Data File

1. Copy the `Resources.xml` you created in the last section into the `App_Data` folder in the solution.

Adding the ComfortASP.NET Group to the Toolbox

ComfortASP.NET comes with some controls that can be used to create specific behaviors. To use these controls in the Visual Studio Designer, you must add them into the Toolbox:

1. Right-click on the Toolbox window, and select Add Tab.

2. Name the tab **ComfortASP.NET**.

3. Left-click the ComfortASP.NET tab.

4. Right-click ComfortASP.NET.

5. Select Choose Items.

6. Click Browse and select `ComfortASP.dll` from the location you placed it in the earlier steps.

7. The new controls are automatically selected — click OK.

You may now begin implementing your first Ajax pages using the ComfortASP.NET framework.

Using ComfortASP.NET

Now that the project is configured to work with the ComfortASP.NET framework, you may begin working hands-on with the framework. The next few sections will walk you through building pages that implement an introductory example, highlight some of the features unique to ComfortASP.NET, and explain how to execute some common operations using the framework.

Example 1: Hello World

The first exercise will take you step by step through creating a Hello World page. In the coming examples, the interaction between the client and server is handled by subclassing ComfortASP.NET's base page class. To Ajax-enable the page, you simply switch on the page's `HiddenFormPostBack` property and the rest of the code-behind remains unchanged from the code used in the traditional postback paradigm.

Figure 9-1 is a screenshot of what the page looks like once it's constructed.

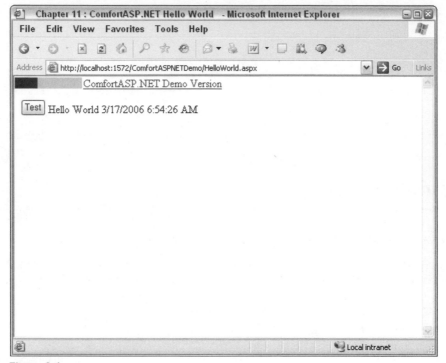

Figure 9-1

When you click on the Test button, the label is updated with the words "Hello World" plus the current date and time.

Implementing "Hello World"

Add a new web form to the solution and name it `HelloWorld.aspx`. Open the HTML editor, and enter the following markup between the `<div>` tags:

```
<asp:Button
    ID="btnTest"
    Text="Test"
    runat="server" />
```

```
<asp:Label
    ID="lblTest"
    runat="server" />
```

Note that the HTML markup is exactly the same as if the page were not using ComfortASP.NET.

Switch to the designer view, and double-click the Test button. This will wire up a click event method to the button and switch you to the code-behind window.

Next, update the `HelloWorld` class to inherit from `ComfortASP.ComfortASP_Page`:

```
public partial class HelloWorld : ComfortASP.ComfortASP_Page
{
    protected void Page_Load(object sender, EventArgs e)
    {
        this.HiddenFormPostBack = true;
    }
    protected void btnTest_Click(object sender, EventArgs e)
    {
        this.lblTest.Text = "Hello World " + DateTime.Now.ToString();
    }
}
```

The `Page_Load` event method will set the `HiddenFormPostBack` property equal to `true`, enabling ComfortASP.NET on the page. In the button click event, update the text of the label to print Hello World and current date and time for the user.

Now you may launch the application in the browser to test your code. Click the Test button, and you will notice that the label is updated. Click the button again, and you can observe that no postbacks are taking place and the time will be updated with each click.

Example 2: Using Complex Controls

You see now that working with ComfortASP.NET is easy, but what about when you want to use more complex controls like the ASP.NET `GridView` control? Databound controls like the ASP.NET `GridView` have a much larger property set as well as custom events. ComfortASP.NET can make developing with these controls just as easy as the Hello World example above.

This example will bind the contents of the `Resources.xml` file to a `GridView` control. When the user clicks on an item in the grid, the `SelectedIndexChanged` event will fire to update the page, notifying the user of the new selected index. The purpose of this demonstration is to show you that the ComfortASP.NET framework makes working with controls that have custom events and extended properties just as easy as the previous Hello World example.

Figure 9-2 shows what the page will look like when you are done.

When you click the Load Resource button, the grid is loaded with data. When you click an item in the grid, the new selected index is printed on the page.

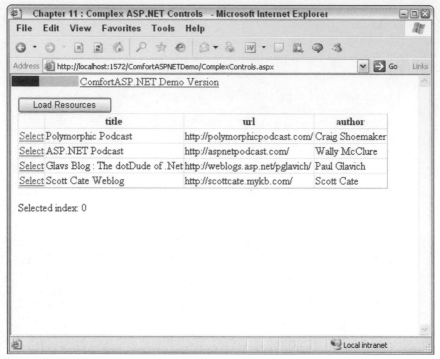

Figure 9-2

Try It Out   Using Complex Controls

Add a new web form to the solution and call it `ComplexControls.aspx`. Switch to the source view and add the following markup between the `<div>` tags.

```
<asp:Button
    ID="btnLoadResources"
    OnClick="btnLoadResources_Click"
    Text="Load Resources"
    runat="server" />

<asp:gridview
    ID="grdResources"
    runat="server"
    OnSelectedIndexChanged="grdResources_SelectedIndexChanged">
    <Columns>
        <asp:CommandField ShowSelectButton="True" />
    </Columns>
</asp:gridview>

<p>Selected index:
<asp:Label ID="lblSelectedIndex" runat="server" /></p>
```

Switch to the source window to update the ComplexControls class.

```
public partial class ComplexControls : ComfortASP.ComfortASP_Page
{
    protected void Page_Load(object sender, EventArgs e)
    {
        this.HiddenFormPostBack = true;
    }

    protected void btnLoadResources_Click(object sender, EventArgs e)
    {
        System.Data.DataSet ds;

        ds = new System.Data.DataSet();
        ds.ReadXml(Server.MapPath("~/App_Data/Resources.xml"));

        this.grdResources.DataSource = ds;
        this.grdResources.DataBind();
    }

    protected void grdResources_SelectedIndexChanged(object sender, EventArgs e)
    {
        this.lblSelectedIndex.Text =
            this.grdResources.SelectedIndex.ToString();
    }
}
```

The page will inherit from the ComfortASP.NET base page and will turn on the HiddenFormPostBack property in the Page_Load method. When the Load Resources button is clicked, you will load the data from the Resources.xml file and bind it to the GridView control. Finally, when an item in the grid is selected, the SelectedIndex is printed to the lblSelectedIndex label on the page.

You can now launch the application in the browser to test your code.

Example 3: ComfortASP.NET Manager Control

The ComfortASP.NET Manager control gives you a centralized place to administer the page's Ajax capabilities. The manager control provides services that implement many common requirements. We will review some of the more common features of the control here, but please refer to the ComfortASP.NET web site for full documentation of the Manager control.

If you want to stop a user from repeatedly clicking on a button that initiates an Ajax call, you might choose to disable the button once the call is dispatched. ComfortASP.NET makes it easy to disable these controls. The manager's DisableFormWhilePostBack property will automate this process of enabling or disabling the controls on a page during a callback to the server. If the property is set to true, then all controls are disabled during an Ajax call; otherwise, the controls are left alone.

Ajax applications face the challenge that the server will not always respond in a timely manner. Consider what the user would think when he or she clicks a button and nothing happens on the page for well over a minute, or perhaps never. The ComfortASP.NET Manager control has a built-in safeguard against this situation. The HiddenRequestTimeout property will define the number of seconds the page should wait until sending a notification that the request has timed out. The user may then decide whether or not to try the request again. The Manager control also exposes a property that will allow you to customize the message displayed to the user in the event of a timeout.

The TransferDifference property will determine if the entire page markup is returned to the client or if just the changed section of the page goes across the wire. The distinction between the two options lies in the use of session state. If you do not want ComfortASP.NET to use session state to persist the page contents, then TransferDifference is false. Alternatively, if you allow the framework to use session to hold page content, then TransferDifference is set to true.

Figure 9-3 shows an example of the "loading" message generated by the ComfortASP.NET framework when the server is engaged in processing. Also notice how the button is disabled. This behavior is implemented by changing some of the values on the ComfortASP.NET Manager control.

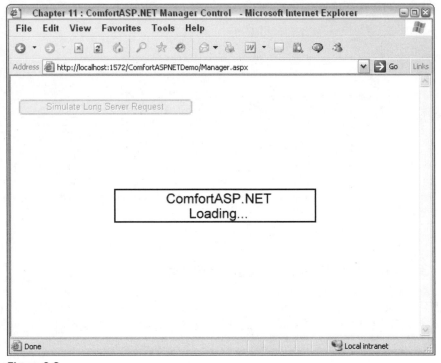

Figure 9-3

Figure 9-4 is an example of how the user is notified when a request timeout occurs.

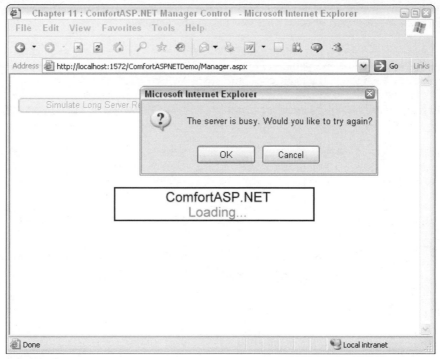

Figure 9-4

Try It Out   Using the Control Manager

Add a new web form to the solution and name it Manager.aspx. Make sure that the ASPX page is in design view, and hover over the toolbar to drag a ComfortASP.NET Manager control onto the page. Switch to source view, and add the following markup.

The ComfortASP.NET Manager control is already added to your page; simply adjust the property values to match what is listed here, and add the markup for the button and label.

```
<cc1:ComfortASP_Manager
    ID="comfortManager"
    HiddenRequestTimeout="20"
    HiddenRequestTimeoutText="The server is busy. Try again?"
    DisableFormWhilePostBack="True"
    TransferDifference="True"
    runat="server" />

<asp:Button
    ID="btnLongRequest"
    Text="Simulate Long Server Request"
    runat="server" />

<asp:Label
    ID="lblResult"
    runat="server" />
```

Switch back to the design view and double-click the `btnLongRequest` button. This action will switch you to the code window and wire up a button click event method.

Update the `Manager` class by inheriting from the `ComfortASP.ComfortASP_Page` class. The only other changes required for this demonstration are to add a short delay when the button is clicked and to print a message on the label when the request is completed.

> *Notice that you are not setting the page's* `HiddenFormPostBack` *property. The ComfortASP.NET* `Manager` *control is responsible for notifying the application that this page is Ajax-enabled.*

```
public partial class Manager : ComfortASP.ComfortASP_Page
{
    protected void Page_Load(object sender, EventArgs e)
    {

    }

    protected void btnLongRequest_Click(object sender, EventArgs e)
    {
        System.Threading.Thread.Sleep(5000);
        this.lblResult.Text = "Done";
    }
}
```

Now run the page to demonstrate its behavior.

Experiment with the manager settings by changing the `HiddenRequestTimeout` property to 3 in the ASPX file. This allows the page to time out before the server is done processing, and you see how the framework will notify the user of a timeout. Change the `DisableFormWhilePostBack` property, and note how the controls on the page are no longer disabled when you make a call to the server. Finally, you can see the effect of the `TransferDifference` property by setting it to `false` and clicking on the button. The ComfortASP.NET demo version includes a bar graph that represents the amount of information sent across the wire. When `TransferDifference` is turned off, you can see by the graph how much more data is transported to the client.

Example 4: PanelUpdater Control (Periodic Refresh)

The ComfortASP.NET `PanelUpdater` is a control that allows you to target specific areas of a page to update. You may decide that you want to change the contents of a section of your page, but the rest of the page should remain unchanged. The `PanelUpdater` wraps up many of the implementation details, allowing you to easily access page segments.

The `PanelUpdater` works by being nested within an ASP.NET `Panel` control. The panel acts as the overall container and the `PanelUpdater`, simply by being placed inside the panel, will expose the container to ComfortASP.NET. The control exists on the page to service interaction between the browser and the server and will not render anything visible to the user.

The ComfortASP.NET `PanelUpdater` is associated to its parent panel, so you may have multiple `Panel`/`PanelUpdater` combinations on a single page.

Imagine for a moment that you want to create a page that will continually engage with the server to see if there are new messages available for the user. The PanelUpdater is a perfect choice for a requirement like this for two reasons:

❑ Reason one is that the control will allow you to target a portion of the page and allow the system to update only that region of the page you have specified.

❑ Reason two is that the PanelUpdater features a timer interval that, once set, will instruct the control to send requests to the server at every *n* number of seconds. This pattern is known as the Periodic Refresh pattern, and you will also implement this same behavior in the next section, using MagicAjax.

The following example implements a page with the requirements just described. Figure 9-5 is an example of how the finished product will look.

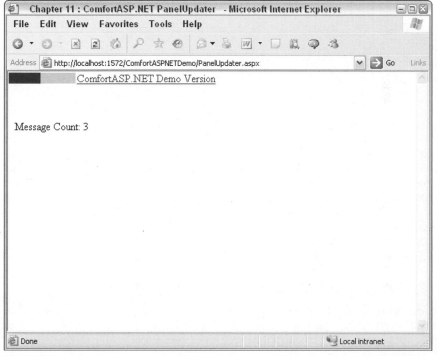

Figure 9-5

The ComfortASP.NET demo version will automatically print the bar graph at the top of the page, indicating the amount of data transferred with a link back to the ComfortASP.NET web site. The full version does not have this feature.

The page includes a panel that will contact the server every 3 seconds to update the page with the new message count.

Try It Out   Using PanelUpdater Control

Begin by adding a new web form to the solution, naming it `PanelUpdater.aspx`. Make sure that you are in source view, and add the following line after the Page directive line found at the top of the ASPX page.

```
<%@ Register Assembly="ComfortASP" Namespace="ComfortASP" TagPrefix="cc1" %>
```

The Register tag will make the ComfortASP.NET framework available to the page.

Continue by adding the following markup between the `<div>` tags:

```
<asp:Panel ID="pnlContent" runat="server">

    <cc1:ComfortASP_PanelUpdater
        ID="ComfortASP_PanelUpdater1"
        TimerIntervalUpdate="3"
        Active="True"
        runat="server" />

    Message Count:
    <asp:Label
        ID="lblMessageCount"
        runat="server" />

</asp:Panel>
```

The ASP.NET panel is the container for the section of the page to update. The ComfortASP.NET `PanelUpdater` control will handle generating the client-side code to create the timeout behavior. Be sure to activate the `PanelUpdater` by setting the `Active` property equal to `true`. The `TimerIntervalUpdate` property will take a value for the number of seconds you want the browser to wait before contacting the server. Finally, the label at the end of the listing will take the latest information from the server and print the message count back to the user.

Now switch to the code window to update the `PanelUpdater` class.

```
public partial class PanelUpdater : ComfortASP.ComfortASP_Page
{
    private int MessageCount
    {
        get
        {
            if (this.ViewState["messageCount"] == null)
            {
                return 0;
            }
            else
            {
                return Convert.ToInt32(this.ViewState["messageCount"]);
            }
        }
        set
        {
            this.ViewState.Add("messageCount", value);
```

```
            }
        }

        protected void Page_Load(object sender, EventArgs e)
        {
            this.HiddenFormPostBack = true;
            this.UpdateMessageCount();
        }

        private void UpdateMessageCount()
        {
            this.MessageCount++;
            this.lblMessageCount.Text = this.MessageCount.ToString();
        }
    }
}
```

As always, the class will inherit from `ComfortASP.ComfortASP_Page` instead of `System.Web.UI.Page`. You will Ajax-enable the page by turning on `HiddenFormPostBack` property in the load method. The `MessageCount` property is a strongly typed wrapper to a `ViewState` entry that persists the message count. If the `ViewState` entry does not exist, the wrapper will initialize the value to 0. Finally, the `UpdateMessageCount` method will simply increment the `MessageCount` property and report the new count to the label on the page.

You can now run the page to demonstrate its behavior.

What You Have Learned

The ComfortASP.NET framework is an Ajax library that is unobtrusive for a .NET developer. The framework allows you to implement Ajax functionality in your ASP.NET pages without having to manually code JavaScript or deal with XML. ComfortASP.NET also features a number of useful controls that allow you to administer the framework's settings and behaviors from a centralized location.

MagicAjax

URL: www.magicajax.net

MagicAjax is a panel-based, changed-HTML framework that makes it easy for you to add Ajax functionality to your ASP.NET applications. The architects of MagicAjax created a framework that integrates into your application with a light touch. Once the site is configured to communicate with MagicAjax, most Ajax functionality can be achieved by adding a MagicAjax Panel to the page. You do not have to inherit from a base class, nor are there any custom controls to declare. Other than adding the MagicAjax Panel to your page, the ASPX and code-behind code is unchanged from how you would write your pages in the traditional postback model.

Setup

Before you begin using MagicAjax, you must first download the files and then reference them in a web project. The following steps help you build a solution that houses all the samples you create for the MagicAjax.

Downloading Files

1. If you haven't already done so, download the zip file containing the MagicAjax DLL from `http://beginningajax.com/downloads/chapter9/Chapter9-Framework DLLs.zip`.

2. Extract the files and place them in a convenient location.

Creating the Solution

1. Open Visual Studio 2005.

2. Click File⇨New⇨Website.

3. Select the ASP.NET Website template.

4. Choose File System under location.

5. Set the path to `c:\BeginningAJAX\Chapter9\MagicAjaxDemo`.

6. Choose C# as the language.

7. Click OK.

Referencing ComfortASP.NET

1. In the Solution Explorer, right-click on the project name and select Add ASP.NET Folder.

2. Choose `App_LocalResources` to create the ASP.NET folder.

3. Copy `MagicAjax.dll` (from the zip file you extracted) to the `App_LocalResource` folder.

4. Create a reference to the `MagicAjax.dll`.

Updating Web.Config

Open the `Web.Config` file and add the following code just after the open `<system.web>` tag:

```
<pages>
    <controls>
        <add
            namespace="MagicAjax.UI.Controls"
            assembly="MagicAjax" tagPrefix="ajax"/>
    </controls>
</pages>
<httpModules>
    <add
        name="MagicAjaxModule"
        type="MagicAjax.MagicAjaxModule, MagicAjax"/>
</httpModules>
```

Your application is now configured to use MagicAjax.

Using MagicAjax

Now that you have MagicAjax set up on your machine, you may begin implementing the examples. Each example will expose a new layer of the MagicAjax framework giving you a taste of the library's features and strengths. The coming examples will demonstrate some of MagicAjax stock capabilities as well as a providing few more involved examples to show you how you might use these techniques in the real world.

Example 1: Hello World

Your MagicAjax examples begin with a Hello World page. With no base class to inherit from and the Web.Config settings exposing the framework to each page, the page-level configuration is minimal. To give a MagicAjax page asynchronous functionality, you simply must declare some ASP.NET controls inside a MagicAjax Panel. This exercise is much like the page you implemented for the ComfortASP.NET framework in that a button click will initiate a request to the server, which in turn will return fresh data to the client, all without a postback.

Figure 9-6 is a screenshot of what the page will look like.

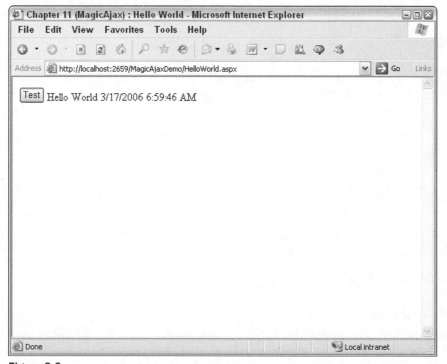

Figure 9-6

When you click the Test button, the text "Hello World" plus the current date and time is returned to the browser.

Try It Out   Implementing "Hello World"

Begin by adding a new web form to the solution and name it HelloWorld.aspx. Switch to source view, and add the following markup between the <div> tags:

```
<ajax:ajaxpanel ID="Ajaxpanel1" runat="server">

    <asp:Button
        ID="Button1"
        OnClick="Button1_Click"
        Text="Test"
        runat="server" />

    <asp:Label
        ID="Label1"
        runat="server" />

</ajax:ajaxpanel>
```

The reason you do not have access to IntelliSense for the `ajaxpanel` *is that you used a configuration option that added the MagicAjax functionality to each page in* `Web.Config`. *If you were to change the configuration to use a* `Register` *directive, then you would see the IntelliSense listings.*

Now switch to the code view, and update the `HelloWorld` class.

```
public partial class HelloWorld : System.Web.UI.Page
{
    protected void Page_Load(object sender, EventArgs e)
    {

    }
    protected void Button1_Click(object sender, EventArgs e)
    {
        this.Label1.Text = "Hello World " + DateTime.Now.ToString();
    }
}
```

Notice that there is *no change* to the code-behind as compared to a normal ASP.NET implantation with postbacks. MagicAjax.NET does all the work by adding the controls into an `ajaxpanel`.

You can now launch the page in a browser to test its behavior.

Example 2: Delay

Every Ajax framework must deal with the likely event that the server will take a few (or perhaps more) seconds to complete a given command. When your application experiences such a delay, you must provide feedback to the user to give them a clue of what is happening. MagicAjax provides a "Loading..." message out of the box to help you keep your users informed of what is happening on the page.

This next example will force the server to wait 5 seconds before returning data to the server. This delay will give you an opportunity to see how MagicAjax responds to such a hesitation.

Figure 9-7 is a screenshot showing what the "Loading..." message looks like.

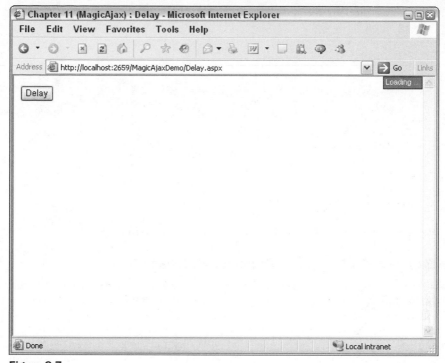

Figure 9-7

Try It Out   Demonstrating the Delay Message

Add a new web form to the solution, and name it Delay.aspx. Open the source view of the page and update the markup between the <div> tags with the following code:

```
<ajax:AjaxPanel ID="AjaxPanel1" runat="server">

    <asp:Button
        ID="btnDelay"
        Text="Delay"
        OnClick="btnDelay_Click"
        runat="server" />

    <asp:Label
        ID="lblDelay"
        runat="server" />

</ajax:AjaxPanel>
```

Now switch to the code view to update the Delay class.

```
public partial class Delay : System.Web.UI.Page
{
    protected void Page_Load(object sender, EventArgs e)
    {

    }
    protected void btnDelay_Click(object sender, EventArgs e)
    {
        System.Threading.Thread.Sleep(5000);
        this.lblDelay.Text = "Done";
    }
}
```

When you click the Delay button, the server will hesitate for 5 seconds displaying the MagicAjax "Loading..." message at the top right of the screen.

You can now launch the page in the web browser to test its behavior.

Example 3: Ajax Call Helper (Periodic Refresh)

If you recall from the examples in the ComfortASP.NET section, you created a page that implemented the Periodic Refresh pattern. The next example will teach you how to implement the same behavior using MagicAjax.

The design goals are the same; create a page that will check the server for changes in data at a regular interval without requiring the user to initiate the request. The page in this example will use MagicAjax's `AjaxCallHelper` class. This class has utilities that help automate your Ajax development. For this example, you will use the `SetAjaxCallTimerInterval` method, which will register a timeout on the browser and create a request to the server every *n* seconds.

Figure 9-8 is a screenshot showing what the page will look like when you are done.

Try It Out   Using the Ajax Call Helper

Begin by adding a new web form to the solution, and name it `AjaxCallHelper.aspx`. Switch to source view, and update the page with the following markup between the `<div>` tags:

```
<ajax:AjaxPanel ID="AjaxPanel1" runat="server">

    Message Count:
    <asp:Label
        ID="lblMessageCount"
        runat="server" />

</ajax:AjaxPanel>
```

The ASPX code in this example is straightforward. You create a label to hold the current count and place it inside a MagicAjax Panel.

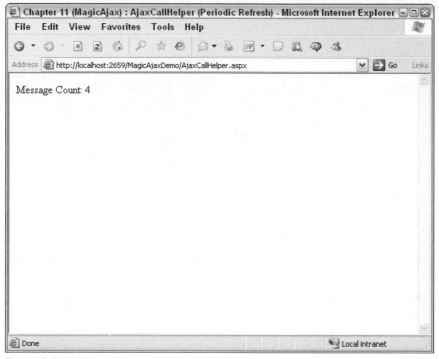

Figure 9-8

Now switch to the code window to update the `AjaxCallHelper` class.

```csharp
public partial class AjaxCallHelper : System.Web.UI.Page
{
    private int MessageCount
    {
        get
        {
            if (this.ViewState["messageCount"] == null)
            {
                return 0;
            }
            else
            {
                return Convert.ToInt32(this.ViewState["messageCount"]);
            }
        }
        set
        {
            this.ViewState.Add("messageCount", value);
        }
    }

    protected void Page_Load(object sender, EventArgs e)
    {
```

```
        if (!this.Page.IsPostBack)
        {
            MagicAjax.AjaxCallHelper.SetAjaxCallTimerInterval(5000);
        }
        this.UpdateMessageCount();
    }

    private void UpdateMessageCount()
    {
        this.MessageCount++;
        this.lblMessageCount.Text = this.MessageCount.ToString();
    }
}
```

If you implemented the ComfortASP.NET demo, this code is familiar to you. The MessageCount property encapsulates the ViewState container for the number of messages for this series of requests.

Upon the first request to the page, you register a timeout on the browser by using the SetAjaxCall TimerInterval method. This command will take care of rendering all the appropriate JavaScript to the page to fire a request to the server every 5 seconds.

When the page is in "postback" mode, the message count increments and the label is updated.

Now launch the page in a browser to test its behavior.

Example 4: Direct Scripting (Micro-content)

In previous examples, you saw how the ASP.NET page event lifecycle is preserved by MagicAjax, allowing you to make drastic changes to a page's contents using Ajax and doing it all from code-behind. This model is powerful and will probably aid you in most of your Ajax development, but what if you need to create interaction on the page that is not native to the ASP.NET architecture? What if you want to update an element on the page when the user clicks away from the control?

The following steps walk you through the process of creating a page that allows a user to directly edit text on the page. For example, when the user encounters the page title, he or she may click on the title text, edit its contents, and continue browsing. In the background, the page recognizes the change and is responsible for contacting the server to persist the latest data.

The Ajax design pattern being implemented in this example is called *micro-content*. The micro-content pattern states that certain areas of a page may be editable by the user without having to manually switch the page into an "edit mode" by clicking on buttons or changing page locations. Small or "micro" areas of the content on the page are open for the user to edit simply by clicking on the text. You will often see this pattern implemented in wikis that are Ajax-powered.

This exercise will make use of not only MagicAjax but also some custom Cascading Style Sheet definitions to power the change in the user interface to give clues as to what is happening.

Figure 9-9 is a screenshot of how the user will first encounter the page.

The page will provide initial clues that parts of the page are editable by drawing a border over the text when the cursor hovers over the editable area. Figure 9-10 shows how the control will look when the mouse is hovering over the control.

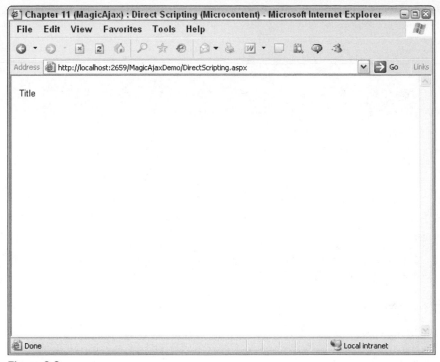

Figure 9-9

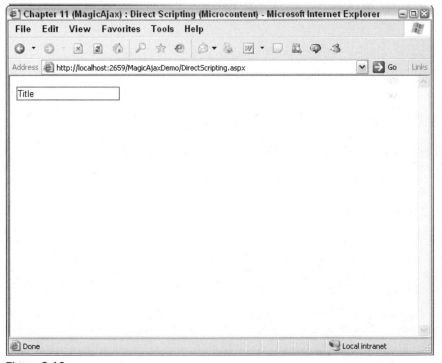

Figure 9-10

The next step is to change the appearance of the control when the user has placed this area of the page in "edit mode." Figure 9-11 shows the page after the user clicks within the border of the control.

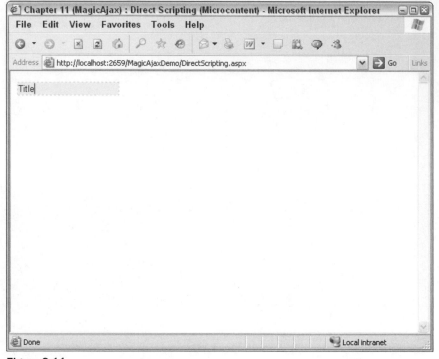

Figure 9-11

Finally, when the focus is lost from the control, MagicAjax will contact the server and allow the back-end processing to persist the latest data. Under normal circumstances, you would probably persist the data to a data store of some kind. For demonstration purposes, this exercise will simply store the information in Session state. This way, after you make a change to the data, you can navigate off the page and return to see your latest changes, but avoid having to implement a data layer just for this example.

Try It Out   Using Direct Scripting

Begin by adding a new web form to your solution, and name it `DirectScripting.aspx`. Next, switch to the source view, and add the following Cascading Style Sheet entries and JavaScript to the page just after the `<title>` tag:

```
<style type="text/css">
input
{
    border:solid 1px #fff;
}
.focus
{
    background-color:#eee;
```

```
        border:dashed 1px #ccc;
    }
    .blur
    {
        background-color:#fff;
        border:dashed 1px #fff;
    }
    .mouseOver
    {
        border:solid 1px #c00;
    }
    .mouseOut
    {
        border:solid 1px #fff;
    }
</style>
```

These style sheet entries give the page the visual clues to help the user understand what is happening on the page. The first entry will place a one pixel white border around the page's input control. This white border is necessary because later you will apply a colored border to the control, and if there is no existing border, the page contents will appear to shift.

The focus, blur, mouseover, and mouseout CSS classes are named consistently with the events that will use them. When focus is brought to the control, the background color is turned a light grey, and a dashed border is applied to the control. When focus is lost from the control, or the focus is blurred, the blur style is applied. The blur style will change the background and border back to white. When the user mouses over the control, the border is turned red as dictated by the mouseover class. Finally, when the user moves their mouse off of the control, the border is returned to the original white state by the mouseOut event and class.

Next, add this JavaScript block directly below the closing <style> tag:

```
<script type="text/javascript">
function ChangeCSSClass(element,className)
{
    element.className = className;
}
</script>
```

This function will handle the work of programmatically applying the stated style sheet entry to a control. The function is defined here and wired up to the control in code-behind.

Next, update the markup between the <div> tags with the following code:

```
<ajax:AjaxPanel ID="AjaxPanel1" runat="server">

    <asp:TextBox
        ID="txtTitle"
        text="Title"
        OnTextChanged="txtTitle_TextChanged"
        runat="server" />

</ajax:AjaxPanel>
```

The markup is simple. A single ASP.NET TextBox control in a MagicAjax panel is all that is required. When the browser recognizes a change to the contents of the textbox, the OnTextChanged event will fire. You will implement your persistence logic in the resulting method.

Finally, switch to the code window, and update the DirectScripting class with the following code.

```
public partial class DirectScripting : System.Web.UI.Page
{
    protected void Page_Load(object sender, EventArgs e)
    {
        if (!this.Page.IsPostBack)
        {
            this.txtTitle.Attributes.Add("onfocus",
                "ChangeCSSClass(this,'focus');");

            this.txtTitle.Attributes.Add("onblur",
                "ChangeCSSClass(this,'blur');" +
                MagicAjax.AjaxCallHelper.GetAjaxCallEventReference(this.txtTitle) +
                " return false;");

            this.txtTitle.Attributes.Add("onmouseover",
                "ChangeCSSClass(this,'mouseOver');");

            this.txtTitle.Attributes.Add("onmouseout",
                "ChangeCSSClass(this,'mouseOut');");

            if (this.Session["title"] != null)
            {
                this.txtTitle.Text = this.Session["title"].ToString();
            }
        }
    }

    protected void txtTitle_TextChanged(object sender, EventArgs e)
    {
        this.Session.Add("title", this.txtTitle.Text);
    }
}
```

When the page is first served to the browser, each event's JavaScript call is wired up to the control. The final portion of this code block inspects Session state for a current "title" value. If the value is found, the control will display the value; otherwise, the page renders the default text defined in the HTML.

While each event function is attached using the familiar Attributes.Add approach, one event stands out among the rest. The blur event is responsible for contacting the server when the user leaves the focus of the control. This type of interaction with the code-behind is not native to the ASP.NET architecture. In order to create a link between the client and server at this time, the MagicAjax AjaxCallHelper class must do the work of talking to the server.

The AjaxCallHelper exposes a method named GetAjaxCallEventReference, which will contact the server simulating a "postback" in code-behind, telling the page that whatever control is passed in as an argument is the sender for the request. Once the server recognizes the request, the page will run the txtTitle_TextChanged event and will update Session state with the latest value. Now when you move to another page and return, this page will have your changed value instead of saying "Title."

You can now launch the page in your browser to test its behavior.

What You Have Learned

MagicAjax is a framework that will make any .NET developer feel comfortable. The panel, changed-HTML-type architecture makes creating Ajax applications easy because the framework is responsible for creating the wireup between the browser and the server. In fact, the only custom JavaScript you wrote in these examples was to update style sheet settings and not to facilitate Ajax scripting. MagicAjax also provides hooks for you to call code written in your code-behind that is not a part of the traditional ASP.NET Event Postback pattern.

Anthem.NET

URL: http://anthem-dot-net.sourceforge.net

Although the Anthem.NET framework features panels and a changed HTML architecture, you also have the option of using custom controls and returning data structures to the client. Anthem.NET is architected to use page Register directives instead of forcing you to inherit from a base class, and you are not required to implement preprocessing to harness its power. Anthem.NET truly represents the best of both worlds.

Setup

Before you begin using Anthem.NET, you must first download the files and then reference them in a web project. The following steps help you build a solution that houses all the samples you create for the Anthem.NET.

Downloading Files

1. If you haven't done so yet, download the zip file containing the Anthem.NET DLL from http://beginningajax.com/downloads/chapter9/Chapter9-Framework DLLs.zip.

2. Extract the files, and place them in a convenient location.

Creating the Solution

1. Open Visual Studio 2005.

2. Click File➪New➪Website.

3. Select the ASP.NET Website template.

4. Choose File System under location.

5. Set the path to c:\BeginningAJAX\Chapter9\AnthemDemo.

6. Choose C# as the language.

7. Click OK.

Referencing ComfortASP.NET

1. In the Solution Explorer, right-click on the project name and select Add ASP.NET Folder.

2. Choose `App_LocalResources` to create the ASP.NET folder.

3. Copy `Anthem.dll` (from the zip file you extracted) to the `App_LocalResource` folder.

4. Create a reference to the `Anthem.dll`.

Copying the Data File

1. Copy the `Resources.xml` you created in the last section into the `App_Data` folder in the solution.

Using Anthem.NET

Since you have had an opportunity to use panels, the coming examples will focus on using Anthem.NET's custom controls. You will also have an opportunity to work with a data structure returned from the server. Working with Anthem.NET's data structures will seem familiar to you because the process is nearly identical to the way you would do it using the Ajax.NET framework.

Example 1: Hello World

Anthem.NET's introductory example will follow the same pattern as the examples for ComfortASP.NET and MagicAjax.

This demonstration will use Anthem.NET controls. The Anthem button and label inherit from the standard .NET controls and extend them for the framework. While the markup for the controls remains the same in this example, you will set a property in the code-behind that will flag the label control for Anthem.NET to use for updating instead of the traditional .NET postback mechanism.

Figure 9-12 shows an example of how the page will look when you are done.

Try It Out   **Implementing "Hello World"**

Begin by adding a web form to the solution and naming it `HelloWorld.aspx`. Now add the `Anthem` register directive to the page just under the `<%@ Page %>` directive.

```
<%@ Register TagPrefix="anthem" Namespace="Anthem" Assembly="Anthem" %>
```

Next, update the markup by adding the following code between the `<div>` tags.

```
<anthem:Button
    ID="Button1"
    OnClick="Button1_Click"
    Text="Test"
    runat="server" />

<anthem:Label
    ID="Label1"
    runat="server" />
```

Finally, update the `HelloWorld` class with the following code-behind.

```
public partial class HelloWorld : System.Web.UI.Page
{
    protected void Page_Load(object sender, EventArgs e)
    {

    }
    protected void Button1_Click(object sender, EventArgs e)
    {
        this.Label1.Text = "Hello World " + DateTime.Now.ToString();
        this.Label1.UpdateAfterCallBack = true;
    }
}
```

When you click on the Test button, the label will update with the text "Hello World" and the current date and time. Click the button multiple times to see that the time will continue to be updated without a postback to the server.

You may now test the behavior by launching the page in the browser.

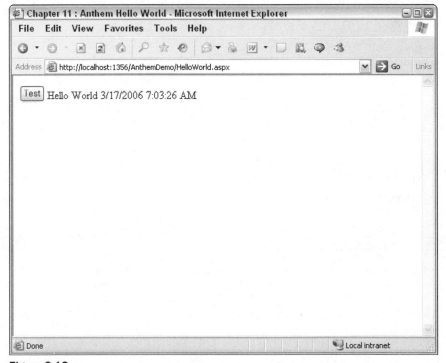

Figure 9-12

Example 2: Complex Controls

Just as you observed with ComfortASP.NET, the framework operates well with a single textbox, but how will the system perform with more demanding controls? This example will guide you through adding a `GridView` control to the page and will use Anthem.NET to respond to the `SelectedIndexChanged` method.

Figure 9-13 is an example of the way the page will look when you are done.

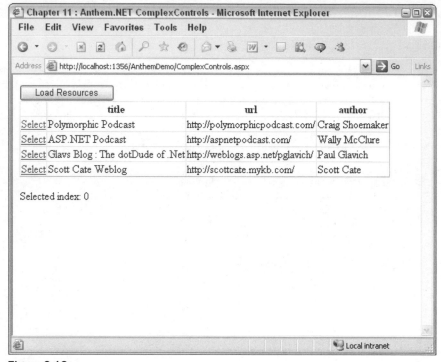

Figure 9-13

Try It Out   **Using Complex Controls**

Begin by adding a new web form to the solution, naming it `ComplexControls.aspx`. Now add the `Anthem` register directive to the page just under the `<%@ Page %>` directive.

```
<%@ Register TagPrefix="anthem" Namespace="Anthem" Assembly="Anthem" %>
```

Next, update the markup by adding the following code between the `<div>` tags:

```
<anthem:Button
    ID="btnLoadResources"
    OnClick="btnLoadResources_Click"
    Text="Load Resources"
    runat="server" />
```

```
<anthem:gridview
    id="grdResources"
    runat="server"
    OnSelectedIndexChanged="grdResources_SelectedIndexChanged">
    <Columns>
        <asp:CommandField ShowSelectButton="True" />
    </Columns>
</anthem:gridview>

<p>Selected index:
<anthem:Label ID="lblSelectedIndex" runat="server" /></p>
```

Finally, switch to the code view, and add the following code to the `ComplexControls` class:

```
public partial class ComplexControls : System.Web.UI.Page
{
    protected void Page_Load(object sender, EventArgs e)
    {
    }

    protected void btnLoadResources_Click(object sender, EventArgs e)
    {
        DataSet ds;

        ds = new DataSet();
        ds.ReadXml(Server.MapPath("~/App_Data/Resources.xml"));

        this.grdResources.DataSource = ds;
        this.grdResources.DataBind();
        this.grdResources.UpdateAfterCallBack = true;
    }

    protected void grdResources_SelectedIndexChanged(object sender, EventArgs e)
    {
        this.lblSelectedIndex.Text = this.grdResources.SelectedIndex.ToString();
        this.lblSelectedIndex.UpdateAfterCallBack = true;
    }
}
```

When you click the Load Resources button, the grid is loaded with data from the XML store. When you click on a Select link in the grid, the text of the label is updated with the selected index value.

You can now test the behavior by launching the page in the browser.

Example 3: Custom Attributes

When Anthem.NET extends web controls, part of the new interface includes some attributes you can define to make working with the controls easier. In some frameworks, you must manually script a feature to disable a button when a call to the server is initiated. With an Anthem button, you may set an attribute that implements this feature for you automatically. You may also find that you want to change the text of a button once the page begins to contact the server. Again, Anthem.NET's button control allows you to declaratively define this behavior.

Figure 9-14 shows an example of how the page will look after you click the button defined with Anthem.NET's custom attributes.

Figure 9-14

Try It Out   Using Custom Attributes

Begin by adding a new web form to the solution naming it `CustomAttributes.aspx`. Now add the Anthem register directive to the page just under the `<%@ Page %>` directive.

```
<%@ Register TagPrefix="anthem" Namespace="Anthem" Assembly="Anthem" %>
```

Next, update the markup by adding the following code between the `<div>` tags:

```
<anthem:Button
    ID="btnTest"
    EnabledDuringCallBack="false"
    TextDuringCallBack="Working..."
    Text="Test"
    runat="server"
    OnClick="btnTest_Click" />

<anthem:Label
    ID="lblTest"
    runat="server" />
```

Finally, update the `CustomAttributes` class with the following code-behind:

```
public partial class CustomAttributes : System.Web.UI.Page
{
    protected void btnTest_Click(object sender, EventArgs e)
    {
        System.Threading.Thread.Sleep(5000);
        this.lblTest.Text = DateTime.Now.ToString();
        this.lblTest.UpdateAfterCallBack = true;
    }
}
```

When you click the Test button, the server will hesitate for 5 seconds before returning a response to the browser. During this delay, you may observe that the button is disabled and the text is changed to "Working...." When the browser regains control of the operation the button is enabled and the text returns to its original value.

Now test the behavior by launching the page in the browser.

Example 4: Client Functions

In addition to custom attributes, Anthem.NET exposes client-side events. These events give you a high degree of control over your page when contacting the server. This example will show you how to implement some custom logic before the framework is contacted, before callback begins, and when the callback is completed.

When you are wiring up code-behind events on an ASP.NET page, the `OnClick` attribute will link the client-side click event to the ASP.NET postback mechanism to contact the code on the server to run the click event method defined in your code-behind. Anthem.NET implements an `OnClientClick` attribute where you may define a function name to run after the button is clicked but before the Anthem.NET framework is invoked. The `PreCallBackFunction` will fire as Anthem.NET takes control of the request but before contacting the server. Finally, the `PostCallBackFunction` will define a JavaScript function that is run once a response is recognized by the browser.

Notice in the example that each JavaScript function is defined passing an argument of `this` to the method. Passing the argument will expose a reference to the initiating control, in this case the Test button. This approach is valuable as you now have an easy way to access the control that originated the request without having to parse the DOM.

Figure 9-15 is an example of the way the page will look when you first click on a button using client functions.

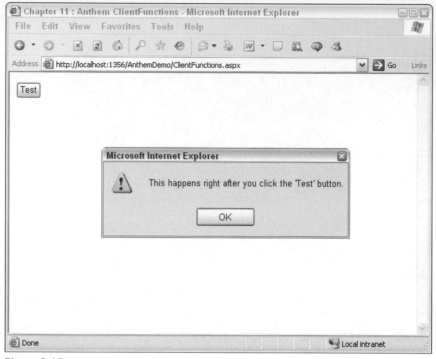

Figure 9-15

Try It Out   Using Client Functions

Begin by adding a new web form to the solution, naming it `ClientFunctions.aspx`. Now add the Anthem register directive to the page just under the `<%@ Page %>` directive:

```
<%@ Register TagPrefix="anthem" Namespace="Anthem" Assembly="Anthem" %>
```

Next, add the following code within the `<head>` tag:

```
<script type="text/javascript">
function btnTest_PreCallBack()
{
    alert("This happens before contacting the server");
}

function btnTest_PostCallBack()
{
    alert("This happens after getting a " +
        "response from the server");
}

function btnTest_Click(control)
{
    alert("This happens right after you click the '" +
```

```
            control.value + "' button.");
    }
</script>
```

Each method will alert the browser of which event is firing. The `btnTest_Click` function will access the originating control's properties to build its statement.

Next, update the markup by adding the following code between the `<div>` tags:

```
<anthem:Button
    ID="btnTest"
    OnClientClick="btnTest_Click(this)"
    PreCallBackFunction="btnTest_PreCallBack(this)"
    PostCallBackFunction="btnTest_PostCallBack(this)"
    Text="Test"
    OnClick="btnTest_Click"
    runat="server" />

<anthem:Label
    ID="lblTest"
    runat="server" />
```

Finally, update the `ClientFunctions` class with the following code-behind:

```
public partial class ClientFunctions : System.Web.UI.Page
{
    protected void btnTest_Click(object sender, EventArgs e)
    {
        this.lblTest.Text = DateTime.Now.ToString();
        this.lblTest.UpdateAfterCallBack = true;
    }
}
```

When you click the button, each event will fire the appropriate JavaScript function.

You can now test the behavior by launching the page in the browser.

Example 5: Invoke Page Method

This example demonstrates how you can use Anthem.NET to call sever-side code without requiring the use of a panel or custom controls. Anthem.NET implements this feature in a similar fashion to the Ajax.NET framework, but instead of creating a proxy object for each page that exposes a method to the client, Anthem.NET has a single function that will take care of communicating with the server.

Anthem.NET's function for interfacing with the code-behind is called `Anthem_InvokePageMethod`. This function may take three arguments.

❑ The first argument is the name of the method on the server you want the function to execute.

❑ The second argument is an array of the server-side method argument values.

❑ Lastly, the third argument is for the callback function and is the name of the function that the browser will call when the server has completed its processing. The callback function argument is optional.

Figure 9-16 is an example of the way the page will look when you are done.

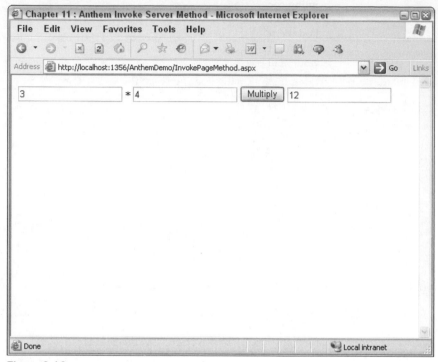

Figure 9-16

Try It Out   Invoking Page Method

Begin by adding a new web form to the solution, naming it `InvokePageMethod.aspx`. Now add the following code within the `<head>` tag:

```
<script type="text/javascript">
function Multiply()
{
    var int1;
    var int2;

    int1 = document.getElementById('txtInt1').value;
    int2 = document.getElementById('txtInt2').value;

    Anthem_InvokePageMethod('Multiply',[int1, int2],Multiply_CallBack);
}

function Multiply_CallBack(result)
{
    document.getElementById('txtResult').value = result.value;
}
</script>
```

The block of JavaScript is responsible for gathering the user input and passing it to the Anthem_Invoke PageMethod function. The first argument in this function is the name of the method on the server that you want to execute. In an upcoming code block, you will define a method on the page named Multiply, which is the code this function will execute. The next argument is an array of values that represent the signature of the Multiply method on the server. Multiply requires two integers to multiply together and returns the result. The final argument is the address of the callback function. After Multiply_CallBack runs, the textbox txtResult's value will contain the product of the two numbers.

You will not add the Anthem page directive to the page in this example. The technique used here will use Anthem.NET's functionality to access methods in the code-behind directly from JavaScript. This approach does not require that you use Anthem.NET controls.

Next, update the markup by adding the following code between the <div> tags:

```
<input
    type="text"
    id="txtInt1" />

<span>X</span>

<input
    type="text"
    id="txtInt2" />

<input
    type="button"
    id="btnMultiply"
    value="Multiply"
    onclick="Multiply();" />

<input
    type="text"
    id="txtResult" />
```

The HTML you see here is a bit different from the type of markup you have defined in the previous examples. In this case, you are not using a panel, nor are you declaring your controls as custom controls. This approach uses JavaScript to directly access the code-behind methods. Each input box is a standard HTML input box, and the work begins when you click the Multiply button.

Finally, update the InvokePageMethod class with the following code-behind:

```
public partial class InvokePageMethod : System.Web.UI.Page
{
    protected void Page_Load(object sender, EventArgs e)
    {
        Anthem.Manager.Register(this);
    }

    [Anthem.Method]
    public int Multiply(int int1, int int2)
    {
        return (int1 * int2);
    }
}
```

The code defined here should immediately be familiar to you from your experience with Ajax.NET. The pattern here is the same as with Ajax.NET. First, you must register the page with the Anthem.NET framework. Then you add the `Anthem.Method` attribute to your method. As stated above, the `Multiply` method requires two factors as arguments and returns the product.

Now test the behavior by launching the page in the browser.

Example 6: Direct Scripting (Micro-Content)

Recall from the MagicAjax section how you implemented the micro-content pattern. You will now implement the same pattern using Anthem.NET.

This exercise uses Anthem.NET as well as some custom Cascading Style Sheet definitions to power the change in the user interface to give clues as to what is happening.

The page will provide initial clues that parts of the page are editable by drawing a border over the text when the cursor hovers over the editable area. (You can refer back to Figure 9-10 to remind yourself of what this looks like.)

The next clue is to change the appearance of the control when the user has placed this area of the page in "edit mode." (Refer back to Figure 9-11 to see an example of this.)

Finally when the focus is lost from the control Anthem.NET will contact the server and allow the back-end processing to persist the latest data. Under normal circumstances you would probably persist the data to a data store of some kind. For demonstration purposes, this exercise will simply store the information in Session state. This way, once you make a change to the data, you can navigate off the page and return to see your latest changes, but you avoid having to implement a data layer just for this example.

Try It Out　　**Using Direct Scripting**

Begin by adding a new web form to the solution, naming it `DirectScripting.aspx`. Now add the `Anthem` register directive to the page just under the `<%@ Page %>` directive.

```
<%@ Register TagPrefix="anthem" Namespace="Anthem" Assembly="Anthem" %>
```

Next, add the following code within the `<head>` tag:

```
<style type="text/css">
input
{
    border:solid 1px #fff;
}
.focus
{
    background-color:#eee;
    border:dashed 1px #ccc;
}
.blur
{
```

```
    background-color:#fff;
    border:solid 1px #fff;
}
.mouseOver
{
    border:solid 1px #c00;
}
.mouseOut
{
    border:solid 1px #fff;
}
</style>
```

The style sheet entries hold the formatting information to give signals to the user as to what is happening. (This is the exact same CSS you implemented in the MagicAjax section, so if you have the code available you can copy it into your file for this example.)

Next, add the following JavaScript just after the style sheet definitions.

```
<script type="text/javascript">
function ChangeCSSClass(element,className)
{
    element.className = className;
}
</script>
```

Next, update the markup by adding the following code between the `<div>` tags:

```
<anthem:TextBox
    ID="txtTitle"
    text="Title"
    OnTextChanged="txtTitle_TextChanged"
    runat="server" />
```

Finally, update the `DirectScripting` class with the following code-behind:

```
public partial class DirectScripting : System.Web.UI.Page
{
    protected void Page_Load(object sender, EventArgs e)
    {
        if (!this.Page.IsPostBack)
        {
            this.txtTitle.Attributes.Add("onfocus",
                "ChangeCSSClass(this,'focus');");

            this.txtTitle.Attributes.Add("onblur",
                "ChangeCSSClass(this,'blur');");

            this.txtTitle.Attributes.Add("onmouseover",
                "ChangeCSSClass(this,'mouseOver');");
```

```
              this.txtTitle.Attributes.Add("onmouseout",
                  "ChangeCSSClass(this,'mouseOut');");

              if (this.Session["title"] != null)
              {
                  this.txtTitle.Text = this.Session["title"].ToString();
              }
          }
      }
      protected void txtTitle_TextChanged(object sender, EventArgs e)
      {
          this.Session.Add("title",this.txtTitle.Text);
          this.txtTitle.AutoUpdateAfterCallBack = true;
      }
  }
}
```

Although much of this implementation is similar to the MagicAjax demonstration, notice the different approaches. Using Anthem.NET you declare an Anthem `TextBox` control and use the built-in mechanism of firing the `TextChanged` event to initiate a request to the server. Once the server is contacted, you can apply the Session value and set the `AutoUpdateAfterCallBack` property on the `TextBox` control equal to `true`.

You can now test the behavior by launching the page in the browser.

Example 7: Server Exceptions

A feature exclusive to Anthem.NET from all the frameworks listed in this section is the ability to deal with unhandled server-side exceptions. In other frameworks, should your application encounter an unhandled exception, the error may bubble up to the user interface as the cryptic and intimidating stock yellow and white ASP.NET error page. While the subject of structured exception management is out of the scope of this book, you will implement an example that will enforce this foundational rule: protect the user from useless error messages.

Anthem.NET will wrap up unhandled exceptions into a JSON error object. When you encounter this object, you may then decide what to do on the client with the error. The response object returned by Anthem.NET includes an error object in its interface. If the error property is not null, then you have encountered an error on the server.

Figure 9-17 shows an example of how the page will appear when Anthem wraps up an unhandled server exception.

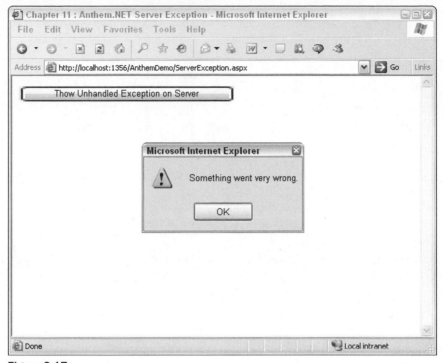

Figure 9-17

Try It Out   Handling Server Exceptions

Begin by adding a new web form to the solution, naming it ServerException.aspx. Next, add the following code within the <head> tag:

```
<script type="text/javascript">
function ShowError()
{
    Anthem_InvokePageMethod('ShowError',null,ShowError_CallBack);
}

function ShowError_CallBack(response)
{
    if(response.error != null)
    {
        alert(response.error);
    }
    else
    {
        alert("No errors here, just keep on working!");
    }
}
</script>
```

This example uses the `Anthem_InvokePageMethod` function to call a method on the server that will throw an unhandled exception. When the callback function runs, the response object is evaluated to see if an error exists. If the error is present, then the error message is displayed to the user.

Next, update the markup by adding the following code between the `<div>` tags:

```
<input
    type="button"
    ID="btnTest"
    onclick="ShowError();"
    value="Throw Unhandled Exception on Server" />
```

Since you are calling the server-side code directly, you do not need to use an Anthem control.

Finally, update the `ServerException` class with the following code-behind:

```
public partial class ServerException : System.Web.UI.Page
{
    protected void Page_Load(object sender, EventArgs e)
    {
        Anthem.Manager.Register(this);
    }

    [Anthem.Method()]
    public string ShowError()
    {
        throw new Exception("Something went very wrong.");
    }
}
```

You can now test the behavior by launching the page in the browser.

What You Have Learned

The Anthem.NET framework opens up options that are not found in most server-side frameworks. One benefit of Anthem.NET is a noninvasive configuration option for integration into your application. You can also choose between methods that simply change the HTML on your pages or work directly with returned data to the client. Throw in support for custom controls, and Anthem.NET may be the best of both worlds.

Summary

You have had an opportunity to review three client-side Ajax frameworks and work with three server-side Ajax frameworks that approach problems in development in different ways.

On the client side, Sarissa, HTMLHttpRequest, and MochiKit provide a lightweight way of abstracting the details away of making `XMLHttpRequest` calls through the browser. Each client-side framework includes much more than just Ajax abstractions, so be sure to examine each library for the best fit with your application before choosing one.

On the server side, ComfortASP.NET and MagicAjax with their changed-HTML-only architecture can make adding Ajax to your pages a painless endeavor. Anthem.NET provides the option of working in a changed-HTML mode but also gives you the option of dealing directly with returned data structures. Each is easy to use, and all are worthy of your time, so experiment more to see which best fits your development environment.

When choosing a framework keep in mind:

❏ **The expertise of developers** — Do you have people well-versed in JavaScript, HTML, and CSS?

❏ **Your page-level architecture** — Do your pages currently inherit from a custom or third-party base class?

❏ **Your application-level architecture** — Does your application use `httpHandlers` or `httpModules` that might cause conflicts with any third-party framework?

The next chapter will begin your introduction to Microsoft's Ajax framework, Atlas, and explain how to use it to quickly develop Ajax applications.

Atlas Client Script

On the surface, Atlas sounds like just another Ajax library that happens to be from Microsoft. While Atlas does provide support for Ajax-style operations, Atlas provides so much more than that. With the Microsoft Atlas package, there is support for generating client-side JavaScript, and this chapter delves into that aspect of Atlas. In this chapter, you look at:

❑ An introduction to Atlas

❑ Calling out to web services

❑ Data objects in Atlas

❑ Extensions to the JavaScript language

❑ Support for a programming model similar to programming in .NET

The Atlas examples and code are based on the March/April CTPs of Atlas. The March CTP is the first version of Atlas that comes with a "Go-Live" license for actual usage in a production application. The April CTP is basically a set of bug fixes to the March CTP. It is our intention to update these files with new versions as breaking changes are made to Atlas. The site for the files is http://beginningajax.com. *Alternatively, you can check for updates on the Wrox web site for this book (*www.wrox.com*).*

Introduction to Atlas

There has been a lot of confusion in the marketplace regarding what Microsoft's Atlas project is. At this time, Atlas will be included in the next version of ASP.NET and the .NET Framework. From a programming standpoint, Atlas may be considered to be at least a couple key things:

❑ **Ajax library** — The part of Atlas that has programmers talking the most is the support for Ajax. With this support, Microsoft has created a library to support the ability to communicate back to the server without the need to perform a full postback from the client to the server.

❑ **Client-side components** — The ASP.NET framework has typically supported the creation of ASP.NET server-side controls. Atlas introduces the concept of client-side components and the ability to create client-side components. Along with those components is an object-oriented paradigm on the web client that includes support for inheritance, interfaces, and such items normally considered to be a part of any modern programming language.

Major Components

Atlas consists of a set of files. These files are:

❑ A server-side assembly (`.dll`). This assembly is named `Microsoft.Web.Atlas.dll`.

❑ A server-side `WebResource.axd` HTTP handler. This file handles streaming the appropriate JavaScript files down to the client. The content of the JavaScript that is streamed to the client is based on the functionality specified in the `ScriptManager` control, which is a control that will be introduced later in this chapter.

❑ The JavaScript files that are streamed to the client are embedded within the `WebResource.axd` HTTP handler. In addition, a set of standalone JavaScript files is also installed. These files are the same as those that are processed in the `WebResource.axd` file.

Server Support

The server-side support for Atlas is provided by the `Microsoft.Web.Atlas.dll`. This assembly provides support for the `Microsoft.Web.*` family of namespaces. Within these namespaces is support for controls, serialization of data, and for communicating with web services.

The `WebResource.axd` HTTP handler handles sending the appropiate JavaScript files down to the client.

JavaScript Files

As mentioned earlier, there is a set of JavaScript files that come with Atlas. These files are as follows:

❑ `Atlas.js` — The `Atlas.js` file contains the core set of Atlas functionality. For example, the `Sys` namespace is defined within this file.

❑ `AtlasCompat.js` — The `AtlasCompat.js` file provides the majority of the browser compatibility layer. This file contains support for Internet Explorer, Mozilla, and Safari.

❑ `AtlasCompat2.js` — The `AtlasCompat2.js` file provides additional support for other browsers.

❑ `AtlasFX.js` — This file contains support for gadgets.

❑ `AtlasRuntime.js` — The `AtlasRuntime.js` file is for performing Ajax-only communication to the server without the need for all of the other files and associated overhead.

❑ `AtlasUIDragDrop.js` — `AtlasUIDragDrop.js` provides the Drag and Drop API for Atlas. In addition, there are a few behaviors that are included.

❑ `AtlasUIGlitz.js` — The `AtlasUIGlitz.js` file contains support for special UI and visual effects. This includes classes that support UI features such as opacity and animation.

❑ `AtlasUIMap.js` – The `AtlasUIMap.js` file provides support for the Virtual Earth Atlas control.

❑ `AtlasWebParts.js` — The `AtlasWebParts.js` file provides support for Web Parts in Atlas.

❑ `GadgetRuntime.js` — The `GadgetRuntime.js` file provides support for gadgets in Atlas.

These scripts fall into the following general layers of code:

- **Browser compatibility layer** — This layer handles the differences between the browsers. By abstracting the differences in the various browsers, the higher-level code does not require `if-else` code to handle browser differences.

- **JavsaScript extensions** — The JavaScript extensions provide support for objects, functions, and data types that are found not in JavaScript natively.

- **Script Core** — The script core provides many features that could be considered to be language extensions to JavaScript. These features include support for namespaces, classes, interfaces, inheritance, enumerations, delegates, and so forth. By providing this layer, Atlas is able to provide features to encapsulate data, logic, behaviors, and such into classes, just like other programming languages. Functionally, this brings JavaScript close to the features available in the .NET languages.

- **Base Class Library (BCL)** — The Atlas BCL is very similar to and is modeled after the BCL in the .NET Framework. This layer provides such things as the `StringBuilder`, `Debug`, `Event`, Disposable support, and `XmlHTTP` abstraction through `WebRequest` and `WebResponse`. In addition, this layer provides support for ASP.NET services, such as Profile and Authentication, to work with the services on the server.

- **Component Model and UI** — This layer provides support for components that can be self-described by their object model.

- **Controls and components** — This layer provides a set of built-in components. Some of these components are the `Timer`, `Counter`, `Listview`, and the `MapControl`.

- **Web Parts and gadgets** — This layer provides support for integrating with external services, such as Web Parts and gadgets

Ajax Support

With Atlas, Microsoft has added many web browser/client-side features. The most talked about feature is support for Ajax. Frequently, Microsoft has been criticized for its lack of cross-platform (or non-Microsoft operating system) support. At the time of this writing, Atlas supports Internet Explorer, Mozilla Firefox, and the Macintosh Safari browsers.

Atlas allows for the calling of a regular web service in a web application through the browser. This allows for the web browser to provide a rich experience to the user without the need for the traditional postback to the web server. Atlas provides the mechanism to consume and expose web services by exposing JavaScript proxies of web services within the browser.

Asynchronous Communication Only

With Atlas, all communication is asynchronous. Most operations that programmers work with are synchronous communication, so it is important to understand the differences. With Atlas, there is no ability to call a web service and wait for its response. This is important. If Atlas provided support for making synchronous calls and a synchronous call were made, the client might very well lock up if the server were to somehow disappear after a request was made. The only way to exit would be to stop the browser task that was running. Other libraries provide support for synchronous operations, but Atlas is currently designed to provide asynchronous communication.

Now that you have heard why Atlas is asynchronous and why synchronous processing can cause problems in a web browser environment, you can actually change this behavior. You have two mechanisms to perform this change:

❑   One of the members of the ASP.NET team has provided a mechanism to perform this. This can be viewed on Bertrand LeRoy's blog at `http://weblogs.asp.net/bleroy/archive/2005/12/15/433278.aspx`.

❑   It is possible to go into the `Open` method of the `XmlHttpRequest` object in the appropriate JavaScript files and change the `Asynchronous` flag to `false`, as opposed to the default value of true.

Please remember that performing synchronous operations is dangerous and not supported in Atlas. If you feel that you must change the Atlas files, you will be making significant changes to the Atlas files and to the programming model. In addition, you will be creating an unsupported implementation.

Adding Atlas Support with the ScriptManager Control

Now that you have down some of the basics of Atlas, you can turn to the question of how you add Atlas support to a web page. In addition to the `ScriptManager`, you will need to add some commands to the `Web.Config` to properly configure Atlas.

The `ScriptManager` control is the mechanism for adding Atlas support to an `.aspx` page. Basically, the scripts needed are added to an `.aspx` page by using the `ScriptManager` control. So, to add the basic support for Atlas (`Atlas.js`), the following code is used:

```
<atlas:ScriptManager ID="Script1" runat="server" />
```

The next step is to add support for calling a specific web service. This is done by adding a service to the `ScriptManager` control:

```
<atlas:ScriptManager ID="Script1" runat="server">
    <Services>
        <atlas:ServiceReference Path="WebService.asmx" />
    </Services>
</atlas:ScriptManager>
```

In the preceding example, you see the `ScriptManager` control. This control provides support for Atlas on the page. The `<Services>` tag adds support for web services that are called by code. In this example, a `WebService.asmx`'s proxy will be placed on a page for calling. The proxy can be called out by JavaScript code running on the client browser.

If only the `AtlasRuntime.js` file is necessary, the `EnableScriptComponents="false"` can be set in the `ScriptManager` tag.

```
<atlas:ScriptManager ID="Script1" runat="server" EnableScriptComponents="false" />
```

You will face situations when additional Atlas (or other) JavaScript libraries need to be loaded. These libraries are added by using the <Scripts> tag. This next example adds several scripts through the ScriptManager control; specifically, the script named AtlasUIDragDrop and the file Script.js file are loaded in the browser.

```
<atlas:ScriptManager ID="Script1" runat="server" EnableScriptComponents="false">
    <Scripts>
        <atlas:ScriptReference ScriptName="AtlasUIDragDrop" />
        <atlas:ScriptReference Path="Script.js" />
    </Scripts>
    <Services>
        <atlas:ServiceReference Path="WebService.asmx" />
    </Services>
</atlas:ScriptManager>
```

In this example code, two ways of calling a script are shown. The first way is that the AtlasUIDragDrop script is added by name. This will be the normal way that an Atlas script is added to a page. A second way to add a script is to add it by path. This is shown using the imaginary Script.js file.

Communicating with Web Services

Calling out to an ASP.NET web service is an important part of Atlas. By default, JavaScript running within a web browser does not know how to communicate with a web service. A web service is built with C#, Visual Basic .NET, or some other language. To communicate with a web service, JavaScript must know how to call a web service, and this is done by generating JavaScript proxies using a feature of Atlas.

Generating the JavaScript Proxies

To generate the JavaScript proxies, you need to add a reference to a web service. Along with that reference, the web service methods must be exposed. This is done automatically when a JavaScript library is added as a service through the ScriptManager control. For example, the ScriptManager produces the following JavaScript code when you add a reference to the WebService.asmx file.

This code is the source code on the web page:

```
<atlas:ScriptManager ID="Script1" runat="server">
    <Services>
        <atlas:ServiceReference Path="WebService.asmx" />
    </Services>
</atlas:ScriptManager>
```

The preceding code will generate the output that follows on the client browser:

```
<script type="text/xml-script">
<page xmlns:script="http://schemas.microsoft.com/xml-script/2005">
    <references>
        <add src="WebService.asmx/js" />
    </references>
    <components />
</page>
</script>
```

This code shows how an external web service proxy is generated. The /js switch instructs the Atlas runtime to create a proxy object. This proxy object will also run on the client.

When you use the previous code, the following JavaScript proxy is generated and loaded on the client:

```
var WebServiceTest = { path: "/Chapter10Sample/WebService.asmx",
GetProjects:function(onMethodComplete, onMethodTimeout, onMethodError)
{return Web.Net.ServiceMethodRequest.callMethod(this.path, "GetProjects",{},
onMethodComplete, onMethodTimeout, onMethodError); } }
```

The following is the web service that will be called by the client and will run on the server:

```
using System;
using System.Web;
using System.Collections;
using System.Web.Services;
using System.Web.Services.Protocols;
using System.Data;
using System.Data.SqlClient;
using System.Xml;

/// <summary>
/// Summary description for WebService
/// </summary>
[WebService(Namespace = "http://tempuri.org/")]
[WebServiceBinding(ConformsTo = WsiProfiles.BasicProfile1_1)]
public class WebServiceTest : System.Web.Services.WebService {

    public WebServiceTest () {
    //Uncomment the following line if using designed components
        //InitializeComponent();
    }

    private string strCn = ".........";

    [WebMethod]
    public DataTable GetProjects()
    {
        string strSql = "select * from tblProject";
        SqlConnection sqlCn = new SqlConnection(strCn);
        SqlDataAdapter sqlDa = new SqlDataAdapter(strSql, sqlCn);
        DataSet dsData = new DataSet();
        try{
            //throw (new ApplicationException("Error on the server."));
            sqlDa.Fill(dsData, "tblProject");
        }
        finally{
            if(sqlCn.State != ConnectionState.Closed)
                sqlCn.Close();
            sqlCn.Dispose();
            sqlCn = null;
            sqlDa.Dispose();
            sqlDa = null;
        }
```

```
                return(dsData);
        }
    }
```

The preceding code is a simple example of a web service. In this example, all of the records from the table `tblProject` are queried and returned to the calling method, which is the web browser.

In an Atlas application, the `Web.Config` file has a new handler for web services. It is defined as follows:

```
<httpHandlers>
    <remove verb="*" path="*.asmx"/>
    <add verb="*" path="*.asmx" type="Microsoft.Web.Services.ScriptHandlerFactory"
validate="false"/>
</httpHandlers>
```

Calling Out to Web Services

Now that you have seen how to generate the JavaScript proxies necessary to call out to a web service, you can look at actually calling out to the web service.

Calling out to a web service from JavaScript is a fairly simple process. An example of a JavaScript call is:

```
Namespace.Class.MethodName(param1, param2, ..., paramN, OnMethodComplete,
OnServerTimeOut, OnServerException)
```

In this example, look at the parameters. The items detailed as `param1`, `param2`, and `paramN` are the parameters that the web service would take normally. The other three parameters are rather interesting. These three parameters, which you will see in more detail in the next three sections, are the callback methods that are used when something happens on the server.

OnMethodComplete

When a web service completes its activities and returns data to the calling application, it needs to have a place to return to. The `OnMethodComplete` event is the JavaScript callback that is called when the web service returns to the application. When this event is called, the method is passed a result parameter. The result parameter is a JavaScript Object Notation (JSON) serialized version of the returned value from the web service.

The syntax of the `OnMethodComplete` method is:

```
function MethodReturn(result)
{
    // Do something with the returned object.
}
```

The `result` that is returned may be anywhere from a simple datatype to a very complicated complex object that is serialized and sent to the browser.

OnServerTimeOut

In the event that the server does not respond within a predefined timeframe, the `OnServerTimeOut` method is called. In this method, it is possible for the application to communicate to the user that the server is not available.

OnServerException

Examine the following code to look at what happens when an exception is returned from a web service.

```
[WebMethod]
public DataSet GetProjects()
{
    string strSql = "select * from tblProject";
    SqlConnection sqlCn = new SqlConnection(strCn);
    SqlDataAdapter sqlDa = new SqlDataAdapter(strSql, sqlCn);
    DataSet dsData = new DataSet();
    try{
        throw (new ApplicationException("Error on the server."));
        sqlDa.Fill(dsData, "tblProject");
    }
    finally{
        if(sqlCn.State != ConnectionState.Closed)
            sqlCn.Close();
        sqlCn.Dispose();
        sqlCn = null;
        sqlDa.Dispose();
        sqlDa = null;
    }
    return(dsData);
}
```

When a server's web service encounters an exception that is thrown back to the calling application, the Atlas OnServerException event is called at the client. This event receives the result object. Take a look at the result object that is returned (there are three parts, but the last two are not required).

❑   get_message() — This is the textual message of the exception that occurred on the server. This is shown in Figure 10-1.

Figure 10-1

❑   get_stackTrace() — This is the stack trace of the exception. The stack trace is shown in Figure 10-2.

Figure 10-2

❑   get_exceptionType() —This is the type of the exception. The exception type is shown in
    Figure 10-3.

Figure 10-3

Passing Types

Applications have methods that require passing various types of parameters. These parameters may be
either simple datatypes, such as numbers, strings, and booleans or more complicated types that are defined
by the developers. The passing of various types is supported within Atlas. Simple and complex datatypes
may be easily sent and received. These include booleans, integers, strings, and other simple datatypes, as
well as datasets and custom objects. These datatypes are easily sent back and forth between the calling
parameters and returned values. The next sections take a look at passing the simple and complex data
types between the client web browser and the server.

Simple Data Types

Let's look at a web page that contains a call using simple datatypes. In this example, the code passes two
integers to a web service and then returns the sum of those values to the calling method through Atlas.

The web service code is:

```
[WebMethod]
public int ServerAdd(int val1, int val2)
{
    return (val1 + val2);
}
```

In this example, the code accepts two integers and returns an integer all through a web service:

```
The code on the web page is as follows:
<%@ Page Language="C#" AutoEventWireup="true" CodeFile="SimpleDataTypes.aspx.cs"
Inherits="SimpleDataTypes" %>
<!DOCTYPE html PUBLIC "-//W3C//DTD XHTML 1.0 Transitional//EN"
"http://www.w3.org/TR/xhtml1/DTD/xhtml1-transitional.dtd">
<html xmlns="http://www.w3.org/1999/xhtml" >
<head runat="server">
    <title>Simple Data Types Page</title>
    <script language="javascript">
            function CallServerAdd()
            {
                SimpleDataTypeWebService.ServerAdd( 3, 4, ServerAddReturn);
```

```
                }
                        function ServerAddReturn(result)
            {
                alert("Result Value: " + result);
            }
    </script>
</head>
<body>
    <form id="form1" runat="server">
        <input type="button" value="Click - Simple Add" onclick="CallServerAdd()"
/>
        <atlas:ScriptManager ID="Script1" runat="server">
            <Services>
                <atlas:ServiceReference Path="SimpleDataTypeWebService.asmx" />
            </Services>
        </atlas:ScriptManager>
    </form>
</body>
</html>
```

In the preceding code, the click of the "Click – Simple Add" button will call the JavaScript method named CallServerAdd(). The CallServerAdd() method calls out to the ServerAdd(...) method on the server. The values of 3 and 4 are passed along with the callback method named ServerAddReturn. When the ServerAdd() method is completed on the server, the client-side ServerAddReturn is called with the data that is returned from the server-side method.

The result of clicking the button is shown as Figure 10-4. It is very simple to call a web service through Atlas with simple datatypes and then to obtain the returned result.

Figure 10-4

Complex Data Types

Now, you can take a look at what it takes to use some complex datatypes. In these examples, you will see some datasets and custom data types.

Datasets

What is a dataset? In .NET, a dataset is an object within the System.Data namespace. A dataset can be thought of as a local subset of data. A dataset contains a set of data tables. These data tables typically contain the results of queries. When developers work with datasets, they typically are used as the result of some database query. It is possible to send datasets from the server down to the client, and that is what we will look at in this section.

Atlas supports the return of datasets to the web browser and then the processing of the dataset on the client. Take a look at an example of calling a web service, returning a dataset, and then processing that dataset.

Here is your web service. It is just a web service that performs a query and then returns a dataset. The web method returns a dataset with a data table called tblProject. Notice that this is the same code that the web service used in the exception example, without the exception.

```
[WebMethod]
public DataSet GetProjects()
{
    string strSql = "select * from tblProject";
    SqlConnection sqlCn = new SqlConnection(strCn);
    SqlDataAdapter sqlDa = new SqlDataAdapter(strSql, sqlCn);
    DataSet dsData = new DataSet();
    try{
        sqlDa.Fill(dsData, "tblProject");
    }
    finally{
        if(sqlCn.State != ConnectionState.Closed)
            sqlCn.Close();
        sqlCn.Dispose();
        sqlCn = null;
        sqlDa.Dispose();
        sqlDa = null;
    }
    return(dsData);
}
```

The following is the client-side JavaScript. It is contained in the page DataTable.aspx page in the example code.

```
<form id="form1" runat="server">
    <atlas:ScriptManager ID="Script1" runat="server">
        <Services>
            <atlas:ServiceReference Path="~/WebService.asmx" />
        </Services>
    </atlas:ScriptManager>
<div>
<input type="button" id="btnGetProjects" value="Get Projects"
onclick="PageLoadMethod()" /><br />
<span id="RowInfo"></span>
</div>
</form>
<script language="javascript">
    function PageLoadMethod()
    {
        WebService.GetProjects(MethodReturn);
    }
    function MethodReturn(result)
    {
        var i = 0;
        var str = "";
```

```
            var strRowsInfo = "";
            var strReturn = "<br />";
            //get a datatable
            var tbl1 = result.getItem(0);
            for(i = 0; i < tbl1.get_length(); i++)
            {
                //tbl1.getItem(i) will return the ith DataRow
                //getProperty("Column Name") will return the column value from a
        DataRow
                strRowsInfo += tbl1.getItem(i).getProperty("ProjectName") + strReturn;
            }
            document.getElementById("RowInfo").innerHTML = strRowsInfo;
        }
    </script>
```

In this code, the reference is created to your `WebService.asmx` file. When the button is clicked, an asynchronous call is made to `WebService.GetProjects()`. The only callback method that you process in this example is the `MethodReturn` callback. The `MethodReturn` function gets the dataset as a parameter in the call to it. To get the data table, the `result.getItem(0)` is called. This will return the data table. Once you have the data table, you can get the number of rows of the data table by calling `.get_length()`. This is then used within the `for` loop to iterate through the rows in the data table. Within the `for` loop, the `.getProperty()` method is used to then get the contents of the column.

> *For some additional information on how Atlas handles data tables, data columns, and the like, refer to the appropriate section later in this chapter.*

Custom Datatypes

Many applications built over the past several years are built with custom business objects. These custom business objects are highly optimized for a specific application. In this example, a custom business object will be created. This example will have two strings as properties of the custom object. These properties are `Name` and `Address`.

The ASP.NET page code for this example is:

```
<%@ Page Language="C#" AutoEventWireup="true" CodeFile="ComplexDataSource.aspx.cs"
Inherits="ComplexDataSource" %>
<!DOCTYPE html PUBLIC "-//W3C//DTD XHTML 1.0 Transitional//EN"
"http://www.w3.org/TR/xhtml1/DTD/xhtml1-transitional.dtd">
<html xmlns="http://www.w3.org/1999/xhtml" >
<head runat="server">
    <title>Complex Data Type Page</title>
</head>
<body>
    <form id="form1" runat="server">
    <script language="javascript">
    function ComplexDataTypeCall()
    {
        var CustName = "ACME Inc.";
        var CustAddr = "WileyVille, USA";
        var objCustObj = new cComplexCustomerType();
        objCustObj.Name = CustName;
        objCustObj.Address = CustAddr;
        ComplexWebService.AcceptComplexDataType(objCustObj,
ComplexScriptCompleteCallback);
```

```
        }

        function ComplexScriptCompleteCallback(result)
        {
            alert("Value: " + result);
        }
    </script>
    <input type="button" value="Click for Complex DataType"
onclick="ComplexDataTypeCall();" />
        <atlas:ScriptManager ID="Script1" runat="server">
            <Services>
                <atlas:ServiceReference Path="ComplexWebService.asmx" />
            </Services>
        </atlas:ScriptManager>
    <div>
    </div>
    </form>
    <script type="text/xml-script">
        <page xmlns:script="http://schemas.microsoft.com/xml-script/2005">
            <references>
            </references>
            <components>
            </components>
        </page>
    </script>
</body>
</html>
```

The code for the complex data type is:

```
public class cComplexCustomerType
{
public cComplexCustomerType()
{
}
    private string _Name;
    private string _Address;
    public string Name
    {
        get { return _Name; }
        set { _Name = value;}
    }
    public string Address
    {
        get { return _Address; }
        set { _Address = value; }
    }
}
```

The code for the web service is:

```
    [WebMethod]
    public cComplexCustomerType AcceptComplexDataType(cComplexCustomerType
objComplexCustomerType)
```

```
    {
        return (objComplexCustomerType);
    }
```

In this example code, the web service accepts the custom business object and then returns the value. There is nothing that would stop the web service from using the properties of the business object that is passed or the web service from returning a string as opposed to the custom business object.

Interrogation of the custom object returns interesting information. The following code will generate the results in Figure 10-5. This figure shows that the `Name` and `Address` properties are available along with an added member — the `__serverType` property. This property defines the type on the server.

```
function ComplexScriptCompleteCallback(result)
{
    var str = "";
    debug.dump(result);
    for(prop in result)
        str += "Member: " + prop + "\r\n";
    alert(str);
}
```

Figure 10-5

A call to `debug.dump()` on the returned result object produces the output in Figure 10-6. The `debug.dump()` method displays the contents of an object in Atlas. This method will be discussed more later in this chapter.

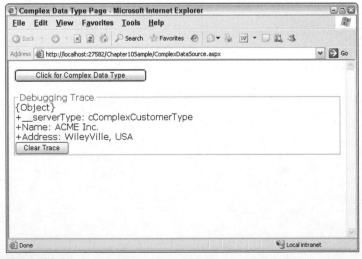

Figure 10-6

Caching Web Services

The data returned from a web service may be cached. This can be helpful in situations where data may not be time critical (for example, a web service that returns the weather forecast for a given location). This is performed in .NET by setting a value on the `CacheDuration` of the `WebMethod()` attribute. As you may have previously done when working with web services, Atlas makes it possible to call a cached web service and get the results of a web service call. Depending on the data and the time that is required to perform the calculation, the time saved by caching may be significant when factored over thousands of possible users.

Take a look at some code and the result. In this example, you are just going to display the time of each call. On the first call, both times that are returned will be the same. Subsequent calls will result in the current time being updated and the cached time being the same, while the cached time is not updated until the cache duration is over.

This is the code for an `.aspx` page:

```
<%@ Page Language="C#" AutoEventWireup="true" CodeFile="CachedWebService.aspx.cs"
Inherits="CachedWebService" %>
<!DOCTYPE html PUBLIC "-//W3C//DTD XHTML 1.0 Transitional//EN"
"http://www.w3.org/TR/xhtml1/DTD/xhtml1-transitional.dtd">
<html xmlns="http://www.w3.org/1999/xhtml" >
<head runat="server">
    <title>Untitled Page</title>
</head>
<body>
    <form id="form1" runat="server">
    <input type="button" id="btnGetServerTime" value="Get Server Time"
onclick="GetServerTime();" />
    <script language="javascript">
        function GetServerTime()
        {
            CachingWebService.GetServerCachedTime(DisplayServerCachedTime);
            CachingWebService.GetServerCurrentTime(DisplayServerCurrentTime);
        }
        function DisplayServerCurrentTime(result)
        {
            var ctrl = document.getElementById("NewTime");
            ctrl.innerText = result;
        }
        function DisplayServerCachedTime(result)
        {
            var ctrl = document.getElementById("StartTime");
            ctrl.innerText = result;
        }
    </script>
        <atlas:ScriptManager ID="Script1" runat="server">
            <Services>
                <atlas:ServiceReference Path="CachingWebService.asmx"
GenerateProxy="true" />
            </Services>
        </atlas:ScriptManager>
    <br />
    Start Call:
```

```
      <div id="StartTime"></div>
      <br />
      New Time:
       <div id="NewTime">
       </div>
       <script type="text/xml-script">
           <page xmlns:script="http://schemas.microsoft.com/xml-script/2005">
               <references>
               </references>
               <components>
               </components>
           </page>
       </script>
       </form>
  </body>
  </html>
```

In the preceding code, on a button click, two remote calls are made out to the server — a call to the
GetServerCachedTime method and one to the GetServerCurrentTime method. The GetServer
CachedTime method on the server returns the current server time when it is called the first time. The
result of this call is cached in server memory. Subsequent calls are returned the cached result for the next
100 seconds, at which point the next request will generate a new time and a new entry in the server cache.
As a result, calls to GetServercurrentTime() will result in the current time of the server being
returned while calls to GetServerCachedTime() will result in a value that is up to 100 seconds old.

The following is the code for a web service:

```
[WebMethod(CacheDuration = 100)]
public DateTime GetServerCachedTime()
{
    return(DateTime.Now.ToUniversalTime());
}


[WebMethod]
public DateTime GetServerCurrentTime()
{
    return (DateTime.Now.ToUniversalTime());
}
```

*Atlas uses UTC encoding for dates and time. This may create confusion for you if you don't remember
it. Personally, my system is set with the time of GMT – 5. As a result, the times that were coming back
were 5 hours off.*

Figure 10-7 shows the results of multiple calls to the cached and noncached web services.

In Figure 10-7, you will notice the two different time values. This shows that calling the cached web service returns the cached value and the noncached version returns the current value of the DateTime.Now
object.

Figure 10-7

Exposing Web Services from a Web Form

All of the examples you've explored to this point in this chapter have used a dedicated web service. It is also possible to have a web service that is exposed within an internal page of a web application. On the surface, it appears that there is no real advantage to this. However, there are two advantages to using web services that are exposed by a web form. These are:

❑   The page and web service are deployed together. There are fewer files to deploy and fewer things that can go wrong.

❑   While not having been announced as this is being written, it appears that Microsoft will be adding some special functionality that will be available only to a web service that is called within a web form. Given the early status of Atlas, more information will come out about this in the future.

This next example calls back to a web service on the same `.aspx` page.

The code for the web page is:

```
<%@ Page Language="C#" AutoEventWireup="true" CodeFile="InternalWebService.aspx.cs"
Inherits="InternalWebService" %>
<!DOCTYPE html PUBLIC "-//W3C//DTD XHTML 1.0 Transitional//EN"
"http://www.w3.org/TR/xhtml1/DTD/xhtml1-transitional.dtd">
<html xmlns="http://www.w3.org/1999/xhtml" >
<head runat="server">
    <title>Internal Web Service Page</title>
</head>
<body>
        <atlas:ScriptManager ID="Script1" runat="server">
        </atlas:ScriptManager>
   <form id="form1" runat="server">
     <div>
     <input type="button" id="btn" value="Call Internal Web Service"
onclick="CallInternalWebService()" />
```

```
    <script language="javascript">
        function CallInternalWebService()
        {
            PageMethods.CallInternalWebService(InternalCallBack);
        }
        function InternalCallBack(result)
        {
            alert(result);
        }
    </script>
    </div>
    </form>
</body>
</html>
```

In the preceding code, note that the calling convention is not `Class.MethodName()`, but `PageMethods.MethodName()`. `PageMethods` is a special class that is used to call the methods internal to a page.

The code-behind file is shown below. Note the addition of the `System.Web.Services` namespace, which is not typically specified in a code-beside or aspx page. The method displayed in the following merely returns a string as an example; however, any number of datatypes can be returned, just like a regular web service and the other examples.

```
using System.Web.Services;
.........
[WebMethod]
public string CallInternalWebService()
{
    return ("Internal Web Service Called.");
}
```

The result of this is shown in Figure 10-8.

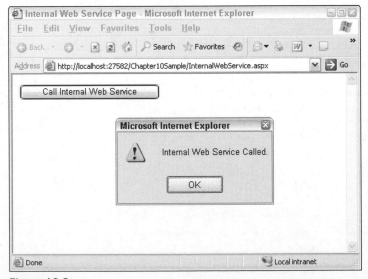

Figure 10-8

Atlas Extensions to JavaScript

Atlas allows for the creation of rich client-side applications that run within the browser. To facilitate the creation of these applications, Atlas has created a set of extensions to the type system in JavaScript. These extensions provide many of the features of the .NET type system to the client-side web browser environment. These extensions include namespaces, inheritance, interfaces, enums, support for strings, and arrays.

Language Enhancements

JavaScript has been around as a language since the early betas of the Netscape Navigator 2.0 web browser appeared in late 1995 to early 1996. Since then, there have been numerous enhancements to the JavaScript language. The latest version of the language is version 1.6. With the shipment of the .NET Framework, Microsoft has released a framework that contains a set of base classes that have features across various languages, including Visual Basic, C#, and JavaScript when running native and server-side applications. Into this, steps Atlas. Atlas provides a set of enhancements on top of JavaScript as it runs in the web browser. The next sections look at these enhancements and extensions.

Controls

Atlas provides a set of controls, classes, and objects that may be used programmatically in JavaScript.

Object

The `Object` class is a client version of the .NET `System.Object` class. The only method that it implements is the `getType(obj)` method. This method will return the type of the specified object.

Array

The `Array` class is similar in concept to the `.NET System.Collections.ArrayList()` class. It has several interesting members such as `length`, `push()`, and `pop()`. A small example is

```
var ary = new Array();
ary.push(47);
alert("length: " + ary.length);
```

In this short example, the user is presented with an alert box with a length of 1.

Date

The `Date` class is conceptually similar to a client web browser version of the .NET `System.DateTime` class. The `Date` object supports a set of methods similar to the `Date()` class in .NET. There are methods to create a date, get various parts of a date, and set the parts of a date. For a quick example, it is possible to create a date:

```
var dt = new Date();
dt.setFullYear(2006, 03, 26);
dt.setHours(10, 12, 13, 5);
alert("Date: " + dt.toString());
```

In the preceding example code, the date that is created is March 26, 2006, 10 hours, 12 minutes, 13 seconds, and 5 milliseconds. The resulting date is then displayed to the user in an `alert()` window.

Number

The Number class contains several methods. There are several methods to parse the content of the number as well as convert it to a string, get the exponential value, and perform other operations.

Boolean

The Boolean class is used for parsing traditional boolean values. It implements several methods for creating a boolean. If the passed value is a string and would return as boolean, the boolean value is returned.

String

The String class is a client web browser version of the .NET String class. The String() class implements some of the methods that are similar to the String() class in .NET. Some of the more interesting members of the Atlas String() class are:

❑ indexOf() — The indexOf(string, startingindex) returns the value of the starting location of the specified string when at the startingindex location.

❑ lastIndexOf() — The lastIndexOf(string, startingindex) returns the value of the starting location of the last time the specified string is found.

❑ substring() — The substring(start, end) returns the substring from the starting location to the ending location.

❑ substr() — The substr(start, length) returns the substring from the starting location of the specified length.

❑ toLowerCase() — The lowercase version of the string is returned.

❑ toUpperCase() — The uppercase version of the string is returned.

RegExp

The RegExp class is a client web browser version of the .NET Regular Expression library. The Atlas RegExp class supports the .parse(value) method.

Built-In Namespaces

Atlas comes with a number of built-in namespaces and classes for managing data, HTTP communication, user interface design, and other things. These are in the Sys.* namespaces. The next sections look at several of the namespaces and their associated classes.

Sys.Net.WebRequest

The Sys.Net namespace provides a set of classes to facilitate HTTP communications between the client and the web server. Though other classes exist within the name, the one we are going to look at is the WebRequest class.

The Sys.Net.WebRequest class provides support for making HTTP requests. The following sample code, for example, makes a web request.

```
var request;
```

```
function MakeCall()
{
    request  = new Sys.Net.WebRequest();
    var url = Sys.Net.WebRequest.createUrl("PageThatIsCalled.aspx", null);
    request.set_url(url);
    request.completed.add(RequestCompleted);
    request.timeout.add(RequestTimeOut);
    request.invoke();
}
function RequestCompleted(objSender, evArgs)
{
    if (blRun == true )
    {
        var obj = objSender.get_webRequest();
        var objWR = objSender.get_data();
        debug.dump(objWR, "Web Content:", true);
    }
}
```

Figure 10-9 shows the output of the preceding code. In this example, the content from the called page is contained within the debug.dump statement as expected. In the preceding example, a call is made out to a web page in the same directory, and its contents are displayed.

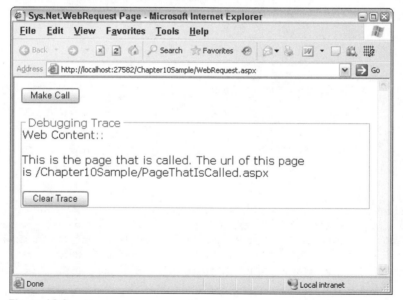

Figure 10-9

Sys.Data.DataColumn

The Sys.Data namespace provides a set of classes that are essentially client-side versions of the similar classes in the System.Data namespace of the .NET Framework. This namespace provides support for classes called DataColumn, DataRow, DataTable, DataView, DataFilter, DataSource, and PropertyFilter.

The `Sys.Data.DataColumn` class allows for the interrogation of column information within a `Sys.Data.DataTable` class. The `DataColumn` exposes the following members. These members will be useful for processing datasets and data tables that are returned from a web service.

Members	Description
get_columnName()	This method will retrieve the column name of a specific column.
get_dataType()	This method will retrieve the datatype of the column.
get_defaultValue()	This method will retrieve the default value of a column.
dispose()	This method will dispose() of the object and perform any necessary cleanup.

The following example code will interrogate a returned dataset. The first thing that is necessary is to get a datatable. This is performed by calling the `result.getItem(0)` method.

```
function MethodReturn(result)
{
    var i = 0;
    var str = "";
    var strColInfo = "";
    var strReturn = "<br />";
    for (prop in result)
        str += "Property: " + prop + "\r\n";
    alert(str);
    var tbl1 = result.getItem(0);
    for(i = 0; i < tbl1.get_columns().length; i++)
    {
        strColInfo += tbl1.get_columns()[i].get_columnName() + ":" +
tbl1.get_columns()[i].get_dataType() + strReturn;
    }

    document.getElementById("ColInfo").innerHTML = strColInfo
}
```

In the preceding code, a web service returns a dataset in the result variable to the `MethodReturn()` JavaScript function. There is a `for()` loop that returns the properties/members of the result object. This is then presented to the user in an `alert()` box. This `alert()` box is only for information's sake. The first table in the dataset is pulled out of the dataset by calling `result.getItem(0)`. Within the first table, the next `for()` loop iterates through the columns returned, gets the datatype, and creates a string, and after the `for()` loop exits, the data is presented to the user.

Figure 10-10 shows the output of the preceding code. One thing to notice is that the `get_dataType()` returns information.

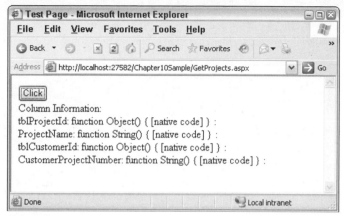

Figure 10-10

Sys.Data.DataTable

The Sys.Data.DataTable class provides all information for integration with the System.Data
.DataTable. The DataTable exposes the following members that may be of interest.

Members	Description
get_columns()	This method will return an array of DataColumns within the DataTable.
get_keys()	This method will return an array of DataColumns that contain various keys within the DataTable.
get_isDirty()	This method will return a boolean indicating whether or not updates have been made on the DataTable object.
get_length()	This method will return the number of rows within the DataTable.
add()	The add method will allow the addition of a DataRow.
clear()	The clear() method will clear the contents of the DataTable.
getChanges()	The getChanges() method will provide a set of DataRows that have changed.
getColumn()	The getColumn() method will provide the specified column.
getItem()	The getItem() method will provide the specified row. This method is very important.
remove()	The remove() will remove the specified row.
dispose()	Performs the standard dispose mechanism.

The following is some code that will iterate through the rows of a `DataTable`:

```
function MethodReturn(result)
{
    var i = 0;
    var str = "";
    var strRowsInfo = "";
    var strReturn = "<br />";
    //get a datatable
    var tbl1 = result.getItem(0);
    for(i = 0; i < tbl1.get_length(); i++)
    {
        //tbl1.getItem(i) will return the ith DataRow
        //getProperty("Column Name") will return the column value from a DataRow
        strRowsInfo += tbl1.getItem(i).getProperty("ProjectName") + strReturn;
    }
    document.getElementById("RowInfo").innerHTML = strRowsInfo;
}
```

In the preceding code, a dataset is returned. The first datatable is obtained by the call to `getItem(0)`. Then the `DataRows` are iterated. This is done by the `for()` loop. To get at the value of a column in a specific row, we use the `getProperty("ProjectName")` method. This method returns the value from the column `ProjectName` in the example. Some example output from the preceding code is shown in Figure 10-11.

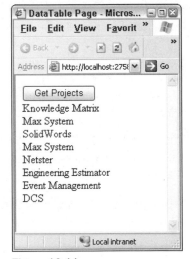

Figure 10-11

Sys.Data.DataRow

The `Sys.Data.DataRow` class is the Atlas version of the `System.Data.DataRow` class. The `DataRow` has a set of properties and is designed for accessing a single row of data from a data table. For example, the `DataRow.getProperty("ColumnName")` method shown in the previous code will return the value of that specific column in that `DataRow`.

For more information about this namespace and classes and others, you can check out http://atlas
.asp.net/ *and* http://atlas.asp.net/docs *for updated documentation from Microsoft along
with the site for this book* http://BeginningAjax.com.

Registering Namespaces and Classes in Atlas

JavaScript is a fairly simple scripting language. When implemented in a web browser environment, it
lacks many features that are common to modern programming languages. As a result, it is necessary for
Atlas to add functionality to create namespaces, classes, and other items that are familiar to developers
who use modern programming languages. There are several different mechanisms to register classes in
Atlas.

Type.registerNameSpace

A namespace is used to group common functionality together. The `Type.registerNameSpace()`
method is used to register a namespace in Atlas-enabled JavaScript. The proper call for this method
is as follows.

```
Type.registerNameSpace('NamespaceName');
```

In this example, `NamespaceName` is a string representing the name of the namespace.

NamespaceName.ClassName.registerClass

A class is a set of methods and data that provide a specific piece of functionality. Atlas provides a mechanism to register classes. This is performed within the following call.

```
NamespaceName.ClassName.registerClass('NamespaceName.ClassName', ParentClass,
InterfaceImplemented);
```

In this example, the `NamespaceName.ClassName` is a string representing the name of the class. If the
class that is being registered is to inherit from another class, that parent class is passed as the second
parameter. The final parameter is any interface that may be implemented within the class.

Take note that not all of the parameters are required.

NamespaceName.ClassName.registerAbstractClass

An abstract class is one that contains methods that are not actually implemented within the class. Also,
abstract classes cannot be instantiated — their only purpose is to be used as a model for child classes.
The definition is performed by the following code.

```
NamespaceName.ClassName.registerAbstractClass('NamespaceName.ClassName',
ParentClass, InterfaceImplemented);
```

In this example, the `NamespaceName.ClassName` is a string representing the name of the class. If the
class that is being registered is to inherit from another class, that parent class is passed as the second
parameter. The final parameter is any interface that may be implemented within the class.

Take note that not all of the parameters are required.

NamespaceName.ClassName.registerSealedClass

A sealed class is one that may not be inherited from. The definition is performed by the following code.

```
NamespaceName.ClassName.registerSealedClass('NamespaceName.ClassName', ParentClass,
InterfaceImplemented);
```

In this example, the `NamespaceName.ClassName` is a string representing the name of the class. If the class that is being registered is to inherit from another class, that parent class is passed as the second parameter. The final parameter is any interface that may be implemented within the class.

Take note that not all of the parameters are required.

InterfaceName.registerInterface

An interface essentially states that a class implements a specific set of methods. The interface is defined by registering an interface. This is performed by the following code.

```
InterfaceName.registerInterface('InterfaceName');
```

In this example, the `InterfaceName` is merely a string representing the name of the interface that is to be implemented. Note that by convention all interfaces are named with a capital "I" prefix.

NamespaceName.ClassName.registerBaseMethod

If a class is going to be specifically overridden in a base class, the method must be marked in the base class. This is performed by the following code:

```
NamespaceName.ClassName.registerBaseMethod(class, "methodname");
```

For example, the class will most likely be defined as the current class in JavaScript (`this`). A good candidate for the method name is the `dispose` method.

Namespaces and Classes

Namespaces allow for the grouping of classes, methods, objects, and data that are closely related. Atlas includes functionality on the `Type` object to add namespaces and classes. These are accomplished through the `Type.registerNamespace` and `Class.registerClass` methods.

Try It Out   **Adding a Namespace and Class through Atlas**

The steps necessary to add a namespace and class to JavaScript through Atlas are:

1.   The `atlas:ScriptManager` must be added to an `.aspx` page. The script manager will add the appropriate script references.

```
<atlas:ScriptManager runat="server" ID="scriptManager" />
```

2.   Register a namespace. This is performed through the `Type.registerNamespace` method. In this example, the string `NamespaceName` is just an example name for a namespace:

```
Type.registerNamespace("NamespaceName");
```

3. Define the contents of a class:

```
ExampleNamespace.cComplexCustomerType = function(Name, Address)
{
    var _Name = Name;
    var _Address = Address;

    this.getName = function() {
        return _Name;
    }
    this.setName = function(val){
        _Name = val;
    }
    this.getAddress = function() {
        return _Address;
    }
    this.setAddress = function(val){
        _Address = val;
    }
    this.Dispose = function(){
        alert("disposing component with Customer Name:" + this.getName() + " @ " +
this.getAddress());
    }
}
```

4. Register the class:

```
Type.registerClass("ExampleNamespace.cComplexCustomerType", Web.IDisposible);
```

5. To add standard methods, such as toString(), to a class, use the prototype member:

```
ExampleNamespace.cComplexCustomerType.prototype.toString = function(){
    return this.getName() + " at " + this.getAddress();
}
```

Adding an item through the prototype member results in sharing of the member between
instances. Sharing of objects defined with the prototype member must be avoided or unusual
results may occur. Conceptually, this is similar to static/shared members in .NET.

Now that a class has been created a program can use the class. The following code will use the class and
display the .toString() value of the customer object:

```
    var objCust = new ExampleNamespace.cComplexCustomerType("Acme", "Wileyville,
USA");
    alert(objCust.toString());
```

Figure 10-12 shows the result.

Figure 10-12

Inheritance

Inheritance is a mechanism to create new classes based on the functionality of an existing class. The new class takes over attributes and behavior of the parent or base classes. This helps in reusing existing code with very little modification. With Atlas, it is possible to provide inheritance in JavaScript:

Try It Out   Providing Inheritance with Atlas

In the following example, you will see a class created called `Animal.Generic`. This class has two properties, `Name` and `Address`. Then the code creates a class title `Animal.Cat` that inherits from the `Animal.Generic` class:

```
<script language="javascript">
Type.registerNamespace("Animal");
Animal.Generic = function(Name, Address)
{
    var _Name = Name;
    var _Address = Address;

    this.getName = function() {
        return _Name;
    }
    this.setName = function(val){
        _Name = val;
    }
    this.getAddress = function() {
        return _Address;
    }
    this.setAddress = function(val){
        _Address = val;
    }
    this.Dispose = function(){
        alert("disposing component with Animal Name:" + this.getName() + " @ " +
this.getAddress());
    }
    this.toString = function(){
        return _Name + " at " + _Address;
    }
}
Type.registerClass("Animal.Generic", null, Web.IDisposible);
Animal.Cat = function(Name, Address, Parents)
{
    Animal.Cat.initializeBase(this, [Name, Address]);

    var _Parents = Parents;

    this.getParents = function()
    {
        return _Parents;
    }
    this.setParents = function(Parents)
    {
```

```
        _Parents = Parents
    }
}
Type.registerClass('Animal.Cat', Animal.Generic);
</script>
```

Note that on the call to `Class.registerClass`, *the parent object is passed as the second parameter in the call to register the class.*

To create the `Animal.Cat` class, you use the following code:

```
function GenerateClasses()
{
    var strReturn = "<br />";
    var strOutput;
    var objCat = new Animal.Cat("Wells", "Knoxville, TN", "Wally and Ronda");
    strOutput = "Cat's name: " + objCat.getName() + strReturn;
    strOutput += "Cat's Parents: " + objCat.getParents();
    document.getElementById("Output").innerHTML = strOutput;
}
```

The output from the preceding code is shown in Figure 10-13.

Figure 10-13

Interfaces

Interfaces are contracts that allow a software program to see if a component/class implements specific methods. Interfaces can be thought of as complementary to inheritance. With inheritance, the base classes provide the majority of the functionality. With interfaces, the new classes are responsible for implementing the required functionality. It is assumed that if an interface is implemented, the methods/ property that the interface defines are implemented.

Try It Out   **Implementing an Interface**

In this example, you take your existing classes `Animal.Generic` and `Animal.Cat`, and you implement the interfaces `IPet` in `Animal.Cat` but not in `Animal.Generic`. Take a look at the following code:

```javascript
<script language="javascript">
Type.registerNamespace("Animal");
// Define an interface
Animal.IPet = function()
{
    this.getFriendlyName = Function.abstractMethod;
}
Animal.IPet.registerInterface('Animal.IPet');
// define a generic base class
Animal.Generic = function(Name, Address)
{
    var _Name = Name;
    var _Address = Address;

    this.getName = function() {
        return _Name;
    }
    this.setName = function(val){
        _Name = val;
    }
    this.getAddress = function() {
        return _Address;
    }
    this.setAddress = function(val){
        _Address = val;
    }
    this.Dispose = function(){
        alert("disposing component with Animal Name:" + this.getName() + " @ " +
this.getAddress());
    }
    this.toString = function(){
        return _Name + " at " + _Address;
    }
}
Animal.Generic.registerClass("Animal.Generic", null, Sys.IDisposable);
// define a specific subclass of the generic class
Animal.Cat = function(Name, Address, Parents)
{
    Animal.Cat.initializeBase(this, [Name, Address]);

    var _Parents = Parents;

    this.getParents = function()
    {
```

```
            return _Parents;
        }
    this.setParents = function(Parents)
    {
        _Parents = Parents
    }
    this.getFriendlyName = function()
    {
        return "Cat";
    }
}
Animal.Cat.registerClass('Animal.Cat', Animal.Generic, Animal.IPet);
</script>
```

In the preceding code, a namespace called `Animal` has been created. Within that namespace is an `Animal`
`.Generic` class. This class does not inherit from anything. It implements `Sys.IDisposable` through the
`registerClass()` method. An `Animal.IPet` interface is defined, and the method `getFriendlyName()`
is defined. A new class is created called `Animal.Cat`. This class inherits from `Animal.Generic`, and it
implements the `Animal.IPet` interface by defining the `getFriendlyName`. This work is handled by the
call to the `Animal.Cat.registerClass()` method.

To call the preceding code, you use the following code. The code that follows tests the `obj` and `objGen`
object. The `obj` object is of type `Animal.Cat`. Given that the `Animal.Cat` class implements the `IPet` interface, the call to the `isImplementedBy(obj)` method returns a true. Given that the `Animal.Generic` class
does not implement the `IPet` interface, the call to the `isImplemented(objGen)` method returns a false.

```
function GenerateClasses()
{
    var strReturn = "<br />";
    var strOutput;
    var objCat = new Animal.Cat("Wells", "Knoxville, TN", "Wally and Ronda");
    var objGeneric = new Animal.Generic("Spot", "Atlanta, GA");
    strOutput = "Cat's name: " + objCat.getName() + strReturn;
    strOutput += "Cat's Parents: " + objCat.getParents() + strReturn;
    if (Animal.IPet.isImplementedBy(objCat))
    {
        strOutput += "Obj does implement IPet." + strReturn;
        strOutput += "This object has a friendly name of: " +
objCat.getFriendlyName() + strReturn;
    }
    if (!Animal.IPet.isImplementedBy(objGeneric))
    {
        strOutput += "Animal.Generic does not implement the IPet interface.";
    }
    document.getElementById("Output").innerHTML = strOutput;
}
```

The result of the preceding code is shown in Figure 10-14.

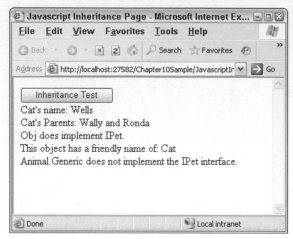

Figure 10-14

Enumerations

The Atlas framework allows for the creation of enumerations similar to enumerations in the .NET Framework. The Web.Enum class supports the method getValues(), which returns a set of values. In this example, the code iterates through the value.

```
function PerformEnumerations()
{
    var strOut = "";
    var strReturn = "<br />";
    var objEnum = Web.Enum.create("Good", "Bad", "Indifferent");
    for (var strItems in objEnum.getValues())
    {
        strOut += strItems + strReturn;
    }
    document.getElementById("Output").innerHTML = strOut;
}
```

Example output is shown in Figure 10-15.

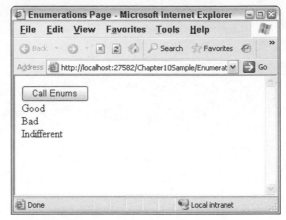

Figure 10-15

Debugging

With Atlas you have two features that are useful for debugging. Each of these built-in mechanisms shows the contents of an object. For more information on debugging see Chapter 13.

Debugging Using debug.dump

The first of these options is the command `debug.dump`. The `debug.dump` command will output the contents of an object and is primarily used with three parameters. An example call takes the following parameters:

```
debug.dump(object, string, boolean)
```

In this call, the object to be interrogated is the first parameter. The second parameter is a string that will be displayed as the object's name in the trace. The last parameter determines if the object will be interrogated within multiple layers below its top level.

Figure 10-16 shows the output of a call to `debug.dump()` with a dataset as the contents that are passed.

Figure 10-16

Debugging Using for() loop

The second option is to interrogate a JavaScript object within standard JavaScript. The code to interrogate an object's properties uses the `for()` loop construction and is as follows:

```
for(prop in obj)
{
    alert(prop);
}
```

This code will display the properties of the object. This code could be expanded out to display all properties of an object through a recursive algorithm.

Special Notes Concerning Atlas Client-Side Script

When working with Atlas client-side script, you should take a few special considerations into account.

❑   `document.writeln()` — The use of `document.writeln()` creates a timing issue within Atlas that may cause the method to fail. As a result, it should not be used.

❑   **Body tag's** `onload()` **event** — The `onload()` event may not properly fire. To create this same type of functionality, the command `<application load="yourFunction"/>` can be added to the XML/script section of your page.

❑   **Timing issues** — There will most likely be other timing related problems, so be flexible. For example, it has been discussed at `forums.asp.net` that the `pageLoad()` method has some undocumented issues in the Atlas environment and may be removed at some time.

Resources Used

Because the Atlas chapters of this book are being written while the software is still relatively new, the documentation available is rather limited. As a result, the following resources were used extensively during the writing of these chapters of the book.

❑   **Wilco Bauwer** — Wilco was an intern on the Atlas team. He blogs about Atlas extensively at `www.wilcob.com`. In addition, Wilco has personally answered a number of my emails and IM questions.

❑   **ASP.NET Forums** — Several forums at `www.asp.net` are dedicated to Atlas.

❑   **Scott Guthrie's blog** — `http://weblogs.asp.net/scottgu`.

❑   **Nikhil Kothari's blog** — `www.nikhilk.net`.

Summary

In this chapter, you have started taking a close look at Atlas. Atlas has allowed you to call to the web server and call methods through web services without having to round trip to the web server. For users, this eliminates the annoying flash that users typically see as well as the loss of user context that result from redirecting the user back to the top of a web page as opposed to where the user has scrolled within the page. In this chapter, we have seen that Atlas supports:

❑   Calling back to the web server through a web service

❑   Passing simple and complicated objects back and forth between client and server

❑   Using features like namespaces, classes, inheritance, and interfaces to provide a set of language extensions

Now that you have looked at some of the client-side building blocks of Atlas, the next chapter will build on this and will look at the controls provided by the Atlas framework.

Atlas Controls

This chapter introduces the concept of the Microsoft Atlas controls. These controls function like other ASP.NET server controls. Once rendered, these controls provide the HTML necessary to communicate back to the server from the client. In this chapter, you look at:

❑ Referencing and creating client-side controls with Atlas

❑ Client-side events — events that are raised by user controls and processed in client-side script

❑ Extending existing ASP.NET controls

❑ Data binding, which allows for the connection of components and controls to manage the flow of data between the two

Controls

With the Atlas framework, the page developer has the ability to create rich applications that do not need to post back to the server on every action that a user performs. Much of this functionality is provided by a set of controls referred to as the Atlas server controls. These controls output the appropriate markup for the web browser client so that actions on the client do not require the dreaded postback.

You start by looking at some generic controls and then move into several more complicated controls.

Buttons

An HTML button is one of the most basic controls in a web application. It is typically used as the last step in some type of user interaction. For example, a user will fill out a form with contact information. The last step in the process is for the user to submit that information to the web server. Atlas has support for working with the buttons in the Sys.UI.Button() class.

Try It Out   Creating a Button and Changing Its Properties

Take a look at an example of dynamically creating a button and then changing one of the properties of the button. Creating a button dynamically can be done through the Document Object Model (DOM):

```
var associatedElement = document.getElementById("divTest");
var btnCreate = document.createElement("button");
btnCreate.id = "btnCreated";
btnCreate.value = "Hi";
btnCreate.innerHTML = "Hi";
associatedElement.appendChild(btnCreate);
```

For more information regarding the DOM, turn to Chapter 3.

Atlas allows a control to be manipulated through JavaScript. The preceding code will hold a reference to a button. After the reference to the button is created, the `visible` and `accessKey` properties of the object are set. In the first code snippet, a button is created using the DOM. In the second snippet, a reference is created to the button. The `visible` property of the button is set to `true`, and the access property is set to `"o"`.

Now that you have a button in the browser, you may need to reference the button in Atlas. To reference a button in Atlas, use the following code.

```
var btnAlreadyThere = new Sys.UI.Button($("btnCreated"));
btnAlreadyThere.set_visible(true);
btnAlreadyThere.set_accessKey("o");
```

While looking at the preceding code, take notice of several things:

❑　The dollar sign ($) is a shortcut to `document.getElementById`. Using the DOM methods means that the method will provide support across multiple browsers that support the DOM.

❑　There is a class titled `Sys.UI.Button`. This class encapsulates functionality of an HTML button and allows that button to be modified through Atlas.

❑　The `Sys.UI.Button` class provides a reference to a button. The class does not provide support for creating a new button, merely for referencing the button.

❑　Setting the properties is easy. The preceding code shows the `visible` and `accessKey` properties being set. These are set by calling `set_visible(boolean)` and `set_accessKey(string)`.

Approximately 40 properties can be set on a button or other user control in Atlas. The most common ones will be the display/user interface (UI) oriented properties, such as `behaviors`, `cssClass`, `enabled`, and other UI properties. It is beyond the scope of this book to go through all the properties of the button control or all the properties of every single control. Suffice it to say, each of the additional UI wrapper controls provided by Microsoft Atlas provides a similar set of properties. You can obtain them by the using the `for()` loop presented at the end of Chapter 10 to interrogate the JavaScript objects.

Sys.UI.Data Controls

The `Sys.UI.Data` namespace provides a couple of key visual/UI-related controls — namely the `listView` and `itemView` classes. We are going to take a look at the `listView` control here.

Try It Out　　**Using listView**

A `listView` is an Atlas control that is used to display a tabular set of data. It is very similar to a `GridView`/`DataGrid` in ASP.NET or an HTML table in classical ASP used to present data. A `listView` is set up within the `<page>` tag of the `xml-script` section of the page. Take a look at the following code using the `listView` taken from the data binding section later in the chapter.

```
<page xmlns:script="http://schemas.microsoft.com/xml-script/2005">
<components>
    <listView id="ProjectResults"
        itemTemplateParentElementId="ProjectTemplate" >
        <layoutTemplate>
            <template layoutElement="ProjectTemplate" />
        </layoutTemplate>
        <itemTemplate>
            <template layoutElement="ProjectItemTemplate">
                <label id="ProjectNameLabel">
                    <bindings>
                        <binding dataPath="ProjectName" property="text" />
                    </bindings>
                </label>
            </template>
        </itemTemplate>
    </listView>
</components>
</page>
```

Notice some of the settings in this `listView`:

❑   The `listView` has an ID of `"ProjectResults"`.

❑   The target element is `"ProjectTemplate"`. The target element from this example is a `div` tag that will receive the tabular results.

❑   The bindings define how data is bound to the element. More information on data binding is found later in this chapter. In this example, the data column `ProjectName` is bound to the label `ProjectNameLabel`.

❑   The `layoutTemplate` defines the layout that will be used for the records. In this situation, the `ProjectItemTemplate` is the element that will hold the contents of data that is bound to the `listView`.

❑   The `itemTemplate` defines the layout that will be used for a single record. Within the `itemTemplate`, there is a binding setup that associates the `ProjectItemTemplate` tag with the layout of the individual records as defined by the `ProjectNameLabel` element.

Server Controls

One of the interesting pieces of Atlas is the support for various server-centric controls and integration with the server-centric ASP.NET way of thinking. The idea behind these controls is to keep the server control model and add support for client-side/Ajax scenarios.

Partial Updates and the UpdatePanel

One of the simplest scenarios is the ability to perform updates incrementally. The goal is to minimize the use of postbacks and whole refreshes and to instead use targeted and partial updates. This scenario is enabled by turning on partial updates through the `ScriptManager` control.

```
<atlas:ScriptManager runat="server" id="scriptManager"
EnablePartialRendering="true" />
```

Setting the `EnablePartialRendering` attribute to `true` causes a postback to be simulated using the Atlas `Sys.Net.WebRequest` class (which is based on the `XMLHttpRequest` object). On the server, the page is processed as if a "classical" page postback has occurred. This works with the server controls, both in-the-box and third-party controls, which call `doPostBack`. The result is that `Page.IsPostBack` returns a `true`, if that is necessary. In addition, server-side events fire as they are designed to, and event handlers continue to be processed.

Try It Out   Using an UpdatePanel

The next step in this process is to determine what to do when the server returns the data. The `Script Manager` needs to determine what parts of the page have changed. The `UpdatePanel` helps the `ScriptManager` in this situation. `UpdatePanels` are used to define portions/regions of a page that can be updated together. The `ScriptManager` will override the rendering of an entire HTML page and display only the content of the `UpdatePanels`. In addition, the `ScriptManager` will handle the updating of page titles, viewstate (and other hidden fields), updated styles, and the like.

Consider this small example. In this example, you will have a drop-down list of employees. When an employee is selected, a `GridView` will be displayed and filled based on the employee that is selected. Here is some ASPX code:

```
<atlas:ScriptManager ID="ScriptManager1" runat="server"
EnablePartialRendering="true" />
        <div>
        </div>
    <div>
<table>
    <tr>
        <td><asp:Label runat="server" ID="lblEmployee">Employee:</asp:Label></td>
        <td><asp:DropDownList runat="server"
ID="ddlEmployee"></asp:DropDownList></td>
    </tr>
    <tr>
        <td colspan="2">
            <asp:Button runat="server" ID="btnSearch" Text="Search"
OnClick="btnSearch_Click" />
        </td>
    </tr>
</table>
    </div>
    <atlas:UpdatePanel runat="server" ID="upSearch">
        <ContentTemplate>
            <asp:GridView ID="gvSearchResults" runat="server"
EnableSortingAndPagingCallbacks="true">
            </asp:GridView>
        </ContentTemplate>
        <Triggers>
            <atlas:ControlEventTrigger ControlID="btnSearch" EventName="Click" />
        </Triggers>
    </atlas:UpdatePanel>
```

How It Works

Conceptually, there are several things you should take notice of in the preceding code:

❏ The UpdatePanel allows the developer to define a region that will be updated.

❏ The <atlas:ControlEventTrigger> allows for the ControlID to be specified through the named property. This allows for Atlas to specifically act on a control.

❏ There is an EventName property. This property "listens" for the specific event as specified by the EventName property. This property works with the specified ControlID property.

Based on the preceding code, you are able to get the screen of results shown in Figure 11-1.

Figure 11-1

Just to show that there is not an update of the complete page, take a look at the source code of the preceding page after the method returns its values.

```
<!DOCTYPE html PUBLIC "-//W3C//DTD XHTML 1.0 Transitional//EN"
"http://www.w3.org/TR/xhtml1/DTD/xhtml1-transitional.dtd">
<html xmlns="http://www.w3.org/1999/xhtml" >
<head><title>
Update Panel Page
</title><style type="text/css">
atlas__delta { font-family:Lucida Console; }
</style></head>
<body>
<form name="form1" method="post" action="PartialUpdates.aspx" id="form1">
<div>
<input type="hidden" name="__VIEWSTATE" id="__VIEWSTATE" value="....." />
</div>
<script src="../ScriptLibrary/Atlas/Debug/Atlas.js"
type="text/javascript"></script>
<div>
</div>
<div>
<table>
<tr>
<td><span id="lblEmployee">Employee:</span></td>
<td><select name="ddlEmployee" id="ddlEmployee">
<option value=""></option>
<option value="ee8d807d-fab3-4e39-948a-67362c61a470">McClure, Wallace</option>
<option value="4d39f850-2b65-477d-9cf4-c90158e26b5f">Coder, Lou</option>
<option value="3a3221a8-5043-46cb-bd61-d12e77195f61">Smith, Joe</option>
</select></td>
</tr>
<tr>
<td colspan="2">
<input type="submit" name="btnSearch" value="Search" id="btnSearch" />
</td>
</tr>
</table>
</div>
<span id="upSearch_Start"></span>
<div>
</div>
        <span id="upSearch_End"></span>
<div>
<input type="hidden" name="__EVENTVALIDATION" id="__EVENTVALIDATION"
value="/wEWBgK9+Yf9BgLO+4f+BgKWzeL+BQL4qeKmDgKdwp/VDgKln/PuCnnVW0Hi59nE7dq0vREhD29F
VgTo" />
</div>
<script type="text/xml-script"><page
xmlns:script="http://schemas.microsoft.com/xml-script/2005"><components />
</page></script><script
type="text/javascript">Sys.WebForms._PageRequest._setupAsyncPostBacks(document.getE
lementById('form1'), 'ScriptManager1');
</script></form>
</body>
</html>
```

The preceding code contains several things it's important to understand:

❑ This is the same code that would be generated when the page is first loaded. The ViewState is at its default setting within the "view source." While the ViewState has been "clipped" for brevity in this example, the ViewState does not seem to hold all the data-bound content of the GridView that you would expect to see from a page that contained the data bound to the GridView and resent to the client. The UpdatePanel has handled the updating of ViewState.

❑ The GridView is not displayed on the page. The UpdatePanel is replaced by the <span> tag. This will be the location where the GridView is placed when the data is returned to the web client. When the data is returned, the data is placed within the <span> tag.

❑ This methodology allows for the integration of Ajax functionality into ASP.NET applications, while preserving the server-centric development methodology that ASP.NET has traditionally provided.

Timed Refreshes

Atlas contains a timer control that provides for timed actions to occur. Situations where this would be useful might be:

❑ Stock symbol updates for an investor

❑ Inventory updates within a manufacturing environment

❑ Retail inventory

❑ Executive information system or dashboard

Try It Out   Performing a Timed Update with the Timer Control

Take a look at some code to perform a timed update:

```
<atlas:TimerControl runat="server" ID="tc" Interval="5000" OnTick="tc_Tick"/>
<atlas:UpdatePanel ID="up" runat="server" Mode=Conditional>
<ContentTemplate>
<asp:Label ID="lblInv" runat="server" AssociatedControlID="lblNum" />:
<asp:Label ID="lblNum" runat="server" />
</ContentTemplate>
<Triggers>
    <atlas:ControlEventTrigger ControlID="tc" EventName="Tick" />
</Triggers>
</atlas:UpdatePanel>
```

The ASP.NET event control is:

```
protected void tc_Tick(object sender, EventArgs e)
{
    lblInv.Text = "Widget";
    lblNum.Text = DateTime.Now.Millisecond.ToString();
    if ( /* Something happened */ true)
    {
        up.Update();
    }
}
```

How It Works

In this example, an Atlas server control called the `<atlas:TimerControl>` is set up. There are two properties that are of interest. These are:

❑   `Interval` — The interval is the number of milliseconds before the `OnTick` event is called. In this example, the interface is set to 5,000 milliseconds. As a result, every 5,000 milliseconds, the timer control will update and run.

❑   `OnTick` — This event fires when the period of time defined by the `Interval` has elapsed.

Along with the timer, the `<Trigger>` in the example shows that when the timer control counts down from 5 seconds to 0, a call is made to the specified method. In this case, the server-side event fires and updates the label controls without the unnecessary page postback. In this example, the inventory listed on screen is updated every 5 seconds.

Figure 11-2 shows what the output might look like.

Figure 11-2

If you look at the source for this page, the code of interest is defined as:

```
<script type="text/xml-script"><page
xmlns:script="http://schemas.microsoft.com/xml-script/2005">
  <components>
    <timer interval="5000" enabled="true">
      <tick>
        <postBack target="tc" argument="" />
      </tick>
    </timer>
  </components>
</page></script>
<script
type="text/javascript">Sys.WebForms._PageRequest._setupAsyncPostBacks(document.getE
lementById('form1'), 'ScriptManager1');
</script>
```

This code contains the definition for the component configuration on the client. This code is generated by the server-side `TimerControl`. When the server control is rendered to the client, this is the code that is generated.

Control Extenders

With ASP.NET, there is a set of controls that developers have become fairly familiar with. These controls include things like the textbox, label, drop-down list box, and many others. One of the questions that Atlas brings to the table is how to provide additional functionality to these controls, while maintaining the programming model that developers have come to be familiar with. Into this problem step *control extenders*. With control extenders, client-side functionality is added to an existing server-side control, while maintaining the server-side programming model. There are numerous examples of these extensions of existing controls.

You are going to see the `AutoComplete` extender control in the next section. The `AutoComplete` extender control is designed to extend the capabilities of an ASP.NET `Textbox` control. The `AutoComplete` control will extend the functionality of the `Textbox` control by hooking it to a web service to get information.

In Chapter 12, the Drag and Drop extender will be presented. It will provide Drag and Drop support through Atlas.

AutoComplete

One of the classic examples of Ajax has been a textbox that is similar in concept to the Windows combo box (similar, but not quite the same). This feature has been popularized by the Google Suggest service.

Atlas provides the capability to extend the `<asp:Textbox>` in ASP.NET 2.0. This extension takes input from the textbox, passes the text to the web service, and the web service returns a list of possible items, similar to the Windows Combo Box. Take a look at the following simple example. Here is the ASPX code.

```
<atlas:ScriptManager ID="ScriptManager1" runat="server"
EnablePartialRendering="true" />
<div>
<asp:Textbox runat="server" id="txtBox" />
<atlas:AutoCompleteExtender runat="server" ID="ace">
    <atlas:AutoCompleteProperties TargetControlID="txtBox"
    Enabled="true" ServicePath="AutoCompleteEx.asmx"
    ServiceMethod="TextBoxAutoComplete" />
</atlas:AutoCompleteExtender>
</div>
```

Look at what is being specified.

❑   There is an ASP.NET textbox. This is the standard textbox in ASP.NET.

❑   There is a new type of server control. This is an extender control, and specifically the `AutoCompleteExtender`. It is a server control that acts on the ASP.NET textbox. The extender control "extends" the functionality in the textbox.

❑   There are series of properties specified within the `<atlas:AutoCompleteProperties>` tag:

    ❑   `TargetControlID` — The `TargetControlID` is the control that will be the target of the extender.

    ❑   `ServicePath` — The `ServicePath` property is the path to the web service that will be called.

    ❑   `ServiceMethod` — The `ServiceMethod` property is the name of the function within the web service.

Now that you have seen the ASPX code, look at the web service:

```
[WebMethod]
public String[] TextBoxAutoComplete(string prefixText, int count) // Seems to be a
problem if the names are not prefixText and count
{
    int i = 0;
    int iLength = 10;
    List<String> Values = new List<string>();

    for (i = 0; (i < iLength); i++ )
    {
        Values.Add(Convert.ToString(prefixText + i.ToString()));
    }
    String[] strReturn = new String[Values.Count];
    strReturn = Values.ToArray();
    return (strReturn);
}
```

The issues with the web service are:

❑   A set of strings in the form of an array must be returned.

❑   The input parameters must be a string and an integer. In addition, at the time of this writing,
    these parameters *must* be named prefixText and count. Naming these values something dif-
    ferent will result in the code not working correctly.

❑   In this example, the code is designed to take an input and add the values 0–9. This code merely
    takes the input and adds a number. It expects a number to be input, but there is no specific
    checking in the example.

Now that you have seen the code, look at the output of the AutoCompleteExtender in Figure 11-3.

Figure 11-3

From there, take a look at the source code generated. Here is the HTML output from the View Source functionality in Internet Explorer.

```
<script src="../ScriptLibrary/Atlas/Debug/Atlas.js"
type="text/javascript"></script>
<div>
<input name="txtBox" type="text" id="txtBox" />
</div>
<div>
    <input type="hidden" name="__EVENTVALIDATION" id="__EVENTVALIDATION"
value="/wEWAgK44YDODwKF+8K0ARfViGhYgqOYxdy6jHmmcbQs826z" />
</div>
<script type="text/xml-script"><page
xmlns:script="http://schemas.microsoft.com/xml-script/2005">
   <components>
    <control id="txtBox">
      <behaviors>
        <autoComplete serviceURL="AutoCompleteEx.asmx"
serviceMethod="TextBoxAutoComplete" />
      </behaviors>
    </control>
  </components>
</page></script><script
type="text/javascript">Sys.WebForms._PageRequest._setupAsyncPostBacks(document.getE
lementById('form1'), 'ScriptManager1');
</script></form>
```

In reviewing this code, take note of the following:

❑   There are no special parameters on the HTML textbox definition.

❑   There is a definition of components.

❑   The definition of components contains a control ID and a behavior. These definitions associate the textbox with the behavior.

Data Binding

Data binding allows for the interchange of data between components and user interface controls. Atlas allows datasources and data controls to directly interact in the web browser without the need to post back to the server. Atlas provides the mechanism to create datasources. These datasources provide services for performing CRUD (create, read, update, delete) style operations. The associated database operations are select, insert, update, and delete.

Atlas supports two types of data binding—declarative and programmatic. Declarative data binding is what most ASP.NET developers are familiar with, but the next two sections look at these both in more detail.

Declarative Data Binding

When a developer ties together data components and user interface components that is known as *data binding*. With Atlas and ASP.NET, there is a further type of data binding known as declarative data binding. With *declarative data binding*, all of the binding information is declared statically within a section of the web page.

You will notice that there is still some code in the example that follows that is programmatic. Declarative data binding is typically not 100 percent declarative.

Try It Out Declarative Data binding

In this example, you will take look at the pieces of code and the steps taken for getting data in a declarative manner:

```
<form id="form1" runat="server">
<atlas:ScriptManager runat="server" ID="ScriptManager1" >
    <Services>
        <atlas:ServiceReference GenerateProxy=true Path="WebServiceProjects.asmx" />
    </Services>
</atlas:ScriptManager>
<input type="button" id="btnGetData" value="Get Project List" onclick="GetData()"
/>
<script language="javascript">
    function GetData()
    {
        WebServiceProjects.GetProjects(OnServiceComplete);
    }
    function OnServiceComplete(result)
    {
        var projectName = $("ProjectResults");
        projectName.control.set_data(result);
    }
</script>
<div id="ProjectResults">
</div>
<div id="ProjectTemplate">
This is a list of all project in the table tblProject:<br />
<div id="ProjectItemTemplate">
    Project: <strong><span id="ProjectNameLabel"></span></strong>
</div>
</div>
</form>
<script type="text/xml-script">
<page xmlns:script="http://schemas.microsoft.com/xml-script/2005">
<components>
<listView id="ProjectResults"
    itemTemplateParentElementId="ProjectTemplate" >
    <layoutTemplate>
        <template layoutElement="ProjectTemplate" />
    </layoutTemplate>
    <itemTemplate>
        <template layoutElement="ProjectItemTemplate">
        <label id="ProjectNameLabel">
            <bindings>
                <binding dataPath="ProjectName" property="text" />
            </bindings>
        </label>
        </template>
    </itemTemplate>
</listView>
</components>
</page>
</script>
```

How It Works

Now take a look at the details of the example:

1. The page is set up just like any other page that uses Atlas. The page has the `ScriptManager` along with a reference to a web service.

2. There is a `<serviceMethod>` tag that defines a web service to call and to create the JavaScript proxy.

3. There is an onclick event defined in the HTML for the `btnGetData` button. When the web service returns data, the `OnServiceComplete` method is called and processing is completed there. Within the `OnServiceComplete` method, a reference to the `ProjectResults` div is obtained and data is bound to the div tag.

4. A "holder" for the final results is defined within the `<div>` tag with an ID of `ProjectResults`.

5. A `listView` control is defined. This `listView` control is associated with the `ProjectResults` `<div>` tag within the script definition.

6. The binding section defines where to get the data from. The `ProjectName` field in the web service's dataset is bound to the `projectNameLabel`.

7. The `itemTemplate` defines the items to be contained within a binding on a per row basis. In this example, the `ProjectNameLabel` output span is bound to the `ProjectName` property.

Programmatic Data Binding

Most ASP.NET developers are familiar with declarative data binding. It is also possible to programmatically set up and perform data binding programmatically. *Programmatic data binding* means you are setting up the data binding through imperative program code rather than through declarative tags and structures.

Try It Out   Programmatic Data Binding

The following example uses programmatic data binding:

```
<atlas:ScriptManager runat="server" ID="ScriptManager1">
  <Services>
    <atlas:ServiceReference GenerateProxy="true" Path="WebServiceProjects.asmx" />
  </Services>
  <Scripts>
    <atlas:ScriptReference Path="~/ScriptLibrary/CustomTemplates.js" />
  </Scripts>
</atlas:ScriptManager>
<input type="button" id="btnGetData" onclick="GetData()" value="Get Project List"
/>
<script type="text/javascript">
function pageLoad()
{
    var listView = new Sys.UI.Data.ListView($("ProjectResults"));
    listView.set_itemTemplateParentElementId("ProjectTemplate");
    var layoutTemplate = new GenericTemplate($("ProjectTemplate"));
```

```
        listView.set_layoutTemplate(layoutTemplate);
        var itemTemplate = new GenericTemplate($("ProjectItemTemplate"),
createItemTemplate);
        listView.set_itemTemplate(itemTemplate);
        itemTemplate.initialize();
        layoutTemplate.initialize();
        listView.initialize();
}
function createItemTemplate(markupContext, dataContext)
{
        var
associatedElement = markupContext.findElement("ProjectNameLabel");
        var projectNameLabel = new Sys.UI.Label(associatedElement);
        projectNameLabel.set_dataContext(dataContext);
        var bindings = projectNameLabel.get_bindings();
        var textBinding = new Sys.Binding();
        textBinding.set_property("text");
        textBinding.set_dataPath('ProjectName');
        textBinding.initialize(projectNameLabel);
        bindings.add(textBinding);
        projectNameLabel.initialize();
}
function GetData()
{
        WebServiceProjects.GetProjects(OnServiceComplete);
}
function OnServiceComplete(result)
{
        var projectName = $("ProjectResults");
        projectName.control.set_data(result);
}
</script>
<div id="ProjectResults">
</div>
<div id="ProjectTemplate">
        This is a list of all projects in the table tblProject:<br />
        <div id="ProjectItemTemplate">
            Project: <strong><span id="ProjectNameLabel"></span></strong>
        </div>
</div>
```

How It Works

Now, take a look at this code in a step-by-step process:

1. The display information is set up exactly like the declarative data-binding example. As a result, the pages work the same.

2. There is a custom template in a JavaScript file that is included by using the ScriptManager control. The custom template is defined as the class GenericTemplate(). This custom template makes it easier for developers to programmatically data bind.

3. The `pageLoad()` event creates and sets up the `listView`, `layoutTemplate`, and `itemTemplate` controls. The `layoutTemplate` and `itemTemplate` are defined using the `GenericTemplate` class that is defined in the included JavaScript file.

4. An item template is created by the `createItemTemplate` method. Within the `pageLoad()` event, the `createItemTemplate` method is passed as a callback to the `GenericTemplate()` class.

5. The `GetData()` method is called when the `onclick` event of the button occurs.

6. The `OnServiceComplete()` method binds the data to the `listView`.

Figure 11-4 shows the output on screen of a call to both the declarative and programmatic code versions.

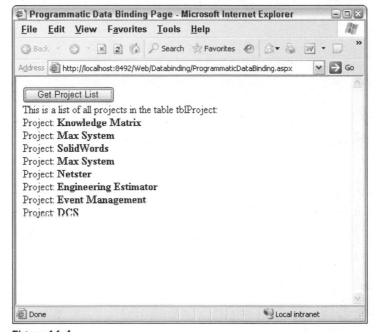

Figure 11-4

The question that you most likely have is why would a developer choose programmatic data binding versus declarative data binding. The simple answer is ease of use versus control. Programmatic data binding depends on the developer to know and understand many aspects of data binding, creating templates, and the intricacies of Atlas, which at this time are not all known. At the same time, programmatic data binding provides an amount of flexibility. Declarative data binding, on the other hand, will most likely be supported by designers, wizards, and graphical interface in a version of Visual Studio .NET after the 2005 release.

Binding Directions

As previously indicated, data binding allows data to be interchanged between components and user interface controls. This interchange may be cast in several directions — specifically, In, Out, and InOut. These directions are defined within the Sys.BindingDirection enumeration. The meanings of these directions are:

❑ In — Defines data going from a datasource into a user interface control

❑ Out — Defines data going from a user interface control in a datasource

❑ InOut — Defines data going back and forth between a user interface control and a datasource

The following code displays the allowed values of the Sys.BindingDirection enumeration:

```
function PerformEnumerations()
{
    var strOut = "";
    var strReturn = "<br />";
    for (var strItems in Sys.BindingDirection)
    {
        strOut += strItems + strReturn;
    }
    document.getElementById("Output").innerHTML = strOut;
}
```

Binding Transformations

Bindings provide the ability to attach handlers and methods for performing operations along with the binding. Two of the built-in transforms are ToString and Invert. The ToString transform converts the data into a string. The Invert transform is designed for boolean operations. It will output the opposite of the input value. Atlas provides the flexibility to create custom transforms.

```
var custBinding = new Sys.Binding();
..
custBinding.transform.add(CustomTransformHandler);
..
function CustomTransformHandler(sender, eventArgs) { .. }
```

The class that makes this possible is the Sys.Bindings() class.

Validation

Validation is a mechanism to verify data input. There are a number of ASP.NET server validators that include client functionality. Atlas provides a set of client-side controls that perform a similar function. The built-in validators are:

❑ requiredFieldValidator — Verifies that data is within the associated control

❑ typeValidator — Verifies the type of data. This may be String or Number

❑ rangeValidator — Verifies that the data within a lower and upper value

❏   `regexValidator` — Verifies the data against the supplied regular expression

❏   `customValidator` — Defines a custom expression handler

Validators are defined together through a collection and are typically fired on a `propertyChanged` event. During this event, the validation is checked, and the validate event is raised. From there, code can subscribe to a validation event. This event is raised after validation. During the validation, the validators are checked. Checking the validators may result in the client-side control `invalid` and `validationMessage` properties being set.

In addition to validators, a special control exists for displaying this information. This control is of type `validationErrorLabel` and is used to display error messages — similar in function to the ASP.NET `ValidationSummary` control. The error messages may be displayed through an asterisk, tooltip, or other mechanism. In addition, validators may be grouped together. A rollup of the validator controls can then occur.

Try It Out   Using a requiredFieldValidator

In the following code, you are going to investigate the use of the `requiredFieldValidator`.

```
<form id="form1" runat="server">
    <atlas:ScriptManager runat="server" ID="ScriptManager1" />
    <div class="description">
        The textbox requires data entry. A requiredFieldValidator is attached.
        Enter a text field, then remove to see the effect.  The validator is shown
        via the tooltip.
        <br /><br />
        <input type="text" id="textboxRequired" class-"input" />
         
        <span id="valRequired" style="color: red">*</span>
    </div>
    <script type="text/xml-script">
        <page xmlns:script="http://schemas.microsoft.com/xml-script/2005">
            <components>
                <textBox targetElement="textboxRequired">
                    <validators>
                        <requiredFieldValidator errorMessage="You must enter some
text." />
                    </validators>
                </textBox>
                <validationErrorLabel targetElement="valRequired"
associatedControl="textboxRequired" />
            </components>
        </page>
    </script>
```

How It Works

Now look at the steps taken to get this code to work.

1.   An HTML textbox and span are defined along with the Atlas `ScriptManager`.

2.   Within the `xml-script` section, there is a set of defined components. The `textBox` is defined, and a `validator` is assigned to the `textBox` control.

3. The `validationErrorLabel` is set up with a `targetElement` and the `associatedControl`.

Figure 11-5 shows the output of the preceding required field validator.

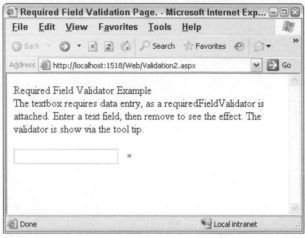

Figure 11-5

Try It Out   Adding Datatype and Range Validation Support

The next step in this example adds datatype and range validation support. By making the changes that follow to the `xml-script` section, the validation is added. In this example, the `<textbox>` tag contains a `<validators>` tag. Within the `<validators>` tag, there are several validators that are set up. The first validator is the `requiredFieldValdiator`. The `requiredFieldValidator` requires that a value be entered for that field. The second validator is the `typeValidator`. The `typeValidator` sets the type that must be entered. In this example, the `Number` type must be entered. The third validator in this example is the `rangeValidator`. In this example, if a number outside of the range from 10 to 20 is entered, a message is presented to the user regarding the number being out of the specified range.

```
<page xmlns:script="http://schemas.microsoft.com/xml-script/2005">
    <components>
        <textBox targetElement="textboxRequired">
            <validators>
                <requiredFieldValidator errorMessage="You must enter some text." />
                <typeValidator type="Number" errorMessage="You must enter a valid
number." />
                <rangeValidator lowerBound="10" upperBound="20" errorMessage="You
must enter a number between 10 and 20." />
            </validators>
        </textBox>
        <validationErrorLabel targetElement="valRequired"
associatedControl="textboxRequired" />
    </components>
</page>
```

Regex-Based Validation

This next example involves the source code to perform a `regex`-based validation. This example is similar to the previous example. There is an `xml-script` section that contains a list of components. In this situation, the text that is entered is validated for being in the form of an email address. In this example, a `regexValidator` is placed within the `<validators>` tag. Within the `regexValidator`, a regular expression is passed for processing by the validator.

```
<form id="form1" runat="server">
    <atlas:ScriptManager runat="server" ID="ScriptManager1" />
    <div class="description">
        Regex Validation Example.  Enter a valid email address. The validator is
show
        via the tooltip.
        <br /><br />
        <input type="text" id="textboxRegex" class="input" />
         
        <span id="valRegex" style="color: red">*</span>
    </div>
    <script type="text/xml-script">
        <page xmlns:script="http://schemas.microsoft.com/xml-script/2005">
            <components>
                <textBox targetElement="textboxRegex">
                    <validators>
                        <requiredFieldValidator errorMessage="You must enter some
text." />
                        <regexValidator regex="/(\w[-._\w]*\w@\w[-
._\w]*\w\.\w{2,3})/"  errorMessage="You must a valid email address in the form of
an email address." />
                    </validators>
                </textBox>
                <validationErrorLabel targetElement="valRegex"
associatedControl="textboxRegex" />
            </components>
        </page>
    </script>
</form>
```

Although the code looks the same as the previous validator example, there is one important difference. The `regex` that is used for the validation has "/" and "/" characters at the beginning and the end of the string representing the `regex` statement.

You may question under what situation a regular expression validation would need to occur. While testing for datatypes, required fields, and ranges can meet many validation requirements, there are situations where looking for pattern is required. In those scenarios, using regular expressions will work well in meeting those requirements.

Custom Validation

Next, take look at a custom validator. The code will look very similar to the existing validator code. There is a `customValidator` within the `<components>` section that will call the custom JavaScript routine. Take a look at the code for this:

```
<form id="form1" runat="server">
<atlas:ScriptManager runat="server" ID="ScriptManager1" />
<div class="description">
    Regex Validation Example.  Enter a value.  Entering the term "fail" will cause
the validation to fail.
    <br /><br />
    <input type="text" id="textboxValue" class="input" />
     
    <span id="valLabel" style="color: red">*</span>
</div>
<script language="javascript">
function onValidateValue(sender, eventArgs) {
    var val = eventArgs.get_value();
    var valid = true;
    if (val == "fail")
    {
        valid = false;
    }
    //You could do something like this to send an alert to to the user.
    //alert("The entry is: " + valid);
    eventArgs.set_isValid(valid);
}
</script>
<script type="text/xml-script">
    <page xmlns:script="http://schemas.microsoft.com/xml-script/2005">
        <components>
            <textBox targetElement="textboxValue">
                <validators>
                    <requiredFieldValidator errorMessage="You must enter some
text." />
                    <customValidator validateValue='onValidateValue'
errorMessage="You entered fail." />
                </validators>
            </textBox>
            <validationErrorLabel targetElement="valLabel"
associatedControl="textboxValue" />
        </components>
    </page>
</script>
```

There are a couple of key things to pay attention to in the customValidator when writing a custom validator.

❑ The onValidateValue method takes two parameters, just like an event in .NET, such as pressing a button in a web form.

❑ The customValidator takes a JavaScript function as the parameter in the validateValue function.

Now that you have seen requiredFieldValdiator, typeValidator, rangeValidator, and regexValidator, I am sure that you are asking, "Why would I need to use a customValidator?" That is an excellent question. There are situations where data must be validated against custom business rules. There might be a need perform a more complicated validation, for example to validate some data against a database. It's not possible to do this through the other validators. The custom validator allows for more programmatic options when validating.

Try It Out   Group Validation

Now that you have seen the code for custom validators, you can tie two or more validators together for a group validation.

```
<atlas:ScriptManager runat="server" ID="ScriptManager1" />
<div id="lblValid" >Valid.  Good data has been entered.<br /><br /></div>
<div id="lblInValid">Invalid.  Bad data has been entered.  Please review your
inputs.<br /><br /></div>
<div class="description">
    This is the group validation page.  This example demonstrates the validation of
two controls together.
    Regex Validation Example.  Enter a value.  Entering the term "fail" will cause
the validation to fail.
    <br /><br />
    <input type="text" id="textboxValue" class="input" />
     
    <span id="valLabel" style="color: red">*</span>
    <br /><br /><br />
    A requiredFieldValidator, typeValidator, and rangeValidator are attached.
    Enter a number between 10 and 20, then remove to see the effect.  The validator
is show
    via the tooltip.
    <br /><br />
    <input type="text" id="textboxRequired" class="input" />
     
    <span id="valRequired" style="color: red">*</span>
</div>
<script language="javascript">
function onValidateValue(sender, eventArgs) {
    var val = eventArgs.get_value();
    var valid = true;
    if (val == "fail")
    {
        valid = false;
    }
    //You could do something like this to send an alert to to the user.
    //alert("The entry is: " + valid);
    eventArgs.set_isValid(valid);
}
</script>
<script type="text/xml-script">
    <page xmlns:script="http://schemas.microsoft.com/xml-script/2005">
        <components>
            <textBox targetElement="textboxValue">
                <validators>
                    <requiredFieldValidator errorMessage="You must enter some
text." />
                    <customValidator validateValue='onValidateValue'
errorMessage="You entered fail." />
                </validators>
            </textBox>
            <validationErrorLabel targetElement="valLabel"
associatedControl="textboxValue" />
```

```
            <textBox targetElement="textboxRequired">
                <validators>
                    <requiredFieldValidator errorMessage="You must enter some
text." />
                    <typeValidator type="Number" errorMessage="You must enter a
valid number." />
                    <rangeValidator lowerBound="10" upperBound="20"
errorMessage="You must enter a number between 10 and 20." />
                </validators>
            </textBox>
            <validationErrorLabel targetElement="valRequired"
associatedControl="textboxRequired" />
            <validationGroup id="formGroup" targetElement="formGroup">
                <associatedControls>
                    <reference component="textboxValue" />
                    <reference component="textboxRequired" />
                </associatedControls>
            </validationGroup>
            <label targetElement="lblValid" visibilityMode="Collapse">
                <bindings>
                    <binding dataContext="formGroup" dataPath="isValid"
property="visible" />
                </bindings>
            </label>
            <label targetElement="lblInValid">
                <bindings>
                    <binding dataContext="formGroup" dataPath="isValid"
property="visible" transform="Invert" />
                    <binding dataContext="lblInValid" dataPath="text"
property="text" transform="onValidGroup" />
                </bindings>
            </label>
        </components>
    </page>
</script>
```

How It Works

In this example, take note of several things:

❑   Two div tags have been added. The IDs for the div tags are lblValid, which contains the text to display when all validators are satisfied with the input, and lblInValid, which contains the text to display when one or more validators are invalid.

❑   A validationGroup has been defined in the xml-script section. The validation group defines the controls that will be validated together.

❑   The lblValid and lblInValid tags have been added to the xml-script section. A set of bindings is defined for each.

Figure 11-6 shows the output of the group validation process.

Figure 11-6

Why would you want to group validators together? Obviously, each individual validator will fire. However, there may be situations where the validation should be done together. For example, it would be valuable for checking required fields when a user signs up for a new service. This is what the validationGroup control in Atlas is for.

Behaviors

A *behavior* is the name of the set of actions that can be performed based on events in DTHML. These events might be click, hover, mouseover, or other client-side events. These sets of actions that are performed comprise features such as auto-completion and Drag and Drop. In other words, behaviors are used to provide a more sophisticated UI and behavioral features beyond standard DHTML In Atlas, behaviors are defined as a collection on a client-side control. In other words, the individual behaviors are attached to a client-side control.

Try It Out   Using Behaviors

Take a look at some code that incorporates behaviors. In this example, a click behavior is set on the lblHide label so that when it is clicked, the visibility of the displayData label is set to false, and the displayData label is hidden from view. When the lblShow label is clicked, the visibility of the display Data label is set to true, and the displayData label is displayed on the screen, if it is not already viewable.

```
<atlas:ScriptManager runat="server" ID="ScriptManager1" />
<div>
<div id="displayData">This is the text that will be hidden and shown based on
clicking the text below.  Pretty cool.</div>
```

```
          <br />
          <span id="lblHide" >Hide</span> 
          <span id="lblShow" >Show</span>
</div>
<script type="text/xml-script">
    <page xmlns:script="http://schemas.microsoft.com/xml-script/2005">
        <components>
            <control targetElement="displayData" cssClass="start" />
            <label targetElement="lblHide">
                <behaviors>
                    <clickBehavior>
                        <click>
                            <setProperty target="displayData"
property="visible" value="false" />
                        </click>
                    </clickBehavior>
                </behaviors>
            </label>
            <label targetElement="lblShow">
                <behaviors>
                    <clickBehavior>
                        <click>
                            <setProperty target="displayData"
property="visible" value="true" />
                        </click>
                    </clickBehavior>
                </behaviors>
            </label>
        </components>
    </page>
</script>
```

Figure 11-7 shows the output of the preceding code. Clicking Hide will hide the text, assuming that the code is visible. Clicking Show will display the code, assuming that it is hidden. The advantage to using behaviors in this way is that no programming must be done in the preceding code. You don't have to set up any JavaScript onclick events or anything to that effect.

Figure 11-7

Resources Used

❑ **Wilco Bauwer**—Wilco Bauwer, a intern on the Microsoft Atlas team provided significant assistance in answering questions regarding many features in Atlas. Wilco's web site and blog are located at `www.wilcob.com`.

❑ **Nikhil Kothari**—Nikhil provided several helpful articles on his blog regarding how to properly use several features of Atlas. Nikhil's web site and blog are located at `www.nikhilk.net`.

❑ **Atlas Quickstarts**—The Atlas web site is `http://atlas.asp.net`.

❑ **Forums on ASP.NET site**—The forums are located at `http://forums.asp.net`.

Summary

In this chapter, you have been introduced some very new and important concepts. These are

❑ Programming controls through Atlas

❑ Working with server controls

❑ Using data binding

❑ Using behaviors

From these you have seen that there is a lot of functionality in the server controls. Along with that functionality is the ability to extend the server control and add new functionality to the server controls. The integration with the server controls is very important as it brings the server-side methodology of ASP.NET and allows it to provide significant client-side functionality.

Now that you have looked at how to integrate Atlas with server controls, in the next chapter, you are going to look at integrating Atlas with membership, profiles, and other services provided by ASP.NET.

Atlas Integration with ASP.NET Services

Microsoft Atlas provides a mechanism to integrate with the services provided by ASP.NET. The integration is provided for services such as:

❑ **Authentication** — Applications must be able to integrate with the ASP.NET authentication services if they are to let only the correct people in and to keep the incorrect users out.

❑ **Authorization** — Applications must be able to control where a user is allowed to go within an application. Authorization is the process of deciding if an application user is allowed to access a portion, or all, of an application. It is typically based on authentication within an application as well as the roles that a user is assigned to.

❑ **Roles** — Applications must be able to provide client-side role-based security. Roles are typically used along with authorization.

❑ **Profiles** — Applications must be able to provide integration with the ASP.NET profile services.

In this chapter, we are going to look at how the client-side focus of Atlas integrates with the server-side ASP.NET services. We'll start by doing a little bit of background on the ASP.NET services and then moving into code and an explanation of how these services integrate with Atlas.

The Atlas examples and code are based on the March/April CTPs of Atlas. The March CTP is the first version of Atlas that comes with a "Go-Live" license for actual usage in a production application. The April CTP is basically a set of bug fixes to the March CTP. It is our intention to update these files with new versions as changes are made to Atlas. The site for the files is http://beginningajax.com.

Examining ASP.NET Services

Before you dive into how Atlas supports authentication, some quick background on the ASP.NET services provided in version 2.0 of ASP.NET is in order. These services are defined and provided by the ASP.NET 2.0 Provider Model. It is possible for a developer to extend these services.

Although it is possible to extend these services by creating custom providers, the examples in this chapter will use the default providers unless otherwise noted.

Authentication

In an ASP.NET application, *authentication* is the process of verifying that a user is who the user states that he or she is. Typical authentication has two parts — a mechanism to request credentials, such as a set of text boxes for inputting a user ID and password, and a data store, such as a database, to check those credential against. The user ID and password are checked against the data store on the initial request. If the initial request is granted, the user is typically granted a token in the form of a browser-side cookie. This browser-side cookie shows that the user has been granted access. Subsequent checks involve examining the validity of the cookie.

ASP.NET supports four types of authentication. These are:

❑ **Windows-based authentication** — Windows-based authentication is controlled by IIS. It is used mainly for internal web applications that run over an intranet, and provides authentication through a Windows-based server.

❑ **Basic authentication** — Basic authentication is similar to Windows-based authentication from the user's standpoint; however, it transmits its information in clear text.

❑ **Forms-based authentication** — Forms-based authentication is a catchall type of authentication that is primarily used to authenticate information against various data sources when a nonstandard data source is used. It is used in a majority of non-intranet ASP.NET applications. Forms authentication provides a mechanism to authenticate users based on custom requirements and code and to then maintain the authentication token (browser cookie, munged URL, or something else).

❑ **Passport authentication** — With Passport authentication, the Microsoft Passport Service is used. If you have used the Microsoft Hotmail service, you are using the Passport Service. With the Passport Service, the user ID and password are stored in a central location on the Internet. This information is managed by Microsoft. With Passport authentication, an application will pass the user ID and password to the Passport system for testing. If successful, the Passport service will hand a token back, similar to forms-based authentication.

Windows Authentication

Windows authentication, also referred to as integrated Windows authentication, uses the Windows operating system account to test the user ID and password (also knows as credentials) against a Windows-based user store, such as Active Directory. If a user makes a request against a web resource that requires Windows authentication, the user must either be logged into the domain that the server is running on, or they must log on to the domain when they attempt to access a protected page. With Windows authentication, the credentials used to test are stored in the Microsoft Active Directory database. The validation is performed using the Kerberos protocol. A major advantage to this authentication scheme is that the password is not sent over the wire. If a user is not already authenticated to a resource, the user is presented with a browser pop-up style window for inputting a user ID/password combination.

Although this is a fairly secure scheme it has several downfalls. The main ones are:

❏ Users must be authenticated against the domain that the server is running against. This would be a large problem for remote users that are not logged on to the network.

❏ Windows authentication is tightly associated with Windows and Internet Explorer. While recent versions of the Mozilla Firefox web browser support Windows authentication when running on Windows, most developers identify Windows authentication as running only on Windows with Internet Explorer.

Basic Authentication

From the user's standpoint, basic authentication is very similar to Windows authentication. If a user is not authenticated to a resource (page, image, or such) that requires authentication, the user is presented with browser pop-up style windows for inputting a user ID/password combination. Behind the scenes, there are significant differences between the two. With basic authentication, passwords are sent over the network using base64 encoding, are embedded within HTTP, and are not encrypted in any way. While not being quite as secure as Windows authentication, basic authentication is supported across multiple major web browsers and server products.

Forms Authentication

Forms authentication is similar to basic authentication. The major difference is that Forms authentication allows a developer to define their own login pages, error pages, and resources to validate users against. With Forms authentication, a login form is created for inputting user IDs and passwords. A button on that form will call a routine to test for the user having the rights to access the resource. ASP.NET provides some built-in methods to test whether or not a user may get to a resource. In addition, the developer may substitute his or her own routines to validate the user.

Passport Authentication

Passport authentication uses the Microsoft Passport system. This is a centralized authentication service provided by Microsoft. It provides a single logon and profile services for member web sites. Passport uses Triple DES encryption. Unfortunately, the Passport authentication system has not been widely accepted outside of the Microsoft family of web sites and is no longer available as public service or for signup by non-Microsoft web sites.

Authorization/Roles

Once a user has been authorized to use a web resource, the next step is *authorization*. This allows developers to specify which resources application users are allowed to access within an application. Grouping users together to manage which resources they may access is referred to as *role-based security*. This allows for users to be grouped as necessary within an application, for example users, directors, application administrators, and other roles.

Within ASP.NET, the authorization rules may be stored within the `Web.Config` file, database, external files, custom objects, or other locations.

Membership

One of the "new" features of ASP.NET 2.0 is that user management capabilities are included in the box. This new feature eliminates the need for writing all of the code necessary to manage users and passwords.

With ASP.NET 2.0, the logon controls provide the default implementation of the membership service. The membership service provides two methods that are of significance. These are:

❑　`login` — The `login` method will validate the user against a data store and return the appropriate Forms authentication cookie.

❑　`validateUser` — The `validateUser` validates the users against a data store; however, it does not return a forms authentication cookie.

Profiles

The profile service is a "new" feature of ASP.NET 2.0. The profile service provider supports the storage and retrieval of user-specific data within an application. Profile information is stored within the `Machine.Config` or the `Web.Config`. Once the application's profiles have been defined, the profile information is available through IntelliSense in Visual Studio .NET 2005.

Web Part Personalization

Web Parts are a new feature of ASP.NET 2.0 that moves web applications one step closer to acting like desktop applications. Web Parts allow an application to be customized by users at runtime. This customization may include the layout of elements on the page as well as the selection of elements that actually appear on a page. The personalization service provides support for persisting Web Part configurations and support for storing the layout and location of Web Parts between sessions for individual users.

Using Atlas to Integrate with ASP.NET Services

Now that you have looked at the basics of the services provided by ASP.NET, you can look at how these services are provided by Atlas.

Authentication

Atlas provides support for Forms-based authentication. This support is provided by the `Sys.Services.AuthenticationService` static class. Inside of that class, there are two methods:

❑　`login` — This method maps to the configured membership provider's `login` method. It contains several additional parameters. The complete calling syntax is:

```
login(username, password, OnLoginComplete, OnTimeOut, onError);
```

❑ validateUser — This method maps to the configured membership provider's validateUser method. This method is different from the previous method in one way. In this method, the only thing that is not done is that if the username and password are accepted, a cookie is not set on the client web browser. In addition to the username and password parameters, there are some additional parameters. The complete calling syntax is:

```
validateUser(username, password, OnLoginComplete, OnTimeOut, onError);
```

Try It Out   Using Atlas to Perform Authentication

Take a look at some source for performing authentication:

```
<atlas:ScriptManager runat="server" ID="ScriptManager1" />
<form id="form1" runat="server">
<div>
<table border="1">
    <tr>
        <td>User Id:</td>
        <td><input type="text" id="txtUserId" name="txtUserId" /></td>
    </tr>
    <tr>
        <td>Password:</td>
        <td><input type="password" id="txtPassword" name="txtPassword" /></td>
    </tr>
    <tr>
        <td colspan="2">
            <input type="button" id="btnAuth" name="btnAuth" onclick="AuthTest()"
value="Auth Test" />
        </td>
    </tr>
</table>
</div>
<script language="javascript">
function AuthTest()
{
    var UserId = document.forms[0].txtUserId.value;
    var PassWord = document.forms[0].txtPassword.value;
    var authObj = Sys.Services.AuthenticationService;
    authObj.login( UserId, PassWord, OnAuthTestComplete, OnAuthTestTimeOut,
OnAuthTestError);
}
function OnAuthTestComplete(result)
{
    if (null == result)
    {
        alert("Auth Test Complete.  Null Result");
    }
    else
    {
        alert("Auth Test Complete. Result: " + result);
        if(true == result)
```

```
        {
            alert("You are now logged in.");
            document.forms[0].txtUserId.value = "";
            document.forms[0].txtPassword.value = "";
        }
        else
        {
            alert("You are not logged in.");
        }
    }
}
function OnAuthTestTimeOut(result)
{
    alert("Auth Test TimeOut. Result: " + result);
}
function OnAuthTestError(result)
{
    if (null == result)
    {
        alert("Auth Test Error.  Null Result");
    }
    else
    {
        alert("Auth Test Error. Result: " + result.get_message());
    }
}
</script>
</form>
```

How It Works

Now take a walk through the code and take note of these important items:

❑ Add in the `ScriptManager` so that the Atlas scripts are properly set up on the client web browser.

❑ Set up the `UserId` and `Password` input elements. It is important to remember to use the type of password for the input element so that the "*" character is used to display input and the input value is not cached at the client.

❑ This example creates an instance of the `Sys.Services.AuthenticationService`.

❑ Call the login method of the `Sys.Services.AuthenticationService` class. When calling the login method, all of the options are handed to the method. These include the user ID, password, callback method on success, callback method on timeout, and callback method on an error.

❑ The user authentication cookie is set automatically for the code.

❑ If a user is successfully authenticated, the user ID and password for that user are removed from displaying on the web page. While not a requirement, zeroing out the form elements is a good idea given that some browsers might have security problems.

Now that the application code has been written, there are several security-related issues (issues that occur because of the security requirements of the various web servers) that you must deal with:

❑   `ScriptFolder` — In this code example, the `ScriptFolder` has been set to allow anonymous access. The Atlas scripts must be available to anonymous users so that the authentication process may be started from the client.

❑   `ScriptServices/Microsoft/Web/Services/Standard` **folder** — This folder is currently the virtual folder that contains the Atlas authentication web service. For authentication to properly call the web service, the web service must be available to the anonymous user. This may be done by adding the following lines to the `Web.Config` file for the application:

```
<location path="ScriptServices">
   <system.web>
      <authorization>
         <allow users="*" />
      </authorization>
   </system.web>
</location>
```

❑   The noted security issues will most likely be dependent on the version of the web server that is being used. For example when dealing with anonymous versus named user access, this application has been developed with the Visual Studio 2005 development–oriented web server and not with IIS 5 or IIS 6. As a result, these security requirements are designed for the application to function properly under it. IIS 5's or IIS 6's security requirements and services are different and will require a different setup. With IIS 5/6, security will need to be set through the IIS management console because IIS, not .NET, controls the access to folders. IIS 7, which is currently under development, will have security services that are different from what is in IIS 6. IIS 7 will have a security modem more inline with the security model and requirements of the web server that ships with Visual Studio 2005.

Figure 12-1 shows the result of calling the login routine.

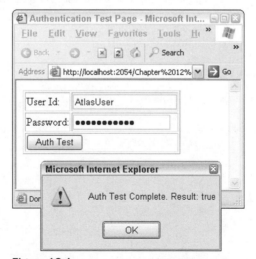

Figure 12-1

Authorization/Roles

Once the problems of authenticating a user to an application has been completed, the next step is to work with the roles that are assigned to a user. While there are no prebuilt web services that are available for a developer to use, it is still possible to use web services to provide this integration. The basic steps are:

1. Create a web service that returns the roles that a user is assigned.

2. Call the web service as needed.

3. Process the returned results and perform any settings on the client that are necessary.

Try It Out   **Working with Roles**

In the example code, there are two roles set up—admin and users. Assume that there are two types of users of the application—the admin users, who have application-level administrative duties, and the users, who are merely regular users of the application. The following web service code returns a list of roles:

```
[WebMethod]
public string[] GetRoles()
{
    return ((RolePrincipal)HttpContext.Current.User).GetRoles();
}
```

This code returns an array of strings. Each element in the array consists of a string representing one of the various roles assigned to the user that is logged in.

> *Although this example shows the return of all of the roles associated with a user, the other methods for a* RolePrincipal, *or any other object, may easily be called also. The only requirement is that a string array be returned.*

Take a look at code on an .aspx page to call this web service:

```
<form id="form1" runat="server">
<div>
<input type="button" value="Get Role Information" id="btnGetRoles"
onclick="GetRoleInfo()" />
</div>
</form>
<script language="javascript" >
    function GetRoleInfo()
    {
        var authObj = Sys.Services.AuthenticationService;
        var UserId = ".....";
        var PassWord = ".....";
        authObj.validateUser(UserId, PassWord, OnValidateUser);
    }
    function OnValidateUser(result)
    {
        if(null != result)
        {
            if (result == true)
```

```
                RoleService.GetRoles(OnGetRolesComplete, OnGetRolesTimeOut,
    OnGetRolesException);
        }
    }
    function OnGetRolesComplete(result)
    {
        var i = 0;
        var bAdmin = false;
        var bUser = false;
        if (null != result)
        {
            for(i=0; i<result.length; i++)
            {
                bAdmin = bAdmin || (result[i] == "admin");
                bUser = bUser || (result[i] == "users");
            }
            alert("User is an Admin: " + bAdmin);
            alert("User is a user: " + bUser);
        }
    }
    function OnGetRolesTimeOut(result)
    {
        alert("Auth Test TimeOut. Result: " + result);
    }
    function OnGetRolesException(result)
    {
        if (null == result)
        {
            alert("Auth Test Error.  Null Result");
        }
        else
        {
            alert("Auth Test Error. Result: " + result.get_message());
        }
    }
}
</script>
```

How It Works

Take a look at what this code does step by step:

1. There is a button, that when clicked, will call the `GetRoleInfo()` JavaScript method. The `GetRoleInfo()` JavaScript method will verify first that the user is valid. This is not strictly required; however, it is a good practice to do so when the user is not guaranteed to be logged in.

2. Within the validate user callback, if the user is a valid user, a call is made to the `RoleService.GetRoles` web service method.

3. Within the `OnGetRolesComplete` callback, the returned array is searched for roles. This search is done by iterating through the result array that is returned. If any of the returned roles are admin or users, the appropriate boolean JavaScript variable is set.

4. Finally, an alert is displayed to the user showing the user his or her status within a role.

Figure 12-2

Accessing Profiles via Atlas

As was mentioned earlier in this chapter, profiles are a mechanism to easily provide users with a custom experience while they use a web application. In this example, you are going to use a fairly simple example of a user's name, address, city, state, and zip code.

Microsoft's Atlas framework provides the Sys.Profile class, which is used to directly access profile information. The class is "static/shared" — it does not require an instance for its methods and properties to be called.

For the ASP.NET profiles in this chapter, your profile will be defined as follows in the Web.Config.

```
<profile>
   <properties>
   <add name="Name" defaultValue ="" />
   <add name="Address" defaultValue ="" />
   <add name="City" defaultValue ="" />
   <add name="AddressState" defaultValue ="" />
   <add name="ZipCode" defaultValue ="" />
   <add name="DragNDropLocation" />
   </properties>
</profile>
```

In this example setup, the properties fall into two groups. The Name, Address, City, AddressState, and ZipCode fall into the area of an address for a user. The DragNDropLocation property is used by the Drag and Drop property example later in this chapter.

Profile Property Names

Atlas provides the ability to get a list of profile names through a standard asynchronous request; however, the semantics of making the call are slightly different from that of making a standard request.

Try It Out   **Retrieving Profile Property Names**

Take a look at some code for getting the names of the properties from a profile.

```
function GetProfile()
{
    var profObj = Sys.Profile;
    profObj.loaded.add(OnGetProfile);
    profObj.load();
}
function OnGetProfile()
{
    var propArray = Array();
    propArray = Sys.Profile.properties;
    if (null != propArray)
    {
        for(m in propArray)
            alert(m);
    }
}
```

How It Works

Consider what happens in the code:

1. An alias to the Sys.Profile class is created.

2. The callback on completion is assigned to the method OnGetProfiles.

3. The asynchronous call is made through the .load() method call.

4. When the callback is made, the code gets the .properties property. The property contains the profile information for a user and the application.

5. The code loops through the returned properties and displays them to the user.

Figure 12-3 shows the output of getting the profile properties.

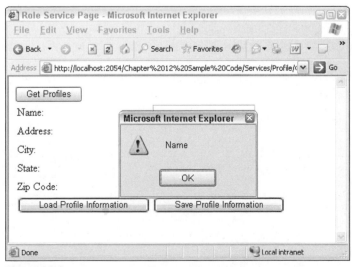

Figure 12-3

Loading Profile Data

Now that you have seen how to get the names of the profile properties, you need to get the actual data within the profile for the logged-in user. To get the data, you go through a set of steps similar to those you used in getting the profile names.

Try It Out   Retrieving Profile Data

The following JavaScript code running in a web browser retrieves profile values for the properties you retrieved in the previous section:

```javascript
function GetProfileData()
{
    var profObj = Sys.Profile;
    profObj.loaded.add(OnGetProfileData);
    profObj.load();
}
function OnGetProfileData()
{
    document.getElementById("txtName").value = Sys.Profile.properties.Name;
    document.getElementById("txtAddress").value = Sys.Profile.properties.Address;
    document.getElementById("txtCity").value = Sys.Profile.properties.City;
    document.getElementById("txtAddressState").value =
Sys.Profile.properties.AddressState;
    document.getElementById("txtZipCode").value = Sys.Profile.properties.ZipCode;
}
```

How It Works

This code performs the following steps:

1.   Creates an alias for the `Sys.Profile` class.

2.   Creates the method to callback once the data is filled. This callback is called `OnGetProfileData` and is created by the call to `loaded.add(OnGetProfileData)`.

3.   Performs the asynchronous load. This is done by the call to `profObj.load()` (a.k.a. `Sys.Profile.load()`).

4.   Once the callback (`OnGetProfileData()`) is called, the various textboxes are filled with the profile values. This done by setting the value of the text field to the profile property value.

   It appears that the profile properties are "early bound." This might get some IntelliSense support in a future version of Visual Studio .NET.

Figure 12-4 shows the output of the code in the previous "Try It Out" Section.

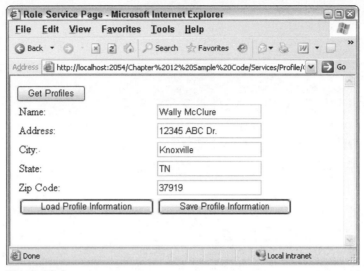

Figure 12-4

Save Profile Data

Now that you have looked at loading data from the ASP.NET profile service, you can look at saving the data in code.

```
function SaveProfileData()
{
    var profObj = Sys.Profile;
    profObj.properties.Name = document.getElementById("txtName").value;
    profObj.properties.Address = document.getElementById("txtAddress").value;
    profObj.properties.City = document.getElementById("txtCity").value;
    profObj.properties.AddressState =
document.getElementById("txtAddressState").value;
    profObj.properties.ZipCode = document.getElementById("txtZipCode").value;
    profObj.save();
}
```

The steps in the code are fairly simple.

1. An alias to the `Sys.Profile` class is created.

2. The properties of the profile are set from the data on the form.

3. The data is saved asynchronously.

This code will save the profile's properties asynchronously. It is possible to receive notification when data is saved. To do that you can specify an asynchronous callback and set a notification to the user with the following code.

```
profObj.saved.add(OnSaveProfileData);
profObj.save();
.............
function OnSaveProfileData()
{
    alert("Profile Data has been saved.");
}
```

Avoiding Profile Service Gotchas

You should keep in mind several important "gotchas" whenever you are using the ASP.NET profile service in Atlas. These are:

❑   `Web.Config` **file** — The `Web.Config` file needs to be set up properly, and there are several settings you need to pay attention to:

    ❑   The `<configSections>` tag must be configured. This may mean adding a section for `authenticationService` and `profileService`. A set of entries should look something like this example:

```
<configSections>
    <sectionGroup name="microsoft.web"
type="Microsoft.Web.Configuration.MicrosoftWebSectionGroup">
        <section name="converters"
type="Microsoft.Web.Configuration.ConvertersSection" requirePermission="false"/>
        <section name="webServices"
type="Microsoft.Web.Configuration.WebServicesSection" requirePermission="false"/>
        <section name="authenticationService"
type="Microsoft.Web.Configuration.AuthenticationServiceSection"
requirePermission="false"/>
        <section name="profileService"
type="Microsoft.Web.Configuration.ProfileServiceSection"
requirePermission="false"/>
    </sectionGroup>
</configSections>
```

    ❑   Within the `<microsoft.web>` tag, the `enableBrowserAccess` must be turned on. This is accomplished within the `<webServices>` like this:

```
<microsoft.web>
    <webServices enableBrowserAccess="true"/>
</microsoft.web>
```

    ❑   The `<profileService>` tag must be configured to get and set the profile's properties. Either the properties may be configured with "`*`", which represents all profile properties, or each property may be listed out individually, such as `Name;Address`. Note that each property is separated from the others by a semicolon.

```
<microsoft.web>
    <profileService enabled="true" setProperties="*" getProperties="*" />
</microsoft.web>
```

    ❑   Properties that are part of groups may be referenced by `GroupName.PropertyName` in the `profileService`, `setProperties`, and `getProperties` attributes.

❑   A special `connectionString` is used. This `connectionString` is called the `AtlasAppServices` connection string. It will need to be set up as follows for Atlas to be able to properly communicate with the ASP.NET application services. Please remember that what you see in the following is an example and will change based on your server environment.

```
<connectionStrings>
    <add name="AtlasAppServices" connectionString="Data
Source=.\SQLEXPRESS;AttachDbFilename=C:\Work Data\Ajax book\Chapter 12\Chapter 12
Sample Code\App_Data\ASPNETDB.MDF;Integrated Security=True;User Instance=True" />
</connectionStrings>
```

❑   **Profile configuration**—Profiles need to be configured properly. As shown earlier, the following is an example for the samples presented in this chapter.

```
<profile>
    <properties>
        <add name="Name" type="String" />
        <add name="City" type="String" />
        <add name="Address" type="String" />
        <add name="ZipCode" type="String" />
        <add name="AddressState" type="String"/>
        <add name="DragNDropLocation" />
    </properties>
</profile>
```

❑   **Login**—For the profile properties to work correctly, the user must have logged in. Although you can use profile properties and anonymous users, these examples are designed for a user that is logged in.

❑   `Sys.Profile.set_autoSave()` **method**—This method will control whether or not a profile's properties are automatically saved when the properties are modified. If a true is passed in, which is the default value, the profile properties are automatically saved on a change. If a false is passed in, the profile properties are not saved on a change. In this case, it is up to the developer to manage the saving of the data.

Implementing Drag and Drop via Atlas

"Drag and Drop" is the generic term for the action of selecting an element with a mouse and moving it on screen. Although Drag and Drop is not a feature of the ASP.NET services, it integrates very smoothly with the Atlas framework's support for the ASP.NET profile services.

Try It Out   **Implementing Drag and Drop**

The following code example shows how to implement the ability to drag text around the screen and save the position of the text with the ASP.NET profile service.

```
<atlas:ScriptManager ID="scriptManager" runat="server"></atlas:ScriptManager>
<form id="form1" runat="server">
<div>
<atlas:ProfileScriptService ID="profile" runat="server" AutoSave="true" />
<div class="dropZone">
```

325

```
    <asp:Button ID="btnRefresh" runat="server" Text="Perform a postback" />
    <asp:Label ID="lblToDrag" runat="server">This is the text to drag around the
screen.</asp:Label>
</div>
<atlas:DragOverlayExtender ID="atlasDNDExtender" runat="server">
    <atlas:DragOverlayProperties TargetControlID="lblToDrag"
ProfileProperty="DragNDropLocation" Enabled="true" />
</atlas:DragOverlayExtender>
</div>
</form>
```

Take a look at what this ASP.NET code does:

1. A new control is introduced. This is the `atlas:ProfileScriptService` control. It integrates with the ASP.NET Profile service so that updates are made to the profile service. The `AutoSave` property is set to `true`. This will automatically update the profile property `DragNDropLocation` as appropriate.

2. The `atlas:DragOverlayExtender` is introduced. This control is a helper control for implementing Drag and Drop functionality. In this example, the Drag and Drop functionality is added to the label with the ID `lblToDrag`, thus the "extender" term on the control name. By clicking on the text, it is possible to drag this text around the screen.

3. By placing a server button on the page, you can show that the profile is indeed updated on a postback and reloaded on the page load. When the page is reloaded, the text stays in its previously defined position.

4. The `dropZone` `div` tag has its height set to some relatively large number. This is to demonstrate the Drag and Drop functionality. If this were not set, the there would be problems attempting to drag outside of the page's body tag.

The next thing you need to do is look at the source code that is created and sent to the web browser:

```
<script src="../../ScriptLibrary/Atlas/Debug/Atlas.js"
type="text/javascript"></script>
    <div>

    <div class="dropZone">
        <input type="submit" name="btnRefresh" value="Perform a postback"
id="btnRefresh" />
        <span id="lblToDrag">This is the text to drag around the screen.</span>
    </div>
    </div>
<div>
<input type="hidden" name="__EVENTVALIDATION" id="__EVENTVALIDATION"
value="/wEWAgLoiZW4DwLAn+vmDOPGFKUwps8DZtEoBXsJWcSnsQOm" />
</div>
<script type="text/xml-script">
<page xmlns:script="http://schemas.microsoft.com/xml-script/2005">
  <references>
    <add src="../../ScriptLibrary/Atlas/Debug/AtlasUIDragDrop.js" />
  </references>
```

```
  <components>
    <profile id="profile" autoSave="true" />
    <control id="lblToDrag">
      <behaviors>
        <floatingBehavior handle="lblToDrag">
          <bindings>
            <binding property="location" dataContext="profile"
dataPath="DragNDropLocation" direction="InOut" />
          </bindings>
        </floatingBehavior>
      </behaviors>
    </control>
  </components>
</page></script>
<script type="text/javascript">
</script>
```

Although most of the data presented in the "source" view is fairly standard, there are several items of note.

❑   The `AtlasUIDragDrop.js` file has been added as a reference in spite of the developer's not having explicitly added it.

❑   The profile service is added in the components section.

❑   Within the `lblToDrag` control, a set of behaviors has been added. This includes a `floatingBehavior`.

❑   Data binding is occurring between the label with text and the profile service. This is defined within the `floatingBehavior` tag.

Figure 12-5 shows this Drag and Drop example as it would be displayed on screen.

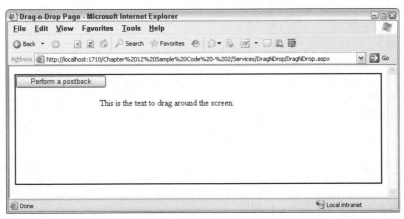

Figure 12-5

Summary

You have covered a lot of complicated material in this chapter. Integration with the ASP.NET services can be very tricky, but the Microsoft Atlas framework has done a good job of abstracting out many of the complications and making this fairly simple. As a result, you have seen how to:

❑   Integrate with the membership services for its support of authentication and authorization

❑   Integrate with the role services for its support for authorization

❑   Integrate with the profile services

❑   Tie these together with a Drag and Drop example

Now that you have explored the integration with the services provided by ASP.NET, the next chapter turns to look at support debugging an Ajax-oriented application.

Debugging

Debugging is the art of identifying and removing problematic code within your applications. Every developer has been required to perform some degree of debugging within their applications at some point in time.

ASP.NET is predominately a server-side development technology, and support for debugging of applications within ASP.NET is quite extensive. Ajax applications introduce some new aspects that make the debugging of applications more involved. The extensive use of JavaScript and the fact that custom data may be transferred through the use of asynchronous postbacks mean that new challenges are introduced when debugging Ajax-type applications with ASP.NET.

This chapter is going to examine the various aspects of debugging Ajax applications within ASP.NET and will cover the following topics:

❑ Server-side ASP.NET debugging

❑ Various methods of JavaScript debugging (in conjunction with Document Object Model (DOM) level debugging)

❑ Debugging and examination of data sent via asynchronous postbacks

As you will see, this chapter covers the full range of areas involving Ajax application development — from the client side, with examination of DOM, HTML, and JavaScript, to the server side, with ASP.NET and the associated server-side language. In addition, we will examine the *in between*, the data that is sent across the network through the use of asynchronous postbacks from the client to the server, and back again.

Server-Side Debugging

ASP.NET is a server-based development environment, and the ASP.NET runtime engine parses and compiles virtually all web pages and code into .NET assemblies.

When an ASP.NET web page is requested (for example, `www.SomeSite.com/SomePage.aspx`), the ASP.NET runtime engine parses the web page and also the code that is associated with the page. This code is usually in the form of a code file present in the `App_Code` directory of a web site, or the code can be embedded within the web page (ASPX) itself. The web page and code are compiled into a .NET assembly and loaded into the assembly cache for execution.

A .NET assembly is a very rich unit of deployment, in that it can contain an extensive amount of information that allows it to be self-describing. This means that the ASP.NET runtime can interrogate the assembly and obtain a large amount of information about the assembly, such as security requirements and other operating parameters. In addition, special debugging information can be included when the assembly is compiled. As a result of this, the debugging experience on the server for ASP.NET applications can be very rich and interactive.

First, let's look at how debugging support and information can be enabled so that a developer can utilize the debugging features available on the server.

Enabling Debugging Support

Debugging support needs to be enabled specifically before debugging can be used. For ASP.NET web applications, this means including the following `<compilation>` setting within the `Web.Config` web application configuration file:

```
<configuration>
  <system.web>
    <compilation debug="true">
    </compilation>
  </system.web>
</configuration>
```

If you try to run a web application using Visual Studio .NET 2005 in debug mode, and the `<compilation debug="true" />` configuration entry has not been set, you will be prompted to enable debugging support (see Figure 13-1).

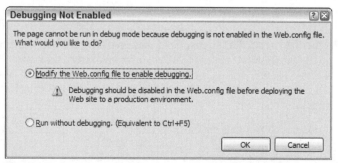

Figure 13-1

For other project types such as class libraries, Debug must be selected as the *active* configuration within Visual Studio .NET 2005, as shown in Figure 13-2.

Figure 13-2

In either case, when the application files are compiled, special debugging information and symbols are produced that enable the Visual Studio .NET debugger to track and accurately show what lines are being executed. You can see this by looking at the output directory of the respective application you are compiling. If the debug build has been selected, or debugging is enabled via the `Web.Config` setting mentioned previously, there will be debug symbol files present, which have a `.pdb` file extension.

For example, if your project produces a `MyApp.exe` assembly, then a corresponding `MyApp.pdb` file will be produced.

Setting Breakpoints

Now that debugging has been enabled, application execution can be tracked on the server. The easiest way to do this is to set a *breakpoint*.

A breakpoint is a marked line of code that tells the debugger to pause execution at the line indicated by the breakpoint when program execution reaches that line. A breakpoint is indicated by a red dot to the left of the line, with the entire line itself also highlighted in red. Figure 13-3 illustrates what a breakpoint looks like (albeit in black and white rather than color).

```
namespace ConsoleApplication1
{
    class Program
    {
        static void Main(string[] args)
        {
            Console.WriteLine("My application is about to start...");
            InitialiseApp();
            Console.WriteLine("Application Initialised successfully.");
            PerformWork();
            Console.WriteLine("Application is terminating.");

        }
```

Figure 13-3

So as you can see, the figure shows that a breakpoint has been set on the line that executes the `PerformWork()` method.

When the application is run, execution is paused at the breakpoint. When this occurs, the application is literally suspended, and this allows the developer to examine various aspects of the programs execution such as values of variables. The developer can choose to continue execution step by step and examine the changing values of variables as the program executes each step. This can be accomplished by pressing the F10 function key or by selecting the Debug menu and then selecting the Step Over menu option. When a method is encountered during debugging, the developer may opt to continue execution past the method, using the Step Over option previously mentioned, or the developer can drill into the execution of each step within the method by either pressing the F11 function key or selecting the Debug menu option and then selecting Step Into.

This debugging environment is very rich and allows a huge amount of flexibility when it comes to inspecting and evaluating the state of your application. Figure 13-4 shows the debugger displaying the value of a variable when the mouse hovers over that variable during a debugging operation.

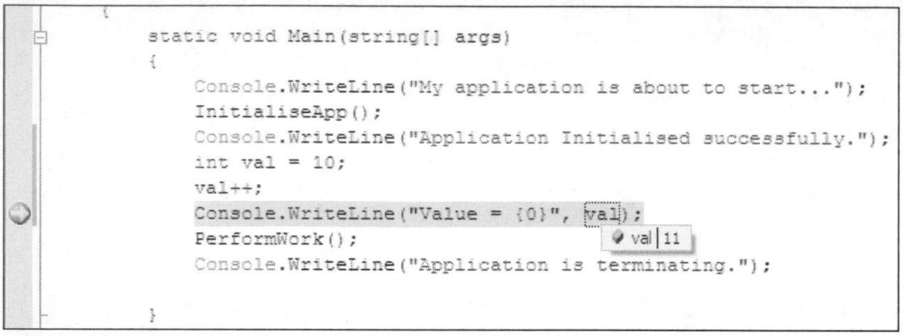

```
        static void Main(string[] args)
        {
            Console.WriteLine("My application is about to start...");
            InitialiseApp();
            Console.WriteLine("Application Initialised successfully.");
            int val = 10;
            val++;
            Console.WriteLine("Value = {0}", val);
            PerformWork();                    val  11
            Console.WriteLine("Application is terminating.");

        }
```

Figure 13-4

This is one of the many ways the developer can interact with the server-side debugger within Visual Studio .NET.

For an exhaustive explanation of debugging applications, visit `http://msdn2.microsoft.com/en-us/library/awtaffxb.aspx`.

This method of debugging should be reasonably familiar to most Visual Studio developers. One of the reasons it is so rich and powerful is that it exists within the domain and execution control of ASP.NET. Visual Studio .NET has intimate knowledge of .NET runtime execution and can, therefore, offer a richer environment.

JavaScript and Client-Side Debugging

JavaScript is a scripting language that executes within the context of the browser. Visual Studio .NET provides ways of creating and developing with this language but offers only very limited support for interactive debugging in the same way that was demonstrated previously with server-side debugging. This is because the browser is outside the Visual Studio .NET domain. Since the execution of asynchronous requests and most Ajax-related functionality relies on JavaScript, it is important to know how to effectively debug the client-side portion of your web applications.

Tools and Techniques of the Trade

Given that execution and processing of JavaScript is outside the direct control of Visual Studio .NET, how then does a developer debug a web application that utilizes rich Ajax functionality and, therefore, makes extensive use of JavaScript?

The answer lies in having an arsenal of tools, techniques, and utilities to suit whatever task is required.

Using Alert Statements

Starting with the most basic and simplistic of options, a developer can intersperse their client-side code with `Alert` statements that either display a value of a variable or simply indicate where in the client script code that execution has reached.

Try It Out   Simple Alert Dialog Boxes

This example simply displays alert boxes at various stages of the code's execution, showing the values of any arguments passed in to the respective functions:

```
<%@ Page Language="C#" AutoEventWireup="true" CodeFile="AlertExample.aspx.cs"
Inherits="Alert_AlertExample" %>
<!DOCTYPE html PUBLIC "-//W3C//DTD XHTML 1.0 Transitional//EN"
"http://www.w3.org/TR/xhtml1/DTD/xhtml1-transitional.dtd">
<html xmlns="http://www.w3.org/1999/xhtml" >
<head runat="server">
    <title>Untitled Page</title>

    <script type="text/javascript">
    function SomeMethod(arg1)
    {
        alert("In SomeMethod: arg = [" + arg1 + "]");
        var counter = 0;
        counter++;
        // ... do some processing
        counter = counter + 2;
        SomeMethod2(counter);
        return true;
    }

    function SomeMethod2(cntr)
    {
        alert("In SomeMethod2: cntr = [" + cntr + "]");
    }
    </script>

</head>
<body>
    <form id="form1" runat="server">
    <div>
        <input id="btnMain" name="btnMain" type="button" value="Test Alert"
onclick="SomeMethod(this.id);" />
    </div>
    </form>
</body>
</html>
```

This approach is obviously extremely simplistic and requires the developer to add extra code to various places within the page. In a complex application, this may not be easy, or even possible.

What would be ideal is to use a rich debugging environment similar to the one provided by the server-side environment discussed earlier.

Code samples from the book are available for download at http://beginningajax.com *and at* www.wrox.com.

Visual Studio Script Debugging

Enabling a rich debugging environment, similar to the server-side environment, is possible. However, this does require some interaction between the browser and Visual Studio .NET; therefore, some quick configuration is required to enable this support that is not normally enabled by default.

Internet Explorer needs to be configured to allow debugging to take place. By default, debugging is not enabled within Internet Explorer. To enable this feature within Internet Explorer, select Tools⇨Internet Options.

A dialog box will be presented with a number of tab options. Selecting the Advanced tab will show a number of options (see Figure 13-5).

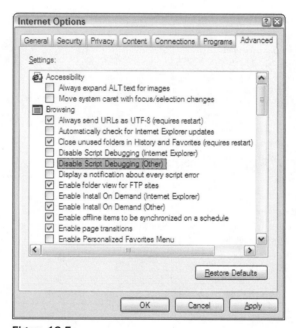

Figure 13-5

Ensure that both Disable Script Debugging (Internet Explorer) and Disable Script Debugging (Other) are *not* selected. Strictly speaking, only Disable Script Debugging (Internet Explorer) needs to be unselected for script debugging to work. Unselecting the Disable Script Debugging (Other) means that debugging will be enabled for scripts hosted outside of Internet Explorer, such as Microsoft Outlook.

For a comprehensive document on configuring and troubleshooting client script debugging, have a look at the following document: www.gotdotnet.com/team/csharp/learn/whitepapers/ How%20to%20debug%20script%20in%20Visual%20Studio%20.Net.doc.

That's all the configuration required to enable script debugging.

Client-Side Script Debugging

To test this, create a new web site project within Visual Studio .NET. Create a new web form/ASPX page, or alternatively edit the `Default.aspx` page within the project. Remove the existing `<html></html>` declaration and everything contained within those tags, and replace it with the following code:

```
<html xmlns="http://www.w3.org/1999/xhtml" >
<head runat="server">
    <title>Test Script Debugging</title>

    <script type="text/javascript">
    function DoSomeWork()
    {
        var cntrl = document.getElementById("txtInput");
        var number = cntrl.value;
        number++;

        var newValue = DoSomeMoreWork(number);

        alert("New Value = " + newValue);

    }

    function DoSomeMoreWork(arg)
    {
        // Do some calculations
        arg = arg * 2 + 32;
        arg = arg + 18 / 2;
    }
    </script>

</head>
<body>
    <form id="form1" runat="server">
    <div>
        <input type="text" id="txtInput" value="test" />
        <input type="button" value="Submit value" onclick="DoSomeWork();" />
    </div>
    </form>
</body>
</html>
```

Ensure that the newly created page is set as the Startup Page within Visual Studio by right-clicking on the page with the mouse and selecting Set as Start Page.

Click the Play button, shown in Figure 13-6 (ensure that the active configuration is set to Debug), or press F5 to launch the application in debug mode.

Figure 13-6

Clicking on the Submit Value button should yield an alert box similar to that shown in Figure 13-7.

Figure 13-7

This behavior is not what is desired, and typically you would expect something more than simply being *undefined*. To fix this, you are going to debug the client-side script within this application. You will set a breakpoint early in the script's execution to see what is going on within the code.

1. Leave the Internet Explorer browser instance running, and click on the OK dialog box button if it is still displayed.

2. Switch to Visual Studio .NET (while Internet Explorer is still running), and select Debug⇨Windows⇨Script Explorer, as shown in Figure 13-8.

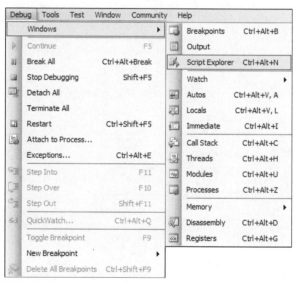

Figure 13-8

3. Once the option has been selected, a Script Explorer window will be displayed within Visual Studio. If your window layout is at the default settings, then the Script Explorer window should appear on the right side of the screen, as shown in Figure 13-9.

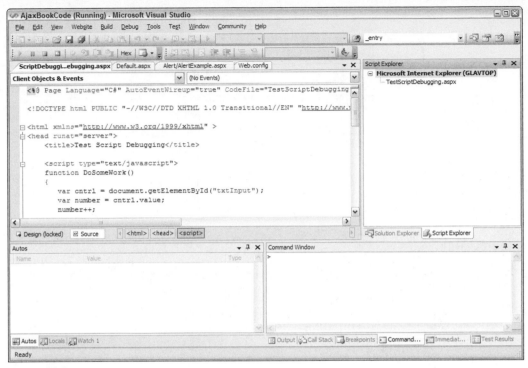

Figure 13-9

4. In the Script Explorer window, you will notice one ASPX page listed, which is the one currently being executed. Double-click on that page within the Script Explorer window. This will list the page within the editor window and will look very similar to the page at design/development time.

The big difference is that you can now set breakpoints and examine variable values as the code is executing in almost exactly the same way you can with server-side code.

5. Within the editor window where the web page is displayed, navigate to the first line within the DoSomeWork JavaScript function, and press F9 or click on the left-side grey sidebar to place a breakpoint on the line. The editor window should now look similar to the one shown in Figure 13-10.

6. Now switch back to the running instance of the browser that is executing the web page. Click the Submit Value button. Visual Studio should automatically become the active window, and execution of the web page will pause on the line that the breakpoint is on. The line will be highlighted in a similar fashion to that shown in Figure 13-11.

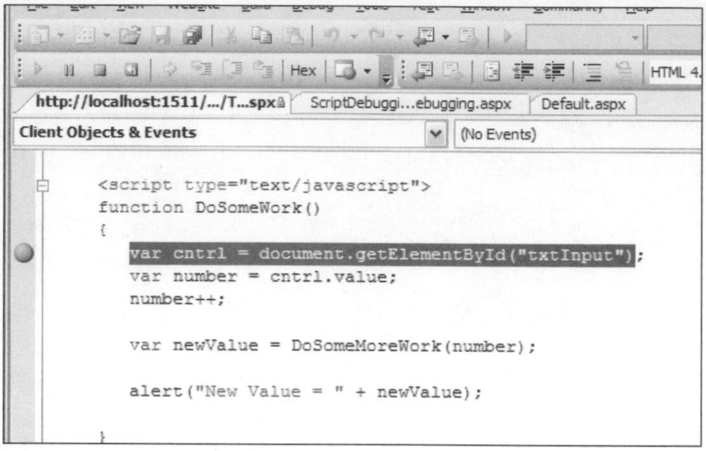

Figure 13-10

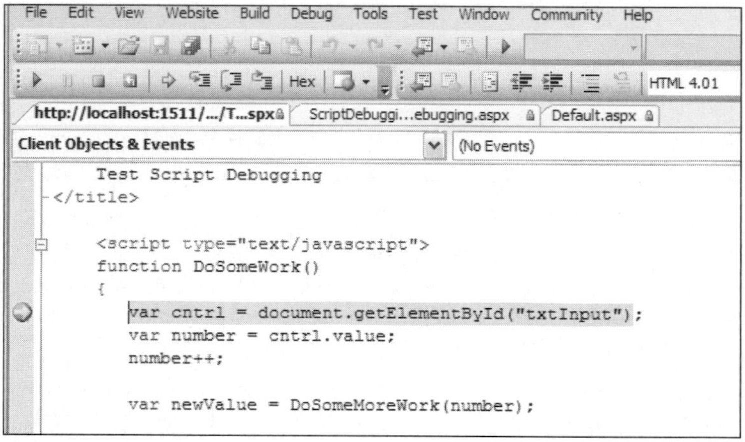

Figure 13-11

7. Press the F10 button to advance the execution to the next line. The next line will now be highlighted. Position the mouse pointer above the `cntrl` variable definition on the line that reads:

```
var cntrl = document.getElementById("txtInput");
```

A small dialog box is displayed, showing the `cntrl` variable with an option to expand the values of this variable by clicking on the + symbol (see Figure 13-12).

Clicking on the + symbol allows a developer to examine the value of that variable and to drill down into the properties of that variable at the current position within the program's execution. This method of examining a variable is very similar to the debugging experience with server-side code.

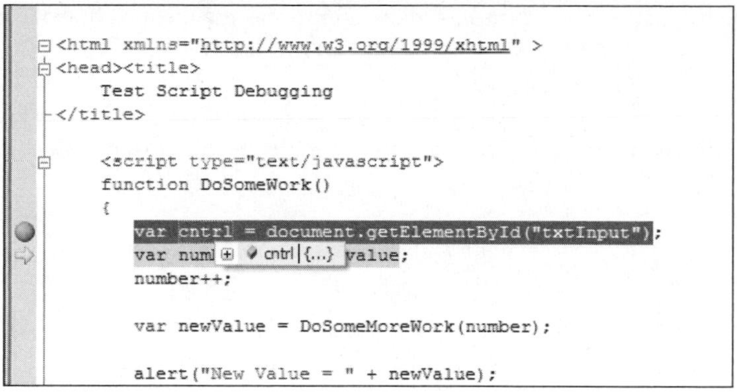

```
<html xmlns="http://www.w3.org/1999/xhtml" >
<head><title>
    Test Script Debugging
</title>

    <script type="text/javascript">
    function DoSomeWork()
    {
        var cntrl = document.getElementById("txtInput");
        var num ⊞ ⎮ cntrl {...} value;
        number++;

        var newValue = DoSomeMoreWork(number);

        alert("New Value = " + newValue);
```

Figure 13-12

Right-clicking on the `cntrl` variable with the mouse brings up a context menu, again similar to the menu presented to users when they are debugging server-side code. Traditional debugging mechanisms are available such as Add watch to add the display of the `cntrl` variable to the *Watch window* at the bottom of the display. These features are discussed in more detail later in this chapter. Alternatively, a developer can open a *Quick watch window* that allows the developer to open a dialog box that provides for easy examination of the variables contents. This window is similar to the Watch window but provides a more direct and prevalent way of interacting with and examining a specific variable. A modal window is presented for the user to navigate; the sole purpose is to display the contents of the selected variable only. The functionality is otherwise almost identical to the Watch window. The only real difference is the availability of a `Reevaluate` button to allow a new variable to be entered into the text entry field and examined.

8. Press F10 again to advance the programs execution to the next line. Program execution should now be paused on the line that reads:

```
number++;
```

9. Position the mouse over the `number` variable. The debugger should display the value of the `number` variable, as shown in Figure 13-13.

Currently, the value of the `number` variable is as expected — that is, it is equal to the contents of the input textbox control defined within the form.

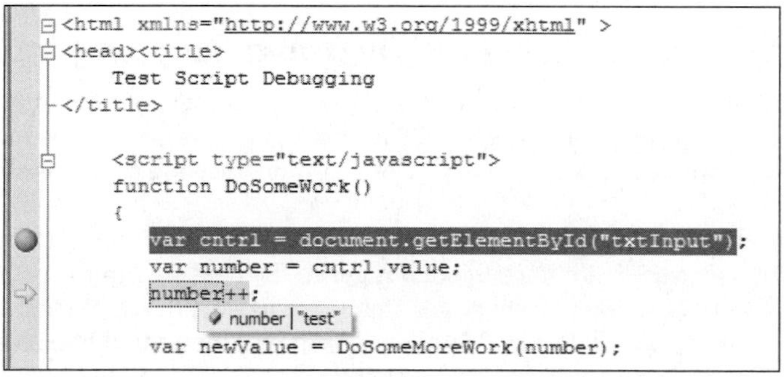

```
<html xmlns="http://www.w3.org/1999/xhtml" >
<head><title>
    Test Script Debugging
</title>

    <script type="text/javascript">
    function DoSomeWork()
    {
        var cntrl = document.getElementById("txtInput");
        var number = cntrl.value;
        number++;
            ⎮ number | "test"
        var newValue = DoSomeMoreWork(number);
```

Figure 13-13

10. Press the F10 key again to cause the debugger to execute the next line of execution. The debugger should now be paused/positioned on the line that reads:

```
var newValue = DoSomeMoreWork(number);
```

Position the mouse over the `number` variable to display its current value. The display should look like Figure 13-14.

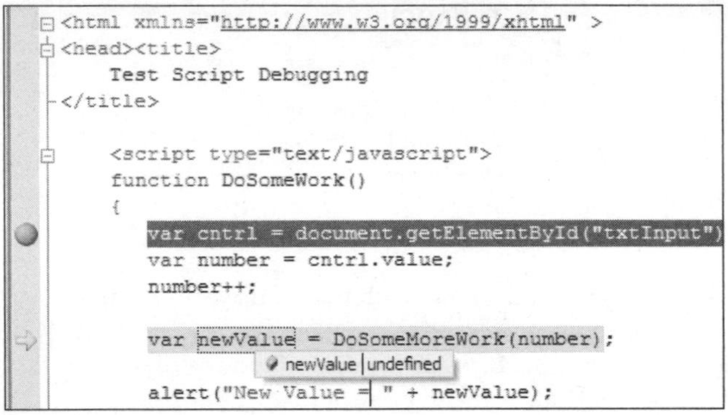

Figure 13-14

You now can see the exact point at which the variable value is turned into something invalid. It is apparent that the value of the `number` value was in fact a textual value of `test`. The next point of execution attempts to perform a mathematical operation on that string value, which of course is invalid. JavaScript is not like the traditional strongly typed server-side languages such as VB.NET and C#. This apparently invalid operation does not yield an exception, but rather, the value of the `number` variable is now flagged as `undefined`, which is exactly what you are seeing output by the browser.

11. Pressing the `F5` key, or clicking the Play button will allow execution to continue as normal, which yields the result seen previously.

You have successfully debugged the script code and identified why the web application behaves in the way it does. Debugging in this manner is a very powerful and intuitive way of examining the execution of script-based applications. Applications can be examined with intricate detail, allowing very accurate determination of any problems within the code's execution.

Stepping Through Code — Stepping Over and Stepping Into

The technique discussed in the previous section works great; however, it assumes that the application starts okay, and then that you can set breakpoints to debug into the operations required. What if you wanted to start debugging the code immediately or examine the code as it was starting?

You can do this by starting the application using the F10 key, or by using the Debug⇨Step Over menu option. Normally, this is used to advance the debugger to the next step in the code's execution or to *step over* the current instruction. Using this step over technique to start the application will start the application as if you had pressed F5 to start it in debug mode but will immediately pause execution on the first instruction, rather than stopping only on a breakpoint.

So far, you have used F10 to advance the debugger's execution. As mentioned in the previous paragraph, this steps over the next line of code. If the debugger encounters a function to execute, pressing the F10 key will call the function, but will not step through each line within that function. In order to do that, you must use either the F11 key or the Debug⇨Step Into menu option. Pressing the F11 key when about to execute a function or call out to another method will have the effect of stepping through each line of that method.

Try It Out   "Stepping into" the Execution of the Method

To see this in action:

1.   Run the application again by pressing the F5 key. Switch back to Visual Studio and ensure that the Script Explorer window is visible as described previously. Double-click on the page within the Script Explorer window, and place a breakpoint on the line that reads:

```
var newValue = DoSomeMoreWork(number);
```

The display should look like Figure 13-15.

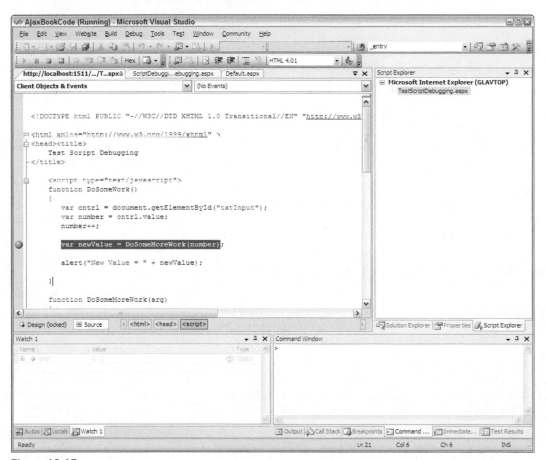

Figure 13-15

If you find you are unable to place a breakpoint on a line, it is most likely that you have not double-clicked on the page within the Script Explorer window, and you are simply examining the source code of the page in the standard Visual Studio .NET display window.

2. With the breakpoint placed on the line that calls the `DoSomeMoreWork()` method, switch to Internet Explorer (which is running the web page) and click on the Submit Value button. Visual Studio .NET will switch to the foreground and execution will pause on the line with the breakpoint.

3. Press the F10 key. Notice that execution is now paused on the next line, which reads:

```
alert("New Value = " + newValue);
```

The method has been executed, and you are now positioned on the next line in the code's sequence. In this case, you have *stepped over* the execution of the `DoSomeMoreWork()` method. Suppose instead that you want to examine execution of the code within that function.

4. Press F5 to allow execution of the code to continue, and the alert box will be displayed as shown previously in Figure 13-7. Click OK in the alert box and then click the Submit Value button once more. Execution should again pause on the line with the breakpoint.

5. This time, press the F11 key. Notice that the debugger has now jumped to the first line within the `DoSomeMoreWork()` method and is paused on that line. Hovering the mouse over the `arg` variable shows a value of `Nan` (JavaScript's method of indicating the value is *Not a Number*). From here you can continue to step through the execution of the code, and the debugger will return to the original place where the method was called and continue execution.

Other Ways of Invoking the Debugger

Previously, we have discussed placing breakpoints in code to pause the debugger at certain positions within the code. While this is a great and easy technique to use, it does have some limitations.

When JavaScript has been generated and registered on the client, it becomes a little more difficult. The JavaScript may be executed on startup and be sufficiently long and complex that you don't want to step through the entire section of code from the beginning using the technique described previously where the application is launched by pressing the F10 key to invoke the debugger.

Try It Out   Using the debugger Keyword

Another way to invoke the debugger is to make use of the `debugger` keyword in your script. In the following example, the code-beside file is registering the JavaScript for immediate execution within your web page. The web page itself contains nothing different from a newly added web form within Visual Studio .NET. Examine the web page and code-beside file in the following example:

Web Page/ASPX Page
```
<%@ Page Language="C#" AutoEventWireup="true" CodeFile="DebuggerKeword.aspx.cs"
Inherits="ScriptDebuggingSample_DebuggerKeword" %>

<!DOCTYPE html PUBLIC "-//W3C//DTD XHTML 1.0 Transitional//EN"
"http://www.w3.org/TR/xhtml1/DTD/xhtml1-transitional.dtd">

<html xmlns="http://www.w3.org/1999/xhtml" >
```

```
<head runat="server">
    <title>Debugger Keyword Test Page</title>
</head>
<body>
    <form id="form1" runat="server">
    <div>

    </div>
    </form>
</body>
</html>
```

Code File/Code-Beside File

```
using System;
using System.Data;
using System.Configuration;
using System.Collections;
using System.Web;
using System.Web.Security;
using System.Web.UI;
using System.Web.UI.WebControls;
using System.Web.UI.WebControls.WebParts;
using System.Web.UI.HtmlControls;

public partial class ScriptDebuggingSample_DebuggerKeword : System.Web.UI.Page
{
    protected void Page_Load(object sender, EventArgs e)
    {
        string script = @"
            var val1 = 10;
            var val2 = 20;
            var result1 = AddValues(val1,val2);
            alert('Sum of values 1 & 2 = ' + result1);
            var val3 = 30;
            var result2 = AddValues(result1,val3);
            alert('Sum of previous values and Value 3 = ' + result2);
            ";
        string addFunction = @"
            function AddValues(v1, v2)
            {
              return v1 + v2;
            }";

        Page.ClientScript.RegisterStartupScript(this.GetType(), "startupCode",
script,true);
        Page.ClientScript.RegisterClientScriptBlock(this.GetType(), "addMethod",
addFunction,true);
    }
}
```

This example will register all the required JavaScript to execute from the Page_Load event of the code file. Running this code (by pressing F5 to execute in debug mode) will produce two alert boxes displaying the sum of some values. You can alter this code to automatically invoke the debugger just prior to the first invocation of the AddValues method.

To accomplish this, you will insert the debugger keyword as part of the generated script. Examine the following code, which just shows the Page_Load method and highlights the modifications:

```
protected void Page_Load(object sender, EventArgs e)
{
    string script = @"
        var val1 = 10;
        var val2 = 20;
        debugger;
        var result1 = AddValues(val1,val2);
        alert('Sum of values 1 & 2 = ' + result1);
        var val3 = 30;
        var result2 = AddValues(result1,val3);
        alert('Sum of previous values and Value 3 = ' + result2);
        ";
    string addFunction = @"
        function AddValues(v1, v2)
        {
          return v1 + v2;
        }";

    Page.ClientScript.RegisterStartupScript(this.GetType(), "startupCode",
script,true);
        Page.ClientScript.RegisterClientScriptBlock(this.GetType(), "addMethod",
addFunction,true);
    }
```

Now execute this application using F5 to start the application in debug mode. The application will start normally but will then jump to the debugger screen and pause execution of the code on the line with the debugger keyword as shown in Figure 13-16.

Other Ways of Inspecting the Value of Variables

As mentioned previously, when in debug mode, a developer can simply hover the mouse over a variable to display its current value. However, having to do this for a range of variables, constantly as each line of code is executed, can be cumbersome. But you do have alternatives.

Using the Watch Window

In similar fashion again to server-side debugging techniques, you can apply a "watch" to variables to monitor their values and interactively perform computations against variables within your application.

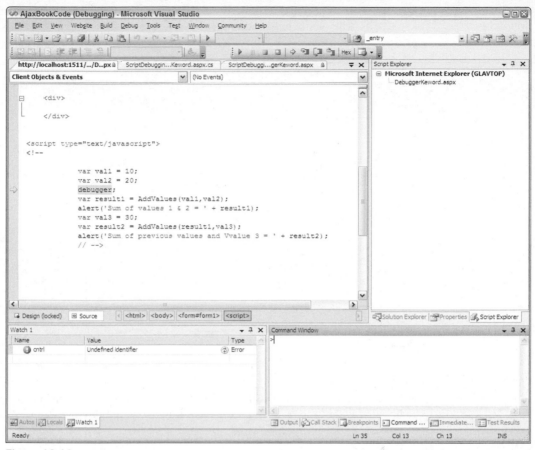

Figure 13-16

Try It Out   Using the Watch Window

Using the previous code example, press F5 to launch the application, which should automatically pause at the `debugger` keyword. When Visual Studio .NET displays the debugger window, using the mouse, right-click on the `result1` variable. This will bring up a context menu. Select the Add Watch option, which will add the `result1` variable to the Watch window. The Watch window is typically located on the bottom left of the Visual Studio .NET environment, as shown in Figure 13-17.

```
debugger;
var result1 = AddValues(val1,val2);
alert('Sum of values 1 & 2 = ' + result1);
var val3 = 30;
var result2 = AddValues(result1,val3);
alert('Sum of previous values and Vvalue 3 =
// -->
```

Name	Value	Type
cntrl	Undefined identifier	Error
result1	undefined	User-defi

Figure 13-17

Notice that the result1 variable is displaying a value of *undefined* in the Watch window. Pressing F10 twice to advance the programs execution past the call to the AddValues method causes the value of the result1 variable to be updated within the Watch window according to the operation within the code's execution.

Multiple items can be added to the Watch window to enable the developer to track the values of variables as execution progresses.

Using the Command Window

Alternatively, a developer may wish to evaluate conditions that are not part of the program itself as the code is executing. To accomplish this, a developer can make use of the Command window. This allows interactive evaluation of ad hoc statements within the context of the applications execution at the point in time that it has been paused.

Try It Out   Using the Command Window

To demonstrate this, again run the previous application by pressing the F5 key to start the application in debug mode. The application will present the debug screen within Visual Studio with execution paused on the debugger statement.

Ensure that the Command window is visible by clicking on the Command Window tab (typically located on the bottom right of the Visual Studio .NET environment) or by selecting the View⇨Other Windows⇨ Command Window (or by pressing *Ctrl+Alt+A*).

The Command window will have a > symbol as the prompt. In the Command window, type the following command and press Enter:

```
? val1 + val2
```

A value of 30 should be displayed. Now try typing the following command:

```
? AddValues(81,42)
```

A value of 123 should be displayed. The Command window should now look like Figure 13-18.

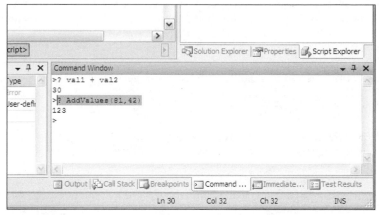

Figure 13-18

Here, you are interactively evaluating variables and executing methods within the application. The question mark (?) symbol is shorthand for *display* or *print*. This technique is an extremely powerful way of evaluating different conditions within your script applications at various points within the scripts execution.

Script Debugging So Far

This method of debugging script code is extremely powerful and is very similar to the way we would debug server-side code. This familiarity means that developers do not need to learn different tools or become accustomed to specialized techniques when debugging script-based code.

Armed with this information, you can now effectively debug script on the client side, as well as debug application execution on the server side (using traditional debugging methods). However, there are still areas that you need to explore and examine thoroughly to enable you to properly debug Ajax-style applications.

Browser Debugging Tools

Quite often, Ajax applications will want to update portions of the browsers display as a result of some background request, typically executed as an asynchronous postback. The browser's DOM is what a developer will typically manipulate to fashion the screen according to the information that has been collected. Although a developer makes a best effort to understand all the implications of making changes to styles, elements, and display items within the browser, sometimes things don't always go as planned.

Both Internet Explorer and Firefox browsers provide tools that allow the developer to interactively examine and manipulate the structural contents of a web page. This allows developers to see any changes that a script may perform interactively as they are applied, and also to apply changes to a web page as it is being displayed.

Internet Explorer

Internet Explorer does not natively provide any tools or support for interactively examining the contents and structure of a web page. However, an external download is provided by Microsoft called the Internet Explorer Developer Toolbar. As we write this book, this tool is currently in beta status, meaning it is not an officially released product yet and may change before it is finally released. It is however very functional and extremely useful.

This tool can be downloaded from the following location: `www.microsoft.com/downloads/`
`details.aspx?familyid=E59C3964-672D-4511-BB3E-2D5E1DB91038&displaylang=en.`
Alternatively, you can also use `http://tinyurl.com/boscb.`

Once the tool is installed, it is not activated by default. To activate the toolbar, open Internet Explorer, and select View➪Explorer Bar➪IE DOM Explorer. The toolbar will open at the bottom of the screen, as shown in Figure 13-19.

From this point on, a web page can be loaded, and the structure of the web page will be displayed within the toolbar window (shown in the previous diagram in the lower left of the screen). Web pages can be loaded from any location on the Internet, or they can be part of an application that a developer may be working on.

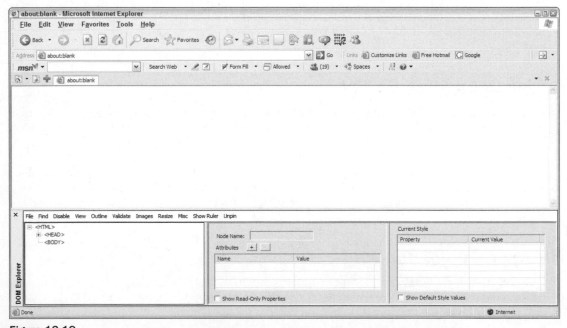

Figure 13-19

Although this section of the chapter is not intended to be a tutorial on usage of the toolbar, some of the toolbar's functionality is worth noting here.

The entire structure of a web page can be navigated using the structural elements of the page, using the tree view display of the toolbar. Each textual, structural, or style-based element can be selected, and its properties displayed for examination or manipulation.

Complex web pages can be difficult to navigate, and so can locating a particular element that a developer may be concerned with. Selecting the Find⇨Select Element by Click menu option of the toolbar allows an element to be clicked on in the web page concerned, and the element itself will be highlighted within the toolbar's tree view display. The element's properties and styles can then be manipulated and examined as required.

One simple but useful feature for developers is the ability to resize the browser window according to standard screen resolutions. Quite often, a developer will be required to ensure a web site/page is displayed suitably within a minimum of screen resolution (for example, a site must display correctly at a minimum screen resolution of 800 × 600). Selecting the Resize menu option from the IE Developer Toolbar menu presents a list of resolutions that may be selected, which will cause the browser to redisplay in the selected resolution. This is an easy way for a developer to test a site at varying screen resolutions without having to continually change the display resolution of their system.

Firefox

When Firefox is installed, an option is provided to install a set of developer tools. Selecting the option to install these tools provides the user with a menu option Tools⇨DOM Inspector. Selecting this menu option will display a window that has a similar look and feel to the IE Developer Toolbar discussed previously (see Figure 13-20).

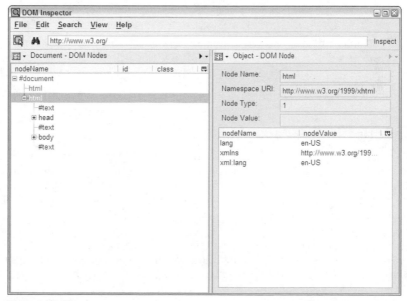

Figure 13-20

The DOM Inspector tool available within the Firefox browser is very similar to the IE Developer Toolbar in that it allows a developer to view the structural and style elements of a web page and any associated attributes or contextual items. The tool also allows some degree of manipulation to certain elements within the page.

Firefox also provides a convenient JavaScript console that displays any errors and warnings encountered while processing the JavaScript code within a web page, in addition to also displaying any Cascading Style Sheet (CSS) errors that are encountered.

Selecting the Tools⇨JavaScript Console menu option displays a window showing any JavaScript or CSS errors encountered thus far in the pages execution and will look like Figure 13-21.

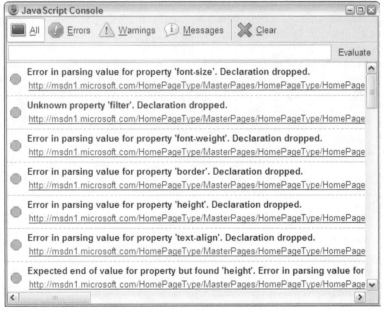

Figure 13-21

Firefox JavaScript Debugger — Venkman

Venkman is a tool that integrates with Firefox to provide JavaScript debugging facilities. It is not a part of the official distribution of Firefox but is a very popular and powerful means of allowing developers to debug JavaScript code within Firefox. Actually, Venkman itself is not specific to Firefox, but works in all browsers based on the Mozilla engine version 0.9.5 and later. Firefox itself is based on the Mozilla browser engine. In addition, Venkman also works on Netscape version 6.2 and later.

Venkman can be downloaded from the Venkman project page at www.mozilla.org/projects/venkman/index.html. This site also contains additional information such as a FAQ and detailed information about the installation and usage of Venkman.

To install Venkman, you should browse to the project home page (listed in the preceding paragraph), using the Firefox browser, and click on the appropriate link. This will launch an install process and install the Venkman tool within Firefox. Once installed, the tool can be accessed from the Tools⇨JavaScript Debugger menu option.

> *Note that the direct link to the download/install location is* `https://addons.mozilla.org/extensions/moreinfo.php?id=216`.

This section does not attempt to provide a detailed examination of the features and functionality of the Venkman debugger, because this is beyond the scope of this chapter. Instead, this is a brief overview provided to give you an idea of what is possible with Venkman. Detailed information and tutorials are available from the link shown in the preceding Note.

Venkman allows a complete JavaScript debugging experience within the Firefox browser. The interface of Venkman is not as intuitive as the server-side debugging experience within Visual Studio .NET; however, it does provide a very usable and powerful way of debugging JavaScript code by supporting standard and advanced debugging features such as:

❑ Setting of breakpoints within JavaScript code

❑ Triggering of breakpoints based on conditions within your code such as a value of a variable or when an exception is thrown

❑ Adding watch conditions to monitor the value of variables within currently executing script code

❑ Supporting of multiple views within the Venkman interface, providing a fully customizable interface

❑ Profiling of JavaScript code to measure the execution speed of your JavaScript application

These features provide a similar client-side debugging experience to that provided by Visual Studio .NET on the server side; however, even advanced features such as profiling are not natively supported by Visual Studio .NET, especially on the client side. Venkman is a free download that not only provides exceptional value, but also provides a powerful array of features that are a valuable asset to any developer doing JavaScript development, most notably developers writing Ajax applications.

The Man in the Middle

The IE Developer Toolbar for Internet Explorer, the DOM Inspector within Firefox, and the Venkman debugger are valuable tools to assist a web developer in debugging, and identifying any issues within a web page or application. These combined with both server- and client-side debugging features previously discussed, provide an excellent set of tools and techniques to identify, debug, and resolve issues within web applications, particularly those that contains a large degree of JavaScript.

However, at this point, one area remains largely unaddressed — that of the actual HTTP traffic that is generated by the web application itself. This is particularly important for Ajax-style applications that can initiate many asynchronous postback operations that are not immediately apparent by just examining the user interface and any associated interaction. Without being able to examine the actual data that form the HTTP communication, a developer can identify issues based only on the effects of the data that is sent and received, and, therefore, make assumptions given those effects.

To make this point clear, Figure 13-22 illustrates what aspect of the web application is being referred to.

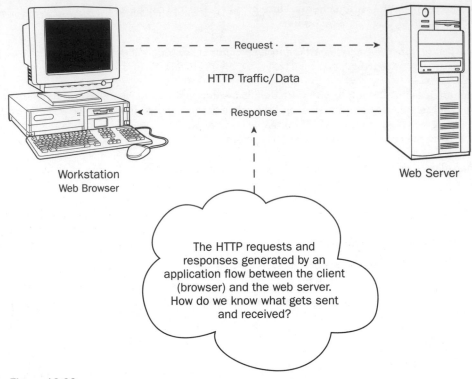

Figure 13-22

Clearly, the actual traffic being sent and received by a web application is crucial to its correct operation, and you would assume that if the code were correct at both the client and server levels, then examining the actual content of the HTTP traffic would not be necessary.

In some cases, this may be correct; however, it is not always apparent when some code is incorrect. Furthermore, assumptions can be made regarding the operation of the application and associated code that result in unexpected HTTP contents that can adversely affect the operation of the application and yield incorrect and/or unexpected results.

This becomes very apparent when dealing with HTTP headers. The HTTP headers that are sent with a request need to be very specific to the operation being performed. For most operations, these headers are implicitly sent along with any requests you make from code, or in some cases, easily mistaken. Examine the following example code:

```
<script type="text/javascript">
function MakeXMLHTTPCall(){

    var xmlHttpObj;

    xmlHttpObj = CreateXmlHttpRequestObject();

    if (xmlHttpObj)          {
```

```
        xmlHttpObj.open("POST","http://" + location.host + "/Chap14/DataFile.xml",
    true);

        xmlHttpObj.onreadystatechange = function() {
            if ( xmlHttpObj.readyState == READYSTATE_COMPLETE )
            {
                alert("Request/Response Complete");
            }
        }

        xmlHttpObj.send(null);
    }
}
</script>
```

When this code is executed, an alert box is presented stating that the request/response is complete, and the code seems to have been successful. If you were to examine the traffic generated by this request, you would see that this request actually generated a 405 error code and was unsuccessful. The problem is that the code specifies a POST operation in the following line:

```
    xmlHttpObj.open("POST","http://" + location.host + "/Chap14/DataFile.xml", true);
```

A GET operation should be used here instead, as shown in the following line:

```
    xmlHttpObj.open("GET","http://" + location.host + "/Chap14/DataFile.xml", true);
```

Without your being able to examine the network traffic and associated error codes, it would not be easily apparent what error was occurring and the fact that the POST verb was the cause of the problem. What is required is a tool that enables a developer to examine and monitor the traffic negotiated between the client and the server — the data that goes over the wire. A tool for just this purpose is the subject of the next section.

In some cases, it may also be necessary to specifically construct the data that is sent to a server, and ultimately, the only way to truly verify that the server is receiving what you *think* it's being sent is to actually examine what is being sent.

There are many tools and network monitors available that will allow you to examine network traffic in various forms. However, the actual function of sending data over the network (whether that network be the Internet or a local intranet) relies on many layers of networking components and protocols acting together. Web developers are typically interested only in the traffic pertinent to their web application. One such tool that effectively provides this functionality is Fiddler.

Fiddler

Fiddler is a freely available tool that installs as a component that can be activated from within Microsoft Internet Explorer and allows the HTTP traffic between a browser and a server to be easily viewed, examined, and manipulated, or *fiddled with* (hence, the name of Fiddler).

The Fiddler home page, where a copy can be downloaded, is located at www.fiddlertool.com/fiddler.

A full set of documentation, instructions, and tutorials exists on Fiddler site, and this is not intended to be a detailed instructional text on how to use Fiddler. However, it is worth discussing how this tool can be used to assist the debugging process within a web application, specifically using Ajax techniques.

Once Fiddler has been downloaded and installed, it can be accessed by selecting the Tools⇨Fiddler menu option. In addition, it appears as a new icon within the Internet Explorer toolbar (see Figure 13-23).

Figure 13-23

Try It Out   **Using Fiddler**

To see Fiddler in action, create a new web site project within Visual Studio .NET. Add a new page (or modify the existing `default.aspx` page) so that the web page and associated code-beside file contain the following code.

TestFiddler.aspx — Web Form

```
<%@ Page Language="C#" AutoEventWireup="true" CodeFile="TestFiddler.aspx.cs"
Inherits="FiddlerExamples_TestFiddler" %>

<!DOCTYPE html PUBLIC "-//W3C//DTD XHTML 1.0 Transitional//EN"
"http://www.w3.org/TR/xhtml1/DTD/xhtml1-transitional.dtd">

<html xmlns="http://www.w3.org/1999/xhtml" >
<head runat="server">
    <title>Test Fiddler</title>
    <script type="text/javascript">
    function OnCallComplete(arg,ctx)
    {
        var dataReturned = arg.split(";");
        var cnt = 0;
        for (var cnt=0; cnt < dataReturned.length;cnt++)
        {
            alert("Data #" + cnt + " returned was: " + dataReturned[cnt]);
        }
    }
    </script>
</head>
<body>
    <form id="form1" runat="server">
    <div>
        <button onclick="DoCallback(null,null);">Do Async Callback</button>
    </div>
    </form>
</body>
</html>
```

TestFiddler.aspx.cs — Code-Beside file

```
using System;
using System.Data;
using System.Configuration;
using System.Collections;
using System.Web;
using System.Web.Security;
using System.Web.UI;
using System.Web.UI.WebControls;
using System.Web.UI.WebControls.WebParts;
using System.Web.UI.HtmlControls;

public partial class FiddlerExamples_TestFiddler : System.Web.UI.Page,
ICallbackEventHandler
{
    protected void Page_Load(object sender, EventArgs e)
    {
        string js = Page.ClientScript.GetCallbackEventReference(this, "arg",
"OnCallComplete", "ctx", true);
        string jsFunction = "function DoCallback(arg,ctx) { " + js + " } ";

        Page.ClientScript.RegisterClientScriptBlock(this.GetType(), "Callback",
jsFunction,true);
    }


    #region ICallbackEventHandler Members

    public string GetCallbackResult()
    {
        System.Threading.Thread.Sleep(2000);
        string[] dataToReturn = new string[] { "Data1", "DataPart2", "SomeData3" };
        // return a hardcoded string array as a single string
        return string.Join(";", dataToReturn);
    }

    public void RaiseCallbackEvent(string eventArgument)
    {
        // Do nothing here
    }

    #endregion
}
```

Ensure that the application runs by right-clicking on the modified page with the mouse and selecting View in Browser. A simple web page should be displayed with a single button labeled Do Async Callback. Clicking the button with the mouse should result in a 2-second delay and then three alert boxes displaying the returned data values of Data1, DataPart2, and SomeData3.

This page is obviously not very complex, but it does utilize an asynchronous postback to execute a server-side method and retrieve some data for display.

Now click on the Fiddler icon shown previously or access the Fiddler tool by selecting the Tools⇨Fiddler menu option.

This will display a new dialog window. Ignore that window for now, but do not close it. Select the previous browser window (that is running the web page previously listed), and click the button labeled Do Async Callback. The same result should be seen within the browser, that is, the display of the three result values.

Bring the Fiddler window to the foreground by clicking in the window or selecting it in the windows taskbar.

You will notice that all requests made by the browser are now logged in the Fiddler window. These will include the original request for the page as specified in the address bar, but also any additional requests for images, script libraries, and other resources that the page loads as part of its functionality and display.

The Fiddler screen should now look similar Figure 13-24.

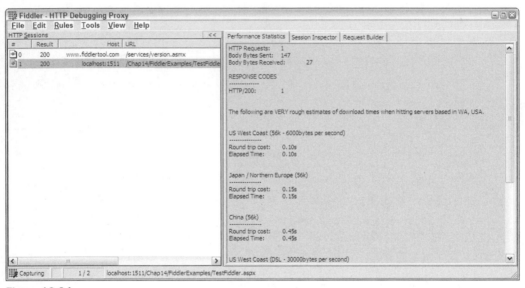

Figure 13-24

You will notice that the asynchronous request issued by the browser has been logged in the Fiddler window in the left-hand pane (indicated in the figure by the `localhost:1511` entry, although the port number may be different on different systems). Select this entry by clicking on it with the mouse. The right-hand section of the display should now show some details about the request.

This initial display shows some simple performance timings as well as the total bytes for the request and response itself.

Click on the Session Inspector tab in the right-hand pane. This will initially display the HTTP headers that were sent as part of the HTTP request in the top right-hand pane. The bottom right-hand pane will automatically have the Transformer section selected. Select the Headers tab in the bottom right-hand pane. This will then display the HTTP headers that were sent from the web server as part of the response. The Fiddler display window should now look like Figure 13-25.

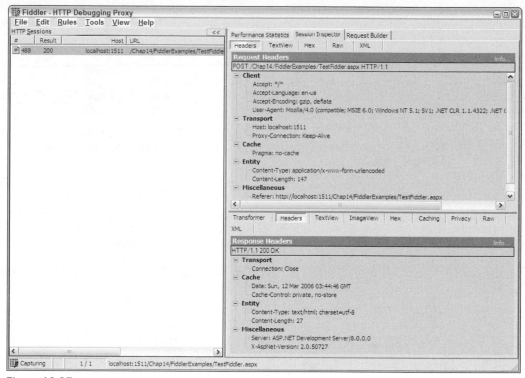

Figure 13-25

This is useful for examining the HTTP headers of the request/response sequence to ensure that the correct headers are being set in an easy-to-view tree-type display. This is especially important when formulating your own Simple Object Access Protocol (SOAP) requests (as demonstrated in Chapter 4 of this book).

However, one of the most useful aspects of Fiddler is the ability to examine the raw contents of the request/response sequence. With the Fiddler display still showing the headers, click on the Raw tab in both the top and bottom right-hand panes.

This display shows the entire request and response data, including header information, as it would be sent by the client and received from the server. In the top-right pane, showing the request, you can see the HTTP headers and also the associated data payload of the HTTP request. This should be something similar to the following text:

```
__EVENTTARGET=&__EVENTARGUMENT=&__VIEWSTATE=%2FwEPDwUJNzgzNDMwNTMzZGRyE%2BruV%2Bh77
fo76pKQAZFknAX7Ag%3D%3D&__CALLBACKID=__Page&__CALLBACKPARAM=null
```

From this, you can get an idea of how asynchronous client script callbacks notify the server of what control generated the callback and what the argument of the call is (via the _CALLBACKID=__Page and __CALLBACKPARAM=null arguments, respectively).

Looking at the request data in the bottom-right pane, again you can see the HTTP headers that form the response and also response data that has been sent back as a result of the asynchronous request. The response data should look similar to the following:

```
0|Data1;DataPart2;SomeData3
```

This enables you to verify that what is being displayed within the browser through the application code is in fact what has been returned by the server.

Try It Out   Using Fiddler Breakpoints to Manipulate Request/Response Data Directly

One of the most powerful features of Fiddler is its ability to allow request and response data to be altered by setting breakpoints at the request and response points. This is completely external to the breakpoints associated with any client- or server-side code. Once a Fiddler breakpoint is hit, request or response data can be examined and/or manipulated and then allowed to continue to its destination with the modified data. This provides an excellent way of debugging and testing your applications.

An example best illustrates this. Create a new web page within Visual Studio .NET and copy the following code into the web page (.aspx file) and the code-beside file (.cs file), respectively.

Web Form — TestFiddlerBreakpoint.aspx

```
<%@ Page Language="C#" AutoEventWireup="true"
CodeFile="TestFiddlerBreakpoint.aspx.cs" Inherits="FiddlerExamples_TestFiddler" %>

<!DOCTYPE html PUBLIC "-//W3C//DTD XHTML 1.0 Transitional//EN"
"http://www.w3.org/TR/xhtml1/DTD/xhtml1-transitional.dtd">

<html xmlns="http://www.w3.org/1999/xhtml" >
<head runat="server">
    <title>Test Fiddler Breakpoint</title>
    <script type="text/javascript">
    function OnCallComplete(arg,ctx)
    {
        alert("The argument returned from the server was: " + arg);
    }
    </script>
</head>
<body>
    <form id="form1" runat="server">
    <div>
        <button onclick="DoCallback('button clicked!',null);">Do Async
Callback</button>
    </div>
    </form>
</body>
</html>
```

Code-Beside File — TestFiddlerBreakpoint.cs

```
using System;
using System.Data;
using System.Configuration;
```

```csharp
using System.Collections;
using System.Web;
using System.Web.Security;
using System.Web.UI;
using System.Web.UI.WebControls;
using System.Web.UI.WebControls.WebParts;
using System.Web.UI.HtmlControls;

public partial class FiddlerExamples_TestFiddler : System.Web.UI.Page,
ICallbackEventHandler
{
    private string _argReceived = null;

    protected void Page_Load(object sender, EventArgs e)
    {
        string js = Page.ClientScript.GetCallbackEventReference(this, "arg",
"OnCallComplete", "ctx", true);
        string jsFunction = "function DoCallback(arg,ctx) { " + js + " } ";

        Page.ClientScript.RegisterClientScriptBlock(this.GetType(), "Callback",
jsFunction,true);
    }


    #region ICallbackEventHandler Members

    public string GetCallbackResult()
    {
        System.Threading.Thread.Sleep(2000);
        return string.Format("The argument received by the server was '{0}' at
{1}", _argReceived, DateTime.Now.ToShortTimeString());
    }

    public void RaiseCallbackEvent(string eventArgument)
    {
        _argReceived = eventArgument;
    }

    #endregion
}
```

As performed in the previous section, using the mouse, right-click on this page in Visual Studio .NET and select View in Browser. Verify that the application works as expected by clicking the button on the web page. An alert box should be displayed with the text similar to that shown in Figure 13-26.

Figure 13-26

The server-side method simply accepts the argument that was sent by the client and returns a string displaying that argument, in addition to the time on the server. In the previous example, the client (browser) sent the string button clicked! as an argument.

Click on the Fiddler icon or select the Tools⇨Fiddler menu option to load the Fiddler display. Select the Rules⇨Automatic Breakpoints⇨Before Requests menu option, or simply press the F11 key. Now click on the button on the web form to initiate the asynchronous call.

On the taskbar, the Fiddler task icon should highlight to indicate it requires some acknowledgment. Switch to the Fiddler application and select the request that was initiated (in the left-hand Fiddler pane) with the mouse. Click on the Session Inspector tab in the top right-hand pane of the Fiddler display. The display should look similar to Figure 13-27.

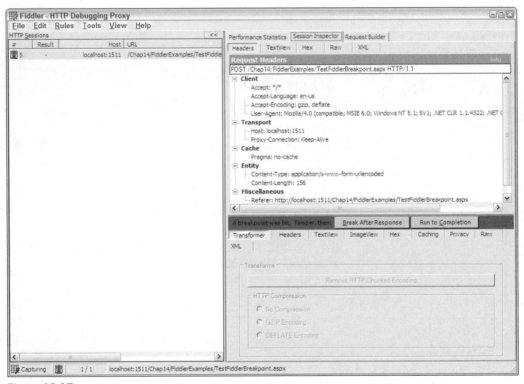

Figure 13-27

Fiddler has intercepted this request, and because you have enabled breakpoints on requests, Fiddler has stopped the request from proceeding until you allow it to proceed.

Select the TextView tab in the top right-hand pane of the Fiddler display. The text content of the HTTP Request data should be displayed and look similar to the following text:

```
__EVENTTARGET=&__EVENTARGUMENT=&__VIEWSTATE=%2FwEPDwUJNzgzNDMwNTMzZGT4go7HPnnHZvVOI
xsR9u48Hce4EA%3D%3D&__CALLBACKID=__Page&__CALLBACKPARAM=button%20clicked!
```

Replace the text `button%20clicked!` with the text `I_am_a_hacker` (note: do not use spaces). The request data should now look like the following:

```
__EVENTTARGET=&__EVENTARGUMENT=&__VIEWSTATE=%2FwEPDwUJNzgzNDMwNTMzZGT4go7HPnnHZvVOI
xsR9u48Hce4EA%3D%3D&__CALLBACKID=__Page&__CALLBACKPARAM=I_am_a_hacker
```

Now click on the Run to Completion button in the Fiddler display. The alert box that is displayed should look similar to the one in Figure 13-28.

Figure 13-28

The alert box is displaying the modified text `I_am_a_hacker`. This is because you intercepted the request, modified the data after the request was issued by the client but before it was actually transmitted over the network. The raw data was modified and then allowed to proceed to the server. The server extracted the data normally, and returned the results, which included the modified data.

Obviously, this is an extremely powerful way to test and debug your web applications because it allows a developer to examine and modify the raw HTTP data as it is being sent over the wire.

Summary

This chapter has covered all the major areas of debugging, focusing on each isolated area of development to provide a complete view of the debugging process and the techniques involved.

❑ First, the traditional server-side debugging methods were looked at. These are easily the most powerful and easy to use debugging methods, and an entire book could be devoted to the subject itself. It is highly recommended that additional time be spent in this area to investigate all the possible features and means of debugging.

❑ Second, the dark art of client-side/client script debugging was examined, and it was shown how the powerful server-side debugging techniques could be utilized within a client script scenario. This type of code has traditionally been very difficult to debug, and Visual Studio .NET makes this task much simpler, enabling the use of familiar debugging methods and techniques.

❑ In addition, techniques to investigate and manipulate the DOM tree were provided to allow a detailed view of how the web page is represented. The DOM is used internally within browsers to represent a web page and its contents, and understanding this is crucial to achieving the desired behavior within web applications.

❑ Finally, a method of investigating, testing, and modifying the data that actually travels between the client and server was examined. The freely available Fiddler tool was used to provide a powerful and easy to use way of viewing, manipulating, and intercepting this data in both a structured display and also in its raw form.

At the beginning of this chapter, we mentioned that having an arsenal of tools is the really the answer to effective debugging. Visual Studio .NET, the IE Developer Toolbar, Firefox, and Fiddler are but a few of these tools. Debugging is a crucial skill for any developer to possess and having this arsenal of tools enhances that skill considerably. Debugging is a skill that needs to be built upon over time, and as a developer, you will also build upon your debugging toolbox as time passes.

Finally, although this chapter has touched upon the various facets and areas of debugging, it is highly recommended that each area be investigated more thoroughly by the developer. Experiment, learn, and expand your knowledge.

To help, the following is a list of URLs relevant to the tools and information discussed in this chapter:

❏ **Detailed information on debugging applications**—`http://msdn2.microsoft.com/en-us/library/awtaffxb.aspx`

❏ **Configuring and troubleshooting client-side debugging**—`www.gotdotnet.com/team/csharp/learn/whitepapers/How%20to%20debug%20script%20in%20Visual%20Studio%20.Net.doc`

❏ **Internet Explorer Developer Toolbar**—`http://tinyurl.com/boscb`

❏ **Venkman Debugger download**—`https://addons.mozilla.org/extensions/moreinfo.php?id=216`

❏ **Fiddler utility download**—`www.fiddlertool.com/fiddler`

XSLT Commands

This appendix provides additional XSLT commands that may be of value to readers.

XSLT Elements

The following are additional XSLT elements that are a part of the XSLT 1.0 specification.

Element	Description
apply-imports	This element applies a template rule from an imported style sheet.
apply-templates	This element applies a template rule to the current element or to the current element's child nodes.
attribute	This element adds an attribute to an element.`<xsl:attribute name="attributename" namesapce="uri">` `<xsl:value-of select="attributevalues" />` `</xsl:attribute>`
attribute-set	This element adds an attribute-set to an element. `<xsl:attribute-set name="name" use-attribute-sets="name-list">` `<xsl:attribute name="attributename">value</xsl:attribute>`
call-template	This element calls a named template. `<xsl:call-template name="templatename" />`
comment	The comment element creates a comment node in the result tree. `<xsl:comment>` `Comment.` `</xsl:comment>`

Table continued on following page

Element	Description
copy	This element creates a copy of the current node with namespace nodes but without child nodes and attributes.
copy-of	This element creates a copy of the current node as well as namespace nodes, child nodes, and attributes of the current node. `<xsl:copy-of select="expression" />`
decimal-format	This element provides the characters and symbols used when converting numbers in strings. This element is used along with the `format-number()` function. This element has a large number of additional attributes.
element	This element creates an element node in the output document.
fallback	This element specifies alternate code to run if the XSL processor does not support an XSL element.
import	This element is used to import contents of one style sheet into another. `<xsl:import href="URI" />`
include	This element includes the contents of one style sheet in another. `<xsl:include href="URI" />`
key	This element declares a named key that may be used in a style sheet with a `key()` function. `<xsl:key name"keyname" match="matchkey" use="expression" />`

message	This element writes a message to the output. This is typically used to report errors back to the output stream.
	`<xsl:message terminate="yes|no">`
	`........output content`
	`</xsl:message>`
	The value of `yes` will terminate processing after the message is sent to the output stream. The value of `no` will allow processing to continue.

namespace-alias	This element replaces a namespace in the style sheet with a different namespace in the output stream. `<xsl:namesapce-alias stylesheet prefix="stylesheet prefix" result-prefix="stylesheetresult" />`
number	This element determines the integer position of the current node in the source. It has many attributes.
otherwise	This element specifies a default action for `<xsl:choose>` element. This action takes place when none of the `<xsl:when>` conditions apply.
output	This element defines the format of the output document.
param	This element defines a local or global parameter.

Element	Description
preserve-space	This element is used to define the elements that should have their whitespace preserved. `<xsl:preserve-space elements="item1 item2" />` This will preserve the space for all of the elements listed in the elements attribute.

processing-instruction	The element writes a processing instruction to the output stream.
	`<xsl:processing-instruction name="xml-stylesheet">`
	`href="stylesheet.css" type="text/css"`
	`</xsl:processing-instruction>`

strip-space	This element strips the whitespace for the defined elements.
stylesheet	This element defines the root element of a style sheet.

text	This element writes literal text to the output.
	`<xsl:text disable-output-escaping="yes|no" >`
	`</xsl:text>`
	A yes means that special characters are output as is. A no means that special characters are output as their encoded versions.

transform	This element is synonymous with the `stylesheet` element.

variable	This element is used to declare a local or global variable.
	`<xsl:variable name="varName" select="expressionValue">`
	`</xsl:variable>`
	If no value is specified for the select attribute, a value may be defined within the `<xsl:variable>` element.

when	This element is used to specify an action for the `<xsl:choose>` element. When the `<xsl:when>` element returns a true, an action is performed.
with-param	This defines the value of a parameter that is passed to a template. For the `<xsl:with-param>` to work, the name in the `with-param` element must match the name in the `<xsl:param>` element.

XSLT Functions

XSLT contains a set of built-in methods. Other methods used in XSLT are available through X Path. These methods from X Path fall into the areas of accessor, boolean, context, datetime, error/trace, node, numeric, OName, sequence, string, and URI. This section covers both the XSLT-only methods and those areas provided through X Path.

XSLT-Only Methods

XSLT-only functions may be called only from within an XSLT processor. These methods are not callable from the Document Object Model (DOM).

Function Name	Description
current	The current method returns a node set that contains the current node as its only member.
document	The document method provides a mechanism to retrieve data from other XML resource from within the XSLT style sheet.
element-available	The element-available method returns a true only if the expanded-name is the name of an instruction.
format-number	The format-number method converts the first argument to a string using the pattern specified by the second argument.
function-available	The function-available method returns true if the function is available in the function library.
generate-id	The generate-id method returns a string that identifies the node in the node set argument that is first in the document order. The node is identified uniquely.
key	The key method returns elements that have been market with an <xsl:key> statement.
node-set	The node-set method converts a tree in a node set.
system-property	The system-property method returns an object that represents the value of the system property that has been identified by the name.
unparsed-entry-uri	The unparsed-entity-uri method returns declarations of unparsed entities in the DTD of the source document.

Accessor

The accessor family of methods provides information about the internal state of a node.

Name	Description
node-name(node)	The method returns the node-name of the specified node.
nilled(node)	This method returns a Boolean value as to whether or not the argument node has been nilled.
data(item, ...)	This method returns a sequence of atomic values.
base-uri() base-uri(node)	This method returns the value of the base-uri property of the current or specified nodes.
document-uri(node)	This method returns the value of the document-uri property for the specified node.

Boolean

The boolean family of methods provides operations that are associated with boolean (true/false) style operations.

Name	Description
boolean(blarg)	A boolean value for a string, number, or node set is returned.
not(blarg)	The boolean value of the opposite of the boolean argument is returned.
true()	The boolean value of true is returned.
false()	The boolean value of false is returned.

Context

The context family of methods provides operations that are associated with location in the XML.

Name	Description
position()	The index position of the node that is currently being processed is returned
last()	The last() method has the index position of the last node.
current-dateTime()	The current date and time are returned along with the appropriate time zone.
current-date()	The current date is returned along with the appropriate time zone.
current-time()	The current time is returned along with the appropriate time zone.
implicit-timezone()	The implicit time zone is returned.
default-collation()	The default collation is returned.
static-base-uri()	The base-uri is returned.

Datetime

The datetime family of methods returns information that is date- and time-related.

Name	Description
dateTime(date,time)	Creates a dateTime from the specified date and time.
years-from-duration (datetimeduration)	Returns an integer that represents the years component of the specified datetimeduration.

Table continued on following page

Name	Description
months-from-duration (datetimeduration)	Returns an integer that represents the months component of the specified datetimeduration.
hours-from-duration (datetimeduration)	Returns an integer that represents the hours component of the specified datetimeduration.
minutes-from-duration (datetimeduration)	Returns an integer that represents the minutes component of the specified datetimeduration.
seconds-from-duration (datetimeduration)	Returns an integer that represents the seconds component of the specified datetimeduration.
year-from-dateTime(datetime)	Returns an integer that represents the year component of the specified datetime.
month-from-dateTime(datetime)	Returns an integer that represents the months component of the specified datetime.
day-from-dateTime(datetime)	Returns an integer that represents the day component of the specified datetime.
hours-from-dateTime(dateTime)	Returns an integer that represents the hours component of the specified datetime.
minutes-from-dateTime(dateTime)	Returns an integer that represents the minutes component of the specified datetime.
seconds-from-dateTime(dateTime)	Returns an integer that represents the seconds component of the specified datetime.
timezone-from-date(date)	This method returns the timezone component of the argument.
year-from-date(date)	Returns an integer that represents the year component of the specified date.
month-from-date(date)	Returns an integer that represents the month component of the specified date.
day-from-date(date)	Returns an integer that represents the day component of the specified date.
timezone-from-date(date)	Returns the timezone from the date argument.
hours-from-time(time)	Returns an integer that represents the hours component of the specified time.
minutes-from-time(time)	Returns an integer that represents the minutes component of the specified time.
seconds-from-time(time)	Returns an integer that represents the seconds component of the specified time.
timezone-from-time(time)	Returns the timezone from the time argument.

Name	Description
adjust-dateTime-to-timezone (datetime, timezone)	Returns the datetime adjusted for the timezone. If no timezone is specified, then the datetime is returned with no timezone.
adjust-date-to-timezone (date,timezone)	Returns the date adjusted for the timezone. If no timezone is specified, then the date is returned with no timezone.
adjust-time-to-timezone (time, timezone)	Returns the time adjust for the timezone. If no timezone is specified, then the time is returned with no timezone.

Error/Trace

The error/trace family provides information regarding errors that are returned.

Name	Description
error() error(error) error(error, description) error(error, description, error-object)	Returns error information.
trace(value, label)	This is used to debug queries.

Node

The node family of functions returns information that is primarily information about the specified node.

Name	Description
name() name(nodeset)	The name() method returns the name of the current node or the first node in the node set passed to the method.
local-name() local-name(nodeset)	The local-name() method returns the name of the current node or the first node in the specified node set without the namespace prefix.
namespace-uri() namespace-uri(nodeset)	The namespace-uri() method returns the namespace URI of the current node or the first node of the specified node set that is passed to the method.
lang(lang)	The lang() method returns a boolean if the language of the current node matches the specified language.
root() root(node)	The root() returns the root of the tree to which the specified node belongs to. If no node is specified, the current node is used. The return value will typically be a document node.

Numeric

The numeric family of functions performs operations that are numeric.

Name	Description
number(arg)	The number() method returns the numeric value of the argument. The argument may be a boolean, string, or node set.
abs(num)	The abs() method returns the absolute value of the argument.
ceiling(num)	The ceiling() method returns the smallest integer that is greater than the number specified.
floor(num)	The floor() method returns the largest integer less than the number specified.
round(num)	The round() method returns the nearest integer to the number specified.
round-half-to-even(num)	The round-half-to-even() method returns the nearest whole number. ½ is rounded towards the nearest even number.

Sequence

The sequence family of functions operates on arrays, or sequences, of lists.

Name	Description
index-of((item1, item2, ...), searchitem)	This method returns the positions within the sequence of items that are within the argument listed as the searchitem.
remove((item1, item2, ...), position)	This method returns a new sequence of items with the item at position removed from the list. If the position does not exist within the list of items, the original list is returned.
empty(item1, item2, ...)	This method returns true if the value of the arguments is an empty sequence; otherwise, it returns false.
exists(item1, item2, ...)	This method returns a true if the value of the arguments is not an empty sequence; else, it returns false.
distinct-values((item1, item2, ...), collation)	This method returns distinct values from the list of items.
insert-before(item1, item2, ...), position, inserts)	This method returns a new sequence with the item list and the value of the inserts argument at the position specified.
reverse((item1, item2, ...))	This method returns a sequence of items that is reversed from the specified list of items.

Name	Description
`subsequence((item1, item2, ...), start, length)`	This method returns a sequence of items starting at the position specified at the starting point and for the length specified.
`unordered(item1, item2, ...))`	This method returns a list of items in an implementation dependent order.

String

The string family of functions performs operations on strings.

Name	Description
`string(argument)`	This method returns the string value of the argument. This argument may be a number, boolean, or node set.
`codepoints-to-string (int1, int2, ...)`	This method returns a string from a sequence of code points.
`string-to-codepoints (string)`	This method returns a list of code points from a string.
`codepoint-equal(item1, item2)`	This method returns true if the value of `item1` and `item2` are equal based on the rules of the unicode code point collation.
`compare(item1, item2)` `compare(item1, item2, collation)`	This method returns a value of -1 if `item1` is less than `item2`, 0, if `item1` is equal to `item2`, or 1 if `item1` is greater than `item2`. This comparison is based on the rules of collation used.
`concat(string1, string2, ...)`	This method returns the concatenation of the strings supplied.
`string-join(string1, string2, ...), separator)`	This method returns a string created by concatenating the string arguments and uses the `separator` argument.
`substring(string, start)` `substring(string, start, length)`	This method returns a string based on the supplied string, which starts at the supplied starting point and is based on the supplied length. If no length is supplied, a substring from the start position to the end of the string is returned.
`string-length()` `string-length(string)`	This method returns the length of the specified string. If there is no string passed as an argument, the string value of the current node is used.
`normalize-space()` `normalize-space(string)`	This method removes the trailing and leading spaces from the string used. All internal sequences of white space are replaced with one space. If no string is specified, the string value of the current node is used.

Table continued on following page

Name	Description
`normalize-unicode()`	This method indicates whether or not the serialization should convert the serialized output to Unicode.
`upper-case(string)`	This method converts the supplied string argument to uppercase.
`lower-case(string)`	This method converts the supplied string argument to lowercase.
`translate(string1, string2, string3)`	This method converts `string1` by replacing the values in `string2` with the values in `string3`.
`escape-uri(stringurl, escres)`	This method returns an escaped version of the string URI specified. The `escres` argument is a boolean.
`contains(string1, string2)`	This method returns true if `string1` contains the value specified in `string2`.
`starts-with(string1, string2)`	This method returns true if `string1` starts with `string2`. Otherwise, the method returns a false.
`ends-with(string1, string2)`	This method returns true if `string1` ends with `string2`. Otherwise, the method returns a false.
`substring-before(string1, string2)`	This method returns the start of `string1` before `string2` occurs in `string1`.
`substring-after(string1, string2)`	This method returns the end of `string1` after `string2` occurs in `string1`.
`matches(string, pattern)`	This method returns true if the `string` argument matches the specified pattern.
`replace(string, pattern, replacement)`	This method returns a string that is made by replacing the specified pattern with the replacement string.
`tokenize(string, patternstring)`	This method tokenizes the specified string based on the `patternstring`.

URI

The URI family of functions provides support for URI resolution.

Name	Description
`resolve-uri(relative, base)`	This method will return the URI given a base URI and a relative URI. The two are put together and a result is returned.

Index

Index

D

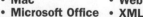